Ancient Israelites and the Eboe (Heeboe, Ibo, Ibu, Igbo) Peoples—a Challenge for Personal and Collective Reinvention of All Ibo (Hebrew) Peoples

Our Common Manners and Customs as Hebrew Peoples

Nkem Emeghara Udum Adah

GoodLuck

WORKBOOK PRESS LLC
187 E Warm Springs Rd,
Suite B285, Las Vegas, NV 89119, USA

Website: https://workbookpress.com/
Hotline: 1-888-818-4856
Email: admin@workbookpress.com

Ordering Information:
Quantity sales. Special discounts are available on quantity purchases by corporations, associations, and others.
For details, contact the publisher at the address above.

Library of Congress Control Number:
ISBN-13:   978-1-955459-31-0 (Paperback Version)
              978-1-955459-32-7 (Digital Version)

REV. DATE: 13/05/2021

OUR COMMON MANNERS AND CUSTOMS AS HEBREW PEOPLES:
ANCIENT ISRAELITES AND
THE EBOE (HEEBOE, EBO(E), IBO, IGBO) PEOPLES

A CHALLENGE FOR PERSONAL AND
COLLECTIVE REINVENTION OF ALL IBO (HEBREW) PEOPLES

By
Nkem Emeghara Udum Adah PhD LLM MA ThM DCR RCDP

"THEY LEFT BLACK...."

The WAR for Israel

When he was asked about peace in the middle east...The late president of Egypt Gamal Abdel Nasser, stated..."*The Jews will never be able to live here in peace, because they left here black but come back white*".

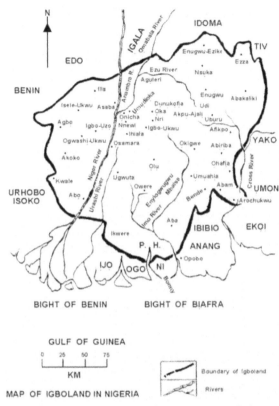

MAP OF IGBOLAND IN NIGERIA

Communities such as, Ogoni, Opobo, Anang, Ibibio, Bonny, Ekoi, Igala Idoma, Umon also fall withn the Heebo, Ibo Country (Colonial Eastern Region). Interviews showed that some of these communities especially those within the Creeks emerged as settlements provided by natives to accommodate rescued slaves by the Ibo (Heebo) brothers. Igboland was historically known as the Ibo(e), Ebo(e) and Heebo country by early European explorers. Early settlement of Igboland is dated at 6000 B.C based upon pottery found in the Okigwe, Oka Igwe and known today as Awka, although another evidence claim 4500 B.C. It is also claimed that Ife was originally inhabited by Igbos prior to 1300 AD.(see black and white films about the Ibo by George Basden 1920s and 1930s in British and Commonwealth Collection British Archives Bristol ref 2006/070, Ngodo excavations, Uturu by Anthropologist University of Benin; 1978 excavations led by Thurstan Shaw, University of Nigeria, Nsukka.

GLOSSARY OF WORDS

Ayah Asha Ayah or Aiyah: The revealed name of the supreme G-d to Moses (Exodus 3: 13). This name has been rendered as YHWH- the so called tetragramaton. This name later was rendered as 'Yahweh" and much later "Jehovah' by Europeans. The claim that G-d did not want his name to be mentioned is unacceptable and has no biblical evidence. David also referred to G-d as Yah in Psalm 68: 4. Ibos say "Ise yah": "as Yah delights so be it." Today shortened to "ise"

Adama: This is the title of the head of the advisory team to the Eze Ala, a title that reminds of the Hebrew word "adama"

Afo, Agho: the third day of the week in Ibo calendar

Agbala: A feminine deity associated with circumcision

Aru, Alu: abomination that which pollutes the land, dis balances harmonious living

Ayolo: (ego) traditional name for money called cowries

Agwu Ukwu: the Circumcision deity

Aguba: locally crafted knife, in the past made from stone (flint)

Ajo ofia: Evil forest where dead criminals were thrown into

Be Chi: The abode of the Chi, the dwelling place of the deity. Chi perhaps became part of Ibo vocabulary following the colonization by the Greek invaders of the Hebrew land that also modified the language. Chi came to mean deity, the owner of destiny, the determiner of destiny. Destiny in this sense means existence and its operations. Chi later came to be used to represent God.

Be: also connotes 'in', just as in Hebrew 'Beth essentiae' in "betselem elohim"- "in the image of elohim"

Chukwu: a version for the name of God literally the great chi

Dibia: Native healer, diviner, prophets

Ede: cocoyam

Uburu- one of the early attempts to pronounce Hebrew (ha-ibhri), some others attemps produced Ibu, Eboe, Heebo, Iboe, Ibo, Igbo etc

Uturu- An Ibo community in the south of the Iboland having a legend that claims to be the "original home of the Igbo people", the other legend around Eri is found among some of the northern part of the land

Edo: beauty red coloured powder

Eke-The traditional first market day; also a name for the war deity

'Udah(Judah):Believed to be the ancestral father of most of the Ibo inhabitants of present Abia state, Rivers State(Etche, Elele etc) and parts of Akwa Ibom state as reflected by names of towns and personal names

Assher: Believed to be the ancestral father of most of the Ibos inhabiting parts of Rivers State (Ikwere, Ugwuocha and area surrounding communities), Imo state (Owerre, Oguta)

Zebulun: Believed to be the ancestral father of parts of Anambra (including Ozubulu and others)

Acchi: Believed to be the ancestral father of Ibos inhabiting parts of Enugu and Ebonyi states etc

Ifit, Ihite, Ivite: Believed to be dialectal names of those Ibo communities claiming Levitical ancestral origin. The communities are scattered all over Iboland and are associated with mysteries and rituals wherever they are; usually identified with the word being suffix or prefix of the name of the town or community inhabiting them such as Ifiteukpo, Oraifite, Ihite...

Ekwensu: Name given to the opposer, Satan, understood as an agent of Chi ukwu (the great chi). Chi is sometimes described as destiny Spirit- also referred toas alter ego.

Elemiri: trumpet carved from the horn of a Ram and used to rally the people

Eze Ala: the title of the High Priest literally King of Ala Priesthood said to be inherited from the lineage of Levites

Eze Nri: The title of the Priestly King of Nri clan (Eri) said to be a descendeant of the Epraimite tribe

Ibi Ugwu: circumcision process

Ibhri: Hebrew, the name of one of the sons of an Ibo ancestor said to have been mispronounced 'Igbo'. The origin of the word was not a name word but a description of a characteristic or activity of the people. Initially Ha ibhri is said to describe a people who "have crossed over" to live in the forest, thus "the forest people"

Heeboes, Eber, Eboe, Eboan, Ibo, Igbo: a corruption of the original word Ha'ibri. A conglomeration of peoples inhabiting what became the eastern region and beyond of the country called Nigeria; usually known as "the Ibo country." Contrary to common perception, the core Igbo peoples are the Ikwere, the Etche, the Ijaw, the Ogoni, Ibibio, Efik, Anang and others (inhabitants of the present day Rivers, Bayelsa, Akwa Ibom, Cross River states). These peoples were first named Ibos and gave and shaped the Igbo core culture. They were the first batch of Igbos to receive the colonial masters and also produced the Igbo grammar syntax and the first Igbo Bible; as well as shaping Christianity as known among the Igbos. They also shaped the Igbo political life and general outlook to life. Other Igbo peoples include the Igbo of the hinterland; notably, the inhabitants of the present day Imo, Anambra, Abia, Enugu, Ebonyi, Delta, parts of Kogi and Benue states

Igwe: the Heavens, some Igbo use it to refer to the Eternal and the title for the all seeing and all knowing, all powerful, the owner and creator of the universe

Areli: one of the ancestral fathers of the Ibo: specifically father of a section of the Ibo including some Owerre, Orlu, Oguta, etc peoples.

Iseyah: Ibo special name for Yahweh; also referred locally as Chiukwu Okike, Chukwu Abiama (abiama and ancient Ibo word, literally is "the people my father" in Hebrew; thus referring to Abrama, or Abraham the father of nations), Chineke, Chiukwu; thus making the Igbo "the Chi People"

Ise: Amen, "may it be so" (implying "as Yah Yahweh has willed it"); full expression is "iseyah"

Izu: Ibo name for week made of four market days

Asaa: Seven symbolizes completeness

Iri: ten

Mbari (embarri) Ibo ritual art gallery

Mgbado: waist beads

Omu ugwo (omugwo): Seclusion following the birth of a child- a period of purification literally the sacred palm frond to depict carrying out the ritual debt that is owed the deity following child birth- an obligatory duty of purification

Ugwo: what is owed, a duty that must be performed

Nri or Eri: the name of the ancestral origin of an Ibo clan according to legend and claimed to be a descendant of an ancient Israelite Levitical order as recorded in the Old Testament

Nwata Ona: the name given for the pectorial mask worn by the Eze Nri

Alah, ani: universal Ibo deity; regarded by some to be same as the Supreme deity of the Ibos that was supplanted by the colonial 'God' concept; perhaps similar to Elah, eloah of the Old Testament times. The Chiukwu originally of the Aro peoples and Igwekala of Umunoha concepts much later rivalled the Alah concept. The Ibos regard these deities to be superior to the western colonial 'God' concept who some claim was created by Chiukwu (The most supreme Chi). Chi could be conceived as referring to the unfathomable sovereign 'Cosmic Mind' from whom all things came and who directs the destiny of everything. Chiukwu is not limited by time and space. Thus is the source of all creation.

Asab, Asaba- lush green territory

Ahab, Ahaba- a place of love, fidelity

Abba, abbah- Father Land

Afru-eka, africa- motherland

Abi ama, abi'am- Father of my people, Chukwu abiama Great Chi of my fathers, God of my ancestors

Nkwo: Ibo fourth day

Obi, Obiri: the shrine of a compound, regarded as the heart and nucleus of an Ibo compound.

Ofo: Staff of moral authority and justice. The Eri (Nri) Levitical High Priest is said to have come to Ibo land with it according to one of the legends (Eri legend).

Ozo, Nze: Ibo titles, the Eze Nri (Eri) coronates people with these titles

Oye, orie: the second market day in Ibo calendar

Otunsi: fetish that is believed to protect a land

Uhie: a beautifying powder, yellow in coloured

Ugwu Nzu: Eri's first residence location according the Eri legend

Uke: ill fortune

Uziza: vegetable for cooking, believed to have curative properties

Ogirishi: an ever living plant used to identify the burial spot of a baby's placenta, the foreskin removed in circumcision and other spots

Mgbe: puberty initation ritual process for females

Omu: Usually omu nkwu: fresh palm fronds used to indicate sacredness, separated, holiness, and the sanctified; different from the profane, ordinary

G-D: used instead of the German-English derivatives, Gott, "God"; and used to refer to Adonai, Lord in place of Yahweh, ha Shem, the sacred name

Nkwu: name for the palm tree

Mbari, embarri: ritual historical art gallery

Ajoku ji: festival marking the Ibo New Year, linked strongly with celebration with yam crop and yam meal; literally 'Yam festival' festival of first fruits

Ipu ala: purification ritual, literally cleansing a polluted the land

Igba ndu: ritualised covenant made between peoples and the deity- often takes a form of sin offering for atonement and commensal meal

Odo: name for egg yolk- applied during circumcision ritual

Igba nkwa- Ibo feast of the Promise- Passover

Onu mkpuru akuku- Ibo feast of First Fruits

Iwa ji, alo mmuo, new yam festival

Onwa asato- feast of Tabernacles

Olaudah Equiano
or
GUSTAVUS VASSA,
the African

Ola Udah Ekwe alua: identified to originate from Iseke Ibo community. He was perhaps an Ikwuani Ibo boy when he was kidnapped and sold into slavery at the age of eleven. He produced the first extant documented evidence that identifies his Ibo people as Hebrews. His name was corrupted by his captors and slave masters

Some Relevant Extracts from Olaudah Equiano: The Interesting Narratives of the Life of Olaudah Equiano, or Gustavus Vassa, The African (Made in the USA Middletown, DE 18 July 2017) Chapter 1(passim): sic:

"That part of Africa, known by the name Guinea, to which the trade in slaves is carried on, extends along the coast 3400 miles, from the Senegal to Angola, and includes a variety of kingdoms. Of these the most considerable is the kingdom of Benen, both as to extent and wealth, the richness and cultivation of the soil, the power of its king, and the number and warlike disposition of the inhabitants. It is situated nearly under the line, and extends along the coast about

170 miles, but runs back into the interior part of Africa to a distance hitherto I believed unexplored by any traveler; and seems only terminated at length by the empire of Abyssinia, near 1500 miles from its beginning. This kingdom is divided into many provinces and districts: in one of the most remote and fertile of which, called Eboe, I was born, in the year 1745, in a charming fruitful vale, named Essaka. The distance of this province from the capital of Benin and the sea coast must be considerable; for I had never heard of white men or Europeans, nor of the sea: and our subjection to the king of Benin was little more than nominal; for every transaction of the government, as far as my slender observation extended, was conducted by the chiefs or elders of the place...."

"... The West Indian planters prefer the slaves of Benin or Eboe to those of any other part of Guinea, for their hardiness, intelligence, integrity, and zeal..."

"...Our land is uncommonly rich and fruitful, and produces all kinds of vegetables in great abundance. We have plenty of Indian corn, and vast quantities of cotton and tobacco. Our pine apples grow without culture; they are about the size of the largest sugar-loaf, and finely flavoured. We have also spices of different kinds, particularly pepper; and a variety of delicious fruits which I have not seen in Europe; together with gums of various kinds, and honey in abundance. All our industry is exerted to improve those blessings of nature. Agriculture is our chief employment; and everyone, even children and women are engaged in it. Thus we are all habituated to labour from our earliest years. Every one contributes something to the common stock; and as we are unacquainted with idleness, we have no beggars..."

"Deformity is indeed unknown amongst us, I mean that of shape. Numbers of the natives of Eboe now in London might be brought in support of this assertion: for, in regard to complexion, ideas of beauty are wholly relative. I remember while in Africa to have seen three Negro children, who were tawny, and another quite white, who were universally regarded by myself, and the natives in general, as far as related to their complexions, as deformed. Our women too, were in my eyes, at least uncommonly graceful, alert, and modest to a degree of bashfulness; nor do I remember to ever heard of an instance of incontinence amongst them before marriage. They are remarkably cheerful. Indeed cheerfulness and affability are two of the leading characteristics of our nation."

"Every woman too, at certain times, was forbidden to come into a dwelling-house, or touch any person, or anything we eat."

"Though we had no places of public worship, we had priests and magicians, or wise men. I do not remember whether they had different offices, or whether they were united in the same persons, but they were held in great reverence by the people. They calculated our time, and foretold events, as their name imported, for we called them Ah-affoe-way-cah, which signifies calculators or yearly men, our year is called Ah-affoe" (present day written: afor, ahor).

"We practiced circumcision like the Jews and made offerings and feasts on that occasion in the same manner as they did."

"And here I cannot forbear suggesting what has long struck me very forcibly, namely, the strong analogy which even by this sketch, imperfect as it is, appears to prevail in the manners and customs of my countrymen and those of the Jews, before they reached the Land of Promise, and particularly the patriarchs while they were yet in that pastoral state which is described in Genesis-an analogy which alone would induce me to think that the one people had sprung from the other." "Indeed this is the opinion of Dr Gill, who, in his commentary on Genesis, very ably deduces the pedigree of the Africans from Afer and Afra, the descendants of Abraham by Keturah his wife and concubine for both titles are applied to her. It is also conformable to the sentiments of Dr John Clarke, formerly Dean of Sarum, in his Truth of the Christian Religion: both these authors concur in ascribing to us this original. The reasoning of these gentlemen are still further confirmed by the scripture chronology; and if any further corroboration were required, this resemblance in so many respects is a strong evidence in support of the opinion."

"Like the Israelites in their primitive state, our government was conducted by our chiefs or judges, our wise men and elders; and the head of a family with us enjoyed a similar authority over his household with that which is ascribed to Abraham and the other patriarchs. The law of retaliation obtained almost universally with us as with them; and even their religion appeared to have shed a ray of its glory, though broken and spent in its passage, or eclipsed by the cloud with which time, tradition, and ignorance might have enveloped it; for we had our circumcision a rule I believe peculiar to that people; we had also sacrifices and burnt offerings, our washings and purifications, on the same occasions as they had. As to the difference in colour between the Eboan Africans and the modern Jews I shall not pressure to account for it. It is a subject which has engaged the pens of both genius and learning, and is far above my strength. The most able and Reverend Mr T. Clarkson, however, in his much admired Essay on the Slavery and Commerce of the Human Species, has ascertained the cause, in a manner that at once solves every objection on that account, and on my mind at least, has produced the fullest conviction. I shall therefore refer to that performance for the theory, contenting myself with extracting a fact as related by Dr Mitchel. The Spaniards, who have inhabited America, under the torrid zone, for any time, are become as dark coloured as our native Indians of Virginia; of which I myself have been a witness. There is also another instance of a Portuguese settlement at Mitomba, a river in Sierra Leone; where the inhabitants are bred from a mixture of the first Portuguese discoverers with the natives, are now become in their complexion, and in the wholly quality of their hair, perfect negroes retaining however a smartering of the Portuguese language. These instances and a great many more which might be adduced, while they shew how the complexions of the same persons vary in different climates, it is hoped may tend also to remove the prejudice that some conceive against the natives of Africa on account of colour...."

Without belaboring the point Dr Olaudah Equiano, as he was called, briefly highlights some of those common manners and customs of his people, the Eboes; that they shared with the Jews of Old Testament Times. He seems to imply that these similar manners and customs they share including skin colour are too many in the Hebrew Text to question their connectedness as one people with a common origin. He also indicated that the Eboes were preferred to other ethnic groups as slaves by the buyers. This is corroborated by the fact that it is known that the white buyers would first ask their sellers if their catch was "Onyeboe". They would shout to their sellers asking: Onyeboe?!!

Onyeboe?!! Onyeboe?!!! Onyeboe?!!!!. It was this exclamation that gave the white person the designation "Oyibo" by inhabitants of then western Nigeria. This has become the name by which every white person is generally referred in that part of Nigeria. The reader will later in the book discover that the native inhabitants of the land referred to the white people as "onyeboe" because of their light skin complexion (just as the Ibos) when the colonial masters first met them. By this time even the natives had corrupted the name Ibhru to heebo, eboe, Ibo.

A BRIEF PREAMBLE

KINGDOM OF JUDAH: KNOWN AS JEWS IN AFRICA WITH A WELL DEMARCATED TERRITORY 1747. ALSO IDENTIFIED AS THE SLAVE TERRITORY. MOST OF THE SLAVES ARE SAID TO BE HEEBOES (HEBREWS, EBOES, IBOS, IGBOS). THEY WERE OBVIOUSLY NOT HAMITES BUT SEMITES. THEY WERE SOLD BY THE NATIVE AFRICANS WHO WERE HAMITES. HAVING FLOODED AFRICA FROM THE MIDDLE EAST WITH ANCIENT ARABS DURING THE VARIOUS MASSACRES AND PERSECUTIONS THEY SUFFERED IN THE HANDS OF THE ENEMIES NOTABLY THE PERSIANS, ASSYRIANS, BABYLONIANS, GREEKS, ROMANS, EUROPEANS, ARABS, AND OTHERS. THEY WERE AGAIN SOLD AS SLAVES AND MOVED TO THE AMERICAS. (Cf ELIZABETH DONNAN: ILLUSTRATIVE HISTORY OF THE SLAVE TRADE TO AMERICA, AND FLAVIUS JOSEPHUS ANTIQUITIES AND WARS)

/ 19 /

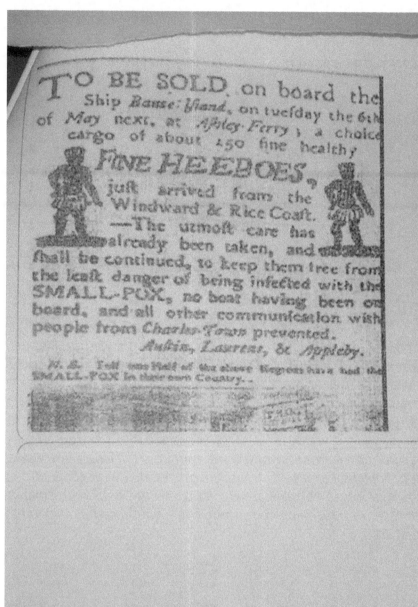

TO BE SOLD, on board the
Ship *Bance-Island*, on tuesday the 6th
of *May* next, at *Ashley-Ferry*; a choice
cargo of about 250 fine healthy

NEGROES,

just arrived from the
Windward & Rice Coast.
—The utmost care has
already been taken, and
shall be continued, to keep them free from
the least danger of being infected with the
SMALL-POX, no boat having been on
board, and all other communication with
people from *Charles-Town* prevented.

Austin, Laurens, & Appleby.

N. B. Full one Half of the above Negroes have had the
SMALL-POX in their own Country.

A BRIEF PREAMBLE

That the Ibos (at least a large majority of them) occupying the Eastern territory (called colonial Ibo country by Europeans) and beyond, of present day Nigeria are Jews (Hebrews or Hebrew ISRAIAH; also referred to as Israelites) is no longer in question. Apart from the native consciousness expressed in many legends constantly pointing to that fact and their manifesting in different forms the characteristics of the Israelites as described in the Hebrew Bible, their recognition and acceptance into the well known Jewish Federation, King Solomon Sephardic Federation International (KSSFI) should attest to this identity to some extent. This universal recognition and acceptance as descendants of ancient Israelites was sealed after rigorous research that included visits to Ibo communities that is said to have spanned a period of at least a hundred years by international scholars including scholars of the University of Oxford, Oxford, United Kingdom (UK). It was during the King Solomon Sephardic Federation International conference held in Philadelphia, USA that it was announced to the whole world that the Ibo peoples of today were officially recognized as descendants of ancient Israelites. So in May 1997 the Ibo peoples of Nigeria were presented with their certificate of membership of the world Jewry of the Sephardim stock. The Eze A E Chukwuemeka Eri, the holder of the Ofor Eri, said to be regarded as the oldest symbol of authority in the world was recognized as the leader of all Ibo Israelites and the coordinator of all Lost Tribes of Israel in West Africa. He was at that conference asked to officially form the Nigeria Chapter of the Federation. King Solomon Sephardic Federation is the umbrella organization representing the Ancient Sepahardic Nations of Eastern Judeans, Hebrews and Israelites. Its primary function is to identify and assist the lost tribes of Israel and Jews in diaspora. It is a non governmental, non-political and non-religious Cultural organization with chapters in Morocco, Ethiopia, Iran, India, the USA, Ghana, Uganda, South Africa, Belgium, Jordan, Zimbabwe, Somalia, Mali, Yemen, Spain, Switzerland, Burundi, Rwanda, and many other nations. The communiqué of this declaration also states that the KSSFI has the capability to bring member nations closer and to cooperate in areas of diplomacy, culture, tourism, business, education, construction, agriculture, medicine, science and technology etc for mutual benefits. The communiqués also emphatically states that the federation is determined to bring the Nigerian Jews (i.e Hebrew-Israiah/Israelites) into the world Jewry, act as a means of cohesion of all Nigerian Jews, establish a permanent relationship with Jewish communities everywhere and provide spiritual, social, and cultural integration of all Nigerian Jews. It hopes to enable the Ibos achieve the status of entering freely into Israel and to seek assistance from Israel including the Oleh Hadash according to the 1948 law of return. The communiqués concludes by calling upon all Ibo peoples to be part of this reinvention. However it is essential to mention here that the ethnic Ibos are not just Jews because they have been registered as members of the shepherdi. They are Hebrews and Jews only because they are children of Jacob who are described as Jews in the Hebrew Bible. Ethnic Ibo peoples have identified themselves in other countries including the Equatorial Guinea, Ivory Coast, Liberia, and in the Caribeans as among liberated slaves notably, St Vincents, Dominica, the Dominican Republic, Martinique, etc and Jamaica where they were said to have arrived as "the Red Ibos." In these lands, they have long claimed to be Israelites in origin. In fact a friend stated to me that "from time immemorial people who are light skinned in Jamaica have been referred to as 'Jamaican Ibo'." This, she explained, also connoted "Jamaican Jew." Thus these Jamaicans, like other unidentified Ibos scattered worldwide through slave trade, are included as Sephardi Jews, this means that they are Hebrew-Israelites of the Sephardic stock also. This also shows that the Ibo nation is far broader than we have known so far. Perhaps, additional to this testimony is this: I met a bearded man somewhere and I was to examine him medically. Initial information involved self identification so in course of the interview he claimed of Caribean nationality but added, "my ethnicity is Ibo according to my ancestors." You can only imagine how shocked I was; a man from the Caribean bearing a Muslim name and with long beard and shaven head. The most interesting part of it was that he insisted I must leave his ethnicity as Ibo. I asked if he had ever been to Iboland? He answered rather proudly: "for sixty four years I have desired to visit the Ibo land, my ancestral home". I asked if he knew Ibos were Jews, the unadulterated Hebrews in existence today? He answered: "Yes, I know: circumstances made me become a Muslim." In addition to these we learn that ethnic Ibos have been identified in various parts of the United States of America (USA) in large numbers. There is today Council of Ibo States in the USA.

On October 23 1997 two Ashkenazi Jews, Yitzhaq David and Zagi David excitedly called upon the Ibos to make a quick come back to reunite with Israel. This was because of the overwhelming evidences convincing them that the Ibos are indeed descendants of ancient Israelites. Earlier on the 28 March 1996 the Israeli Ambassador to Nigeria made a special gift of olive and oil to Eze Nri, a gift he confirmed was only offered to Kings of Israel. We can also recall that the Anglican missionary to Iboland, the Reverend George Thomas Basden long ago advised his fellow missionaries intending to come to Ibo country to first farmiliarise themselves with the Old Testament laws before coming to the Iboland if they must "make a better witness to the Ibos." This is because according to him what he saw of the Ibo life style was all Old Testament practice characterized by belief in the one true God, circumcision on the 8th day following the birth of a baby boy, animal sacrifices that followed a carefully regulated pattern, feasts and laws similar to the laws of Moses, belief in clean and unclean animals to mention just these. It was on the basis of these observations and testimonies that some people argue that Ibos are not to be called Jews rather they are to be regarded as the original Hebrews of today. This is to differentiate them from those who claim to be Jews but who are not Jews by ethnicity. These non ethnic Jews claiming Jewish ancestry are often referred to as "synagogues of Satan." These nonethnic Jews are many in number and have been claiming the control of the affairs of the world Jewry for perhaps a very long time. One example often cited is those of the Khazarian stock said to be converts to Judaism who established the present day Judaism of the Ashkenazic stock. They are said to have been responsible for interpreting much of what is known as Jewish today including establishing a Zionist political movement, the Jewish nation, its flag and symbols as well as the Star of David, and even claiming the sole right of determining who should or should not be regarded as a Jew or who should be given the qualification to belong to the world Jewry etc. They are said to have adulterated the Hebrew language by introducing the German version known as the Yiddish. However, there should be no reason why converts to Judaism cannot have the right to claim Jewish ethnicity including pursueing the well being of the Jewish people. What the world Jews need today is forging a common front to fight injustice and reinvent themselves and pursue a common task of carrying out the instruction of Yahawah (Yahweh). It was the failure of the true Hebrew Israelites to fulfil this task of Yahawah that ignited the curse on them (Leviticus 26 and Deuteronomy 28). The world Jewry is expected to collectively fight and emancipate themselves from oppression wherever they are; it is hoped that Ibo Hebrew-Israelites will achieve their liberation with the cooperation of their fellow Jews just as the present day state of Israel has been achieved.

Further evidences were also observed to characterize the testimony of Ola udah (meaning "the glory of Judah") Ikwuano or Ekwealua, (corrupted as Equiano) when he first read the Old Testament. He and his sister suffered the effect of the curse of Leviticus 26 and Deuteronomy 28 and its inherent blessing also. Having been taken into slavery with his younger sister who was perhaps about three years old, at the age of eleven; he later learnt to read and write in the English language. Thus reading the Hebrew Bible culture for the first time opened his eyes to the similarities in practice and belief among his people. This observation was corroborated by the opinion of scholars he cited above.

It is therefore the true worship of Yahweh that makes a person a true Jew, not just by belonging to an ethnic group. Any body can claim to be Hebrew but any identification with the Jew calls for scrutiny of your life style, worship, beliefs systems and allegiance. Yeshua, ha Maschiach stated this fact in the Berit Hachadasha (The New Testament) when he states that True worshiper of Yahweh must worship Him in Spirit and Truth. Paul the Apostle and all other Apostles also testify to this when they realized that claiming to be a Hebrew does not make a person right before Yahweh. Rather it is by being a true worshipper of Yahweh that is needed to be a Jew. We must not confuse being a Judaizer with being a Jew. A Judaizer practices Judaism, the type of religion Yeshua condemned as Hypocritical. Thus being a Jew is a commitment to serve Yahweh in truth and Spirit as the Mosaic laws require. It also includes being allegiant to the cause of the Jews and Israelite peoples all over the world, including fighting their wars and battles of survival. For this reason the writer of this study tends to prefer to address Ibos as Jews rather than as Hebrews. As Jews to have a calling to worship the God of their father Abraham in Spirit and Truth and to correct immorality, hostiltity, injustice and evil in the world, though they are truly Hebrews being children of Jacob and therefore Abraham(Abiama) as the Hebrew Bible refers to them.

The Deserts of Seth found in Africa

Deserts of Seth – West Africa 1747 map located within the district of Biafara where most of the Ibos still inhabit

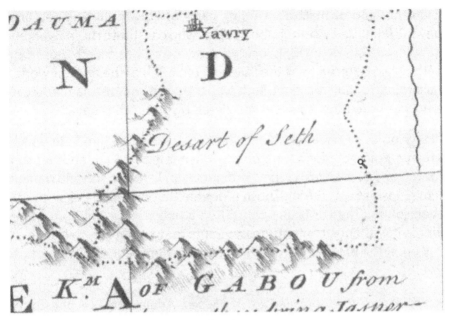

Deserts of Seth 1747 map

By 1777 the name Seth disappears from the map and prominently Biafara seems to dominate

Even the land of Biafara including parts of Equatorial Guinnea and beyond inhabited by ethnic Ibo peoples who constitute the indigenous peoples of Biafara (IPOB) is located within what was called "Desert of Seth" (also referred to as the "Deserts of Seth") of the ancient world. According to Bible account Seth was the third son of Adam and Eve who was born after Abel was murdered by his brother Cain.

"Later on Eve gave birth to another son and named him Seth which means "granted"; for as she put it, God has granted me another son for the one Cain killed." When Seth grew up, he had a son and named him, Enosh. It was during Enosh's lifetime that men first began to call themselves "the Lord's People."(The Catholic Living Bible) In other words it was Enosh and his descendants that first began to invoke or call upon the name of Yahawah: "Leqra beshem Yahweh."(Genesis 4: 25-26)

According to the Apocalypses of Moses, Adam and Eve had thirty children, however only three were mentioned in the Bible. The Book of Jubilees mentions five of their children namely: Cain, Luluwa, Abel, Aklia and Seth. Adam and Eve were advised by the creator to descend to the lower level of the holy mountain and reside in the Cave of Treasures below paradise on the western border. Apparently Cain and his descendant later descended from the mountain and began to populate the plains below in the land called Nod to the East of Eden Gen 4: 16. No land was named after Cain. However when Seth began to multiply, the book goes on to say, Satan began to skim for an interaction between Cain and Seth's children by Canem who had multiplied into a large city north of West Africa. Thus the desert of Seth in West Africa was named after the righteous son of Adam called Seth by his descendants. It was perhaps intermarriage between Cain's descendants and Seth's descendants that probably led to the flood in which only Noah and his family were preserved. However according to Amanda Trayce (2013): "by 1777 AD the name Seth had disappeared from the map of the Europeans and in the modern times is located the Republic of Biafara located in the Southeast and dominated by the Igbo (Ebo, Heebo, Ibo) peoples who have long been recognized as a remnant of the lost tribe of Jacob." Unfortunately another form of conspiracy by sworn enemies of the Ibo (Hebrew) peoples has removed the name Biafra on the map, from identifying the same area.

Seth was perhaps the most likely ancestor of the Semites as Noah, his descendant who survived the flood and his household had three sons Ham, Shem and Japhet. Shem became the father of the Semites of which the ethnic Hebrew-Israiah (Israelites) are the main survival stock. The ethnic Semites are facing persecution worldwide including the Hebrew /Israiah, (Israelite) Ibos. As an observer sucintly stated: "Thus the world's best kept secret" of the Jewishness of the Ibo peoples is no longer a secret as the G-d of the fathers of the Ibos who the Ibos refer to as "Chiokike Abiama (Abrama, Abraham)" has at his own time exposed the Jewishness of the Ibos to the rest of the world and comfounded enemies of this fact. Thus His Royal Highness (HRH) King Opigo, an izhon ('Ijaw') and through oral tradition, are believed to belong to one of the Jewish tribes (Hebrew- Israelite), intelligently and wisely suggested the name "Biafara" to the new nation in 1967, in the bid to unite all Ibos as descendants of Seth and in line with the Europeans calling the whole of the then Eastern Region Ibo country.

The origin and meaning of the name Biafra has been given different explanations. However the concensus seems to be directed to a generic term derived from the root word "Ephraim." Mr Simon Ukegbe suggests that the republic of Biafra of 1967 should be named The Christain Democratic Republic of B'Ephraim. According to him the "B'" should be referring to the Bight or bay bearing the name Biafra. According to him the Europeans at that time called the Bay variously Biafar/Biafara/Biafares. Researchers also hold the view that the area is inhabited by the descendants of Ephraim. Mitchell map of 1839 states that the important esturaries from where the rivers flow into the ocean is called Ephraim town which is located 60 miles from River Nun which was part of the Ibo country, and today is in the present day politically and artificially created South-South Nigeria. The river is said to be named after Nun the father of Joshua of the tribe of Ephraim. The Biblical meaning of the name Ephraim is 'God has made me fruitful in the land of affliction.' In actual fact this reflects the fate of the Ibo peoples inhabiting this area, notably, the following peoples as some people have artificially and politically demarcated today: All the Igbo speaking peoples, the Ijaw made up of speakers of Kalabari, Edoid, Izon languages; the Ibibios, Effiks, Ogojas, Idomas, Igalas, and others. This means that these peoples and their kith and kin in Guinea Bissau, Kameroons, Gabon, Equatorial Guinea, Sao Thome, and others have been coexisting thousands of years before colonial unslaught that divided them into separate countries. As perhaps stated earlier, in Hebrew the word that is perhaps the root of the Baifrah is "Behphrah" that means disturbance, affliction, interference, interruption, distraction, intrusion and such like. It is a name word. B'Ephraim (be'ifra) thus becomes self explanatory, as the land of Ephriam.The "B" in Hebrew language being taken as either "Beth essentiae" or regarding it to mean strait forward simply "in". That would mean "as ifra" or "in Ifra": perhaps "in affliction". Thus "in a land of affliction." It was perhaps corrupted by European pronunciation and perhaps also plus the attempt to disconnect the inhabitants from their Israelite roots and from their associated superior status compared to the various colonial masters. This also means that the English who colonized the area like their fellow Europeans' understanding of the indigenous Ibos was very limited. It is also possible that the word pronounced as "Biafara" is perhaps more a European creation being probably Portuguese in origin but derived from the original Hebrew name. I also understand that there is a town in Portugal called "Biafra"; this could confirm the foreign origin of the corruption of the name from its original pronunciation. The Portuguese also called Africans "Negroes', a word that they later gave a derogatory connotation as it came to refer to the black complexion as inferior. Others refer to inhabitants as "Ebony" (perhaps derived from Eboany) perhaps later used to specifically describe those Africans who are of jet black beauty. However the Hebrew-Israelite Ibos are Semites while the descendants of Ham are not as some scholars have propounded. These scholars propound that it was the Hamites that sold the Semites into slavery while the descendants of Japhet were the slave owners and remained their torturers. While the sons of Abraham through Ishmael and later Keturah Abraham's wife and others became known as the Arabs especially the North African Arabs. The descendants of Japhet became known as the "white race." This is in spite of being referred to as being red in colour (Edomites) being descendants of Esau. This perhaps includes those who are said to be the Khazarians who among other achievements played a part in establishing the modern Ashkenazic Judaism with its superiority portrayals. Even Christianity, the religion of the so called "white" colonizers was used to brain wash the Africans that they are inferior; painting G-d and Yeshua the Messiah "white", and reinterpreting their natural complexion as white instead of the Biblical reddish colour as recorded in Genesis 25: 25. As stated earlier Genesis 25: 25 identifies these colonizers as descendants of Esau and consequently Edomites. Revelation 1: 13, 14 present Yeshua (Jesus) as having a wooly hair and other features of the black race being a descendant of Jacob through Judah as enunciated in Hebrews 7: 14 of the Christian New Testament. Also as stated earlier, the present day photograph popularised to be Jesus the Christ is a photograph of a European man called Caesare Bogias who was said to be a child of a certain Pope Alexander. This deception has caused so much confusion to the uninformed Christian world for centuries. This is such that some people tend to claim that Iesous/Jesus/ Yeshua do not refer to Yashaiah but to a pagan spirit derived from Zeus, Djaus Piter, Jupiter etc that was incorporated into paganised version of Christianity when Constantine the Emperor was christianising Europe. This is because the Greek word Iesous literally means "son of Sous". Thus (son of Zeus) who was also same as Djaus Piter (father Zeus, and same as Jupiter)

So called Blacks of the world have been given different denigrating tags and names by foreign invaders especially the Europeans. This is probably because the Europeans abused the right of being the first to explore other peoples' lands and wrote the peoples history and created maps. This right was given to them because the Black race being Hebrew Israelites as Jews are suffering the stigma placed on them by G-d of their fathers for backsliding from serving Him (Deuteronomy 28) see also Deut 7:6 Leviticus 26). Yet it could be argued that the present day version of colonial Christianity notably the western versions are a distorted versions of the original version; the result continues to bring about rivalry, suffering and lack of peace in the world. Unfortunately the majority of the Ibo people has embraced these corrupt versions and consequently continues to distant themselves from the true worship of the G-d of their fathers. This calls for the need for personal and collective reinvention.

As the reader would come across in this book, the word Africa was derived from the fact that going by historical accounts of Josephus Antiquities and confirmed by Olaudah Equiano's testimony, Africans descended from their forefather Apher (Afer, also called Aphron), one of the sons of Abraham, "the Ibhri", descendant of Heber (Eber). Abraham is said to be a descendant of Heber (Eber). The word "The Ibhri" is literally "Ha Ibhri" in the Hebrew language. This is not a name word but a description or designation of a characteristic. Some claim this designation to refer to "Abraham, the forester", or 'the dweller in the forests', "the forest person." And lastly the word was transcribed and anglicised as "Hebrew." The reader could also easily discover that the name variously written as Heebro, Ibo, Ebo, Ebo(e), Eboan, Heebo, Igbo is derived from the word "ibhri', 'eber', heber, as various people attempted to pronounce it. Pronouncing the Hebrew 'rough breathing' letter 'bh' has been known to sometimes take the form "v", "gb", "b", and how it is pronounced will perhaps depend on the thickness of the lips pronouncing it. There is no other ethnic group in the whole world today identified as the original Hebrews apart from the Ibos. Consequently the Hebrew-Israelite Ibos are the only people of the world today still referred to as Hebrew though corrupted to Ibo (Igbo). The claim that the word Igbo is found among other ethnic groups in Nigeria does not change the original name of the Ibo. Among the Yorubas the word may not be a name word and even if it means a name word said to mean "forest" could be describing the features of the Ibos and perhaps the original meaning of the word "Ibhri" as "people of the forest." This perhaps agrees with the Bible use of the phrase "Abram, the Ibhri" "Abram, the forester" because he crossed over the river to dwell in the forest. One Ibo legend holds that an ancestor of the Ibo called Eri began the journey of migration along with Oduduwa the founder of the Yoruba (Yaarabi) race said to have his own origin traceable to Nimrod, "a strong and powerful man" and "a great hunter" (Genesis) and said to be the architect of the building of the Tower of Babel and consequently the founder of Babel territory (Babylon). The Yorubas today still refer to him as Lamurudu. This could point to the fact that the two ethnic groups understaood themselves and still maintained the designation by which the Hebrews were known in ancient times. However the word could be different in both languages. Nimrod is said to be the husband to Samiramis, the

Queen, who begot the dreaded Tammuz. Tammuz on the other hand begot Horus...who is said to have presented features that have been attributed to Yeshua by some scholars, a very controversial issue that has been disproved and rejected by most evangelical and biblical Christian scholars today.

Also some people claim that the word "Igbo" means "slave"(actually "servant") in some parts of Nigeria; including parts of Delta State. This is because as the story goes, some Ibos were taken by a certain Oba of Benin, in very remote time, to serve in his Kingdom. They mixed up among the people some of whom were Ibos their brothers. Being naturally very hard working and more attractive to the women, the Oba is said to have these servants castrated to ensure they did not cohabit with his many wives. So the word "Igbo" came to acquire the connotation of "servanthood" through the years among some of these Deltans. However the story cannot be concluded without further aftermath of this saga. This is because the Oba is said to have favoured some of these servants. In addition to other favours, the Oba did not castrate them. They got married. One in particular was most favoured. He got married and his children rapidly expanded as Ishan community. He was said to have later remembered his native home and relocated to meet his brothers across the Niger. His brothers are said to have allocated a portion of land by the sea side. They were referred to as "people of the area of Ishan", literally in the Igbo language "onumara Ishan". This designation passed through many linguistic modifications including "Onuma Ishan" and eventually to "Onuishan" and finally corrupted by the colonial Anglicising to "Onicha." The veracity of this saga is perhaps the fact that some time ago the Onitcha people were mistakenly not regarded as truly Ibo. A cololary to this experience is perhaps the emergence of the community called Kwankwaso in Kano, Northern Nigeria. A community that derived its name from the founder one Mr Okonkwo who set up a business he tagged as "Okonkwo and Sons." The name "Okonkwo and Sons" is said to have undergone many linguistic pronunciations as the natives Hausanised it through the years. The name of the area eventually came to be known as "Kwankwaso."

In the same vein my research shows that the mba miris (the coastal areas) is inhabited by Ibo people from the interior who were taken into slavery but were evacuated along the coast by their captors when the travel to overseas was foiled in the run up to the ending of the trade. These evacuated Ibo were given land to settle by their brothers who inhabited the coast. This explains the origin of communities we know today inhabiting the whole coastal areas. These include the Ijaws, Ogonis, Bonny (Ubani), etc and why the dialectremain either as Igbo or related to Igbo. Being first to come into contact with the colonial masters gave them many advantages over their brothers in the interior making them the ones to lay the foundation for the growth and development of their brothers in the interior, notably Ibos of the so called Southeastern states some of whom are wrongly singularly called Igbos.

Also I was told by a Ghanaian that when she was a child she was told that the Igbo people were "a forest people" (bush people), lived in the bush, and who were regarded to eat human being (carnibals). This perhaps refers to the notorious Abam warriors, "Abam head hunters" as they were called in today's Abia state. They terrorized other Ibo communities and beyond even during my time as a boy in the early to mid 50s until independence in 1960.

The above brief at least shows that the word, "Ibo (Igbo)" has come to mean different things to different peoples depending on the connotation given to the experience of the peoples with the Ibos. In every experience, the name has faced hostiltity, persecution, enslavement, and stigmatization, like the people it represents since the time of Abraham, (who was perhaps, "the first Eboe, Heeboe, Ibo, Igbo") but who have still survived and triumphed. There are indications that the Ibo country will live forever as they are in fact found all over the world.

The truth is that today the Ibo peoples have come a long way in realizing who they are and have been confirmed to be the original Hebrew Israelite (also called Jews); as stated earlier some Igbos prefer to regard themselves as the only surviving pure Hebrew people. This group of Ibos have the habit of sticking to this belief about the Ibos in spite of the claim that the total world population of Jews is only fourteen and a half million, perhaps, a misinformation championed by certain quarters. The population of the Ibo Sephardis alone today is at least eigthy million and their habitation goes beyond the boundaries of the Niger River and Benue River and should naturally include all those inhabiting the Atlantic coastal lands and beyond rather than just those inhabiting the interior of the current South Eastern, Kogi, Benue and Delta states of Nigeria.

It is on record that on the occasion of the first national conference of Nigerian Sephardi Jews that took place in Jos Plateau State Nigeria in 1997, I was appointed and given the privilege by the Eze Chuckwumeka Eri to act as the secretary and take the minutes of the Executive Meeting. During that conference important discussions included planning the hosting of a planned International conference of the World Jews in Nigeria, the writing of the History of

MAP OF BIAFRA
LAND OF RISING SUN

Land of some of the heebo; certainly the heebo peoples include far more than these as they extend to the Middle Belt, Equatorial Guinea and Cameroon and even beyond as awareness of this common ancestry increases

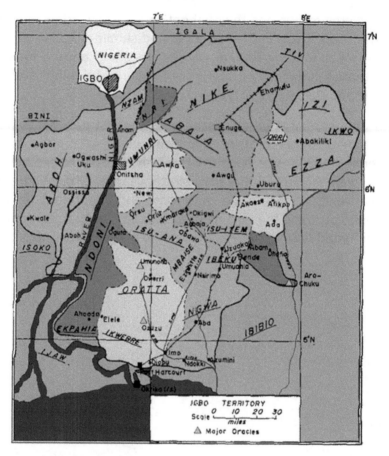

the Ibos, and many other important associated matters surrounding security as well as ways to prevent challatans from deceiving people under the guise of being "Ibo Jews" as was observed to take place in 1997 when because of nationwide excitement many guillible Ibos were duped.   Many other important issues were discussed at that convention that I consider to be too private and sensitive to include in this book. I do recall that an Ashanti was the West African General Secretary of the Shepardic Jews and he was present at the conference. Most the women who were present proved to me that they had long begun to reinvent themselves as Hebrew women, mothers and wives as the Old Testament teaches and as was practiced by Ibo ancestral mothers and wives. I was personally challenged and impressed by the fact that reinvention was very practicable in spite of modernity.

This book is therefore not aimed to prove to the Ibos that they are

Hebrews or Jews, if by that is meant descendants of Jacob who was later in his life renamed 'Israel', and as conceived in the present day. In fact majority of the Ibos already know they are Jews in that sense of the word; perhaps only very few may still be in denial of this fact.

There maybe inhabitants who by their own collective consciousness understand that their ancestors belong to the group of original native inhabitants of the territory who the Ibo ancestors might have met and who are now absorbed into the Ibo ethnicity and nation. Some of these original natives have been identified as the Kwas, the Alukus, the Ituris, and the Pigmies (referred to as Dwarfs). Perhaps these were of the Hamitic stock. These have got so mixed up and have become so absorbed by the descendants of the ancient Ibo ancestors that it has become difficult to separate the ancient Ibo descendants from the natives of the land. Some species might have died off (e.g.the pigmies/dwarfs). However in Nigeria as we know thus far the common practices binding all Ibo peoples include in addition to circumcision, the practice of the New Yam festival and other first fruit festivals, and other agricultural rituals, laws and festivals as commanded by Moses in the Hebrew Bible. This celebration follows a common ritual pattern and carries a common significance among the peoples. For example the New Yam festival also marks the Ibo New Year and falls within the same period as the Jewish Rosh hashana (New Year). There is also the need to state that all children of Ibo women married to non Ibos are regarded as Ibos just like the Jews of ancient Israelite times. This is because it became difficult to know who actually fathered a child in a world that rapes women during wars and persecutions. It was believed that the Jewish gene can also be transmitted through a Jewish woman. This means that the Ibo peoples are spread all over, world wide, as stated above, not just within the enclave of former eastern states, Delta, and territories within present Benue and Kogi states and territories that were formerly referred to as Ibo Country by the colonials.

The aim of this study is also not to convince the world that the Ibos are Jews or the only true Hebrews of today. Such identity proof is, anyway, neither necessary nor needful of any people on this earth. Peoples remain who they consciously believe they are and nothing can alter this consciousness. Moreover the question of what constitutes a Jew has been made so unclear and politicized that it is becoming more and more difficult to know who is truly a Jew. Some claim the Davidic line is the only true Jewish identity route; some claim the Ashkenazi rabbinic interpretation of the Halakhah as the only yardstick of Jewish identity etc. Nevertheless the Sephardic and other Jewish groups have recognized the possibility of more descendants of Jacob and other Hebrews perhaps for centuries. I still contend that the true identity of a Jew cannot in addition to self consciousness, go beyond the choosing to voluntarily be "a people of Yahweh" in Spirit and Truth and live as such.

The route of descent has also been traced through the line of either a human figure regarded as representative or a popular rabbi that lived in the past. Others claim that genetic test can identify a Jew. Yet we know that genes do mutate and alter and there is no religious gene if Jewishness is a religious designation. Even the assertion that a Jew must be a person born of a Jewish mother has failed to prove or disprove the Jewish identity of a person as that is only possible if the mother can be proved to be a Jew. Thus we are still left with the question, 'who is a Jew after all these religious and politically motivated unreasonable reasonings?' This has even made some ask, "should we rather, not be talking of who is a Hebrew, instead of who is a Jew? Hebrew is an ethnic identity but Jewishness can be made a myriad of claims: religious, political, and even unsubstantiated arbitrary claims. However not all Hebrews are Israelites although every Israelite has the right to claim to be a Hebrew. In what Christianity calls the Old Testament times, to be a Jew seems to be strictly patriarchal in line in the sense that only through the father including all his human possessions in his household could a person be regarded as a Jew and of course also as Hebrew. However forced marriages, rape, suffered by the Jews during very many pogroms, inquisition, the holocaust and wars including the Biafran wars etc as stated earlier many children were fathered by non Jewish men (goyim, gentiles). Jewishness became matriarchal since such a child would only know their mother and would not know who the non Jewish father was. A person could also become a Jew through adoption by a Jew. And there are Ibo communitteis that are still matrilineal today and hold strongly to that tradition.

The lineage of the priest may also be strictly Jewish in the sense that it is believed that such a gene could only be transmitted through the father who himself must have inherited the gene. This is observed among the Ibo Levite communities commonly called the Ifite, Ihite, Ivite communities scattered all over Ibo land. This means that a person can be a Jew if either of the parents is a Jew even in this sense. However I still reiterate that only a true believer and true worshipper of Yahweh can be called a Jew. This includes observation of relevant Mosaic laws that fits the age we are living in.

There is also a claim that certain illnesses are associated with people of Jewish origin. This is also difficult to use as a completely reliable proof. One of such illnesses is Amylloidosis that also affects the Ibos. But this can not be a reliable proof of a Jacob or Israelite descendant due to same reason of gene mutation and indiscriminate cross breeding of the human species etc.

This book is also not aimed to prove to the Israeli government that the Ibos are Jews because there are indications that the Israeli Knesset already know this fact to be true. This includes the fact that there are many Ibo who are still practicing the ancient Hebrew religion today unadulterated by modern times. The Knesset know this fact; including the proof of an Ibo man said to have been made to undergo DNA test that eventually proved his claim to Hebrew origin in courts in Israel. This test was said to have been necessitated by marriage intention to a Jewish Israeli woman. There are Ibos openly seen all over the world including in Israel practicing Judaism. The religious Jewish population in Nigeria is rapidly growing as many synagogues are spreading all over the Iboland. As Ibos discover their Jewish roots they quickly reconvert to Judaism. However my response to them is this: being in Judaism does not necessarily make you a Jew in actual fact. Moreover, you are already a Jew by birth but there is need for you to reinvent your roots and abide by the true worship of the Yahweh, G-d of your fathers. Joining Judaism will lead you into another colonialism; a perhaps more dangerous one as modern version of Judaism is not necessarily true to Yahweh worship.

Therefore this Book is not aimed to make a case for Ibos to be accepted as belonging to the present day Israel. Citizenship of any nation does not hinge upon cultural or ethnic identity only. It is a matter of choice and political convenience, a legal definition. It could even be purchased with money.

Also the study is not aimed to arrogate to the Ibos that smug elitism that is often associated with the "chosenness" of the Jewish people strongly associated with favouritism by G-d for the Israelites over all other nations and peoples: "religious racism", so to say. Unfortunately the Ibos fell foul of this elitism in the past with dire consequencies in a spate of genocides against the Ibos that co-ominated in the Biafara war. This smug elitist feeling and display is being rejected by even many practicing Jews today especially following the Spanish, British, Nazi, etc persecutions, inquisition, and genocide against European Jews before and during the second world war and has continued in today anti-semitism. However this does not deny the fact that the idea of G-d choosing ancient Israelites is a scriptural truth (Deuteronomy 7: 6, Isaiah 41:8, 1Chronicles 16: 13, Psalm 105: 6, Psalm 135: 4, Zechariah 8: 23, Genesis 15: 4, 7, Genesis 18: 18-19, Genesis 12: 1-3, Genesis 13: 14-17, Hosea 6: 3 etc) and that according to scripture this 'chosennes' is forever and ever and carries with it known advantages and privileges with expected responsibilities, to the children of Jacob all over the world including the Ibos who are in fact the core children of Jacob today upon whom other children of Jacob look up to for guidance.

בשבילך הם עם קדוש לה ' אלהיכם

. יהוה אלהיכם בחרה בך

מכל העמים עלי אדמות להיות לעמו

היקר שלו דברים 7 possesion .

For you are a people holy to the Lord your G-d. The Lord your G-d has chosen you out of all the peoples on the earth to be His people, His treasured possession- Deuteronomy 7: 6.

This study is also not an impetus to motivate the secession of Biafara or the Ibo country. The scripture does not tell the chosen children of Yahweh to secede from the land He has given them and form a separate nation in the sense of modern state structure. In fact Yahweh commands the Israelites to occupy any land He has given to them. They are to become dominant and take over control for the benefit of the inhabitants. He told his people that anywhere they step upon has been given to them for a possession. That is the core of Yahweh's blessing upon His people. The Ibos are placed in their present habitation to take over the realm of things and build the place for the benefit of all. "Through you all the families of the earth shall be blessed" is the primary promise of Yahweh to His chosen people. The present Ibos should realise that it is only a question of time and they will eat the fruit of their habitation. Nevertheless, let exiting the present country be at Yahweh's appointed time when Yahweh will make the need for their separate existence very obvious and inevitable. He will, if He wants it, give the Ibos a separate nation 'on a plater of Gold', so to say. The agitation for a separate existence should however continue as a way of creating awareness of an unflinching desire for separate development and identity among their descendants and neighbours and to create awareness of fight against marginalisation and carefully politically crafted dividing the Ibos for organised political and economic exploitation and oppression by their enemies. It is no longer hidden that being part of the nation Nigeria is a major reason for the loss of self awareness, loss of self fulfilment, and loss of identity. The Ibos should be the foundation for the development of other Hebrew peoples because they are the only so far known original Hebrew on earth. It is an extra privilege Yahweh has given them. They are to take their position as leaders and protectors of their brethren worldwide. There is no need to remain intimidated by their current status because they have backslidden from the G-d of their fathers and joined gentile ways and manners including current version of Christianity. This has made then loose awareness of their mission on earth. This is why this book is a call to Ibos to reinvent themselves individually and as a collectivity. Without strong political and religious alliance, first with all fellow Ibos in this part of the world and in the diaspora, Jews in the world and then with friends of the Jewish peoples any attempt for Biafra secession will be impromptu and ill timed. The first effort to have Biafra failed because the leadership failed to have credible alliance and support. They were unable to achieve this alliance because the secession was illtimed and impromptu. The leaders worked very hard and are exonerated judging from the little they had at that time. Today is different; the Ibos should be wiser than they were previously and seek the ways, especially wisdom of Yahweh to achieve freedom and justice. They should give enough time to make alliances. This is the season for that. This is not the season for war or fighting for separation unless war cannot be avoided for defence purposes. Make haste slowly and wisely and you will eat the fuit of the Land Yahweh your G-d has given you. The easiest way to prolong Yahweh's blessings is to be impatient. Your persecution is contrived and executed by the enemies of your progress who are near and far.

According to Lord Macauley's address to the British Parliament on 2nd February 1835:

" I have travelled across the length and breadth of Africa and I have not seen one person who is a beggar, who is a thief such wealth I have seen in this country, such high moral values, people of such calibre, that I do not think would ever conquer this country, unless we break the very backbone of this nation, which is her spiritual and cultural heritage and therefore, I propose that we replace her old and ancient education system, her culture, for if the Africans think that all that is foreign and English is good and greater than their own, they will lose their selfesteem, their native culture and they will become what we want them, a truly dominated nation." And the success of the colonialists is manifest everywhere today. The missionary educators in Ibo country were instructed to "make sure you do not teach them technical subjects, rather to teach them only the 3Rs." By the 3Rs they meant reading, (w)riting, and (a)rithmetic, having observed that the Ibos were already very strong in cultural technology including smithing and iron works etc. The political 'divide and rule' system still continues as they have torn the Ibo nation apart through politicians' lies, many of whom have remained their stooges. They have spread corruption including lies to parts of the Ibo nation telling the guillible that they are not Ibos and convinced some communities to believe their lies. The onslaught of Christianity as a claimed superior faith with claimed superior practices and the forceful introduction of colonial education, colonial political systems, colonial economic system, and colonial value systems in the name of political correctness and civilisation, as well as unequal distribution of economic proceeds and opportunities have forced the Ibo to engage in very destructive practices that are contrary to the responsibilities the G-d of their fathers expects of them. Their self esteem has been hammered to such an extent that some are ashamed of being called Ibo. Many have sold their birthright for the biblical "pot of portage."

Like Moses said to Pharaoh, "Let my People go that they might serve the G-d of their fathers as He has commanded them to" should be the watch word of the Ibo. Yet Yahweh has to be the one to direct and operate and make it to come to fruition. As I said earlier there is the need for the Ibos to make haste slowly and let Yahweh be in control. Those who are impeding the progress of the Ibo will one day repent of their misguided hatred and fall down to plead to the Ibos to take control. This is because the Ibo are a blessed people and their neighbours know that as the case. Let us not forget that it was the action of one misguided so called Ibo (Ifeajuna) that contributed to the collapse of Biafra during the Biafra war, otherwise the Nigerian army would have surrendered in battle within three months of the start of the war. Also the betrayal by some other Ibo elders especially of the riverine part was due to misguiding, by misinforming and disinforming of the elder and young people by the enemies of Ibo progress. The interest of the enemy has been to control and exploit your resources. They seem to have done this successfully by vilifying some of your brothers (the Igbo) who they identify as too strong to overcome by any other means. As the honourable Oko Okon Edem, the Biafran spokesman used to exclaim and warn during the Biafra war: "they want your prosperity and not your progress." He added a call, "Biafra fight them to a finish." This time, what are needed are not a physical war but intellectual, diplomatic, battle of wits and spiritual and moral battle. The Ibo everywhere needs to first reinvent himself and herself no matter your present status.

Yahweh allowed all this to teach the ethnic Ibo the lesson of the disadvantages of loss of self identity and disunity among brethren. Yahweh allowed it because for the Ibos to have a viable nation, they must know who they are and who their kith and kin are; they need a reinvention of themselves. Yahweh allowed that so that betrayers of their brothers, like Edom in the book of Obadiah, may suffer the same fate as Edom. Edom the sons of Essau are wiped out in history because of the curse of Yahweh on them for betraying their fellow Israelite brothers to their enemies during war. They betrayed their brothers when their brothers needed their help more than ever. These "EDOMITES" betrayed their brothers into the hands of the enemies that murdered them in the different parts of Nigeria during the genocide against the Ibos of the 1960s to 1970 and is continueing. A European lady sitting in Kaduna tells them that their fellow Israelite brethren are no longer their brethren and they believed. They obeyed her Jezebelic, devilish advice and modified their native language by changing a letter 'U' to 'R' etc in other to claim pretended separate ethnicity from their own blood brethren. This has become embarrassingly superficial and stupid to their young ones, one of whom is the writer of this study, who now "sees no basis for this stupidity" as one of the Youth from this part of Rivers stated, "How easily did these betrayers forget that blood is thicker than water and that truth does not dissolve in the blood of a person?" Even the "Nigerian Mafia" who are using the service of the betrayers for their self interest has a saying that, 'Gaskiya ta fi kwobo': "truth out weighs financial gain." Truth will always prevail and will always endure while material gain fritters away and fame gained by that remains ephemeral.

G-d blessed Gad, who is believed to be one of the ancestral fathers of the Ibo according to oral traditions, saying, "Gad, a troop shall overcome you but you shall overcome at the last" (Genesis 49:19). This should be comforting to the Ibos. The G-d of their fathers; the G-d of Abraham, who the Ibos refer to as "Chukwu Abiama", is in control of history and has promised that they shall rise again and overcome.

An additional blessing states that: "blessed is he that enlarges Gad, he dwells as a lion, and tears the arm with the crown of the head" (Deuteronomy 33: 20). These blessing were proclaimed through the mouths of Jacob the father of Gad and Moses who led the children of Israel in their course to the Promised Land. God also blessed the children of Asher who are identified as the Ikwere, Etche, Owere,

Oguta, and most inhabitants of present day Bayelsa, Rivers and Imo states that their foot shall be dipped in oil etc. This blessing has remained the envy of others. Is it not a shame that the same children of Asher produced those who began to champion the division and disuniting of their own people thereby selling their birthright for a mere "pot of potage"?

According the Chronicles of Jasher, Moses reminded all Israel the importance of observing all the words of G-d's law that he had given them "and to walk in the way of the Lord your G-d; turn not from the way which the Lord has commanded you, either to the right or to the left." And Moses taught the children of Israel statutes and judgments and laws to do in the land as the Lord had commanded him. And he taught them the way of the Lord and his laws; behold they are written upon the book of the law of G-d which he gave to the children of Israel by the hand of Moses (Jasher 87: 5-8).

The emphasis placed on this instruction of Moses by Jasher indicates how serious and vital to life the demands of G-d should be regarded by the Israelites. The question is: did the Ibos keep to this advice? The enemy came and sowed the seed of loss of identity and image in them. Neverthe less the Hebrew Bible states that in the final words of Moses he advised...let Asher be blessed...let him be the most privileged of his brothers and let him bath his feet in oil Deut 33: 24. If the writer is correct in asserting above and below that the inhabitants of the Rivers, Bayelsa, and Imo communities belong to the tribe of Asher as evidenced by this statement of Moses in describing their status, it is perhaps not wrong to assume that the Rivers people are being addressed here as also blessed with oil and the whole Ibo Israelites are being advised to ignore the current attitude of some of them. One commonality among the Owere, Ikwere, Etche and the children of Asher in the Bible is the common name Amad/Amadi among other common practices and traits. Is it a mark of ignorance or deliberate idiocy that a person by the name of Amadi from Ikwere was among those who championed the disunity we are talking about? We also have many other Ibo words and names that are pronounced the same way and mean the same. An example is 'Abba', the name of a town in Igboland. Abba is Aramaic/Hebrew word that means 'father' specifically by implication, "my father" (please see below for the section on Hebrew-Igbo language similarity).

Thus the aim of this study should be to contribute in clarifying and reiterating with implications a question of identity of a people which has been talked so much about for centuries and to identify who the Ibo (ibhri) peoples are and enable them recover their pride of identity in place of present apparent crises of identity and lack of self awareness. By self awareness is meant enabling the Ibo (ibhri) to understand himself better especially as regards his language, philosophy, mannerisms, attitudes, propensities, ethical and moral expectations, and collectivity (kith and kin) etc. The crisis of self confidence and identity in the Ibo is mostly a product of foreign ideologies and influences inflicted upon him by colonialism, foreign helenistically influenced religion of Christiandom, and resultant lack of clarity as to who they actually are; and who are their natural relatives and brothers. Consequently an average Ibo person, man, woman, boy or girl is confused as to who they are, where they are from and why he/she appears to be different in attitude and expectations from the rest of the people around them? Why has there been so much hostility against their people by other peoples especially by Muslim Nigerians? And why is the Ibo so enviously ambitious and yet successful and progressive and continues to feel so stifled and unfulfilled; consequently so unsettled in mind? The more they are persecuted the more they are progressive. Their enemies being aware of this ignorance of who they are have been successful in sowing seed of discord and disunity among them. Perhaps this study will also enable all the Ibo peoples to reinvent themselves, renounce their ignoble present attitude to materialism and immorality, by looking back to their noble past and calling, as part of the chosen people of YHWH, the Creator. It is hoped that reading this book should enthuse all inhabitants of the former Ibo country (former eastern region) and Deltans and kith and kin in current Benue and Kogi states, all who constitute the Ibo nation: all Ibos in diaspora, all the Ibo governors, elders, tradional and religious leaders and youths and all those willing to align with them, to have a rethink of their motivating values, get united and operate cooperatively for the enhancement and reinvention of the values of the Ibo peoples. The leaders should come together to educate the youth living in every part of the Ibo land their noble history as a people and the need for them to identify the trick of the enemy to disunite the Ibo in their common heritage. They should work to overcome the negative influences of the enemy of the Ibos. They should work together to disabuse the minds of the Ibo youths that they are disparate peoples in different ethnicities and states. If achieved this awareness to unite should help produce development in all ramifications of their life. It is perhaps then that the talk of a separate nation may begin if still considered necessary at all. Reinvention should come first before any talk of forging a common front for a separate existence whenever necessary. Any agitation for Biafara today should be seen as short term goal and a conscious effort to keep the spirit of Biafara alive. However such agitation should look forward to a long term goal for eventual independence at what is usually called G-d's own KAIROS: the most appointed time. They should collectively fight to overcome the ever growing 'Ibophobia' that has mentally inflicted Ibo neighbours and the former colonialists.

So many Ibos are turning to Judaism today not without spate of persecutions from the front line Christianities and christiandom. By Christianities I mean the variegated forms of the helenically influenced Christian religion which prides itself a superior place, yet represented by a myriad of doctrines, and practices, leaving a legacy of doctrinal and ethical confusion, practice of injustice, racism, political incorrectness as unhealthy compromises and discrimination, crave for inordinate wealth, even to the embarrassment and chagrin of the rest of the religious world. All this is due to the fact that they are practicing a religion devoid of the Old Testament as basis and foundational to what they profess. Is this not "paganism" and witchcraft in practice? There is no word referred to as "Christianity" in the scriptures, thus what we see today as christiandom is manmade. Christ himself even placed the Old Testament in a position of exaltation above any other teaching. The New Testament became helenised (Greek culture influenced) and politicized and became used to support and to serve human aims and caprices. Thus many sincere Ibos seem to see themselves as 'going against the grain' in a society where everyone seems contented with worshipping of money, mediocrity, lies, pretenses, and falsehood. Unfortunately some of them (Ibos) have imbibed these vices and many are still imbibing them as fashionable because of foreign influence including the influences of Christianity for very many decades.

This means that many Ibos still present as ignorant of who they are by descent and associated expectations; they seem to have allowed themselves to be carried along in this state of affair by situations they have helplessly found themselves. Many have succumbed to the pressures of mediocrity, sycophancy, immorality and corruption around them. It is saddening to see the Ibo society degenerating ethically and morally, losing the high morality and sacredness by which it was originally known and for which Ibos were originally proud of and for which they were envied by their neighbours. It is as if the pride of race for which they were known has completely waned.

I consider the above situation of things as the direct consequence of growing ignorance and lack of appreciation of who they are and their Yahweh given role in the world as children of Abraham through Israel, the father of faith in the Almighty creator. Abraham and his descendants through Isaac were called out by the creator, as explicated by Ibo ancestor descendants of Israel (Jacob) to live an exemplary life; not necessarily to preach to the world rather to live out an example of a life of morality and justice, equity and emancipation from forces of evil; a way of life that is in harmony with the spirit forces, nature and all of creation.

It is noteworthy that, perhaps, political pressures seem to have hindered and delayed open recognition by the Israeli Parliament (Knesset) that Ibos have ancient Israelite roots and so are their brothers with whom they could work together toward achieving a better world. The Israeli Knesset have united with some other non-Israeli Jews like the Falasha (literally "unwanted stranger") of Ethiopia. The Knesset refused to welcome Ibo visitors as their brothers. Yet Ibos are prominent member of the King Solomon Sephardic Federation International (KSSFI), a federation of Sephardic Jews well known and recognized by the United Nations Organisation (UNO) and by Israeli governments. Also the Israelis have paid visits to the Ibo community at different times when it was politically necessary for them to do so. Some visits were obviously aimed at discrediting the notion of the Jewishness of the Ibos even when it was too late to imagine such. For example in 2004-2008, a certain rabbi Yaacov Behrman after visiting Ibo communities in Nigeria concluded that there was lack of evidence to prove the Ibos are Jewish; so he is said to have refused to recognize the Ibos as such. This is in spite of the recognition of many influencial Rabbis, including the chief rabbinate that accorded such recognition of the Ibos as reported in Israel Today 2006 and Musaf Haaretz in 2005 and the witness of many scholars world wide; there is even the existence of Ebo-Gad community in Tel Aviv Israel. Not to talk of popular dailies spreading the news in Israel that the Ibos are Jews and several court sessions including DNA tests, religious and secular debates regarding the identity of the Ibos.

Whatever maybe the case what is important is how a people regard themselves. Moreover an Ibo saying states: "you can only introduce a person to his brother (a close relative), but you cannot introduce a person to his friend". It is hoped that the two peoples will one day come to accept each other as children of the same ancestors, a fact the whole world seem to be acknowledging.

Perhaps this book will be a food for thought to those Ibos who are oblivious to the present day clamoring of the Ibo to belong to where posterity has placed them, I mean those who claim to be of Ibo descent, yet, who for political and economic gain and convenience and perhaps cowardice are trying to fight against the true Ibo descendants who are calling for the physical, spiritual and possible political identity with present day Israel and World Jewry. As stated earlier it could be said that these opponents of the Ibo-Israelite consciousness are perhaps descendants of the natives of the land whom the Ibos had absolved into their culture and lack the subconsciousness of being of Israelite origin all true Ibos have. This could explain why there are at least six historical accounts on the sources of the Igbo race. On thing common to all of the accounts is that they are children of one father though details may differ slightly. What is perhaps expected is that the more advanced culture absorbs the rest. Above all the immigration into this part of the world occurred at different times and stages and phases: from the North, South, West and East. It also began from very remote antiquity perhaps from as far back as at least some 10,000 years ago and has continued to evolve as time goes on.

The book should be helpful to clarify issues for the searching mind, particularly, of that young Ibo person whose parents have told them that their forefathers originated from the lineage of Jacob, of ancient

Israel, that he or she is a descendant of Abraham but who has heard nothing further about it. It should be helpful to clarify the facts to a young Ibo girl who desires to be a mother and wife and whose mother has told her that "you must always remember you are different and so must not imitate wrong marriage practices" but who lacked knowledge of the facts of why she is different and what constitutes these wrong marriage practices.

The Book should also enlighten those who think that for someone to be Ibo that they must be able to speak the Ibo language as spoken today. Yes, as important as language is for cultural identity ethnic identity involves far more than being able to speak a language. Many are, who speak an Ibo dialect yet are ignorant of who they are and what ethical life is really expected of them as a people. As stated earlier some have for political reasons and for other self centred excuses denied they are Ibos. More disheartening and shameful is that the enemies of the Ibo race have convinced some native Ibos to deny their Ibo identity. These Ibos who have 'sold their birthright for a pot of porridge' are no doubt living a false life. They need to abandon this false life and reinvent themselves for the benefit of posterity and for their sanity and the sanity of their children and grand children. Denying their identity is tantamount to denying the Yahweh, the G-d of their fathers. Above all self determination cannot be achieved by any people who are disunited, worse still disunited by deliberate misinformation and manipulation, a lack of identity cannot achieve self rule and consequently such a people remain servants of their overlords. Such remain emasculated forever having no reason to live and fight for.

As a different people the young Ibos who read this book should seek to find out what makes them different as Israelites or Jews in all aspects of life. This does not mean that the book aims to encourage people to join Judaism. No! it is to create an awareness that every Ibo needs to live an ethically acceptable life, having identity as of different in origin and expectations; to enable them understand themselves better and be more proud of who they are.

The book should also help the Ibo to begin to know and appreciate who actually are their close relatives among groups in Nigeria, Africa and the world at large. For example the book brings to the fore why the Efiks, Ibibios, Idomas, the Ikweres, the Etches, the Ogonis, the Ijaws, the Igbos, and all of the former Ibo country (Eastern region of what became Nigeria); the Igalas, the Idas, the Benei Israelites of Ondo state, the people of the Jemaa Federation of Kaduna, the Angas of Plateau State and other groups known to be of ancient Israelite origins in Nigeria, Africa and the world, are their closer relatives. Many of these (perhaps, except some of those in the Middle Belt areas), are Ibo peoples and so also accepted as Sephardi Jews in addition to the inhabitants of the present Bayelsa, Rivers, Akwa Ibom, Cross River, Ebonyi, Anambra, Imo, Enugu, Benue, Kogi and Delta. There are those peoples among them that prefer to be called Igbo. This is to reiterate that not every Ibo is Igbo. But every Igbo is Ibo being descendants of the same Israelite ancestors called "Ibri" that has come to be rendered as "Ibo" collectively.

Some examples of relatives of the Separdi Ibos from Africa are: Jews of Equatorial Guineas, Jews of Sao Thome, the Lembe of Zimbabwe, the Falasha of Ethiopia, the Ashanti and others who belonged to the old Black Jewish Empire of Ghana, West Africa, North Africa, East and South Africa, the Kamnuris, to mention just these. Many of the present day inhabitants of the area called Biafara immigrated from Sao Thome and Equatorial Guinea.This will be better appreciated when we realize that there was no such boundaries between these territories before colonial demarcation was imposed on Africa because of the scramble for territory.

Other close brothers of the Ibo Sephardi include the so called lost tribes located in other parts of the world. An example are the so called Marranos, a derogatory name given to those Jews who were forced to eat pigs by those who murdered and persecuted them in Spain; those Jews in different parts of the world who were forced to convert to Roman Catholicism. I mean those generally referred to as Anusim. Many of these who today live in the USA and the Americas are also to be regarded as closest relatives of the Ibos. The Scriptures tell os that the great ancestor of the Ibos, identified as Gad had other sons Ziphion, Haggi, Shuni, and Ezbon (also called ozni, ezhon) apart from Eri, Arodi and Areli who have been identified through oral tradition to be among the direct ancestors of the Ibo nation. The question is where are these Gad's sons located? There have been claims that Gad settled in the Nordic/ Scandinavian countries majorly Sweden from where they spread to the British Isles where they are known as Goths and numerous other tribes. Gad countries have also been associated with Austria, Germany, Prussia, Mexico. Does this recognition of Ibos as their brothers explain why Sweden and Portugal were in sympathy with Biafra during the Biafra war? Unveiling this fact should help clarify and establish where strong cultural, economic and political identity for a common cause and for the protection and uplifting of one another should be extended. Ibos should now know that all members of the King Solomon Sephardic Federation are included as their blood brothers as well as all genuine Jews of the world. By genuine Jews I mean true worshippers of HaShem (the Aiah Asha Aiah: I am that I am). We know that it is not everyone that claims to belong to Judaism that is a true child of Abraham. Many have distorted the faith of our forefather Abraham with political incorrectness and political and economic ambition that has led to compromises and corruption of true worship of Ayah Asher Ayah: "I am who I am" (also referred to as YHWH, Yahweh), the G-d of Abraham, Isaac and Jacob- ethical and the Holy one of Israel whose character is of justice; who handed the ofo rod as the staff and symbol of justice and morality to Ibo ancestors. The Lord and Messiah, Yashayah, who western world call "Jesus" said that a time would come when those who worship Ayah Asher Ayah will worship Him in truth and in Spirit rather than worshiping in one place. Did "Chukwu Abiama" not tell Abraham to walk before Him and be perfect before even asking him to circumcise all males in his Household? (Genesis 17:1ff). AYAH ASHER AYAH (YHWH) demands pure and sincerity of heart and worship more than anything else and has called his children to show example in this. Thus as Yashaiah has stated, for the Ibos as ever, the time is today so only the true worshippers of HaShem are those worshipping him "in Spirit and in Truth." These are those bonded to ensuring that Justice reigns in the world as Abraham their father did. Thus the current clamour of some Ibo Jews to seek affiliation and recognition from Israel and modern Judaism that was imported from the western world is unwarranted and needless. Rather Ibo Jewish practices, past and present, are more original and should be made to form the standard practice for all Jews to emulate. Let us not forget that Judaism as we know it today is not the religion of the Old Testament peoples. Judaism began in Babylon during the time of the exile of the Israelites in that part of the world. In order to sustain the tradition of their fathers, gatherings that became synagogues were set up in Babylon. When Cyrus came to power he allowed the Israelites to go back home under the leadership of Ezra. Ezra who became the spiritual leader and Nehemiah who was appointed Governor of Judea set to reestablishing the proper traditional worship of their forefathers and created again the nation of Israel under the Temple worship with Jerusalem as base. However by the time of the Roman rule Judaism had taken strong root and had metamorphosed into about twenty four groups with the Sadducees, Phariseee and the Essenes as majority. This period was characterized by the following: apart from rival religious sects, a religious cabinet known as the Sanhedrin, a powerful high priest; and strange doctrines which interpretations were most often politically motivated, as well as merchandising and marketising of the traditional religion and values. It was when the Romans sacked the whole nation of Israel including the destruction of the Temple in Jerusalem, in 70 Anno Domino-in the year of our Lord Jesus Christ (AD) that the final scattering of the Jews into foreign lands including Spain (ancient name as Sepharad), Portugal, and Germany (ancient name as Ashkenaz) e.t.c perhaps began and in massive numbers. Judaism had become the official religion of the Jews and shortly after (1000AD) split into Ashkenazic and Sephardic traditions. The Ashkenazi interprets the identity of a Jew to be someone who practices Judaism, who is born by a Jewish woman. This is different from the interpretation of the Sephardi Jews as a reader of this book would soon discover.

Thus the backsliding of the Jewish peoples from the religion of their fathers continued and perhaps came to the climax when they abandoned the name of AYAH ASHER AYAH to adopting the English word 'God' (G-d) represented as YHWH etc. Consequently this understanding makes me use the word Yahweh reluctantly. The English speaking believer uses the word "God" or Yahweh (YHWH) to refer to the one true God. However what does the word "God" actually represent or mean? There is suspicion that the word could have a proto- Indo- European Sanskrit or Proto-Germanic 'Got' (500BC- 500 AD) idea of the divine. The suspicion is that the etymology could be connected to Odin, sacred cow, idol, libation and all sorts of connections that are idolatry. The word "GOD" is also used to refer to a variety of deities; so could be a sort of generic "no name" label for any divine being. Unfortunately this word has overshadowed the conception of the divine all over the world; a product of political domination of the Helenistic western world and underdevelopment of the rest of the world including Africa and the Blacks everywhere- a product for dehumanization, genocide, and colonization.

This same political manipulation is observed in the use of the Greek name 'Iesous', that was transcribed to "Jesus" instead of the original name Yashaiah ha Machiach Another word used for Yashaiah is Yeshua, a word that means Wealth rather than salvation as the Angel instructed Mary in Matthew 1: 21. We have already stated that the word Iesous means etymologically "son of": "Ie" and "sous": ZEUS. It was the same Helenized mind set of looking into G-D that the name 'elohim refers to a plurality of the deity. We the Ibo know that 'elohim is honorific name exalting the G-D of creation. In Ibo understanding plurality is accorded seniority. On the other hand ancient Israelite ancestors were given a name by which the true G-d was to be conceived but it seems to have been abandoned. Thus we have AYAH ASHER AYAH as the true name G-D gave to Moses(Exodus 3: 13): "I am that I am" and was never stated that this name should not be used freely except using it in vain like the pagans do with the name of their g-d. Israel was privileged to be handed over the true conception of G-D for the world. The name of the divine gives Him a character to be identified with. Neglecting this character of the divine has lead to a loss of true worship that has also lead to dire consequencies. It is the realization and appropriation of this basic fact by the Ibos that will perhaps begin the foundation to the survival of the Ibo nation.

I feel that it is needful to clarify the above issue in the minds of the reader to make it easy to appreciate that by the time Judaism was formed some Ibo ancestors, (perhaps the first set of Ibo ancestors) might have left that territory and immigrated into the Niger River area (long before 1305-2000 Before Christ was born BC) and perhaps, preferring to settle to the East, the area of the rising sun that is believed to face in the direction of Jerusalem. With time and as events unfolded in the Middle East other Ibo ancestors began to join this first batch of immigrants and inflow from different directions into the Niger River area continued including the so called 'Niger Delta' area, that the whole world knew was Biafara and that is still the land of Biafara (Biafra). Therefore by the time the reader finishes reading this book, it is hoped that they would realize that questioning if Ibo peoples can be regarded to be Jews on the bases of Judaism is an unnecessary question as not all Jews are of the Judaism religion. Our Ibo ancestors who were the first to leave were perhaps, not subject of abandoning the true name and true worship of AYAH ASHER AYAH. Neither should the Jewishness of the Ibo be judged by the practices of Judaism today as interpreted by the western helenistic Ashkenazi version of rabbinic Judaism. The reader will also realize why colour is not a factor in determining a Jew.

Concerning the approach to the study I gave more credence on those beliefs, customs, and practices that I consider likely peculiar to the children of ISRAIAH (also called the Israelites) in the Hebrew Scriptures that are reflected among the Ibo past and present. This includes giving a prominent place to only those customs and practices; including words and expressions of some the present day Ibo language dialects that are pronounced the same way and mean the same or similar as the Hebrew equivalent especially the Biblical Hebrew. Hebrew and Aramaic are perhaps the main languages of the ancient children of Israiah (Israel). Modern Hebrew is no doubt a derivation of these ancient languages, though the language has been modified by European influences on the Jews especially the Ashkenazi or German derived Jews bringing into play Yiddish and other version of Modern Hebrew. This study is focused on ancient Biblical Hebrew for obvious reason that the language of our ancestors must have been closer to the most ancient version of the Hebrew. Biblical Hebrew and perhaps Aramaic are likely to be such versions, just as the Biblical customs and manners and some ancient practices and beliefs are closer to the traditions of our ancestors in view of the time they first began to emigrate.

I am aware that this approach has narrowed the vocabulary to just a few words in view of the thousands of years that has elapsed and usual changes in language use and intermixture. Yet that there are still similarities in these two languages is close to a miracle and perhaps buttresses the fact that Ibo ancestors are actually of ancient Hebrew origin. Moreover the language similarity investigation will certainly continue beyond this work and I believe that more relevant and useful words and expressions to the investigation will unfold as words from the many and various dialects within the Ibo languages come to light. The Ibo nation is large and wide in geographical entity as stated above. For example closer study of the Abakaliki, Udi, Ikwere, Ijaw, Ogoni, Kalabari, Kogi, Ika Ibos, etc dialects needs to be carried out in the light of their Hebrew roots. I speak only colloquial Hausa, and some Arabic, Yoruba and Ibo. My Ibo dialect is just one of the dialects of the Ngor Okpala, Ovunze people of the many Owerre dialects. So my Owerre dialect is too limited and minuscule to claim expert justice to this study. My knowledge of the ancient Hebrew, Aramaic, Ugaritic, and Arabic is also very limited. Yet still I am not trained in philology.

My present approach is aimed to begin to eliminate present approach of some writers, especially known Ibo scholars who make arbitrary connection of words and expressions in Ibo as Hebrew; words and expressions that have no connection with the Hebrew, ancient or modern that these people are introducing, thereby trivializing such a serious study. One discovery that fascinates me and that should fascinate any Ibo reader is how the Ibo word "miri", "yem miri" among other words and expressions came to be in use. In addition to this, is how the Ibo Northern neighbours (Hausa-Fulanis) gave us the name "ya miri", or "aya miri" as it came to be corrupted today. This is discovered to be linked to the miraculous supply of water in the wilderness of which the presence of Miriam played a major role.

Also on the use of the nomenclature for the "Ibo" - it is observed that there have been many renditions of it in literature. These include 'Heebo', 'Heebro', 'Ebo', 'Eboe', 'Ibo' and 'Igbo'. Also words like Oyibo, Qaibo (kwaibo), Jamaicalbo, Ikalbo, to mention just these are derived from the original word.

Perhaps the earliest mention of the Eboe is in an account of a group of slaves referred to as the Eboe tribe who the writer of the article informs us referred to themselves as the 'Messiah tribe'. They were associated with bearing the hand and gold key which is interpreted as symbolizing the belief that "God opens all doors". They were also said to have tattoos on their bodies, of different designs but significant in design. One such is a snake biting its own tail referred to as "Aido-Wedo", the god which connects the Heavens with the Waters. Among the Ibo of today the symbol of snake biting its tail is a common symbol which is interpreted as referring to "eternity" representing the Omnipotent. Another is said to be referred to as "Aberewa ben" design patterns. The narration presents the Eboe tribe as a proud and diehard people who chose to drown than go into slavery. As the narration reads:

"The chief among the slaves wore a robe woven with a message inspired from a 'Kente' design. This design is called 'Aberewa ben' and the message on it means "He is Omnipotent". The chief carries the staff from the Messiah tribe bearing the hand and gold key which means 'God opens all doors'.

The art and crafts in everyday life are symbols stemming from African religion. This was in every part of their lives; it can be seen in jewelry, pattern on clothes, cooking utensils, homes and religious ceremonies.

The Ebo (sic) landing art is a small moment in the historical southern past. The legend that remains is a reminder of a life and tragedy of slavery. Women and men from the Ebo (sic) tribe were brought from Nigeria, the southern part of Africa, to Savannah to be auctioned off as slaves. Two families from St Simons Island purchased them and had them shipped to the Island on a ship named Morovia. The captains own slave was the first to commit suicide by drowning in Dunbar creek. Then the Eboe (sic) chief began chanting:

'The sea brought me and the sea will bring me home'

There was no questioning the chief's decisions. They all began chanting together. Chained one to the other they came into the port and were lead into the dock. But instead of walking to the bank into a life of slavery, they all turned and followed their chief into the depths of Dunbar creek." (see Ebo Landing Painting-Dee Williams Oil on Wood Coastal Centre for the Arts Ibo(e), Ebo(e), Eboans, or Heebo; Igbo: ndi Igbo; Poupard Dennis; Mark Scott, Gale Research Company. Literature Criticism from 1400 to 1800 1st ed. Gale Research co. pp 185-187 Retrieved 24 Nov. 2008. See also Floyd, E Randall 2002 in the Realm of the Ghosts and Hauntings: Harbor House: p. 51 (uses Eboe); See also Lovejoy Paul 2000: Identity in the Shadow of Slavery: Continuum International Publishing Group: 58(uses Eboe); Cassidy, Frederick Gomes; Robert Brock Le Page 2002: A Dictionary of Jamaican English 2nd ed. University of the West Indies Press p. 168; Equiano, Olaudah 1837: The Interesting Narratives of the Life of Olaudah Equiano 1, Knapp: 27(uses Eboe) Obichere, Boniface 1982: Studies in Southern Nigerian History: A Festschrift fur Joseph Christopher Okwudili Anene 1918-1968 Routledge 207 (uses 'Heebo'), "Ibo" in Encyclopedia Britannica 11th ed. 1911(uses Ibo).

The word "Aberewa" is commonly used among the Owerri people.

There are legends on the version 'Igbo'. One legend is claimed to be the name change of the Eri in a dream; this he later gave as name of one of his sons whose activities popularized the name. This son was said to have been originally named 'ibri' (Hebrew). This son is said to have been apparently, later banished by his brothers because of his recalcitrant attitude. He is however said to have become the dominant person among his brothers. His descendants became famous and spread so rapidly that their name "Igbo" became a more common nomenclature by which some particular Ibo people are referred. I decided to play down on the use of this nomenclature 'Igbo' and majorly used 'Ibo' as the main nomenclature to represent our peoples. I must be quick to state that the two words are so fused together in use that it has become difficult to speak of the Ibo without referring to them as 'Igbo'. So any appearance of 'Igbo' or 'Ndigbo' in this work should please be regarded as contextual reference to a particular group of Ibo people, mostly of the present southeastern and Delta states. The word Ibo in this work is used to include all members of the past Ibo country and beyond who have been known to have ancient Israelite roots. This is same as the colonial Yoruba country that is today referred to as Yoruba Nation and the colonial Hausa country. 'Ibo Peoples' is also used to include all those who are known to have ancient Israelite roots living in Nigeria. These are scattered all over Nigeria especially in the area south of the Benue River. As stated above a common factor among the Ibo peoples are circumcision and New Yam festival; some others are farming festivals, wedding, marriage, family life customs and common concept of their identity with the ancient Israelite peoples as their root. Many others are descendants of the Ibo peoples.

The section of this work on Reinvention calls all the Ibo peoples to accept that they have a common origin as Jews. This realization should act to unite them with the common goal to be the special people God has called them to be and work towards achieving the purpose for which they have been chosen by God. When this is achieved the realization of the long desired and natural yearning for cultural, political, social, economic etc emancipation will become easily achieved. The realization of the desired separateness as a people will be easily enhanced. It will give them a common philosophy of life as well as a way of life, a soul as a people.

I am thankful to those researchers whose works have been very helpful in the writing of this book which research effectively started in 1997 though could be said to have begun even much earlier if the years of research for my major work on comparative study of Ibos and Hebrews should be included. This was as far back as 1983 and continued when I became the General Secretary of the King Solomon Sephardic Federation Nigeria (KSSFN) based in the University of Jos under the Hebrew –Ibo research committee. The first KSSFI West African conference took place when I was the secretary of the University of Jos chapter, during which I was privileged to record the minutes of that conference.

Due to the subject and the nature of the issues surrounding this work, the reader may please forgive the writer because many points might be repeated in different sections or chapters of this book. Someone has said that 'repetition is the principle of deep impression'.

Permit me to use this opportunity to encourage everyone to accept the inevitable especially my fellow Ibo peoples, that they have the same origination, the same ancestors, with the Jews of the world. No other group in Nigeria claims such origin in their legend or history. The Yorubas, west of the Niger River claim to originate from Lamurudu (said to refer to Biblical Nimrod and Arabia) a son of Cush: And Cush begat Nimrod; he began to be a mighty one in the earth. He wasa mighty hunter before the Lord: where it is said, Even as Nimrod the mighty hunter before the Lord (Gen 10: 8, 9). Nimrod was born at a time when life was hard and dangerous for the inhabitants of the earth just after the flood; movement was from the east until they inhabitants found a plain land in the land of Shinar and dwelt there. This was the land where Babylon and later called Mesopotamia was founded. There were threatening wild animals (Exodus 23: 29- 30). Thus Nimrod was born as deliverere and savior to the inhabitants and this endeared him to the people and made him very influential. Legend also has it that Nimrod was said to be a strong medicine man, a famous and "mighty hunter" and the first king of Babylon. The name of his wife was Samiramis; her child was Tammuz. His kingdom was the first to be mentioned in the Bible (Genesis chapters 10 to 11) Following his death, he was greatly mourned by his people; his wife made sure that he became deified and worshipped, pieces of his body were said to have been burnt and the ashes were sent to various areas (cf similar practices in Judges 19: 29, 1 Sam 11: 7). His wife further made sure that Nimrod was deified as the sun god and ritual fires and candle light was introduced as the symbol of worshipping him. Nimrod also became worshipped as Baal, (Master), and various symbols of worship were introduced such as sun images, fish, trees, pillars, and animals. Thus Babylonian idolatry became rife all over. And as time went on the Samiramis taught the people to believe that her son Tammuz was the reincarnation of Nimrod, the hero (Josephus Antiquities of the Jews: 1: 4: 2, 3; Jewish Encyclopedia vol 9. 309; Hislop A: 1959 (1853): 12ff). Furthermore she claimed her son, Tammuz, who was said to have been born even after the death of Nimrod, was supernaturally conceived. Tammuz, himself became worshipped. Later the worship of his mother Samiramis followed. This idolatrous worship spread all over following the invasion and expansion of the Roman Empire. The worship of Tammuz and Samiramis, who became the Queen of heaven, also spread as far as Asia and Egypt. And took various forms and names including, Osiris, isis, istar etc and the concept of the holy mother and holy child pair in religions (e.g Madonna) of the world. Examples are the Chinese Shingmoo or the holy mother pictured with child in arms, the Scandinavians called her Disa, The Etrusnans called her Nutria, the Druids virgo-patitura, mother of God, In India she is called Indrani, The Greeks called her Aphrodite or Ceres, Nana to the Sumarians; in Rome as Venus or Fortuna and her child called Jupiter; we also have Devaki and Krishna as mother with child in her arms, we also have Isi, the great goddess and child Iswara. In Asia also we have

Cybele and her child Deoius. Among the ancient Israelites she was known as Ashtaroth or Ashtoreth (Judges 10: 6, 1 Sam 7: 3, 4; 12: 10, 1Kings 11: 5; 2Kings 23:13), the queen of heaven (Jeremiah 44: 17-19), In Ephesians she was encountered as Diana(Acts 19: 27). In Egypt the mother was encountered as Isis and her child as Horus. Thus by the time of the Roman invasion and spread this worship of the Great mother had also spread to the whole Europe and had become very popular among the peoples.Also if Nimrod became known as Baal, his wife Samiramis as great mother goddess would become Baalti. In English this word means "my lady"; in Latin it would be Mea Domina and later to be corrupted in Italian language as "Madonna."(Hislop: 20). Among the Phoenicians the mother goddess was known as "the lady of the sea" (Harper's Bible Dictionary: 47). One significant observation of scholars in their studies is that most of these pagan goddesses were associated with the moon including Astarte, the Phoenician goddess of fertility as represented on the metallic medal with the crescent moon with stars surrounding her head (Kenrick "Egypt" vol 1, p 425, Blavatsky "Isis Unveiled" p 49; see also Smith: 1953) This interpretation of events was later to result in significant theological developments as could be observed in the Christian New Testament book of Revelation (see Revelation 17-19) and as some have believed, on certain important Christian beliefs and theology as Christianity encountered it as a rival influence on early converts and later development of practice (please see Romans chapter 1, 2Thes 2: 3, 7; 1Tim 4: 2, Jude 1: 3, 4).

According to Dr Olumide Lucas, said to have been the first Yoruba to obtain a doctorate degree, all the gods in Yorubaland are traceable to Egyptian origin; perhaps, implying the origination of the Yaariba peoples and their attitude to life. The Ibo neighbours are said to have referred to the Yaariba people as oru oba, which means "slaves of the oba (king)" perhaps by their different attitude to rulership and relationship whereby "every man is a king in his own house" and overemphasis on individual achievement. This word became the universal name by which the Yaariba peoples became called following the translation by the colonials as "Yoruba." Also some of the Binis claim to be of same origination as the Yorubas through Eweka, although these claims are being seriously questioned as there are many Ibo peoples surrounding the Binis. Yet some claim the Edo people descended from the Edomite tribe, a claim that is yet to be verified.

May I also state that the Jews who are opposing the recognition of Ibos as their kith and kin might need to be reminded that the state of Israel today was founded on the promises of the Bible, not on human promises made on paper, nor on declarations of organization and nations, but on the word of God that is believed to be settled in Heaven eternally. Therefore as it was with the founding of Israel so it shall be that whatever God has written shall come to pass. This is not a statement of faith, rather it is a statue of God and Gos's supremacy must prevail. The Bible states that G-D's word is forever settled in Heaven (Psalm 119: 87). The Jewishness of the Ibos can therefore not be negotiated. The two peoples who are related are challenged by the fact that rather than belonging to a worship built on human being and idolatry as briefly related above, the effective Divine names are revealed to their fathers. And when these names are used answers are received as such. The gods of other nations do not respond because they are not identified by any character to their names. Thus Baal could not respond to the cries of its prophets like the "I AM THAT I AM", the divine of Elijah. The Ibo also sometimes refer to AYAH as ISEYAH and as " Chukwu ABIAMA" the G-D of our fathers (or literally "the Great G-d of the fathers of my people"). In Hebrew the Hebrew word for father is "ab", and Hebrew word for people is "'am." Thus the expression, "Abi" in Hebrew expresses 'my father'. Thus we have it that the compound word "Abi ama", could be rendered as "the father of my people". Chi-ukwu also expresses the greatness of G-d.

....

Some Personal Reflection

Permit me to indicate that embarking on this study was with mixed feelings and hesitations. This was partly due to my initially being one very diehard opposer to this belief of Ibo Israelite origination, but majorly due to the unfriendly behavior of some of the professors who claim to be Ibo involved in the Igbo-Hebrew Research Project of the University of Jos, Nigeria which group I belonged. As the Research Secretary of the Igbo Hebrew Research Project I frequently was tempted to resign and quit from the post due to attitude of some participants who were self centred, profit seeking, selfserving and self promoting, obsessed colleagues on the committee. However their negative and discouraging presentation was turned into positive results when by a flicker I realized that the research could be a means to enable the Ibos reinvent themselves. This was not the original purpose of the research. There is therefore a reason to thank these over ambitious colleagues as well as thank those people, professors and students, who remained close and encouraging to me throughout the period of the research and writing. This includes specifically Professor Umezilinwa, Professor John Ihenacho, Dr Anigbogu, and others whose patience, tolerance, encouraging words and dedication inspired me to not give up in spite of trying times. I also wish to thank the members of the King Solomon Sephardic Federation International who recognized the Ibo as Hebrew in 1997and registered us as members of the federation during my days as research secretary although the Ibos may not regard themselves as belonging solely to that federation of Jews being indegineous desendants of Israelite Hebrews. I thank also Eze Chukwuemeka Eri and his executives (Nigeria and West Africa chapters). His humility, high intelligence and enviable patience and tolerance gave me so much to measure up to. He appointed me as the scribe of the first minutes taken on the first convention of the King Solomon Sephardic Federation. It was a National Convention although delegates from West African chapter attended. The convention was held in Jos Plateau.

I must also thank the Israeli Embassy in Nigeria for sending me Hebrew language lectures which I received in print and audio free of charge. It was a great encouragement to me.

My thanks should go to those Ibos who encouraged me by accepting to be interviewed by phone from the United Kingdom when domestic reasons forced me to relocate to the United Kingdom. I thank the leadership of the King Solomon Sephardic Federation West Africa region for remaining in contact with me until communication was no longer possible. I also thank those Ibo rabbi who freely spoke to me and told me stories of their experiences. I very much admire your humility, listening ears and willingness to learn.

Above all I am indeed thankful to those students who carried out research interviews in Ibo villages. My thanks is especialy to Ms Regina Obi, a native of Ora Eri who spent so much time investigating on the relevant issues while researching on "Female Circumcision among the Ora Eri People" under my supervision. Much useful materials came from her research interviews. Also worthy to be thanked are the many students who participated in investigating various aspects of this study that spanned so many years. God will reward you all for your efforts and sacrifice. The successful publishing of this work is an indication that the efforts of all participants in this study were not in vain.

I also thank those Ibo musicians whose lyrics played a part in providing me Ibo words, idioms and sayings that enlarged my vocabulary of the Ibo words needed for the writing of this book. These were particularly helpful in the aspect of language study.

I should also thank those people who have made efforts in researching and publishing on the origin of the Ibos. Their efforts must be commended though some of them have been heavily criticized. I commend particularly Professor Alaezi for his efforts in spite of the fact that this field is not his area of specialization. He would perhaps be more helpful if he narrowed his research in contributing in the area of his specialization in Education. Same goes to others who made the brave effort to delve into this area of specialization where they do not belong and have no expertise. Our brother Remi would do us a great favour if he would research into how the ancients reasoned on matters of law including laws of agriculture, and certain cultural issues like circumcision, marriage, family life, purification, and such like. Nevertheless their efforts are highly commendable.

I thank also the team of the Messianic Bible and the Jewish groups that communicated with me and sent me weekly Parashas and lessons. These were of immense help to me.

I should also thank both those who made life difficult for me in the United Kingdom in various forms and manners as I thank those who endeavoured to assist me to overcome my difficulties. I came to a point I had to try various jobs and felt like "a square peg in a round hole", so to say, in some of the jobs; all to enable me finance the research and publishing of this study.

Mostly to be thanked is the Almighty AYAH ASHER AYAH, ISEYAH!! And Lord and savior Yeshua, Lord Jesus Christ, who have taken me through various experiences including providing me scholarship to study the Hebrew people in very renowned universities in Europe and the UK contrary to my life ambition. They provided me the opportunity to study under the best scholars in the world on the Biblical, Hebrew Bible, Hebrew and Ancient Near Eastern peoples, a study spaning from 1984 to 2018 and continuing.

ISEYAH healed me when I was sick of cancer and gave the guidance, wisdom, comfort, consolation and care when I was abandoned by those closest to me. All praise, benefits and glory from this study belong to Him alone.

This study is dedicated the only Field Marshal of the Biafran Armed Forces, General J. Achuzie who continued fighting for the cause of Biafra till he was gathered to the fathers, and to all those children of Abraham by blood everywhere who are willing to reinvent themselves after reading this book. May the G-D of Abraham help us redirect our lives towards upholding the values for which He chose Abraham our common Ancestor: Amen!! Iseyah!!!!

TABLE OF CONTENTS

SECTION ONE
ISSUES SURROUNDING IBO PEOPLES
AS ISRAELITE IN ORIGIN

CHAPTER 1

BACKGROUND TO THE STUDY

The Search for Identity and Origin of Ibo Peoples

That it has been noised around for, perhaps, very many centuries that the Ibo peoples from ancient times have a common genealogy with the Hebrew peoples of the lineage of Jacob(Israel), is perhaps, no longer news. This is belief has persisted in spite of contrary opinions who believe that the Ibo race existed thousenads of years before the origination of the Israelites.

A perhaps well known written testimony of Ibo –Israelite originations is that of the well celebrated Olaudah Equiano, who some Ibos think should be originally trendered as (Ola Udah Ekwe Alua/ ikwuano). Historians have identified him to have been a young 'Ebo (e)' (Ibo) slave who through hard work was later able to buy his freedom. He is said to have described his 'Heebo' peoples and Hebrew people, as being of a common genealogy. This is one of such extant documented evidences. His local origin has been traced to be Ikwuano in Umuahia in what has become Abia State today.

Also a certain Eldad ben Mahli, also known as Eldad the Danite, a nineth century well learned Jewish traveler, said to be a native of the Black Jewish Empire of Ghana and a historian, identifies the Ibo as not just Hebrews but Jews. He states that his tribe Dan, with Napthali, Gad, and Asher migrated from the land of Israel. The people of the clan of Dan, he says, left the land of their forefathers to avoid participating in Yeroboam's wars of secession and resided in the land of Havilah beyond the land of Ethiopia. According to him, the other three tribes, Naphthali, Gad (from which some Ibo groups claim to have descended), and Asher, later joined the Danites in Havilah. According to Eldad this was during the wars of Sennacherib. Eldad the Danite perhaps regards the wars of Jeroboam and the wars of Senacherub as taking place at the same period. The wars of Senacherub he mentions, perhaps, were the same wars that led to the evacuation of the Northern Israelite Kingdom. The Northern Kingdom came into existence following the seccession of Northern Kingdom under the leadership of Jeroboam against Rehoboam's of the Southern Kingdom's hostile leadership. Rehoboam was a descendant of Solomon.

Also Biblical history states that King David and Solomon, his son, had earlier sent people on exploration to Tarshish. King Solomon in addition made friends with King Hiram both of whom sent merchant fleets far afield into lands far and near to explore and trade. They made gains of gold, silver, exotic animals and fruits from different parts of the then world.

One of the prominent Ibo legend, among others, claims that Eri, one of the descendants of Gad and said to be part of the Levites, with his priest called Adama, emigrated and settled in, and raised children among the land that today has come to be referred to as Iboland. This legend dates Eri's immigration into Iboland 1305 BC. However the first immigration into this part of Africa is said to have been earlier than 3000 BC of the Nok people. The Eri and his entourage of Semitic Hebrews first settled among this people and later moved on into the Niger River basin. He was said to have been accompanied by his two brothers Arodi and Areli, his wife Ishamal and other relatives including Ezhon(claimed to be present day Ijaw) an offspring of Zebulon, Edo, Igala, and Idoma, said to be likely descendants of Esau/ Edom. These Semites are said to have pre-empted the coming persecution in Egypt so decided to leave to safety. The same oral tradition claims that they were accompanied by a Babylonian Arab man named Oduduwa who is also claimed to be the ancestor of the Yoruba peoples through Lamurudu (perhaps referring to Biblical Nimrod) and his own relatives. As they journeyed it appears that the various companions settled at various points. It was Eri and his brothers who finally went east and settled at the confluence of the Omambala River. Eri was said to have in possession the Ofo staff of moral authority and justice and the Alor.

Another ERI legend claims that he and his entourage must have been part of the groups that branched off from the Elephantine Jewish settlement on the bank of the Nile River about the fifth century BC when that settlement was being attacked.

Other oral traditions think Eri and his companions left much earlier sensing an attack on the Elephantine settlement before it occurred. It is likely that an earlier immigration of the Jews into Ibo country must have been a branch off from the Exodus or pre-Exodus entourage of Moses. This group perhaps settled in what became enlarged as the Elephantine settlement as more Jews joined their brothers and then scattered during the attack on that settlement at about fifth centryru BC. The Eri entourage must then have been part of this entourage who headed towards the Niger River confluence and subsequently settled there.

Eri and his entourage are said to have arrived and settled close to the confluence of Ezu and Omambala (later corrupted as Anambra) rivers which are tributaries of the River Niger. Eri is said to have built a shrine in honour of his ancestor, Gad. In a dream his name was said to have been changed to 'Igbo' which is said to mean, "I PURU GBOO", "IPU GBOO" " YOU LEFT THE PLACE MUCH EARLIER", "DID YOU DEPART THE PLACE LONG AGO?' The name is thus because Eri was said to have departed Egypt before a great persecution against the Hebrew children struck Egypt. His sharp instincts told him of the impending persecution and he obeyed his instincts and left Egypt by the route that led him to the confluence of the River Niger known then as oshimiri Ogbaru. He later named his fourth son "Ibhri"(ivri) (corrupted as "Igbo") and through him Eri's descendants spread far more rapidly than his brothers throughout the area. This means that "Igbo" was a contraction of the word "ivri," to Ebo, Ibu, Eboe, "Heebo" and finally 'Igbo''.

Another legend claims that Eri was one of the merchants King Solomon sent far afield and who came down to the territory and founded the Ibo Gadite clan. Being Levites they set up the priestly class that guided the known rules of the Ibo peoples as traditions and rules of the land (omenala). Another group might have left much later after the first group. The group possibly witnessed the establishing of the Levite priest class some of whom later joined their brothers in Ibo land. It is also likely that there were Levites even in the first Eri exodus.

Yet another legand, rather a mixture of myth and history claims that about 900AD Eri descended from the sky, sent by Chukwu to establish order. It claims he and his entourage came from southern Egypt and passed through Sudan(under ancient Ethiopia), to Chad, Lokoja, traversing what became the wester region of Nigeria as Yoruba country, including Igala, and finally settled and established a community in the middle of present day Anambra(Omambala) river valley at Eri-aka. Eri married two wives from Eri-aka. The first wife Nneamaku had five children- Agulu (thus Agulu Eri literally Agulu of Eri descent), Menri (thus Umunri literally descendants of Nri), Onugu, Igbariam and Ogbodolu (later called Amanuke). The fifth child was a girl called Iguedo who is said to have given birth to the founders of Nteje, Awkuzu, Ogbunike, Umuleri, Nando, and Ogboli in what came to be called Onisha (Onitsha). Menri is said to have left Aguleri and settled east of Eri called Okpu. He founded Nri, Enu Ugwu ukwu, Amanuke Nawfia, Enu ugwu- Agodi and Igbo- ukwu.

The second wife of Eri called Oboli gave birth to Onoja, the son who founded the Igala kingdom in present day Kogi state.

The Umueri and Umunri clans became the most influential and powerful dynasties of priest and diviners among their brothers and their influence spread all over Igboland and to neighbouring territories such as Bini, Igala, Idoma and surrounding areas. Eri and his children are said to be responsible for the Igbo Ukwu sites including the art and metal works, the Igbo four market days, the Ozo and Nze title systems, ikpu ala (purification), and other ritual practices of the Igbo and their neighbours. It was in the Igbukwu Metal art that the STAR of David was carved on one the Artifacts. This Star of David attracted the attention of the colonial Europeans who inscribed it on the first coin in West Africa. Another version claims that the star of David was dug out of the ground in the 18th century AD. (However the star of David may not be of much significance to this study as there are questions surrounding its existence). The same tradition claims that Agulu inherited the Ofo from Eri and handed it over to Enu Ugwu his third son before he died and decreed that Enu ugwu descendants should uphold the traditions of the ofo, and the rights of kinship associated with that holding the ofo including making kings in Igboland. However the same tradition claimes that non of these early leaders made themselves kings rather were content with remaining spiritual, cultural elders and leaders.

The same tradition claims that one of the six sons of sons of Eri called Oba settled south of Eri his father. He founded Ugwu Ogodo and that his kingdom was ended by Edom by treachery. Thus the territories of modern day Edo and Benin tribes of Nigeria are claimed to originally belong to Oba. The other five children of Eri are Agulu, Atta, Igbo, Meneri and a daughter called Ada mgbo.

Some of the experts mentioned above, following the invitation of the Oba, later migrated to settle in places such as Bini and spread rapidly among their hosts. They became so progressive to the envy of their hosts that they were expelled. At the order to leave the territory some moved out of Biniland by way of the coast and founded or settled in coastal area and founded coastal territories. This is said to account for the many Ibo inhabitants of the states by the coast of the Atlantic down to Cross River State, Akwa Ibom and beyond to the Cameroons.

Apart from the legends surrounding Eri, a professor told me that his own peoples legend claim that their ancestors were Ephraimites and that they were part of the "Bnei Israelite in the western region." I later came to understand this Bnei Israelite to refer to the Bnei Israelites of Ondo. The professor also said that their ancestors came through Morocco.

Yet still a small group of scholars claim that the Igbo had been the original inhabitants of the territory of West Africa. They claim that archaeological finds from Igbo Ukwu, Okigwe, and Nsukka have proved this claim to be true and reliable. They also argue that the "Igbo" complexion is different from that of the Jews or Hebrews. This work does not only disagree with this small number of scholars but also makes a distinction between 'Igbo' and 'Ibo' as many renowned scholars in different parts of world have made as well as showed that the complexion of the Jews was same as the complexion of the Ibos. In fact the word 'Oyibo' is an Anglicised version of "Onyelbo" as the word Yoruba is an Anglicised version of Oru Oba, a term by which the Ibos referred to the Yoruba before it was anglicized to Yoruba. In Ibo, Oru Oba means "slave to the Oba". Ibos did not recognize Kingship or monarch so referred to their Yoruba neigbhours as worshipping their king who is called 'Oba'.

However we now know that present day scholarship has proved that the last point is informed by ignorance of how the ancient Hebrews actually looked and no one should be surprised that we have variation in the legend on how the Ibo came to settle in this part of the world. One common fact is that the legends point to a common ancestral linkage, to Eri and other ancients Hebrews. The variations in legends are only embellishments which commonly characterize such stories passed on orally among peoples. In fact so called variations are actually not significant enough to detract any central fact of Ibo commonality of tradition of origin of the peoples. The legends also confirm that we can conveniently speak of Ibo peoples.

Also the testimony of Eldad, the Danite, seems to connect the long standing and perhaps dominant old Ibo legend claiming that the Ibo (at least some of them) belong to the tribe of Gad. The same Eldad throws light to the whole account by stating that the river Sambation, beyond which the ten Israelite tribes were dispersed by the Assyrian Army, 722BC, was in Africa and that the initial migrants were of the tribes of Dan, Asher, Naphthali and Gad. The legend also states that some other migrants later joined from the other lands including those lands that later became called Libya, Portugal and Syria. These migrants are said to have joined the company at different periods through the land that became referred to as West Africa today, around 740AD, 1484AD, and 17th century AD.

There were also descendants of those who had fled the land of Judah, for reason of hostilities meted on them with the invasion of the land of Judah in 169BC under Antiochus 1V and in 70AD. In 70 AD, during the invasion of Titus the Roman Empire took over Jerusalem completely. The second temple was destroyed and polluted and they expelled millions of people to Europe as slaves and very many people were massacred.

Historians have evidenced the fact that very many tribes emigrated from Judah into Africa at different times. These either moved into different parts of Africa. Others were forcefully taken to Europe. This dispersal and settlement must have been what James had in mind when he stated, James, a servant of God and of the Lord Jesus Christ, to the twelve tribes which are scattered abroad, greeting(James 1: 1) in the first century AD. Those addressed must have included knowledge of those Israelites settled in Iboland by the time first century AD. This means that the presence of the Ibos in Africa was a common knowledge to the Apostles and Disciples of Christ.

Following further persecutions, especially by the Roman Catholic rulers of the lands of Spain, Portugal, Syria beginning from the fifteenth century onwards further migrations occurred into the area of the River Niger (oshimiri ogbaru) confluence into the land that became the Iboland. We also know that forced Jewish settlement of Sao Thome must have supplied settlers into Ibo country.

According to historical accounts, on 2 January 1492 the Moorish stronghold of Granada was conquered by Queen Isabella and Ferdinand, having been ruled by Muslim Moorish armies since 711. The victory of Ferdinand and Isabella brought the whole of Spain into Christian control under Ferdinand and Queen Isabella. On 31 March 1492 Ferdinand and Isabella promulgated the decree to expel all Jews from their kingdom. They accused the Jews of corrupting the Marranos to be disloyal to Christianity. It is estimated that at least 100,000 Jews left Spain and Portugal. These were scattered all over the Mediterranean coasts, Europe, Italy and Turkey. Most of them moved into North and West African Muslim dominated countries where persecution was less. Persecution was reduced because their complexion was same as the inhabitants so they could blend easily with the natives. These black Jews founded the Black Jewish communities including that of Ashanti, Angola, Dahomey, Morocco, Libya, Egypt, Algeria, and Yoruba (beni Israel- 'sons of Israel', of Ondo state) and must have inhabited the Desert of Seth that included Bight of Biafara and of course from where they must have entered interior into what became Ibo land thereby connecting with their brethren who had long settled there. This area inhabited by current and Bayelsa, Rivers, Cross River, Akwa Ibom states by the coast and possible joining Delta, Edo, Imo states in the interior. These must certainly have joined together with all the children of Gad who had settled already eventually.

Jewish communities in North Africa also included the Ait Moussa (bait Moussa-'house of Moses') or Beni Moussa, 'sons of Moses'. Leo Africanus, a Moorish convert to Judaism states that the North African Jews were hybrid in quality as they had intermarried and proselytized among the Greeks, Vandals, Romans, Spaniards, and Portuguese (see Leo Africanus alias Hassan ibn Mohammed el Wazzan el Zayyati History and Description of Africa trans Pory 1600; Hakkluyt Society 1896 cited in Windsor 2003: 117)

The black Jews of Africa also founded Hebrew Academies (e.g at Sijilmasa), that became centres of great learning in Grammar, Talmudic law, Poetry, and Philology to mention just these. The scholars held public debates, and lectures. Eldad the Danite, a Hebrew from the Jewish Kingdom of Ghana was said to have visited these schools in the ninth century (Windsor, 2003 115-135, Godbey 1930, Cowper 1897, Williams 1931). Therefore Eldad the Danite's account on the Ibo stated above must be credible as he must have communicated with these Jewish scholars and was versed in the history of the Jews. It is also very likely that some of these Jewish scholars formed part of the current Ibo known for their learning and priestly art that influenced most parts of the southern part of Nigeria especially the part that came to be known as the 'Ibo country'(former eastern region of Nigeria).

The period of Jewish learning came to an end by the invasion of the Almohades (Muslim Unitarians) in 1145 that destroyed Sijilmasa. The Almohades unleashed destructive assault on non-Muslim communities. This confirms Eldad's claim that the Ibo lost most of their Jewish identity because of persecution. According to him the Ibo lost all documents and religious texts and retained oral stories and some practices including the Book of Joshua, the main text which they had retained. This text must have been also lost or destroyed by human action or climatic and environment factors like all other historical artifacts.

In 1484 King John II (Joao II) of Portugal unmercifully took away 700 black Hebrew children from their parents and relocated them to the Island of Sao Thome. Sao Thome which was founded in 1471 as a Portuguese territory is located by the coast of today's Ibo country, Cameroon and Gabon. These Jews are described as serious minded, reserved, and wealthy and were said to have held most of the trade in their hands.

Thus we can confidently extrapolate that what we know as the Iboland today is occupied by these migrants who came to constitute the Ibo (Ibo) peoples. This variety of black Jewish migrants into Ibo country could account for why there are various Igbo peoples each having its own different legends, yet all pointing to a common origin as Israelite tribes. For example some claim to belong to the clan of the Levites, some claim they belong to the Ephraimite clan. There are those who claim Benjamite; another claims of the Moussa (Moses) clan. They are today referred to as Ibo peoples because they inhabit what was referred to as the Ibo country by the colonialist. They are a people whose history traces them to the stock of Jewish immigrants who dominated trade, were serious minded, ambitious, intelligent, priestly, scholarly and wealthy, achievement oriented.

The colonial masters also created boundaries, demarcations, and divisions as they are till today. This place, variously spelt as 'Heebo', 'Ebo', 'Eboe', 'Heebro', and later 'Ibo' country by different colonial, missionaries and early native writers includes all the land of the former eastern region. Today, we know that the Ibo peoples also occupy lands beyond the river Niger into parts of present Kogi, Benue, Ondo and Rivers, Cross River, Akwa Ibom and Delta states. The other parts of what became Nigeria as demarcated by the colonialists were called 'Hausa' country to the north and 'Yoruba' country to the west. The Jews from different parts of what became Africa (north, south, west) must have been attracted to settle on the fertile coast of the River Niger(oshimiri ogbaru) and from here moved into the hinterland spreading all over the area that became Iboland.

Regarding the Ibos to be Jewish (not just Hebrews), Eldad the Danite in his recollections of the Jewishness of the' Ibos' went further to state that the ancient Ibo in Africa had an entire body of scriptures except the books of Esther and Lamentations. According to him the Ibo knew nothing of the Mishna and the Talmud. Rather they had their own 'Talmud' which contained all the Jewish Laws but in the name of the biblical Joshua. These Jewish laws included, perhaps what present day western scholars, like G. von Rad have identified as the Hexateuch. Eldad described a specific law on the killing of animals for food which is strictly kosher. According to him due to frequent hostilities from enemies of the Ibo Jews, notably Muslims and Christian rulers, the Ibos lost all inherited important documents because they were forced to be in constant movement and many of the scriptures were also destroyed by these enemies. Consequent upon the experience of threat to life and property and for fear of extermination as a people, according to Eldad, the Ibo Jews practiced their faith in secret and could only retain the history of their origins and religious practices in memory. An example of a common word that lives today is perhaps, the word, 'opoto'. This word is up till this day used as one of the words that refer to 'the land of the dead'. It is perhaps a reference to their experience in O'Porto (ancient name for Portugal) during the mass murder of their ancestors that took place there; that forced their Ibo ancestors to flee to what came to be called 'Heebro' (also spelt 'Heebo' 'Ibo' and today 'Ibo') country.

Some of these secret practices of the 'Ibo Jews' according to Eldad included: Circumcision of every male on the eighth day after birth, observance of kosher dietary laws, separation of men and women during menstruation, celebration of holidays such as yom kippur, Rosh Hashanah, Sukkot, and Passover. Much later, celebration of Hanukkah and Purim which were not known to their ancestors were added. The most reminiscent of all the ancient practices is perhaps the agricultural ahiajoku yam festival which mirrors the feast of weeks (Shavuot) of Deuteronomy 16: 10 and the new maize celebration among other agricultural observances including presentation of agricultural produces in the village shrine before the priest usually of Ala deity or Amadioha deity as the case may be. Although the original observances are lost among the Ibo as a result of persecution I can testify to the fact that as a child I also met the time when there was strict method of killing an animal, a season when 'strange' rituals were carried out solely by the local chief priest, the ritual cleansing practice, including the ritual washing and separation of all utensils, and the fact that a menstruating woman was not allowed to cook or serve food to her husband and a wife cooked food and served the food with her head completely covered and must ensure that her hands were well washed before serving the food. Also I do remember that my community and compound was averse to pigs. Those who reared pigs were derided and they sold the pigs to other peoples. Pigs were never reared, eaten or killed in our compound. Although I did not understand why these practices were observed I can vividly recollect them. And above all circumcision was taken as given for every male on the eighth day following birth although some people carried it out as a puberty rite, yet still some others carried it out earlier than eighth day following birth; and the baby's mother's purification period lasted about thirty days for a male child and longer for a female. The end of the purification period was marked by a big feast. Another practice I can remember is the removal of all mirrors from the room where a corps was laid before burial. Where the mirrors were not completely removed they were turned with their reflective surface to face the wall. Also although there was elaborate funeral ceremony the corps was never laid for more than a week usually four days after death before being buried and burial places were close to home and carefully marked with a particular special tree that was regarded as an ever-living plant (ogirishi). A stone was used to mark the head of the buried and the head nust face in a particular direction which I later discovered was towards the east. I also later understood the east to point towards Jerusalem . However I am not sure that everyone understood this practice to mean pointing towards Jerusalem because Jerusalem has not been of any significance to the people. This is perhaps one of those lost important observances that indicate the origin of the people from the land of Israel. I also noticed, as a child, incantations in strange language by priests following strange ritual practices of virgin goats. The priest also wrote signs on the wall some of which I realize look like Hebrew alphabets.

Also noteworthy is the practice of referring to one's father and uncle as 'papa'. The uncle is also addressed as 'dede' and aunt as 'dadah'. A mother is addressed as 'mma', 'imma', 'mama'. An elder father or uncle is addressed as 'nna anyi' or 'nna ani' (our elder father) while an elder aunt is addressed as 'nne anyi', 'nne ani' (our elder mother). I can also recollect the eating of achicha (iri achicha), perhaps locally baked unleavened bread within family circles compulsorily at certain times or seasons of the year or occasion; I can also remember the time during which only bitter leaf was eaten, and when the utazi leaf is cooked in all households. There was also the practice of cooking without oil for a season and the women made sure they must not mix items of food or utensils. Milking of livestock was avoided completely. This separation was extended to agricultural produces and farm crops. Certain crops must not be planted in the same place although mixed planting of crops was practiced. It was regarded as abomination to violate this rule of separation as doing so would require ritual purification to establish orderliness and peace with the deities and the ancestors. Also I remember the driving away of evil (I chu fu agbara) ritual in which the blood of sacrifice is placed on all door posts including and especially entrance to compounds following ritual purification (I pu Ala-cleansing of the land), I ma ntu (covering with ashes- perhaps reminiscent of Sukkoth celebration among the ancient Hebrews) and observance of a day of rest on Eke day that is reminiscent of Jewish Sabbath although the Ibo calendar has doubled four days making up an 'izu' (eight days) similar to European week made up of seven days. The Ibo days are called Nkwo, Orie, Afor, and Eke. Eke is treated as a sacred day. I also remember that in counting an Ibo day we began at Sun down (in the evening) also reminiscent of Hebrew day. The calendar observed was that of the moon. Another practice I can remember is the taking a new born son to the shrine of Ala deity. This practice is carried out by the parent usually after weaned the child of breast milk. A gift is presented to the deity and believed to be presented to Chukwu (supreme destiny) through the Ala deity. The gift of carefully selected goat or ram is given. This is perhaps a remnant of Jewish son presentation, redemption and dedication. There was also the ritual lustration to mark the end of seclusion following delivery by a mother. This ritual lustration took various forms ranging from dipping the feet in the village stream to complete bathing, and accompanied by young maidens while the husband carried along a young carefully selected goat for presentation to the deity for sacrifice by the priest. This marked the end of her purification period following child birth. There was also the iru mgbe carried out by girls beginning from childhood and culminating at puberty till about age eighteen years when it was expected to terminate and the girl is from then fit for marriage. I also remember the period of seclusion of young maidens who built the mbari. The Mbari is a complex art representing all the skills and trades and deities of the peoples' life and history in a period of time (usually in a type of shrine, so to say). These practices (iru mgbe and the mbari) are perhaps reminiscent of Jewish Bat mitzvah.

For the male the joining into the masquerade cult and learning the secrets of the land is perhaps equivalent of the female iru mgbe and reminds of Jewish bar mitzvah (Basden 1966, Ogbalu 1979, Achebe 1958 Munonye 1966, Ganzfried et al 1961, Nwapa 1966)

It might be needful to note that some of these observations have either been, renamed, modified or abandoned as a result of persecution, syncretism, compromise and neglect due to lack of continuity. This lack of continuity must have perhaps been exacerbated by intermarriages with non Jewish neighbours and conversion to Christianity especially Roman Catholicism. For example the present day Ajoku ji festival which marks the Ibo New Year falls within the same time of year as the rosh hoshana, the Jewish New year. Thus syncretism could be at play here and on some other practices explaining why the Ibos seem to have lost their ancestral heritage and embraced foreign customs and practices. We can also appreciate how unpopular it was to remain Jewish in European colonial and Roman Catholic dominated territory in those days.

Writing in 1789 Equiano remarks:

'the strong analogy which...appears to prevail in the manners and customs of my countrymen and those of the Jews, before they reached the Land of Promise, and particularly the patriarchs while they were yet in that pastoral state which is described in Genesis-an analogy, which alone would induce me to think that the one people had sprung from the other'

Among the customs and manners Equiano has in mind is expressed in this his observation:

...agriculture is our chief employment, and everyone contributed something to the common stock, and as we are unacquainted with idleness, we have no beggars (Narrative 7, please cf Lord Macauley's statement to the English Parliament quoted above).

The collections made in the common stock as observed by Equiano were for the needy. Also the law of gleanings at harvest which required the owner of a farmland to leave some crops behind while harvesting his farm produce was for providing food for the needy and the foreigners who would then go at their own convenience to collect food. This can also be compared to the ancient Israelite practice as recorded in Leviticus 23: 22. It was this strong kinship spirit that enabled the fathers' people to 'live and let live'-and no one would think of misappropriating or embezzling 'what belongs to all of us' (corporate ownership) for private ownership or profit. Adding to this would be blood solidarity whereby the offence of one person affected everyone else and could endanger the existence of the whole kindred community just as it was among the ancient Israelites. Thus theft, incest, homosexuality, bestiality, oppression of anyone especially the orphans and the widows, false witness, desecrating the boundary demarcations, defaecating on farm land, breeching the law of cross breeding, breaching of marriage laws, fornication, becoming pregnant while unmarried, adultery, breaking the laws of virginity, to mention just these were treated as abhorrent. All agricultural laws, Land laws, fertility laws, and laws of interpersonal relationship and community preservation were never to be breached. These were regarded as sacrosanct. This is because my people like the Israelites believed that there was a strong linkage between kin, cult practices, land and the afterlife. These manners and customs still linger to this day among some Ibo peoples, though colonial ways and imitating western lifestyle have come close to obliterating them. Many Ibo are crying out loud and continually lamenting against the situation of things today. The true Ibo manners of old seem to have eroded faster than could have been imagined by our ancestors when they were walking this earth. This erosion of our manners and customs seems to have been hastened by the type of forced colonial Christianity introduced among the inhabitants of the Ibo country in addition to some other beliefs acquired through syncretism and intermarriages. The Biafra war and modern persecutions have accelerated this degeneration of morality as the Ibo struggles for survival.

We have abandoned the G-d of our fathers and are abandoning our ways, manners and customs. Consequently our generations are now suffering. We are almost losing our identity completely, our uniqueness as Ibo people (see kinship relationship below please). The Ibo ancestors must be reeling in their ancestral world because of the degeneration of Ibo society. There is an urgent need for a rethink of present day values among the Ibo. We are politically divided as our children are being made to imitate moral degeneration.

Israeli Interest and Visits

I have been made to understand that apart from the 1997 visit from Israel, the Israeli Prime Minister Yitzhak Rabin had sent a team of researchers in 1995 to Nigeria 'in search for the lost ten tribes of Israel'. A visit to the Ibo peoples was also made in 1988 when Nabhi Moshe visited the Ibo people and discussed this common genealogy with his 'Ibo brothers'. These visits or incursions if proved to be true certainly indicate that even in Israel there seems to be an understanding that the Ibo peoples are their blood brothers. Yet I am made to understand that some Ibos were denied entry into Israel to settle in 1988. It is my opinion that Ibo seeking to settle in Israel may be taking the wrong step. As stated earlier being of the Hebrew or of ancient Israelite origin does not automatically guarantee citizenship of Israel nor does ethnicity guarantee citizenship of a nation. Also having genealogical linkage with ancient Israel does not necessarily make a person a Jew. Yet still that the state of Israel claims to be a Jewish state is a political claim yet to be ratified by the United Nations and by people who believe in justice for all citizens. This is to say that people who are claiming citizenship of Israel on the basis of genealogical linkage are doing so because they are ignorant of the real situation of things. They need to be better educated about what citizenship of a nation involves. Also you do not have to be a Jew to be an Israeli citizen as there are non Jewish Israelis today.

Whatever might have led to this search for the Ibo by politicians from Israel one thing would be certain about embarking on this search: there must have been some clue to the possibility of evidence that there are Jews (Israelites) in this part of the world to warrant this search. Already some Israelis and some western Rabbis and educators are today sponsoring the building of synagogues in Ibo land and supporting them. There are many younger Ibo boys and girls joining Judaism, others are becoming rabbis of Yeshua, the Messiah Movements. There has also been increase in the number of Sabbath churches among the Ibo in place of the traditional Christian churches. This is perhaps an indication that there is growing awareness of their Israelite/Jewish roots or some positive force motivating them towards Judaism. My opinion is that the Ibos should make hast slowly with regard to this in order to avoid being colonized again by the wrong religious/political beliefs. There is no evidence that Judaism as practiced today is the true worship of the God of Abraham. The Ibo must be proud of their undiluted form of worship of Yahweh as handed down by our fathers through Abraham and Moses.

The Ibo, even the modern Ibo who have embraced Judaism have not been accorded any political recognition by any of the Israeli governments, nor by all the branches of Judaism in spite of being registered as Shepardi Jews. According to certain powerful quarters in Israel and elsewhere, they are seeking for convincing documented evidence to support this very long standing claim before granting the Ibo full international political recognition as fully fledged blood brothers of ancient and modern Israel. According to this school there is no extant proof of any historical or religious connection, as the Hasidic, with the Ibos, making such a claim futile. These politicians and religious leaders are aware of the fact that in this part of the world it is near impossible to preserve all such artifacts due to the climatic conditions and nature of the soil. This assertion seems to further imply that the Ibo peoples never had their own Hebrew or Jewish practices and are incapable of following their own form of Jewish worship even today. This again is reminiscent of the colonial Christian mission that undermined native approach to worship and westernized the Christianity among the Ibos- a type of Christianity that aimed to serve the interest of the colonizers. The result is what we have seen today, a Christian version that colonised the minds of the people with denominational and sectarian indoctrination and mind control through parochial education systems; a nominal form of Christianity that has compromised the traditional moral fabric of the people, a failed form of Christianity in this part of the world.

On the other hand, in spite of opposition from powerful known quarters it is close to being taken as given by all and sundry that the Ibo peoples of the world understand themselves to be Hebrews, as they are descendants of Jacob, even if there were no so called documented evidence linkable to any ancient Hebrew forefather(s) along the lineage of Jacob or Jewish religious lines. By documented evidence I think these people mean witness among ancient Hebrew ancestor(s) archaeologically extant. Even oral histories and legends among the Ibo today do not seem to be accepted by these so called powerful.

Those so called powerful quarters that oppose the view that Ibo are Hebrew (modern Jews) have not themselves presented any documented evidence to prove their case, or disprove this consciousness that the Ibo peoples have common ancestral linkage with Israel.

While the proponents base their argument on native awareness of the Ibo as Hebrews, the opponents seem to base their disagreement with the proponents for selfish and parochial reasons, and for reasons of political convenience.

It is also, perhaps, needful to say to the proponents that they should appreciate, no matter how sadly it might be, that it has not been enough to convince these people by merely declaring that 'the Israelites and the Ibo are brothers' and by tracing the exodus of Ibo ancestors from the area today called the middle east at be it pre-exodus or exodus times or the time of the Assyrian conquest and evacuation of the northern kingdom, and so on, nor is it enough to say that the Ibo ancestors came from a catalogue of places where Hebrew (Jews) had emigrated from as is being claimed for long. These places as stated earlier include today's Spain, Syria, Portugal, Libya, and other North and coastal African countries into their habitation today, though these may be historically relevant especially if valid archaeological evidence can back them up at least to satisfy the doubters who claim that oral evidences, collective consciousness and personal awareness are not enough. Not even the fact that it was the Israeli Jews themselves who began the search for the Ibo peoples and not the other way round.

The Roman Catholics have opposed the view that Ibo peoples are linked to ancient Israelites genealogically for centuries but their reason for this opposition are becoming increasingly exposed to be influenced by self serving and parochial motives, while the politicians, especially in the Israel of today and parts of the western world, oppose it for political paranoia and economic convenience, perhaps, based on fear of the consequences of such recognition. Perhaps if Biafra had survived as an independent nation state, oil and other mineral resources found in Biafra would have produced a different attitude from these politicians towards the Ibo claims and request for closer relationship with Israel.

I have heard of court cases instituted against the Israeli government including the political saga involving three people said to be Ibo business men who were arrested in Israel for overstaying their visa. It was said that they challenged their deportation in court of law in Israel, claiming that as descendants of Jacob (Israel) they had the right to live, work and do business in Israel so they claimed they had come back to their forefathers' original land. The case as I learned lingered on as an international news item for a while but suddenly fizzled out of circulation. Some politicians were said to have challenged their claim in the court while some others including some Jewish bodies supported the businessmen's claim. So it was claimed to have become a nutty political battle with its implications.

However, rumours had it that the businessmen were quietly granted leave to do business or remain under certain conditions to prevent a legal precedent which would grant legal rights to other Ibo to claim Israeli citizenship. Other rumours claim that the business men were deported home. The details of what really happened are yet to uncover. The point being made here is that the issue of whether Ibo peoples are Israelis by blood has attained a worldwide political fame and importance and perhaps, notoriety.

It is, perhaps, essential to be noted here that although many Ibos are in Israel already working in the farms (Kibutzim) and as traders, the Ibo peoples should not in actual fact be interested in leaving their present habitation to permanently inhabit anywhere else, not even to Israel. The Ibo population (70 million to 80 million) is very many times larger than the whole Israeli population so also is the Ibo territory or land mass very much greater. Moreover, the Ibo land of today is far richer and better endowed with resources than anywhere else in the world. All the Ibos are asking for is to be allowed their G-d given opportunity to develop themselves. They are asking governments to stop stifling them; to stop seeing them as a threat, rather encourage them to help in cultural and economic emancipation of their peoples and allow them to develop the world with their G-d given talents and intelligence which they consider their primary calling on earth. They claim that they share in the blessing upon Abraham; so through them the families of the world shall be blessed (or shall bless themselves). Yes, it might be true that the land occupied by ancient Israel might have been very much larger than what Israel is today, yet geographically it cannot accommodate even one tenth of the Ibo peoples. This is perhaps one of the reasons some Ibo scholars think the Israelites should rather think of coming back home to Ibo land from where their forefathers left to Palestine, especially as they have incurred so much trouble for themselves. According to this school of thought, the history of Ibo peoples predates that of the Israelites of old. These scholars claim that the Ibo origin is 8000 years old while the Israelite history of origin is 4000 years old. Some claim that the Igbo race is among the oldest in the world; still some others though the very minority claim the Igbo are the oldest race in the world.

In her book, They Lived Before Adam: Prehistoric Origins of the Igbo The Never-Been-Ruled, Catherine Acholonu claims that Igbo oral tradition is consistent with scientific research into origins of humanity. Speaking at the Harlem Book Fairs, Acholonu surmarised the content of her argument as follows:

"Our research includes the origin and meanings of symbols used in every religion and sacred literature all over the world. In these, we found that the Hebrew Bible, the Kabbalah of the Hebrews and the Chinese, the Hindu Vedas and Rmayana and the recently discovered Egyptian Christian Bible called the Nag Hammadi are of immense importance in revealing lost knowledge. Wherever we looked we found evidence confirming the claims by geneticists who have been conducting mitochondrial DNA research in four leading universities here in the USA that all mankind came from sub-Sharan Africa, that Eve and Adam were black Africans... Igbo oral traditions confirm the findings of geneticists, that by 280,000 BC-280,000BC- human evolution was interrupted and Adam, a hybrid, was created through the process of genetic engineering. However, our findings reveal that the creation of Adam was a downward on the evolutionary ladder, because he lost his divine essence, he became divided, no longer whole, or wholesome. All over Africa and in ancient Egyptian reports, oral and written traditions maintain that homo erectus people were heavenly being, and possessed mystical powers such as telepathy, levitation, bi-location, that their words could move rocks and mountains and change the course of Rivers. Adam lost all that when his right brain was shut down by those who made him."

Catherine Acholonu died on 18 March 2014 at the age of 62 from a year long renal failure.

However many people disagree with our great researcher. One of whom is Harold Johnson (on March 29, 2010) who argues thus:

"If you are a serious researcher you are going to be disappointed at this work (That refers to Acholonu's research and conclusions above). As a linguist, I was upset at the fact that this work is riddled with folk etymology. In no sense was the comparative method used for her cross cultural analysis on lexical items between languages. If you are to compare terms, you back it up, if it is basic vocabulary, with words in known related languages. This was not done. Also it is very Igbo centric and assumes, not based on demonstrated linguistic, genetic or archeological evidence that the Igbo are the oldest people: thus that the oldest languages and customs on EARTH are Igbo. This is silly when genetics demonstrate that the Khoisan and the Oromo/Habasha of Ethiopia are your oldest people. They didn't and don't speak Igbo.

Secondly, a lot of the conclusions Acholonu, et al, came to assumed that the myths were true. So instead of treating the Genesis stories and Sumerian stories (for example) as myths, the authors treat the stories (Adam and Eve, etc.) as if they are ESTABLISHED truths. You would have to first convincingly prove the stories to be true and then compare your findings to known findings written prior to your work. This was not done. She should have consulted the works of GJK Campbell-Dunn and Modupe Oduyoye for her linguistic work. Then she would have a leg to stand on.

Thirdly a lot of her resources are good resources (sic) (perhaps Johnson meant to say, 'are not good resources'). They would never be approved for a Master's or PhD thesis. Some of her resources don't have any references.

My main issue is her methodology and her lack of thoroughness in the research. I only give it a three because there are some claims in the book that I can back up but with evidence and sound linguistics. These same methods will render a lot of what she claims to be incorrect. I am impressed however with the research done on the Ikom Monoliths and will be purchasing the Gram Code to analyze it. I do feel however that it will suffer from the same issues as this book. There is so much information out now that could provide evidence for some of her conclusions, but because the research wasn't thorough, she missed an opportunity to make a strong case"

Another reaction by Olu Oguibe dismisses the claim that Igbo is Jewish by arguing that: "Most Igbo groups and clans do not recognize or accept the tradition of Eri ancestry. The Mbaise, Ngwa, Owere, Orlu, Nsuka, Ohafia, Abakeleke and Aro Igbo, to name but a few, most certainly have no oral traditions of Eri ancestry. In most part, the attempt to project a universal Igbo tradition of Eri common ancestry is the work of one man: M Angulu Onwuejeogwu. The Nri and Aguleri probably descend from a common ancestor named Eri. For the rest of the Igbo, that's just another cock and bull story without scientific foundation. It's as though in his work, Onwuejeogwu set out to revive the mission of Nri hegemony, this time foisting it over Igbo history. Much credit to him for his assiduous work to lay the foundations of an articulate, collective Igbo history. Unfortunately, much of that work is baseless. And if Eri is not some kind of common ancestor of the Igbo but of only a town or two, then, it doesn't really matter much where he came from. What the science tells is that on the chromosomal tree of human evolution, the Igbo are an older people than either Egyptians, Jews, or any Afro-Asiatic group. On the mitochondrial evolutionary tree, the Igbo belong to the L1 group, which follows immediately from the L0 group at the beginning of human existence. In other words, we carry matrilineal DNA that goes back 107,300 - 174,000 years. The oldest mtDNA haplogroup in North Africa including Egypt is only 50,000 years old. We were around for at the very least 50,000 years before Egyptians evolved. Jews are even much younger on the evolutionary tree. On the patrilineal Y-chromosomal tree, the dominant DNA strand among the Igbo places them in the much discussed but often misrepresented E1b1a haplogroup. It's probably the most controversial haplogroup in sequencing, but only because people ignore the science and make up all kinds of idiotic, fantastical claims. Some of the misleading claims come even from the scientists who discovered the parent stem of the group. Long and short of it, though, is that no, Egyptians do not carry the E1b1a Y chromosome. So, if Eri is the common ancestor of the Igbo and he came from Egypt, he probably lost his Y-chromosome in the Sahara before making his way to Nri. Now, for those who want to be Jews, science has some starkly disappointing news. Beside the fact that the matrilineal DNA pools show that Jews are at least 75,000 - 140,000 years more recent as a group than the Igbo, the patrilineal evidence also places the greater percentage of Jews in the E1b1b1 haplogroup, another smaller but substantial percentage in the J haplogroup, and the rest in the R1 haplogroup. No Jews are known to belong in the same haplogroup as the Igbo, namely, the E1b1a. Needless to restate that the E1b1a haplogroup also predates the E1b1b1 haplogroup by thousands of years. Like most Central and coastal West African groups, we are an ancient people. According to science, we predate the Egyptians and the Jews by tens of thousands of years. We should be proud of that."

There are some other Books that have been in circulation that need mention in this study. One is the book by Remy Ilona titled The Igbos and Israel: An Inter-Cultural Study of the Largest Jewish Diaspora: 2014, which was a very commendable effort in providing some already known cultural evidence based on Ibo Omenala (traditions and practices) comparable to the practice of the ancient Israelites. However, Ilona who studied law would have more effectively contributed to the study if he had focused on the legal features that link the two peoples as that is the area of his expertise, leaving the Anthropological and Biblical-Theological-Philosophical aspects to the experts in those fields. His book also failed to bring to the fore what is unique to the Ibo and the Israelites as a people as many of the practices and beliefs he attributed to the Ibo and Israelites could be found among other peoples. He also did not clarify or define who the Igbo are. Yet the book is highly commendable since originating from a non biblical non philosophical/ theological scholar. Perhaps he might consider helping us decipher how the laws of the Hebrew Bible and that of the Ibo omenala appeal to reason both in the ancient times and today. Thank you my brother for your efforts.

The other book perhaps worthy of mention is the work by one Rabbi Yehudah Tochukwu Ben Shomeyr and titled "Finding Gad: The Quest for the Lost Tribe of Gad": 2015. If I understand him he found Gad in Iboland. I thought Gad was not missing, it was rather his child Eri Gad that was missing. He perhaps found Eri descendants among the Igbo as he was told by the people around him and who influenced his conclusions when he visited Iboland. Secondly the book is poorly organized and lacking in any new information. Yet the worst aspect of the book was too much dependency on the opinion and influences on a previous work by one Professor Alaezi. The most unattractive aspect of Rabbi's Finding Gad is the language connection. As a Rabbi one would have expected a clearer treatment and clarification on the language connection. Unfortunately what I thought should attract readers, especially Ibo scholars of the Hebrew and Ancient Near Eastern and Ibo languages became the most unscholarly and unattractive aspect of the book. This does not mean that the other aspects of the book are any useful or relevant. Someone described the book as a rehash of old traditions, worne out stories. The information therein is a retelling of what people he met during his visit told him. Worst still the book is annoyingly and disappointingly expensive raising questions as to what the aim of the writer was (the reader may want to see Professor O. Alaezi's IBOS: Hebrew Exiles from Israel, Amazing Facts and Revelations 2012; also "Ibo Exodus" published 2006) Now I contend that the Ibos should not be described nor conceived as "Hebrew exiles from Israel." They are not on exile and do not see themselves as such. Our forefathers did not teach that we are on exile as if we belong elsewhere. The fact is that there was need for Yahweh's relocation of the Hebrew peoples, as did most other peoples of the world, at different time in their history, and the Yahweh relocated the Hebrews to the present West Africa and settled them here for thousands of years. This does not fit into the feature of a people on exile.

My reaction to the other earlier opinions above goes thus: first the Ibo do not claim one source or legend on their origin. This means that we agree that the Eri legend is not a universally circulating Ibo legend. We have the Uturu legend alongside. The Eri legend is popular majorly among those who claim the nomenclature "Igbo" as representing them. Please note that Eri is not said to be an

Egyptian. He was a Hebrew who had inhabited in Egypt. The legend may not be popularly circulating among the Owere, Mbaise, Ngwa, Orlu, Nsuka, Ohafia, Abakeleke, Aro, Annang, Ebuno, Eket, Ejagham, Ikwere, Etche, Ijaw, Ibibio, Delta and Benue and Kogi Ibos areas etc as aledged. Therefore these should be considered to have the right to exclude themselves from being referred to as 'Igbo' if they so wish, however only a very minority seem to do so. "Igbo" seem to have absorbed every eboe people as a generic nomenclature. However clearly this does not exclude any of them from being of the Hebrew origin. Above all they all have a collective understanding that they are Hebrews by origin, at least a good majority of them. The Heebo race is an enigmatic group, as enigmatic as the name sounds. Some groups were obviously absorbed into a common ancestry with the Ibos. This is the main reason I refer to them as Ibo (Heeboe) peoples in this study and to highlight their common customs and manners as Dr Olaudah Equiano stated. This is also perhaps, why such issue as the place of language should become important in a study such as this. Also I wish to quickly reiterate that there is a complete mixing up of the groups such that it is difficult to separate the peoples called Ibo. This is more difficult to do with regard to those closest to the "Igbo" group. It is also possible that influences of 'Igbo' and his singular descendants have spread so widely that other Ibo peoples are almost completely absorbed into those "Igbo" people who claim Eri ancestry. Thus even if Eri was the father of only a town or two the legend is still very significant in tracing Igbo origins to Eri. In fact it mixing up could cause people to deemphasis the importance of legends of origin, as commonalitiy of manners and customs become very obvious and more significant. What is important is that all Ibo legends and history in one way or the other claim Jewish/ Hebrew-Israelite origin and ancestry and that they present features, manners and customs that portray them collectively as such. The Owerre people (people of former Owerre province) most of whom are said to have Areli ancestry, present closest affinity to the Hebrew and ancient Israelite, both in language, customs and manners than perhaps any other single Ibo ethnic groups. The Asher ancestry is also evident. Also research of this nature never terminate as new facts emerge scholars should be humble enough to drop their previous biased conclusions. This is more so when the so called western scholarship values and methods are used in such study. For example would it not be arrogant to claim to be the oldest race in the world and would it not be considered more naïve to base such a fact on result of a single DNA test. Already recent tests have also shown that the Ibo are of the Semitic DNA. DNA mutation is becoming too rife to rely on such a test to draw conclusions. Ibos are not asking to be identified as Ibos by DNA. They already know they are of the Hebrew stock.

The objection that Ibos are not Hebrew and so not Jewish from genetic haplography does not hold any grounds. Those who are using that argument perhaps need to update their knowledge of genetic research. The research on gene mutation has proved that there has been so much gene-mixing that it is difficult to separate origins of people by using DNA. Moreover everyone has the genetic make up of the first human and that genetic make is continuously (not continually) being generated and exists in all human beings. Genetic differenciation for demarcating human species was a colonial tool to dominate peoples politically and mentally. Also it is disheartening that Africans including researchers and writers who are not themselves genetic researchers depend so much on these old colonial theories and in fact still cling onto them even when those who previously were involved in the research had abandoned those old theories. I was close to being made to rely on genetic proof and in fact had brought out my credit card to pay for a genetic test but the timely advice of one of the researchers I contacted on phone advised that genetic test may not give final proof of a person's genealogical origin. In other words being told that you have Jewish gene, does not make you Jewish. This is because many so called gentiles could still have same or similar gene. This he said was due to gene mutation and mixing up of genes through intermarriages, rape, and so much fornication and adultery of today's world.

Finally once again the claim that the Ibos or any other ethnic group are the oldest ethnic group on earth is too controvercial to address here. What was Adam's tribe? Was he an Igboman? Was he a Khoisan, or Oromo, or Habasha? He was certainly not. Making this sort of claim should not be encouraged. As stated, it smacks of arrogance and perhaps ignorance. Moreover anybody and everybody could make the same claim. Above all as stated earlier Jewishness is not a genetic factor. Jewishness is a faith, a system of beliefs that creates a collectivity of believers under some form of leadership that could be manipulative of other peoples.

There is however, no further proof to warrant any further serious attention to the objectors' theory. Moreover their assertion does not nullify the fact that the Ibos and the ancient Israelites are blood brothers. It is either the Ibos are Hebrews or the ancient Hebrews who located to the orient.

Also it is very probable that not up to one hundredth of the Ibo peoples would be willing to relocate to the Israel of today nor would any Israeli wish to relocate to Ibo land. In fact it is more likely that more present day Israelis would prefer to relocate to Ibo land than Ibos would. The world should stop comparing the Ibo with the Falashas of Ethiopia. The word Falasha means, "the UNWANTED STRANGER". The Ibos are not unwanted they are very much in control, needed and wanted in their present location and do not intend to exchange it for anywhere else. The Igbo are not wandering; they are a well settled people though envied by their neighbours who fail to appreciate their egalitarian attitude to life and proud of themselves. This is perhaps one of the reasons they were seen as possessing "upity" by their colonial enemy. So Israeli government should have no fear or expect any massive exodus to Israel from Iboland.

Moreover in the modern world, as stated earlier, being a Hebrew or Jew does not confer the automatic right of citizenship of Israel just as being English does not confer citizenship of England or the United Kingdom.

It is true that accepting the Ibo as Jews in the sense that they are also the children of Abraham along the lineage of Jacob will be of mutual benefit to both the Ibo country and present day Israel. In fact there are obvious indications that it will be of greater benefit to Israel than to the Ibo peoples politically and economically. Politically the Ibo peoples are numerically stronger and are scattered all over the globe and so will be a force to promoting the political interest of the Jews worldwide and Israel in particular. Economically they are a very hard working and intelligent people. Also it is perhaps the huge achievements of the Ibo in terms of corporate size in land mass and population that should be the land mark of appreciating the fulfilling of the promise to Abraham that his children would be as many as the sand of the sea and through his descendants the families of the earth shall be blessed. The size of the Ibo population could help propagate the true Hebrew faith to the inhabitants of Israel. Yes, as Yashaiah has fulfilled this promise spiritually it is the collective efforts of all Abraham's children in this earth that would fulfill it in the physical and material realm. It is when all Jews of the world unite as one people: think together, fight together, survive together, work together, plan together, and make this world a better place that the physical dimension of Abraham's promise will be fulfilled. The promised blessing to Abraham by "the I am that Iam" is to be interpreted as holistic by including the physical and spiritual dimensions. It is a calling, a mission for all Jews no matter their colour or location.

The ploy to dissociate themselves from the so called 'haters and murderers of

G-d's son' that the Roman Catholics have for centuries blackmailed the Hebrews with, has contributed to their opposing any attempt, perhaps for centuries, to associate the Ibo peoples with Hebrew origins. This explains why the Roman Catholic priests in Ibo country have for centuries sought to exclude the Ibo peoples from this idea. There is also the fear that the Ibo having similar traditional beliefs and worship with the ancient Hebrews, would reconvert to Judaism in droves. This would deplete the population of the Roman Church, which we know is purely colonial in intent, and for which the Ibo are the majority in that part of the world. They are perhaps the most populous Roman Catholic territory in Africa. As an example I wish to cite that the church and colonial educators in the Ibo country today have not explained why the final 'h' in certain original Ibo words and names were suddenly dropped beginning in the late 1960s; and every Ibo child has continued to be taught to spell those Ibo significant nominal words without final 'h'. I am sure many Ibo peoples today do not know that certain significant nominal Ibo words that end in vowels especially 'e' and 'a' are originally supposed to be followed by final 'h'. Thus name words like 'Oparah', 'Ibeh', and 'Adah', to mention just these have been denied the final 'h'. The reason for dropping final 'h' is to rid Ibo words of any linkage to Hebrew roots evidencing common manners and customs in which the final 'h' refers to and reverences AYAH ASHER AYAH (yah) the 'I am that I am'; Lord and King; our forefathers believed that He alone deserves to be worshipped and served by all peoples on earth; He alone should be King. The Ibo have never reverenced or worshipped any human figure such as the pope. Also I have heard Roman Catholic priests whisper to me time and time again 'please stop connecting the Ibos with being 'Israelites' or 'Jews''.

As stated earlier the Roman Catholic wish is corroborated by those Ibo scholars who claim that there are alternative theories. One of which stated above is that the Ibo history predates that of the ancient Hebrews. Also as stated earlier these reiterate the claim that it was the Hebrews who emigrated from the Ibo habitation and migrated to their ancient Palestinian habitation. It is these that assert that the present Jews should rather come back home to their Ibo habitation. However what we are still saying to these Roman Catholic priest and supporters is that both ancient Hebrews and Ibo have a common genealogy that must be acknowledged and appreciated for the common well being of the two peoples and for the benefit of all peoples as Yahweh has promised the world that He would bless the whole humanity through us, the descendants of Abraham by blood. Then spiritual dimension of this has been accomplished in Yashaiah the Christ, the Ibos need to be recognised to participate in actualizing the physical dimension of this promise alongside others related by blood and calling.

Common Peculiar Cultural Dimension Explored

Therefore if the present documented evidence of Hebrew linkage seems not convincing enough to those that matter or has been ignored, I have decided to examine and explore the cultural dimension including language and select manners and customs in this study. The old missionary anthropologists' observations that are often cited were able to provide similarities in ritual practices between the Ibo and "the Old Testament" religions. However some of these similarities often cited could be regarded to be somewhat universal among traditional peoples in most parts of the world unless these peoples are also to be regarded as Jewish. Certainly, mourning ritual for a specific period of time, celebrating the new moon and conducting weddings under a canopy, just to mention these among other claims as evidences, could not be peculiar to only Ibo and Hebrew peoples. Also circumcising males on eighth day of birth, refraining from eating so called unclean food are not reserved rites for the Ibo and Hebrew alone. Almost all Ibo neighbours practice the same rituals, though it is not unusual that these neighbours are also linked to Hebrew genealogy as they could be counted as belonging among the Ibo peoples or copied them from the Ibos or vice versa.

What I think is needed is a study on those cultural aspects, notably beginning with language, ritual practices, festivals, beliefs and manners that appear peculiar to the ancient Hebrews and the Ibo peoples.

Understanding the word "Ibo" "Heebo" "Eboe"

The Anglican missionary George Thomas Basden (1938) can be said to have started on a more relevant note when he observed that the word 'heebo'(Ebo, Ibo, later to be confused with 'Igbo') could be a corruption of the 'Hebrew' (ibhri, ivri) as the two words sound alike. As stated earlier, the word Ibo has been rendered variously by foreigners through the generations beginning with the earliest as 'heebo', 'ebo', 'heebro', 'Ibo (cf Equiano: 1789)'. The claim that the white man's inability to pronounce 'gb' does not necessarily stand as evidence that the correct rendition should be 'Igbo'. The origin of the word is deep into antiquity; perhaps as enigmatic as the word "Ibhri" 'ivri' from which the word ha ibhri (the 'ibrew, ha ibrew, thus Hebrew) is derived-a word that describes a people rather than a name word as it has come to be regarded today. The definite article the (ha) clearly shows this. The enigma can be solved if it is accepted that the Hebrews derived their name from their key ancestor Heber, Eber.

Also the claim that it was the Yoruba people that corrupted the original word to 'Igbo', in attempt to pronounce it as a result of their thick lips seems not plausible. This claim states that the original name was 'Ibhri' but that they (the Yorubas) in attempt to pronounce it pronounced 'ibhri' 'ivri' to sound 'Igbo' since the bh is pronounced as 'vu' or 'gb' .

Yet another claim is related to one of the descendants of an Ibo ancestor called Igbo. He was said to have become very famous, hard working, achieving, but so arrogant and recalcitrant that he was banished among his brothers. However his fame made him some what the major figure among his brothers. This resulting division and banishment enthused him to work harder and to spread his influence far and near to such an extent that his name overshadowed the others and became the name by which the Ibo nation came to be called by the natives of what became Nigeria. Unfortunately his infamous behaviours became regarded as the feature of all Ibos. Consequently where ever his brother spread to they were referred to as 'Igbo' people especially as they presented similar physical features. Thus when the Onicha Ibo asks, 'if you will marry the daughter of Igbo' they are not implying that they are not Ibo rather they are questioning the wisdom of marrying a descendant of the known recalcitrant. Also when the early missionaries accused the Ibo of being stubborn and ungovernable, they were probably not referring to all Ibo, rather they were describing the characteristic of the descendants of Igbo. Yet the descendants of Igbo seem to have been easily identified as the names of their communes reflect the name Igbo even today. An example is Umuigbo, Amaigbo, Obigbo, Igbokiri, and such like names. This does not mean that every Igbo descendant presented recalcitrant behavior.

The natives of the land who the Ibo ancestors perhaps met and perhaps, absorbed, as stated earlier included the Kwa, the Alloku (Allokoo, aluku), the Ituri and the Pigmy (also called dwarfs). Although some of these tribes must have majorly died off(e.g the pigmies), their culture and practices must have been eventually absorbed by the Ibo dominant culture and ways of life and have tremendously influenced the ways and manners of the Ibos to such an extent that it became difficult to separate one group of people from the other. In fact the influence on the Ibo makes it almost difficult to carry out any research on the Ibo as Hebrew. The syncretism has been such that even the Ibos adopted the names of the deities of the natives and reverenced and worshipped them, practicing their rituals, observing their days and adopting their names. Yet the natives were said to have been influenced by the hard working and achievement orientation of the Ibos that when the colonial masters came the natives across the Southern part of Nigeria are said to have referred to the colonialist as onyibo, oyiri ibo (literally 'Ibo look-alike', 'Ibo act alike'). Some scholars have tended to regard this experience as indicating that the original Ibo must have been of light complexion. Perhaps there was a similarity in complexion with the 'white' colonialist as it was said that most of the early Ibo ancestors, including Eri, were somewhat of lighter complexion than the surrounding natives. There seems to be little plausibility for this whole claims and assertions. All the Jews of Africa are described as Black Jews by historians. This however may not imply that they were all jet black or olive black. Some African Jews might have been light complexions due to intermarriages with Japheth's descendants (see below) but it could not be comparable to being so called 'white' as to make the natives to compare the white colonialists with the complexion of the Ibo ancestors at that time. It is very probable that no one thought of people or imagined people as 'white' in complexion at that time. The origin of the word 'Onyibo' for the white or light skin should therefore be sought elsewhere. The Ibos today call the light skinned 'onye ocha' (literally "Whiteman") and/or "Bekee" (onye bekee) said to have been derived from the name of the first colonial representative sent to visit the Iboland who was called Mr Baike. Perhaps the phrase, 'Ibo Act alike' might suffice as the origin of "Onyibo". Another version is that because the white slave buyers always preferred the Ibo slaves, they were always heard to inquire by asking, Oyibo (onyeibo). Consequently, they became referred to as "Onyibo" by way of mimicry in the whole southern Nigeria and this was eventually shortened to Oyibo. It was said that the Yorubas popularized calling the slave buyers "oyibo."

Yet another claim is that it was the missionaries themselves that reduced the name 'heebro', 'eboe', 'ebo' and 'heebo' to 'Ibo'. Today some scholars including those of Ibo origin insist the rendition should be 'Igbo' and Ndigbo (literally Igbo people), a claim that, perhaps, has no basis except, as explained above, it represents one of the Ibo family heads who dominated his brothers. Some of his brothers are named as: Edozie, Ogbe, Oba, Ata, Ishi, Nri, Agu and others. The other descendants of the Ibo peoples named after the Ibo ancestors including Eri include: Agulu Eri, Umu le Eri, Ora Eri, Mbi Eri, Owu Eri(Owerre), Ama Igbo, Umu Igbo, Ura Ata, Agu ata, Ish Agu, Ama Ishi, Oba, Ama Oba, Ama Ogbe, Umu Ogbe, just to mention these(please see below for more on this). According to this legend the Ibos expanded in land and settled all over current Ibo heartland and later spread all over Southern part of Nigeria making incursions into Benin, Yoruba country, and the coastal areas. In fact it is claimed that there was a time the coastal Kings of New Calabar, Bonny, Opobo, etc were of Ibo descent (cf Adams: 1975 esp 231-232) and it is also claimed that some Igala and Edo peoples are directly linked to the Ibo. One account is that there was a time when Ibo medicine men and traditional doctors inhabited the Benin Kingdom. They became too influential as they expanded. However, there arose a King that did not know how the Ibos immigrated into Benin; so he expelled them. Some of the group of Ibos that emigrated went to inhabit along the coasts of the Atlantic. Their descendants are found in the present day Rivers state, Bayelsa, Akwa Ibom, Cross River state, Delta and other parts of the Niger Delta. Notable among these are the Bonis, Ogonis, Ikwere's, Okrikas, inhabitants of Port Harcourt, Etche, Elele, Opobo and many others scattered all over the coastal regions of Nigeria. Some of the Ibos who did not emigrate remained, and got absorbed into the Edo groups. Even today names of towns are being changed to refelect non Igbo. An example is the town originally called Igbokiri that has been changed to Igbanke.

It is also noteworthy that the scholars advocating the adoption of the name 'Igbo' or 'Ndigbo' as universal might have forgotten that the Ibos had what was called 'nnu hiburu (Ibru)' probably 'ibhri salt' originally understood as special type of sea salt produced by those called the 'ibru' people. I can remember that as children we were taught to believe that the 'hiburu' salt was brought along to what became the Iboland; it was not originally produced by the natives. This implies that the Ibo never lost their original universal nomenclature 'ebo' to 'Igbo' completely even at this early period. This also further confirms that there were native owners of the land when the children of Eri (Gad) and other Semites in his entourage arrived some of which have been mentioned above. This also perhaps concludes that not all inhabitants of the present Iboland can be said to have originated from ancient Israel. Eclecticism and Syncretism must have been rife and rapid through cultural integration of the children of Eri (Gad, Ibo Hebrews) and the natives they met and perhaps whom they eventually absorbed majorly into the cultural web of the Hebrews (Ibos) while the Ibos lost their religious and national roots. This integration must have been hastened by intermarriages and colonial and religious persecutions. As stated earlier persecutions must have forced the Hebrews who were mostly 'black' in colour to mix practices and abandon their original beliefs and practices. The question today is how to filter the real Ibo who are descendants of the Hebrew ancestors and the natives their ancestors met. In my own case and my kith and kin our great grandfather managed and retained his native Hebrew name, Udum Adah and some beliefs that have unveiled our Hebrew roots. And as the approach of this study any name that does not present similar pronunciation and meaning as the Hebrew equivalent cannot be regarded as Hebrew in origin. This approach as stated above is adopted to avoid arbitrary connection of words and names as Hebrew.

Also Olaudah Equiano, in his narratives, was able to reflect on what seems to be peculiar words and practices to the Ibo peoples and Hebrews such as 'mbrechi' mark of facial scarification. This mark is perhaps same as the marks on the faces of the judges called Umbares (supreme judges) that Solomon's son King David Menilek I of Ethiopia brought along to rule with him when he took over as ruler after the death of his mother, Queen of Sheba around 986 BC. Among these judges and specialist was Azarias, the son of Zadok, the former high priest who was said to have carried along with him a Hebrew transcript of the Law to Ethiopia. It is possible that the descendants of these judges and priest are among the Ibo descendants that continued the legacy of specialist priesthood (please see below for more on this).

Also the popular universal 'three back-hand' greeting readily comes to mind and has been noted as common only to the Ibo and the ancient Hebrew peoples. It means 'forward ever, and backward never' among both peoples and reflects the common Ibo salutation to each other and to one another to "continue the hard work" (ji sie ike). It might be interesting to note that many young Ibos salute one another with ji sie ike, "continue the hard work" without applying the back hand greeting. This is because they probably do not know what the three back hand greeting practiced by the older Ibos symbolizes. Rabbi Moshe, who was among the visitors to Iboland in 1988, said, it literally means "kadi maya omela" in Hebrew which means also 'forward ever backward never' and is also observed in the same manner as the Ibo three back hand greeting. Moshe Nathan, an Ibo rabbi was present when Rabbi Moshe visited and narrated this testimony and details of the visit to me. I can also remember the elders putting on what looked like the present day prayer shawl (tallit) of the Jews as formal dressing, although the shawl became majorly used to drive away flies.

How the Ibo Peoples view themselves

The consciousness of a people is most essential in determining who they are. I had heard, like perhaps every Ibo of my age group, when I was younger, that our people are Hebrews (Jews, Israelites). And there have been some write ups claiming same for our people, although, again, mostly by foreign writers and missionaries who narrated similarities between Ibo beliefs, rituals, and practices and the book of Leviticus in the Bible (e.g Basden: 1938). Many of these practices, beliefs and rituals were discarded as devilish by some missionaries.

Evidence of lost tribes of ancient Israel

I first saw information on this claim of common genealogy in an old geo-political atlas published around 1933 in the University of Oxford United Kingdom in 1990. It was based on a research carried out by some Oxford University scholars on the Diaspora Jews and was tagged 'search for the lost tribes of Israel.' The introduction stated that the researching scholars travelled around the world for very many years, costing quite a substantial amount of money to fund. They claimed to have examined legends, and claims and pruned peoples alleged to have been thought to belong to the lost tribes of ancient Israel. Their investigation, however, confirmed only a select number of peoples around the world as among the lost tribes of Israel, and that includes the 'Ibo' of West Africa (benei Israelites as they were called) and the Falasha, (beta Israelites as they were called) of Ethiopia. The word 'benei' is Hebrew word that means 'sons of'. Thus 'Benei Israel' means 'sons of Israel'. I came across this atlas when I was a research student at the University of Oxford and the atlas showed that as far back as 1933 the world scholars had concluded that the Ibos of Nigeria and the Falashas of Ethiopia are descendants of Jacob. However I was rather very angry that such a connection was made with my people by non Ibos. I readily discountenanced and regarded the whole saga as an insult. My contention was that my people could not have been lost. Moreover the information was not relevant to my research interest. However subsequent experience lead to my convinction and submission to the research findings of the Oxford Scholars and I eventually became a researcher in the field.

In sum we can observe that the Ibo being Jews seem to have been settled historically by the accounts of well respected researchers including Eldad the Danite. We also observe that the etymology of the name Ibo reflects Hebrew connection. Doubters and opponents like me have to learn and change their minds on this issue including those who are questioning the Jewishness of the Ibo for parochial or political reasons. There is more evidence for the Ibo being Jewish than not. More so that the Ibo believe they are Hebrews from their collective consciousness.

Chapter 2
Some Brief History

According to the Works of Josephus (Antiquities) the Jews were called Hebrews because their progenitor was Heber. Heber was the son of Sala who was the son of Arphaxad from the lineage of Aram. The Greeks called the Aramites, Syrians. And all were descendants of the lineage of Shem.

However the Hebrew Bible(the so called Old Testament) account seems to indicate that the origination of the word Hebrew is attributable to Abram who was described as "the Hebrew" or "passenger over Euphrates" as translated by the Septuagint that used the Greek word "perate's"(crossing over). Shem has been called the father of all the children of Heber (all Hebrews) long before Abram passed over Euphrates (Genesis 10: 21). Abram is a descendant of Shem through the lineage of Phaleg. Phaleg means "division" and he was named to commemorate the time of the division of the people into various nations. His brother Joctan had many sons and their descendants were numerous and spread all over the area. Abram's father was Tera, and he died in Haran in the land of Mesopotamia formerly called Babylonia founded by Nimrod who was born of Cush in the land of Shinar as perhaps the whole area was named..

In Genesis 14: 13 Abram is referred to as 'the Hebrew'. This is rather used as an appellative rather than as a proper name (Antiquities of the Jews translated by William Whiston Massachusetts: Peabody: 32)

Nevertheless according to the Hebrew Bible (Old Testament) Abraham was called out by "El Shaddai" whom he had never heard of, on a special mission to the world. He became the first Hebrew (ha ibhri) as the neighbours referred to him as 'Abram 'ha 'ibhri". This came to be transliterated as "Abram, the Hebrew." One of his descendants who was named Jacob at birth is said to have had an encounter with this God of his forefathers and his name was changed to Israel. Israel became the point of focus in the drama of this theocratic nationhood.

Jacob (now Israel), had twelve sons each of whom was to constitute a clan in the saga of multiplying 'Abraham's descendants as many as the sands of the sea' according to promise; and through whom all the families of the earth shall be blessed, even as the promise of 'El Shaddai' to him is also re-echoed (Gen 12:3, Gen 17: 5 Rom 4: 17, 18). 'El Shaddai' had earlier come to identify himself as AYAH ASHER AYAH "I AM THAT I AM" (often referred to as YHWH- 'Yahweh' by western/European Christendom) to another descendant of Abraham called Moses in another dramatic fashion, in a bush which though on fire was not consumed by the fire and through which the voice was heard where he identified his name as I am that I am (Exodus 3: 13). It is important to note that, perhaps, no other people today claim that their ancestors had worshipped their object of worship by the name 'I am that I am.' This is, perhaps what is most unique about the people called Hebrews. Their G-d is unique and introduced himself as the greatest and only G-d over and against idols. "I AM THAT I AM" appointed prophets to hone home this lesson and message to all peoples beginning with the Hebrew nation. "I am" was to be their all in all as a nation. This was sealed in an everlasting covenant with the Hebrew people wherever and in all time. Some of the prophets preferred to call Him "HaShem', which means "the Name" to reflect his sacredness, holiness and separateness from everything else; as He is sovereign. He revealed himself to Abraham as the Babylonian G-d El Shaddai "the Almighty" and to Moses as Ayah Asher Ayah "I am that I am", which is to be understood as 'I am'. His name is perhaps sacred and holy, so it is to be regarded as not like any other name, "Above All." And to Jacob he introduced himself as the 'God of his fathers'.

The children of Jacob (Israel) that made up the nation of Israel were from four wives notably:

The first wife was Leah who gave birth to Reuben, Simeon, Levi, Judah, Issachar, and Zebulun.

His second wife was Rachel and she gave birth to Joseph and Benjamin.

The third wife was Bilhah and she begot Dan and Naphtali.

The fourth wife was called Zilpah and she gave birth to Gad and Asher.

These children were born to him in a place called Padan-aram (Genesis 35: 22ff).

These twelve sons of Jacob had become the twelve clans that made up Israel as the only historically recognized Hebrew peoples.

As Abraham's descendants increased and progressed, what could be regarded historical exigencies caused a split among the dominant lineage of Jacob whose children had become the major players in the saga of this theocratic nation. The sons of Jacob had formed the nation of Israel as a kingdom ruled by human kings instead of by 'Yahweh' as covenanted with their forefather Abraham. Later these clans constituting the kingdom split into the North and South kingdoms in the rebellion led by Yeroboam; with the North larger with about ten and half of the clans out of a total of twelve. Thus only Judah and half of another clan constituted the south kingdom. Disunity led to Disintegration which led to things falling apart among them as a people and eventual military defeats, and sacking as a nation with consequent dispersing and scattering to other lands. Firstly by the Assyrian army that dislodged and dispersed the northerners in 721 BC and later the Babylonian army dislodged and dispersed the southerners in 586BC.

Of particular interest to us is the tribe of Gad the seventh son of Jacob from which perhaps the majority of Ibo peoples claim to have originated.

We read that the descendants of Gad by their clans were as follows:

through Zephon, the Zephonite clan,

through Haggi, the Haggite clan,

through Shuni, the Shunite clan,

through Ozni, the Oznite clan

through Eri, the Erite clan,

through Arodi, the Arodite clan;

through Areli, the Arelite clan.

According to the book of Numbers chapter 1:1-4, 14, 18, 24-25 when census was taken of 20 years and above we have 45650 in total. However the total discovered from the census recorded in Numbers 26: 1-4, 15-18 is 40500. This leaves a difference of 5, 150 people. The question is: where did the 5,150 go? Does this indicate that not all children of Gad actually entered or remained with Moses during his led Exodus? Does this give credence to the narrative that some of Gad's children headed elsewhere? It is possible that withdrawal from entering into the promised land along side Moses and others occurred intermittently and at different times during the trip. As these withdrew they headed to join their brethren who had left. The most likely direction must have been towards Africa according to Ibo legend of Eri and his entourage into Ibo land.

It is also perhaps needful to note that the Gadite clans that continued into Canaan with Moses and the rest of the Israelites did not possess the land of Canaan; rather they possessed the land of the Amorites, and the Bashaites. This perhaps means that they were separated from the religious reforms that took place among their kith and kin across in Canaan. Also they might have been exposed to syncretism and backsliding from the forefront religion of their people. Also they might have been among the first set to be evacuated and scattered as refugees and consequently must have begun migrating out of Palestine into Egypt and from there to other parts of what became Africa including what has become the present location as Ibo land. The Elephantine community in Africa seems to testify to this immigration to Africa even as early as this period.

According to one Ibo legend of origins, a certain Gad claimed to be the seventh son of Jacob had sons who settled in the present day southeastern Nigeria which is predominantly inhabited by the Ibo. Those sons Eri, Arodi, and Areli (perhaps a fourth son as is being speculated by some scholars) are said to have fathered clans, established kingdoms and founded towns still existing today including Owerri (Owu eri), Umuleri, Arochukwu, Aguleri. However we read in the Old Testament that the Gadites built up Dijon, Ataroth, Aroer, Shoran, Jazzier, Jobehah, Beth Nimrah, and Beth Haran as fortified cities and built pens for their flock. Does this difference in account indicate that the biblical account recalled only Gadite cities in ancient

Israel, ignorant of other cities located far off lands? Secondly, how are the proponents sure that it was not another Gad (please see 2 Samuel 24: 18).

Nevertheless it is probable that, Eri, Arodi, Areli were the first to cross over from Egypt having been forced by persecution to what became called Africa and founded the Ibo peoples as one of their descendants or their only descendants. They were joined by other Israelite relatives from the East at different times in the Israelite history. Yet we also understand that another Ibo oral legend of migrations claims that certain Nri (Eri) families may have been descendants of Levitical priests who are thought to have migrated from the area that has come to be called North Africa. Another legend mentions Moses as their ancestral route of origin. The other claims Ephraim from the lineage of Joseph the beloved son of Jacob who was famous in Egypt during the days of famine and on whose wisdom the Pharaohs relied upon to overcome the famine on land.

A tradition focusing on the Davidic line claims that the descendants of David also entered Africa through Egypt. This ruling family (malkhut Beit Dawud), Kingdom of the house of David, entered Africa and could still be identified today. David had bought the lands of the present day Temple Mount, built an altar to the Lord there and sacrificed burnt offerings and fellowship offerings (2 Samuel 24: 24-25). David had at least one daughter and at least twenty-two sons. One of his sons, Solomon succeeded him as king and built the first Temple in Jerusalem. As stated earlier, at the end of Solomon's rule ten out of about twelve tribes of Israel rejected the Davidic line of kings and seceded from the rest as the northern kingdom of Judea. By 597BC/587 the Babylonians sacked the territory of Davidic descendants who scattered all over the world: Mesopotamia, the Levant, Egypt and the Mediterranean basin seeking where to live as Jews. As stated earlier while some remained in Spain, Portugal, France, and Italy, others later moved on into other parts of Europe. They separated into Ashkenazi, Sephardi, and other groups. Migration into the Americas was begun by the Sephardic from Spain, Portugal, Africa, and the Middle East in the 1600s. By the 1730s Ashkenazi Jews from Eastern Europe, Germany and France massively entered the Americas. This massive migration into the Americas is said to have ended in 1924. Some of the Davidic lines especially those of the rabbinic descent carefully maintained their identity and seem to seek to reestablish their authority. They insist that to be identified a Jew one must be able to trace their descent to one rabbi or scholar of the Davidic line. Consequently it appears that only a genealogical connection with some famous rabbis and scholars have become the only identity needed to be recognized as authentic Jew in the Ashkenazic tradition.

Other migrants disagree and trace their Jewish root through the Sephardic line back to Hezekiah of Bagdad who fled to Spain. In Spain he left two sons Yitzhak and David. Shealtiel is one of the famous Sephardic family surnames said to have descended through Hezekiah.

The common account of the separation of the children of Jacob confirms that the north was in the majority while the south was made up of only Judah and perhaps half of another clan born of Joseph called Manasseh whose brother was named Ephraim although it appears that the Davidic line remained dominant in the south.

The same common account confirms that historical accident forced the termination of the nation completely by stronger military powers. The South was known to have been evacuated to Babylon (586BC) and was later known to have returned as remnants of the descendants and rebuilt that part of the nation centred on the temple in Jerusalem. This is an indication of the dominance of the Davidic line during the days of exile. According to Scripture God had advised David to purchase the land of Moriah. This is the place the Temple was eventually built.

That day Gad came to David and said to him,

"Go and build an altar to the Lord on the threshing floor of Araunah the Jebusite." So David went to do what the Lord had commanded him. When Araunah saw the king and his men coming towards him, he came forward and fell flat on the ground with his face in the dust. "Why have you come? " Araunah asked. And David replied, "to buy your threshing floor, so that I can build an altar to the Lord, and he will stop the plague." "Use anything you like," Araunah told the king. "Here are oxen for the burnt offering, and you can use the threshing instruments and ox yokes for wood to build a fire on the altar. I will give it all to you, and may the Lord God accept your sacrifice'." But the king said to Araunah, "No, I will not have it as a gift. I will buy it, for I do not want to offer to the Lord my God burnt offering that have cost me nothing." So David paid him for the threshing floor and the oxen. And David built an altar there to the Lord and offered burnt offerings and peace offerings. And the Lord answered his prayers, and the plague was stopped (The Catholic Living Bible 2 Samuel 24: 18-25).

We can also observe that the Old Testament includes known designated names for the High God of other nations, Elah (perhaps Alah) and Eloah. Elah is perhaps, first used in the Bible by Ezra and may have been adopted from the Babylonian exile. El first appears in Genesis 14:18 when Melchizedek, King of Salem, appears on the biblical scene, so Elah was adopted as a name. It is perhaps this universal High God El who is revealed to Israel as Yahweh in Exodus 6:3.This high God was named Elohim in early part of Genesis. Thus Elohim, El, Elah, Eloah, were adopted names of the creator God before He finally introduced himself as Yahweh. It might interest the reader to note that the universal deity of the Ibo people is named 'Alah' (ani) usually referred to as the Mother or Earth goddess, the source of all life.

So also we have the names 'God', 'theos', 'Dieu', 'Gott', the names of the pagan European High God was adopted by early Christian missionaries. Isaiah refers to Him as 'Immanu-el' which literally means "El with us". The Christians identify Yeshua as Yahweh because Yahweh is the God of salvation to the earth. The Greek version of the name is Iesous while the Latin version is Jesus. The name Jesus has been adopted by the English and other peoples pronounce it in local dialectal versions. Some orthodox Jews have decided to make a mockery of the name by referring to him as 'Yesu', giving it a negative connotation.

As Yahweh Immanu-el, Jesus remains the Christ, the Messiah, and the bringer of Salvation to all of mankind. The Old Testament condemns the existence of lesser deities in competition with Yahweh worship. Thus Baalim, Ashtoreth, Moloch must never be tolerated by Yahweh's children. So also should all lesser deities of nations never be tolerated by Yahweh's chosen People. This includes the worship of Mercury, Jove, etc of Europe and deities of Africa and any peoples.

One may ask: what about the days of the week named after the worship days of these ancient deities that seem to have come to remain? The answer is perhaps that the names of the days adopted since Roman times for political convenience does not amount to worshipping those Roman deities. Thus we follow Monday, Tuesday, Wednesday, Thursday, Friday, Saturday, and Sunday but never to worship the elements thereof or seasons associated with their worship. In the same manner the Ibo have adopted the native African days as Eke, Orie, Afor, Nkwo, an indication of religious syncretism and diffusion.

Thus we see that the Israelites were allowed to adopt names of the God of other nations but not to indulge in their idolatrous practices as listed in Leviticus 18: 21-25; Deuteronomy 12: 29- 31, Deuteronomy 18: 9-13. Yahweh does not condone idolatry, human sacrifice, Sexual perversion of any type including homosexual practice, bestiality and all sexual deviations. Also to be abhorred are fortune telling, divination or other spiritistic practices. Any deviation from God's instruction would be punished.

Thus prophet Amos stated:

'You only have I known of all the families of the earth; therefore I will punish you for all your iniquities' (Amos 3:2 RSV)

What we see unfolding is that chosenness by Yahweh as His people involve responsibilities; such responsibility that should not make the chosen proud. Yahweh is infinitely Holy while the human is too finite and unholy in nature to be associated with Yahweh. This cannot evoke elitism but fear and trembling; nor does it evoke religious racism. This perhaps explains why many Jews abhor being referred to as the chosen of God. Historical experience of failure and sufferings of children of Jacob (Israel) seems to contradict this feeling of special relationship and 'chosenness'.

Following splitting of Israel the majority Northern Kingdom was evacuated much earlier (721 BC) than the South and were never recovered but are assumed to have been absorbed completely into other nations. They were absorbed into the religion and practices of their captors. They also scattered to different places around the world.

Scholars have been making efforts to piece together information aiming to identify these so called lost tribes said to scatter around various parts of the world. This means that the interested scholars are searching for every tribe of Israel with the exception of Judah.

However, there was a scattering that had taken place much earlier under King Solomon when his territory expanded through wider trade links, marriages and procreation. Peace and stability during Solomon's time provided atmosphere for development; and trading opportunities were worldwide. Consequently people immigrated to other parts of the world voluntarily while some others were sent to represent King Solomon as trading merchants or emissaries. Some of these perhaps, did not go back to the land of Israel; rather settled in their newly found richer and perhaps, more comfortable haven.

Although the Ibo of West Africa and the Falasha of Ethiopia (in the East Africa region) were initially identified as the only peoples in Africa researchers thought to be among the lost tribes of ancient Israel, with time, however, other African peoples have been discovered. These include the Lemba (Zimbabwe) and the Ashanti (of the old Black Jewish Empire of Ghana) to mention just these. Also Ibo ethnic peoples are scattered all over Nigeria. We find them in Benue state, Kogi state, Bayelsa state, Akwa Ibom, Cross River State and Delta, and perhaps Edo states. So also are the Beni Ephraimites of Ondo State who trace their origin to Ephraim, son of Joseph, a brother of Gad and Levi; all these are among the various clans claimed to be ancestors of the Ibo peoples. The Beni Ephraimites of Ondo are referred to as Yoruba Jews by historians because they are located in one of the Yoruba states called Ondo state commonly referred to as the "Emo Yo Quaim" or "Strange People" by the native Africans, they seem to have failed to absorb the surrounding cultures due to their small numerical strength. They call themselves by the Hebrew name "B'nai Ephraim" or "Sons of Ephraim". They claim ancestral migration from Morocco. Supporting this claim Professor Godbey observes that their language is a mixture of Maghrebi Arabic and local Negro dialect. An example is they use 'yaba' to refer to father (abu), and umm to refer to mother. Hebrew 'em' is 'ima'. They are mostly influenced by the surrounding Yoruba culture socially. They claim that their ancestors were driven from place to place because of Muslim persecution. From

Timbuktu they migrated to the present site. They preserved portions of the Torah, observed only some of the Jewish customs such as holy days (Windsor 2003:131 citing Godbey 1930: 244-256).

Thus we can identify some of the African Jews to include the following groups: The Moroccan Jews, the Libyan Jews, the black Jews of Dahomey, the black Jews of Angola, Guinea, Senegambia, Kamnuria, and Lamlam. Lamlam was situated about two hundred miles west of Timbuktu. The Hebrew merchants in Lamlam are said to have monopolized the trade and are said to have fought wars to maintain their control of trade. In addition in the year 1012BC the Queen of Sheba named Bilkis, Queen of Ethiopia visited King Solomon. She got infatuated with King Solomon and is said to have become pregnant for him. This child was born as David or Menilek I. The Queen returned to Ethiopia with her son Menilek I for a while and was sent to Solomon by his mother where he was educated. Menilek was eventually crowned king of Ethiopia and accepted the name David. The king returned with eminent lawyers in 'the Law of Moses' who became judges under Menilek I. One of these was Azariah the son of Zadok, the former high priest who brought Hebrew transcripts of the law. The Falasha, and the Emperor Haile Selassie, all the black Jews of Ethiopia claim descent from those Jews who returned from Jerusalem with Menilek I. The Queen died 986 BC after reigning for forty years and Menilek I took over (cf Windsor 2003: 38ff).

Noteworthy about West African Jews is the fact that there were also only two towns south of the Jewish Kingdom of Ghana. History states that at puberty the youth in these towns were branded on the countenance or at the temple with fire leaving identifying marks. They built their dwellings on the bank of the river which they claim flowed into the Nile (possibly the Niger River). Like the Hebrews they also carried out ritual purification, observed new moons, had a designated period of weeping for the dead during which time they wore sack cloths and ashes; sacrificed animal and sprinkling the blood on the door posts and altar of shrines. They also divided the tribes into different families, into twelve parts; observed formal processions, circumcisions, and various other practices. The native Africans observed these practices without knowledge of their origin or the object intended to be commemorated. Many of these purifications were purposed to protect from evil forces threatening or to secure some favours or just as cultural formality handed down by the ancestors. In fact many of these West African peoples have lost their Hebrew nationality. The Ibo are no exception to this ignorance of their Hebrew nationality. It is possible that many of these African Jews, especially those of the present day West African stock gathered in the part of the world that could be rightly called Ibo World. The Iboland is located in the East, a delight for the Jewish and all Middle Easterners, close to the Niger River shores, and close to the Atlantic shores, fairly black in complexion limiting making identification of the Jews who are also perhaps fairly black almost impossible, has similar weather as the ancient Israel, and well forested with arable land for sheep and goat rearing and fertile land for agricultural.

Loss of National Identity

Some of the factors identified as leading to loss of Hebrew nationality by these peoples are:

The fall of the Hebrew kingdoms

Lack of communication with Hebrew educational centres

Intense, persistent and sustained persecution including deliberate blotting out of their minds the fact that they are of Hebrew nationality

Cultural and Religion diffusion (cf Windsor 2003: 122-124)

Describing the attitude of these persecuted Jews Slouschz states, " In most cases these Hebrews by race and Mussulmen by faith seek to hide their origin, which has become a burden to them" (quoted in Windsor 2003: 123) Also it was said that in Portugal Jewish parents would not divulge the secret of their religion to their children until they had attained the age of reason because they believed that denial of the Hebrew religion would eventually lead to denial of nationality (Roth: 1959: 358 cited in Windsor 2003: 123). Scholars of History proved by experience of history show that if a people deny their culture and nationality over a long period of time they are likely to totally forget their root through the resultant process of assimilation that takes place (cf Windsor: 2003: 124).

Perhaps, noteworthy in present day examples of deliberate cultural disintegration is the massacre of the Ibo for the reasons of being Ibo, too industrious, too competitive and arrogant to be tolerated by their neighbours. Politicians have been attempting to divide and separate the Ibo peoples. This, perhaps, came to a crescendo during the genocide against them in the 1960s; it continued during the war fought against them (the Biafra-Nigeria war) and has remained till date. This ploy to divide Jews, geographically, politically and socially must not be allowed to succeed anymore; it must be resisted collectively, continuously and persistently for the common good of the Jewish posterity. A common ancestry should be the rallying ground for a united front not just among themselves but also with their kith and kin in West Africa, Israel, the Middle East, and other parts of the world. It is said that blood is thicker than water. Blood solidarity should provide the cooperation and fighting spirit that is needed to survive in the midst of hostility. The King Solomon Separdic Federation is already providing this common front for fight for collective survival.

The Modern State of Israel and the Aliyah issue:

Afer being in exile for about 2000 years with untold misery, suffering, vilification, holocaust slaughtering, and mockry to say the least, Israelites living all over the world breathed a sigh of relief when on the 15 May 1948 the leaders of the Zionist Movement, the political pressure group of Israelites and Hebrew community proclaimed the independence of Israel as a sovereign state. This was achieved in the midst of so many odds that militated against it including respectable states reneging on their promises, and state declarations. It was a struggle started by the vision of Theodore Herzl many years earlier to be brought to fruition by the dogged efforts of Chaim Weizman and Ben Gurion and others. For example in 1922, the League of Nations entrusted Great Britain to oversee the establishment of a Jewish nation in the Land of Palestine, having recognized the historical connection of the Jewish people with Palestine and not anywhere else. However the British government under pressure from the Arabs, reneged on their earlier promise to effect this policy. It became anti Zionist and issued a White Paper of 1930 and 1939 which restricted immigration to Palestine and stopped the purchase of lands in Palestine. This white paper was issued in spite of the ranging slaughter of Jews in the Nazi

Holocaust that was going on at that time in Europe. The Israelite Zionist and movement and Hebrew communities defied policy of the White Paper. In addition the world had become aware of the slaughtering of millions of Jews that had been on going in Europe. Following the end of the Second World War in 1945 the United Nations adopted a resolution of 1947 which asserted the partitioning of Palestine into a Jewish land and Arab land.

Ben Gurion who was born David Gruen on 16 October 1886 in Polansk became the first Prime Minister of the new state. It was his idea that the new state should be named Israel. He immigrated to Israel in 1906 at the age of 20. He was the one who made the broadcast declaring the state of Israel on 14 May 1948 during a ceremony at the Tel Aviv Museum of Art. Hours after this declaration and as the world was celebrating with the Jews, a coalition of Arab countries attacked the young state of Israel in a bitter war that was to last a year with a loss of 600,000 Jewish lives. The war ended with victory for the small, fragile and newly founded state of Israel. The coalition of Arab states was made up of Egypt, Syria, Jordan, Iraq, and Saudi Arabia.

Ben Gurion's focus was the return of the exiles. He began the development of infrastructure to accommodate the returning exiles to their homeland. He set about setting up and encouraged the setting up of Kibutzim (farm settlements) beginning in the desert of Negev. Ben Gurion also saw the independence of Israel as a miracle and a fulfillment of prophecy and a challenge to continue the God given task of being a light to the rest of the world, a task he said was begun but terminated in the middle. Israel's task also involves the "bequeathing to the entire world the eternal Book of Book..."

" Anyone who does not believe in miracles is not a realist" Ben Gurion

It is commonly believed that scripture passages especially the Old Testament prophets state that there would be a time when YHWH (HaShem) the Merciful, would return all lost clans of Israel to their fatherland and reunite them as a people. Today, this is referred to as the 'aliyah' and there has been increase in coming back to Israel since the modern state of Israel became independent in 1948; and this has continued and will continue to be so. Some of the passages include Deuteronomy 30:4-5; Jeremiah 32:41, Obadiah 20, Isaiah

66:19; 1Kings 9: 26; 2Chronicles 8: 17; Zechariah 8: 7-8. We also have passages of the Talmud alluding to this return.

In Deut 30: 4-5 we read as Moses prophesied:

"Even if you have been banished to the most distant land under the heavens, from there the Lord your God will gather you and bring you back. He will bring you to the land that belonged to your fathers, and you will take possession of it. He will make you more prosperous and numerous than your fathers..." NIV

And according to Zechariah 8: 7-8: "this is what the Lord Almighty says: 'I will save my people from the countries of the east and the west. I will bring them back to live in Jerusalem; they will be my people, and I will be faithful and righteous to them as their God.'" NIV

Isaiah had prophesied that the people would be scattered: 66:19: "I will set a sign among them, and I will send some of those who survive to the nations- to Tarshish, to the Libyans and Lydians, to Tubal and Greece, and to the distant lands that have not heard of my fame or seen my glory. They will proclaim my glory among the nations. And they will bring all your brothers, from all the nations, to my holy mountain in Jerusalem as an offering to the Lord..." NIV

Then Isaiah 11:11 states:

"In that day the LORD will reach out his hand a second time to reclaim the remnant that is left of his people from Assyria, from Lower Egypt, from Upper Egypt, from Cush, from Elam, from Babylonia, from Hamath and from the islands of the sea. He will raise a banner for the nations and gather the exiles of Israel; he will assemble the scattered people of Judah from the four quarters of the earth."

The rest of the chapter goes on to speak of how great Israel will become when their brothers are gathered again from where they had been scattered.

Obadiah 1: 20, 21 states: "This Company of Israelite exiles that are in Canaan will possess the land as far as Zarephath; the exiles from Jerusalem who are in Sepharad will possess the towns of the Negev". And verse 21 states: "Deliverers will go up on Mount Zion to govern the mountains of Esau. And the kingdom will be the Lord's. Ordinarily Sepharad is regarded as referring to Spain but could be regarded as 'far lands'."

Amos 9: 14- 15

" I will bring back my exiled people Israel; they will rebuild the ruined cities and live in them. They will plant vineyards and drink their wine; they will make gardens and eat their fruit"

" I will plant Israel in their own Land, never again to be uprooted from the Land I have given them, says the LORD Your God".

Jeremiah 33: 7

"I will bring Judah and Israel back from captivity and will rebuild them as they were before."

Jeremiah 30: 18

"I will restore the fortunes of Jacob's tents and have compassion on his dwellings, the city will be rebuilt on her ruins, and the place will stand in its proper place"

Perhaps we can include the following information as further evidence (1kings 9: 26 and 2Chronicles 8: 7-8) that clearly show that King Solomon sent trading emissaries to foreign lands. "King Solomon also built ships at Ezion Geber, which is near Elath in Edom on the shore of the Red Sea. And Hiram sent his men –sailors who knew the sea- to serve in the fleet with Solomon's men. They sailed to Ophir (probably Africa- see below) and brought back 420 talents of gold, which they delivered to King Solomon." We next read of how wealthy King Solomon became as he extended his trading links with far and near including Queen Sheba of Ethiopia and the rest of the land that we know today as Africa. He also multiplied wives and concubines for which practice he was condemned due to the resultant extreme syncretism and spiritual adultery. King Solomon is finally said to rest with his fathers and was buried in the city of David his father and Rehoboam his son succeeded him as King. It is noteworthy that it was during the reign of his son Rehoboam that the sons of Jacob split into the northern and southern kingdoms and were eventually defeated and evacuated to be scattered all over the world. These exiles are now returning to the modern Independent state of Israel as the prophets foretold. What is perhaps significant is that Israel is set up to be a Jewish state; this means a state where Jews are to dwell and abide by the Jewish Laws and ways of life.

In 2010 the Israeli Prime Minister Benjamin Netanyahu stated: "Our ability as a collective to determine our own destiny is what grants us the tools to shape our future- no longer as a ruled people, defeated and persecuted, but a proud people with a magnificent country and one which always aspires to serve as "Light Unto the Nations."

The question is: who and what determines what this Light should be? (cf Zechariah 12: 10).

On the question of colour

It is often asked how could the Ibos, in fact, any black African be linked to ancient Israel or Hebrews 'as they are of different skin colour'? According to these critics the Ibos have black skin colour while the Israelites are of light skin colour or 'white.'

My response to such question and assertion is to ask, how people arrive at such a conclusion that ancient Israelites or Hebrews were of so called "white" skin colour. It is clear that although we cannot say for sure the colour of Adam and Eve it is obvious that Adam and Eve could not have been of white complexion. This is because they were said to have been made from the dust of the earth (clay Genesis 2: 4-7). They would perhaps be possibly dark brown; but this can only be by inference and depends on the colour of the clay from which they were fashioned. Perhaps they were also given a natural potential for gene mutation and gene change.

Nevertheless, the book of Genesis teaches that the inhabitants of the lower Tigris – Euphrates valley were descendants of Cush through Nimrod. Flavius Josephus calls them Ethiopians (Antiquities: Whiston: 31). We read that Nimrod descended from Cush and that Nimrod grew to be a mighty hunter and warrior before the Lord. He ruled the following area: Babylon, Erech, Akkad, and Calneh, in Shinar. And from here his territory expanded to Assyria, where he built Nineveh, Rehoboth Ir, Calah, the great city. Cush is of black complexion, and a descendant of Ham. His brothers were Mizraim (Egypt), Phut (Libya) and Canaan. The descendants of Cush through his sons were Seba, Havilah, Sabtah, Raamah, and Sabteca (Genesis 10:8). Josephus Antiquities adds other descendants including Ragmus whose descendant, Judadas, fathered Western Ethiopians. And as we have read, Nimrod (Lamurudu in Yoruba tradition), a descendant of Cush, conquered and built the land of Shinar located at the mouth of the Persian Gulf (Genesis 11: 1-9). Shinar is also called Sumer. This would mean that all the inhabitants of Sumer were possibly dark or black complexioned being descendants of Cush and of the region of Havilah (Genesis 10: 7, Genesis 2:11), the Persian Gulf (Genesis 10. 22, 26-29). This means that the whole area was Cushite, namely: Babylon, Akkadia, Sumer, the Chaldea, all the land watered by the rivers Tigris and Euphrates, Pishon, Gihon, the great Zab, little Zab, the Diyala river and surrounding areas that were well watered and were called 'the Garden of Eden'. This also shows that Terah, Abraham's father was not light skinned; Abraham was more likely not light skinned also. He was more possibly dark skinned. This whole area was called Babylon until there was confusion of language that scattered the inhabitants forming various languages and nations consequently. The area was also called Sumerian land. Another name for the Sumerians in the ancient times was Ethiopians. This area now includes Iran, Afghanistan, Pakistan, and northwest India (cf Genesis 10:10, Genesis 11: 1). The black Sumerians (Shinar) founded cities in this area as early as 4000BC. These included Eridu, Lagash, Nippur, Kish, and Ur. Therefore it could be stated without contradiction that originally inhabitants of the earth were not white but possibly black or dark in complexion, including perhaps Noah and his family (cf Windsor 2003:13-17) although it has been suggested that Noah was born albino or what is unacceptedly called "half cast" today.

Noah and his descendants

The account of the Bible in Genesis Chapter 9 refers to Noah and his descendants. Here we read that after the first human race had been destroyed God reserved a family to continue the existence of the human being. This man and his household was Noah, his wife, his three sons and their wives, and their livestock. The Ark in which they were saved from the flood rested on a high land called Ararat. Mount Ararat is today located in the land of Armenia. The sons of Noah who survived after the flood and who later repopulated the world are named as Shem, Ham and Japheth.

The descendants of Shem inhabited the following territory: Assyria, Elam (i.e Persia), East of the River Tigris, Eastern part of Syria, and Parts of the Arabian Peninsula.

The descendants of Ham controlled the civilization soon after the flood (4000BC) through the conquering and hunting efforts of his descendant Nimrod. They inhabited and controlled the following territories: Africa, The land of Canaan including Israel, Parts of Arabia, Syria, Phoenicia, Turkey, Babylon, Southern Persia, East Pakistan, and a large part of India.

The descendants of Japheth inhabited the 'Isles of the Gentiles', the shores of the Mediterranean Sea in Europe, and Parts of Asia Minor. They dispersed northwards and entered the entire Europe and parts of Asia. They occupied the Caucasus Mountains, Parts of Turkey, Southern Russia, and Cadiz (Spain).

Japheth's descendants also included Gomer, Magog, Javan, Tubal, Meshech, and Tiras (Gen 10:2). Gomer's descendants were the Cimmerians, the Cimbri including the offshoots of the Celtic family, Gaels of Ireland, Scotland, and the Hebrides Islands. Homer described the Cimmerians as inhabiting in a remote place of mist and gloom and located north of the Black Sea.

Magog became the father of the Magogites also called the Scythians who were wandering tribes and dwelling close to the Black and Caspian Seas. These were also regarded as "lacking in intelligence and civilization" (Windsor 2003 citing Homer)

Another descendant of Japheth, Madai became the father of the Medes and his descendants were located at the southern part of the Caspian Sea. They later united with the Persians to form one race, Medo-Persia.

The fourth descendant of Japheth called Javan had the Ionians and all the Greeks as his descendants.

Tubal, the fifth son of Japheth, is associated with Javan (Isaiah 66.19). Messhech and Tubal (Ezek 32.26 and 39.1) are in the North from Israel and are associated with Iberia, and Georgia.

Tiras became the father of the Thracians who inhabit the north of Turkey, Asia Minor, and Northeast of Greece.

Japheth's descendant called Ashkenaz formed the Germanic race. Thus Jews who moved to Germany during persecution are called the Ashkenazi Jews; while those who went south to Africa and other lands are called Sephardic (or Spanish) Jews. By the 378AD the Germanic tribes began to move under the following names: Lombards, Burgundians, Franks, Saxons, Angles, Jutes, Ostrogoths, Visigoths, Suevis, and Vandals. These ten Germanic barbarians settled all over Western Europe as we know them today. All these tribes were descendants of Japheth.

How did these children of Japheth become called white in colour? They are called white probably because their skin is of thinner layer and so was light-coloured rather than dark clay or dust. We know that there is no white coloured race. White later became a political and oppressive designation to depict "innocence" as against black which is depicted as "evil". Again it is pertinent to reiterate that it is not possible to arrive at the exact reason why some people have lighter and thinner skin colour. This is made more difficult because we have no records of the complexion of Japhet's female children and in fact no information about their existence in the Bible or history texts.

A number of suggestions have however been postulated on how Japheth's descendants became light skinned. One is that Japheth asked God to turn him to a light skinned man which came to be wrongly designated as 'white', and God answered his request and he turned to light skin. There is however no evidence to warrant this suggestion as historians have observed (please see Windsor 2003). However, there are evidence of people being turned into white as snow in the Bible for specific lessons. It is therefore possible that God could change the gene of a person.

Another explanation is racial whereby it is claimed that Japheth and the whites were made out of inferior and adulterated material by

God. There is no room for such insult just as there is no room allowed for the claim that black depicts evil or dark forces and weakness.

The other explanation given is that there was a mutation in the genes due to climate and environment. Thus as the years went by their skins turned white as the melanin by which they were naturally endowed faded. Being inhabitants of a very cold and darker part of the world with the sun remote from them, there is likelihood of gene change for adaptability in addition to melanin depletion. According to medical science, a very cold weather as the territory of the descendants of Japheth is; would obviously produce a light skin tone. This is because there is reduced sun to enhance the production of melanin, the element that accounts for the black colour of the skin experienced by the inhabitants of the tropical and Mediterranean environment of Africa and elsewhere. Yet there must be a genetic environment to make this skin colour change possible in the first place. Thus there is evidence that the original colour of human being must be dark or black as melanin is natural product of the human. None can become light skin and develop melanin later in life. It is usually the other way round. It could also be possible that Japhet inherited the gene through his father Naoh who was said to have been albino or half cast in his natural complexion.

Others who inter-married with Japheth descendants and procreated with them will certainly produce light skinned children and descendants. However the fact remains that Japheth was not of white complexion originally neither were his brothers and parents. His descendants must have later become of a different complexion due to this gene mutation and loss of natural melanin. The intermingling with Germanic tribes occurred in the Middle East between 2000 and 1500 BC, and between Arab conquerors and white women in North Africa etc. It is also perhaps, significant to note that the white gene remains the recessive gene and can easily be dominated by the dominant black gene. This is perhaps additional evidence that the original human gene is probably the black gene.

For the concern of this work we can testify to the existence of black Jewish kingdoms in Africa and elsewhere. Most Ashkenazi Jews are light skinned while most Sephardic Jews are brown, red or black. This could be explained by the fact of gene mutating to adapt to climatic conditions. The Ibos were originally known as "Red Ibos" because some had "olive oil" and some "near white/red tint" complexion; pointing to the non black complexion of their ancestors. This variety of colour is maintained by the majority of the Ibos today.

Perhaps a major proof that Abraham and his descendants were not white as we conceive it today is that Josephus Antiquities seem to attest to the fact that Africans are descendants of Abraham through Keturah. After the death and burial of Sarai, Abraham married Keturah. Keturah had many children including the nation called "Troglodytes".

Abraham's six sons through Keturah are described as men of courage and of sagacious minds. They were Zambran, Jazar, Madan, Madian, Josabak, and Sous. The sons of Sous were Sabathan and Dadan. The sons of Dadan were Latusim, Assur, and Luom. The sons of Midian were Ephas, Ophren, Anoch, Ebidas, and Eldas.

These sons and grandsons of Abraham founded and settled in colonies, took possession of Troglodytis and the country of "Arabia the Happy", as far as to the Red Sea. Ophren made war with Libya and conquered them. The children of Ophren who inhabited Libyan territory changed the name to Africa so as to immortalize their grandfather. Josephus supported his account of this ancient history of the Jews with information from other historians with slight modification. For example one account by Cleodemus the prophet, who was also called Malchus and wrote the history in agreement with the history of Moses, their legislator, relates that there were many sons born to Abraham by Keturah including Apher, Surim, and Japhran. From Surim emerged the land of Assyria while the other two Apher and Japhran the country of Africa took its name because these men were said to be auxiliaries to Hercules when he fought the Libya and Antaeus. Hercules was said to have married Apher's daughter who gave birth to a son, Diodorus (Ant. XV Whiston, 37-38). Following the accounts of the ancient history of the Jews as narrated above we can conclude that Abraham and his descendants could not have been of white complexion almost all Africa is not light skinned but dark or brown skinned.

It is perhaps necessary to state that the above account of Josephus that connects Africa as closely related to Abraham shows that Africa has a noble historical development. It is not a dark continent as has been portrayed through the centruries. In fact as Windsor well illustrates, African nations and Asia remained in the highest position even by the middle ages. Africa was greatest politically, and welded economic, education and military influence in the world. Europe on the other hand existed in darkness for thousands of years until in the seventeenth century and later when it began to emerge in influence. At this time some Europeans including the Germans began to imagine themselves as being a superior race than other races of the world. Africa became the target for this castigation and relegation. Notably among these over ambitious Europeans include Johann F Blumenbach (1752-1840), a German who began to divide the human race into skin colours. He classified five races of mankind as the Caucasian, the Mongolian, the Ethiopian, the American (American Indians), the Malayan. He placed the Caucasian race as top and superior over others as the original race. This sort of classification never existed before this time (Windsor: 2003: 21 citing the Columbian Encyclopedia 3rd ed New York. Macmillan 1963. 1757 see also the Encyclopedia of Social Science New York. Vol 1-11: 605). This means that, by implication, among the Caucasians the Germans shall be regarded as superior. He therefore propounded that the purest white people originated from the Caucasian mountains situated between the Black Sea and the Caspian Sea. Other racists like Blumenbach include J A Gobineau and H S Chamberlain. They sought to promote the supremacy of the white Nordic race and its culture (please see Herbert Wendt 1964. It Began in Babel. New York: Dell Company: 403-405 cited in Windsor 2003: 21). These racists that attributed Psychological value and importance to race introduced a vicious racial philosophy that led to the relegation of the black and all non white peoples; race prejudice leading to the introduction of the philosophy of Nazism and eventual persecution of Jews worldwide, the Second World War and the near extermination of the Jews of Europe. The introduction of race divide and race persecution seems to have contributed to the rewriting of History beginning with these western anthropologists. It seems that they have succeeded in convincing the world against the truth that civilization began in the Africa and the Middle East among non white peoples. If any race should claim superiority over others it should be the black and Jewish people who are kith and kin.

The Backslidders from Judaism

According to halakhic Judaism of the Ashkenazi rabbi, there are different types of backsliding in Judaism that have been identified so far. These include the 'anusim', 'crypto Jews', the 'Meshumad', the 'Mashadi' and the 'Min'.

The Anusim

The Anusim refers to those persecuted adherents to Judaism religion who secretly practiced Judaism but publicly professed to belong to another faith, specifically Roman Catholicism or Isalm. Their persecutors coerced them to abandon Judaism against their will. The Hebrew word, "anus" means, "coerced" (singular); the plural form is, "anus'im'. It is a term derived from the Talmudic phrase "averah b'ones" which means "a forced transgression". In Hebrew the term is, "ones".

The Crypto-Jews

The crypto-Jews referred to those Jews who publicly profess a different faith but secretly practiced their Judaism during persecutions especially during the 1391 anti-Jewish pogroms and the expulsion of Jews by the Alhambra decree in Spain (1492) and its aftermath on the Jews and various Islamic persecutions that occurred at different times. The word kryptos is Greek for "hidden". The decree required Jews to compulsorily convert to Roman Catholicism or be expelled from Spain. Consequently numerous so called converses publicly professed Roman Catholicism but privately adhered to their Judaism in private. This practice can also be traced as far back as the time of the Spanish Inquisition.

Although the Ashkenazi influenced the interpretation of the Halakha; condemned and isolated the crypto Jews, Maimonides is said to have preferred and encouraged this hidden practice of Judaism to martyrdom.

The crypto Jews and the Anusim are not counted as Jews, as according to the orthodox interpretation, majorly informed by Ashkenazic versions, claim that these backslidden Jews do not have evidence of Jewish maternal lines and do not meet the requirements of orthodox halakha as Jews(see The Jewish Year Book 2007).

The Meshumad

This term refers to those who are treated as heretics in Judaism. They deliberately rebelled against the observance of the Jewish law.

The Mashadi Jews

These are similar to the Anusim and the crypto Jews described above who succumbed to hiding their Jewishness during the Persian (today's Iran) persecutions. They lived dual religious lives of Jewish-Muslim.

The 'Min'

The halakha refers to the "Min" as apostate because they abandoned the faith completely. They have basically denied the existence of God.

The reaction to all the backsliders is that none of them is accepted as Jewish anymore until perhaps there was a reconversion and evidence of practice of the Jewish rites. It also means that not even their decscendants are accepted as Jews.

However Hakham, one of the most respected Sephardic Sages after the expulsion in Spain stated:

"Indeed, when it comes to lineage, all the people of Israel are brethren. We are all sons of one father, the rebels (reshaim) and criminals, the heretic (meshumadim) and the forced ones (anusim), and proselytes (gerim) who are attached to the house of Jacob. All these are Israelites. Even if they left God, or denied Him or violated His Law, the yoke of that Law is still upon their shoulders and all will never be removed from them."

Hakham BenSion Uziel, the chief Sephardic Rabbi of the state of Israel, stated in the 20th century:

" And we still have to clarify on the subject of Anusim, to whom the government forbids them to perform Halakhicaly valid marriage, if it is necessary to say that their wives must have a 'Get' to permit them to marry another man, for the reason that, by force of the Law Hazaqah, a man does not have intercourse for promiscuity (zenut)... In our very case, we deal with those who converted and kept Torah in secrecy and hid their religion because of the gentile surveillance, we say that they do have intercourse for the sake of marriage". This means that Hakham Uziel considers anusim as Jews, because only Jews can give or receive a 'Get', a Jewish divorce.

Rabbi Moshe ben Maimon (Maimonides) stated:

"But their children and grandchildren of Jews in rebels, who, misguided by their parents,... and trained in their views like children taken captive by the gentiles and raised in their Laws and customs, whose status is that of an 'anus, one who abjures Jewsih Law under duress, who, although he later learns that he is a Jew observes them practice their Laws, is nevertheless to be regarded as an 'anus' , since he was reared in the erroneous ways of his parents...Therefore efforts should be made to bring them back in repentance, to draw nearby friendly relations, so that they may return to the strength-giving source i. e. the Torah" (the Mishneh Torah, Sefer Shofetim. See also R Se'adya ben Maimon Ibn Danan 16th century; Hhemdah Genuzah 15b www. wikipedia.org/wiki/anusim; Gitlitz, David "Secrecy and Deceit: The Religion of Crypto Jews" Albuquerque, NM: University of New Mexixo Press 2002; The Jews and the Crusades: The Hebrew Chronicles of the First and Second Crusades, translator and editor: Shlomo Eidelberg. Madison: University of Wisconson Press 1977; The Chronicles of Solomon bar Simon-The Chronicle of Rabbi Eliezer bar Nathan- The Narrative of the Old Persecutions or Mainz Anonymous; Crisis and Leadership: Epistles of Maimonides; Texts translated and Notes by Abraham Halkin; discussions by David Hartman. Philadelphia: Jewish Publication Society of America 1985; Henry Kamen, The Spanish Inquisition: An Historical Revision. London: Weidenfeld and Nicolson 1997; Jose' Faur: In the Shadow of History: Jews and Conversos at the Dawn of Modernity. Albany, NY: State University of New York Press, 1992)

On the Question of DNA Evidence for the Ibos

This was a concern to me because of the numerous numbers of people to be tested and the difficulty of convincing people to participate in testing for DNA. It will also require time to educate the Ibo peoples; and cost would be prohibitive. I had heard of the anusims of Mexico and other parts of the world submitting to DNA test. But the population of these people is fewer compared with the population of the Ibo. According to experts in Jewish genetics less than 1% of non-Semites, but more than four times the entire Jewish population of the world possessed the male-specific genetic Cohanim marker. The Cohanim are of priestly descent, this means that not all Jews are meant. Some 38 of 78 Latinos tested in New Mexico (38.5%) were found to carry the Cohanim marker. This will imply that apart from the general gnetic test for all there would also be need to identify those who have priestly descent among the Ibo. However I was reassured that Genetic test may not be necessary to identitfy a person of Hebrew descent when I found out that there is no specific Jewish DNA marker. This was through a letter sent to me by the DNA testing company I contacted to carry out my own DNA test. This was to have cost me more about six hundred British Pound (600) Sterling just for a single test. Also I had all the while felt that the Ibo or any peoples do not need to prove their Jewishness through a DNA test. This is because DNA undergoes mutation and adaptability and there has been so much mixing up of DNA through intermarriages and change in the environment of habitation. The Ibo are now a mixed multitude and do not need any DNA test as evidence for their being Hebrews or Jews. Above all Jewishness is a religious community and Ibo of today are not necessarily seeking to be identified with a religious community as much as they just want their Hebrew roots as children of Abraham through the line of Jacob called Israel. However in spite of all this the writer of this work, submitted to DNA tests from two different companies that identified him as of the Haplogroup E1B1A1 which I understand identifies him as of the native Judaen lineage. By native is unadulterated first generation Jew. According to the information I got experts are yet to identify some Jewish gene types (2-6) and that the first type is rare to comeby. Interestingly I happen to fall within the category 1 type. Thus I am said to belong to the native Jew. The question is how did this come about? I have to leave the question to the experts to provide answer. Nonetheless since Udum is an ancient

Judaen name for Adam, that should somewhat provide an explanation to the question of my native unadulterated Jewishness.

As the Ashkenazi rabbi focus on interpretations of the Halakha rather than the Bible account and advice, underscores why there is strict adherence to so called halakhic requirements to be accepted into a Jewish community as a Jew. The Sephardim to which the Ibo are said to belong at present are more inclined to interpreting Judaism from the point of view of the Bible and consequently would not be expected to follow the Ashkenazic rigid interpretation of the Halakha. Moreover, these rabbinic interpretations of the halakha are based more on human reasoning than the spirit of the original Jewish community that produced them and often coloured by the pastoral authority of the rabbi interpretating. The Ashkenazic approach to Judaism could be seen to be based more on intellectual commentary of the halakha than on holistic approach to the Law and life generally as it affects human relationships. I personally think that a religion based on such narrow and reductionistic approach to life faces the danger of being more backslidden than those they condemn. The danger of burdening adherents with dos and donts must also not be ignored.

In sum we see that there is evidence that Jews entered the Iboland from different directions. Abraham was a Hebrew being a descendant of Heber the father of the Hebrews who later became refered to as Jews by some people. Abraham's descendants through Keturah inhabited Africa. The other entry routes were through the coast of West Africa, North Africa and from Ethiopia; there was massive entry into this same area as far back as the time of Solomon, Jeremiah and Sennacherib during the Jeroboam wars. The children of Queen of Sheba through Solomon are inhabitants of Ethiopia and Northern and Eastern Africa. The River Niger, called originally "oshimiri ogbaru" in Igbo language provided a fertile coast for such habitation and the fertility of the Land and its "East" geographical location to Jerusalem, must have made settlement more attractive; therefore Niger River confluence and coasts seem to have suited the psyche of the settlers who are Ibo ancestors. The skills, business acumen, wisdom and priest craft and education of the Ibos endeared them to their neighbours who invited them to inhabit in their midst and made use of their skills and abilities. However as they multiplied in influence they became a threat to some of the hosts who asked them to leave. An example is the Benin Kingdom that expelled the Ibo inhabitant after hundreds of years of living with them. While some of the descendants of the Ibo settlers chose to live within the vicinity of their unwelcoming neighbours, others emigrated and took the route of the Atlantic coasts thereby forming new settlements; yet others moved on to settle and inhabit areas known as Opobo, Boni, Ikwere, Eche, Ogoni, Izhon (Ijaw) etc and other areas in the present day Rivers, Bayelsa, Akwa Ibom, Cross River etc, states. Other places the Ibo ancestors settled are Igala, Idah, Otukpo, Igumale, Nkpa, Utonkon and as Idoma speaking peoples of Benue state, etc as claimed by legends of migrations of Eri and his brothers and relatives from Israel and different parts of the world as they migrated to what became the Niger River area that became Iboland.

On the question of complexion we have also understood that the world population was black or non white in complexion from Adam and Eve through Cush and all through the generations that followed. That Japheth's descendants became white is perhaps an accident due to gene inheritance or mutation generated by environmental adaptation. This is perhaps, indicated by the one fact that the white complexion is recessive gene. Most of the Jews that entered Africa were black or non white in complexion because Africa provided a safe haven where the people were of same complexion and where it was easier to evade persecution due to easy mix with their kith and kin in Africa.

A look at the history of migration legends shows some similarity to the experience of Ethiopian Jews and the Ibo ancestors into what became Ibo territory; in fact it could be claimed that, in a sense, the entering of the some Hebrews into what became Ibo territory is tied strongly to their migration into Ethiopia although Ibo Jews may have settled in the land (4000BC-3500 BC) long before further entry through Ethiopian route began.

1200 BC: Some scholars claim that in about 1,200 BC some Hebrews who left Egypt with Moses during the time of the Exodus, never made it across the Red Sea. Instead, they traveled out of Egypt into Ethiopia. According to an Ibo legend the migration of Ibo ancestors from the Middle East through Egypt must have begun about 2000-1305 Before Christ was born (BC) and it is possible that entry into the Ibo territory continued as these migrant Jews sought to join their kith and kin in around the coast of the Niger River.

900 BC: The story of King Solomon and Queen Makeda of Sheba is a well-known legend told by people over the centuries. This has already been stated above. About 1200 BC King Solomon of Israel invited the Queen of Sheba to his Palace. She was said to have visited Solomon but stayed very long time. Sheba is thought to be located in Northern Ethiopia or Yemen. The Queen later left Israel and went back home where she began to rule the people with the help of people she took from Israel. The Queen was said to have become pregnant for Solomon and gave birth to the future ruler who became Menelik 1 of Ethiopia. On reaching adulthood Menelik 1 was said to have gone to be with, King Solomon, his biological father, and later to come back to Ethiopia to rule after the death of his mother in 986 BC. Menelik 1 was said to have come back with a larger entourage of renowned Israelites than his mother, most of whom were learned and of the "House of Moses" as well the Ark of the Covenant said to be kept in St Mary's Church in the holy city of Axum today. His mother had come back with about 18000 Israelites. An Ibo legend claims that descendants of this 'House of Moses' migrated to Ibo land and became part of the Ibo ancestors who they claim contributed in setting up the priestly class.

8th century BC the sacking of the Northern Kingdom by the Assyrian army forced many Israelites who escaped the Asyrians evacuation to emmigrate to Africa through Egypt. One of those tribes was the tribe of Dan. The Ibo legend also claim that many of these Israelites entered into Iboland to become Ibo ancestors.

587/586 BC Babylonian army sacked the Southern Kingdom and scattered Israelites again moved to different places. They entered Ibo land to join Ibo ancestors, their kith and kin.

Also Jews of the Elephantine community in Egypt, where there was a large Temple by the 6thc century BC also were attacked and scattered by the 4th century BC Persecutions. The inhabitants of the community moved south and entered into Ibo land to join their fellow Hebrews who had become Ibo ancestors. They claimed to have passed through Ethiopia to the Niger River Coasts where their brethren already were settled. They joined their kith and kin in this friendly, devoid of all hostilities, and more conducive part of the world to life in Egypt etc.

1stC BC-1stC AD: Some scholars theorize that the Beta Israel is descended from a group of black Cushites, the Agaw, who were converted to Judaism 2,000 years ago by Jewish merchants from Yemen. The beta Israelites are called "the Falasha."

169 BC The Maccabean revolt also forced more Israelites to join their kith and kin in the Niger River coasts to later become Ibo ancestors

70AD The Roman sacking of the Temple in Jerusalem in the final unslaught against the Israelites who by now are called Jews forced some to join their kith and kin in Ibo land. Other important dates of entry into the Niger River basin are 900AD, 740AD, 1145 AD, 1484AD, 17 Century AD.

According to an Ibo legend the ancient Israelites (Hebrews) entered into the land that became Ibo land by 2000-1305 Before Christ (BC); far earlier than the Jews entered Ethiopia (c. 1200BC). Ibo legends on Hebrew entry also claim that migration into Iboland occurred from different directions and included those who entered from Ethiopia, North Africa, Egypt, West Africa, Sao Thome, Elephantine community, the Middle East. As the Nile River attracted migration to Egypt and through the Ethiopian route, so the River Niger and the Delta regions of what later became the Ibo country attracted migrations into the land as Ibo legends explained above. It is possible that the River Niger must have been mistaken for the River Nile by historian. It is likely that the River Niger was thought to be a tributary of the Nile River.

Chapter 3
Doubts, Controversy and Challenges

Nevertheless, not every Ibo accepted the claim of a common ancestral identity with the ancient Israelites although every Ibo seem to believe they are different from their neighbours in the same country. In the past, I personally, discountenanced opinion of the Oxford scholars on the Ibo peoples and Falasha being among the lost tribes of ancient Israel, though I am Ibo. In fact their conclusion seemed to identify only the Ibo and the Falasha as the lost tribes of Africa at that time of the research (published 1933). Such information was not of any importance or significance to me at that time in the late 1980s and early 1990s when I was a student researcher at Oxford University. And in fact I had detested any talk or information regarding so called 'the lost tribes of Israel'. My reasoning then was that if they were lost why border looking for them. Let people be left to seek their roots themselves rather than being told by other people that they are lost. A lost person does not need anybody to tell them they are lost. They should be able to see evidence of their being lost. I did not think at that time that as Ibo I needed anyone to tell me or my forefathers that we are lost from our roots. This is so in spite of the apparent restlessness and feeling of being stifled and hated by others including the colonial country. Neither I nor any Ibo person felt they were lost. I also argued saying that all peoples are lost if we come to realistically view the issue of lostness of peoples in this sense. People do migrate from original habitations and relocate for various reasons such as wars, natural disasters, economic convenience, social convenience, to mention just these. Emigration and relocation has been part of human habit. The question is should this experience be regarded as being lost, I often argued? I also questioned the idea of long migrations and rejected theories and claims based on long distant migrations.

I was one of those who in discussions opposed the idea of any peoples being lost. And as time passed on I became more and more averse to the idea that the Ibo were one of the lost tribes of ancient Israel, and in fact I once suggested that it was possible that the present Hebrews rather emigrated from Ibo land to the ancient Israel, so called. This assertion was buttressed by the common belief among some Igbo people, especially of the Owerri axis that all the events of the passion of "Jesus" took place in Igbo land around the Owerri axis. This fable identified Naze community as short form of Nazaret, Also Bethany, Jerusalem, and related nativity towns are also identified within the same area. However ther is not enough evidence to take this opinion any as serious. All the same, all this talk about Ibo being lost, to me, sounded like another colonial ploy to tell us that we are too intellectually inferior to know who we really are. This was how I felt at that time and I think there might be some others still thinking in this way. In my childhood days I was an ardent Roman Catholic, an altar boy, who nursed the idea of becoming a Dominican priest and was taught to believe that the Jews killed Jesus Christ and participated in singing a popular song among my people whose lyrics emphasized hatred for the Jews who killed Jesus.

Yet through personal reflection I did know that, associated with the Ibo peoples, was arrogance and pride of race just like the Jews are often accused. However, I did rationalize and often stated that one could say that arrogance and pride of race 'is part of every people'; however, to me I sometimes felt that my people's arrogance and pride of race could be said to have been extreme, even an obsession. I came to this conclusion from the utterances of Igbo politicians who dominated the politics of Nigeria. In fact one of them Dr Nnamdi Azikiwe in an address in 1949 as if it was taken as given that the Ibo race was created to rule others. My people presented themselves as in some manner superior to other races, this superiority was regarded as given, not just in relating with tribes within the same country; but in relation to all races; not even the claims of western European superiority changed this feeling about who we are. The success of the Europeans in colonizing our people was regarded as a fluke, and was permitted by G-d (Chukwu) as punishment on our people for being preoccupied with land- an attitude that was traditionally regarded as an abomination. According to warnings by Ibo prophets before the colonialist entered, God was going to punish our people for committing abominable evils especially for their changed attitude characterized by irrevernce to land and nature. This attitude included deliberate acts such as falsely changing boundaries of land, using land to oppress the widow and the orphan, selling land, burning land, ignoring the traditional laws forbidding sexual intercourse on farm lands, ignoring the rule of gleaning crops and seed, the laws of jubilee, ignoring rule of crop mixing, theft of crop from farmlands etc; but the people never hearkened to the prophets' warnings; so it was believed that 'God allowed white foreigners to take over our lands and wealth as punishment, as observed by an older uncle (cf Isichei: Igbo Worlds)

Yet there used to be frequent talk, or say, claim of being specially sent to the world by "Chiukwu Abiama (God of the father of the people from the Hebrew words ab (father) and 'am (people) for a mission. As a young boy it was drummed into our heads always that we were of different destiny from all other peoples. You were constantly reminded that as Ibo you were expected to excel in everything and in every competition with other tribes. In business you must outwit other peoples. In academic work, in government offices, just anywhere you were you saw it as a birthright to be ahead of all others. The obsession to excel was such that the name IBO was changed to represent "I Before Others", by other tribes. You were expected to take your work more seriously and more importantly than you take your physical existence because you could only be remembered by your work after you were dead and death could strike at anytime. My people sing that: 'ihe e ji echeta mmanu wu oru': 'A person can only be remembered by their work'. It was believed that the fruit of your labour was more important than you.

Above all just as Equiano pointed out above, you must not for any reason beg for food or for anything, and must not allow your brother to beg for food rather you were constantly reminded that you were created to provide for other peoples around you. You must not marry non Ibo woman and not even get into any intimate friendship and if you were involving in such you must keep in mind that you were the superior. The areas to take a wife were well defined as women from then Eastern Region, now made up of Rivers, Bayelsa, Akwa Ibom, Cross River and the current south eastern states; and from Ibo parts of Delta, Benue and Kogi states. You were not even allowed to befriend girls from non Ibo areas.

This sentiment extended to religion. There were certain religions and peoples that you must not associate with. Of particular mention were Islam and the Arabs; and the reasons given were: in addition to your being created to guide, that all other religions and peoples were retrogressive and so associating with them would set you backwards. There was an innate dislike of anything Arab. In fact the word "Arab" was used as euphemism for those considered to be "osu" among Ibos. It was a euphemism for "the people of the left" (osu is dedicated as a cult slave by choice). The principle was that all religions were retrogressive and the Ibo were to accept only those aspects that added value to his existence; including the survival and immortalisation of the community that extended to the ancestors and those yet to be born in a strong matrix between kin, cult and the afterlife. Roman Catholic missionaries apparently capitalized on this mind set and provided an evangelistic strategy that was based on benefit such as education, and medicines, that is to say, 'carrot evangelism', sustained with indoctrination. Thus the boast of one of their key pioneer missionaries to the Ibo: 'give me a neonate and I will make him a catholic forever' was successful among the Ibo as about ninety-nine percentage of the Ibo population was at that time Roman Catholic. The strategy was that to get medicated for malaria or to get any favours from the church, you and your sick child and children must be baptized Roman Catholic.

As this was a time when the white man's medicines were popular and indispensable and fast replacing traditional cure methods as our people were brainwashed to believe they were, after a period of sustained resistance, many Ibos eventually caved in as they had no other choice but to do so lest they or their relations would die or be denied other benefits especially western education. Become a Roman Catholic or your sick child or children would be denied medicines and western education. Western education posed a challenge to the Ibo psyche; so they took the bull by the horns, so to say, to make sure they did not lag behind neighbours who had already begun embracing the system with obvious advantages. The traditional Ibo religious beliefs and sacrifices, though they followed the patern of ancient Hebrew religion, including the healers who were very many and very efficient were relegated as the church claimed the traditional herbal medication and practice were of demons or evil spirits engineered. It is disheartening that even our mothers who were inherently herbalists, being knowledgeable in medicinal vegetation and cooked with them were forced to look down upon their useful G-d given skill and knowledge for healing and diet. An example is the eating of bitter herbs and practicing vegetarian. Our fathers and uncles were mostly strong, handsome, tall and healthy looking. They are today replaced by unhealthy, malnourished and stunted descendants who are dependent on failed, deceitful western church systems with their sinful and pollutant systems. Unfortunately, today is not any better as we have seen a resurgence of 'carrot evangelism' even propagated by some misguided Ibo pastors today in the form of 'Prosperity Gospel' with its promise of benefits of wealth and material possessions without hard work. This is contrary to the belief inherited from our ancestral values of hard work and honesty. The result is the further moral decadence, armed robbery, kidnapping, get-rich-quick syndrome, betrayal and callousness etc among the Ibo people, especially politicians. Brotherhood solidarity and kinship strength are waning fast.

However, there seems to be a resurgence of pride of race as there has never been since the Biafra war ended. One would have thought that the lessons learned in the Biafra war should have put an end to racial superiority among the Ibos.

Also the values of our forefathers have remained inherent among many Ibos. Evidence is that young Ibo youth including of my time are still being warned that colonial religion and religious ways would set them backward in life if they are not careful to adhere to the Ibo ways of life and expectation. The tension has continued, between pressure to compromise your values and to remain true to their inherent desires and aspiration as a people.

Nevertheless, generally speaking, the average Ibo have still remained a people strongly controlled by strong desire for personal achievement and success through hard work and trust in the guiding spirit of Chiukwu Abiama (Chi okike) to help accomplish their destiny allocated to them by God as a birthright.

When I was contemplating getting married to a Yoruba, a much younger cousin to me who visited me in the student hostel, opposed it on the ground that "she will set you backward; if you marry her you will never progress; there are many Ibo girls out there who will understand the achievement oriented nature of our people and our own culture and customs and will give you the needed support you need to progress," he emphatically warned me. This warning was repeated to me when I visited a friend in Ibadan, Nigeria and told him of my intention to marry a Yoruba. My friend was emphatic: "we are different, they can't understand but they know we are different, don't do that, or you will regret it", he warned me.

The most challenging of it all was, perhaps, the moral expectations from an Ibo boy and girl. You dare not disgrace your race by embarking on immorality of any sort. These included sexual immorality, prostitution, begging for food, theft, telling lies, cheating, disrespecting an elder or a senior person, bearing a false witness, betrayal of any type, cheating a fellow Ibo in a foreign land, 'behaving British', to mention just these. Any boy who tried to prove he is clever by playing on the intelligence of an elder was publicly called 'British"- behaving British. Every young girl must marry as a virgin and proof must be provided by the girl and her parents.

Any girl who got pregnant without being married was first disgraced publicly, and then the parents, especially the mother, had their own form of disgrace for failing to bring their daughter up in the traditionally (omenala) expected ways. No one dared eat pork. Im very sure that many Ibo youth do not know that there was no word for prostitution in Ibo language. It was never mentioned or imagined. The word for a prostitute, "akwunokwuno" was foreign language from a neighbouring tribe. However, because of imposition and compromise from Christianity, where pig rearing was practiced it was sold only to "outsiders." Rearing and trading on pigs was abhorred generally. Such a person was pitied. When I traded in livestock for my father during the Biafra war, I was strongly warned never to buy pigs. In fact pigs were never seen in any market.

Challenges and Questions

I completed my studies in Lagos where I studied my first profession and went on to work in the University of Jos Teaching Hospital and shortly after I was sent to go and set up the Xray department in

Plateau Specialist Hospital Jos. However having become born again some four years earlier, I realised that I spent more time preaching to my patients with only a cursory discussion on medical issues. So I later left to train in one of the Baptist Seminaries and there became a Baptist in my final year after spending four years; it helped me understand the Baptist systems and beliefs. Shortly after a spell in lecturing at the Samuel Bill Theological College, Abak and Cross River State University, Uyo (part time), I went to study for some postgraduate in Europe (Switzerland) with the aim of specializing in Church History. But hostility or as God would have it, so to say, I found myself specializing in the Biblical Studies: Old Testament with strong emphasis on ancient near eastern languages with emphasis on Hebrew and Greek grammar in addition to German, French and Latin. I later completed my thesis in Religious Studies specializing in Hebrew and Ibo Comparative Studies (Philosophical Theology) with a research that involved a lot of Hebrew, Greek and Ancient Near Eastern languages. A requirement for the doctorate was a working knowledge of Arabic grammar plus German or French. I chose to study Arabic and French since I had already learned German while a student in Zurich Switzerland. However, I had no intention or interest of studying Ibo-Hebrew genealogical links; but the research widened my knowledge to include beliefs of all peoples and religions of the world, ancient and modern and issues around death, burial and the afterlife. I must confess that this area of specialization was a most controversial and difficult area to specialize at that time. I struggled with the amount of ancient grammar involved: Ugaritic, Akkadian, Aramaic, Arabic, Classical Hebrew, ancient Hebrew, Greek, Ancient Ibo words, phrases and sayings and Philosophical courses. Above all I was not a specialist philologist and had to rely heavily on philologists all of whom were of European origin. My relying on European philologist was not acceptable to my highly knowledgeable supervisors at Oxford University, so I had to begin again; at a point I even wanted to relinquish my scholarship funding and give up the study but for encouragement of the principal of my college (Wycliffe Hall) and my supervisors, I was therefore motivated to continue with my studies. I accepted the challenge and continued with the research on Death and the Afterlife among the ancient Hebrews. This study covered every aspect of Hebrew life and was under the supervision of one the best Old Testament scholars in Europe and perhaps in the world, Professor Hans Mallau and Professor Schmidz of the University of Zurich who was also the rector of the University of Zurich at that time on the one hand; and Professor G Wenham, Professor McConville of Oxford University on the other hand.

I thank the Lord that in spite of the oppositions from people who deliberately put impediments, the force that motivated me led me to success and triumphant. It was shortly after that I realized the reason for it all: My Motivator, Provider and Sustainer was equipping and preparing me to be the instrument for this study of Jewish peoples and Ibo peoples' linkage. Yes, the Almighty, the God of our fathers (Chukwu Abiama) wanted to use me to play a part in a purpose: that the present world may know His purpose for His people (Jews) everywhere in the present day political, social, religious, and economic sphere. This was completely different from my life ambition and expectation, which was to become a scientist and a medical missionary in 'a far away country.'

I got a position to teach in the University of Jos, Nigeria in 1991. It was in the year 1997 that a friend came to my house; pleading, he said, 'Lucky I beg you in the name of God come and help our people.' (Goodluck is the name by which I am known in family circles since it is my childhood name. It is shortened as 'Lucky' by my people, peers, friends and everyone else). I asked my visitor, Mr Oscar Nneli what his statement meant. He said, 'there is a project by Ibo people going on in the University and they are looking for specialists; I know you are going to be helpful.' I asked what it was about. He said he did not know but said it involved Ibo and Jews; then mentioned the names of the professors involved. I said to him, 'I hope they are not seeking to prove that Ibos are Hebrew or Jews'. He said he thought so; then I answered him in my characteristic arrogant nature and said, 'I'm sorry I do not believe in that' and added that he should tell them that 'I am not a specialist in the Hebrew language and culture, my calling is to teach pastors, that is why I am in the university as a teacher.'

Oscar was not ready to give up in his persuasion. Two days later he came back to me to repeat the same request. Then I told him that I did not want to be involved with Ibos as I did not want "their trouble" and added "you know that many of them are dubious, even university professors"; I was aware that this statement was too blunt and arrogant, with 'a holier than thou' tone. My aim was to stop him from speaking further about it. He responded by saying that I was "dodging my responsibility" to my people and that he knew it was my specialist area because when I was on research holiday from Europe and UK I talked so much on this and asked him questions on Ibo words and practices.

It was about a week later that I accompanied Oscar to the meeting place, a university of Jos professor's house, and the research committee was meeting that day, they were also electing officers. I was surprised that they unanimously chose me to be the secretary of the project. One of the professors I respected a lot said to me, "Dr Nkem (just the way students addressed me) as the secretary it means you are now in charge of the project; its success and failure is in your hands." My protest that I only came to survey what it was all about and that I was not a specialist in that area of research, did not carry. I accepted the post because of the highly respectable people present including the dean of my faculty who addressed me earlier.

A Visits from Israel

During the sessions of discussions by the Ibo-Hebrew Research team of the University of Jos Nigeria, for which I was by now the Secretary of the research team, information that were considered significant began to come up. One of these was that in 1988 the Ibo people got unexpected visitors from Israel. The visitors claimed that they had "come to visit their brothers, the Ibo peoples." According to our informant who had become an Ibo rabbi, they were religious Jews. According to him the visitor identified "the three backhand strokes" of the Ibo as same greeting among the ancient Hebrews and that it meant 'forward ever backward never' spoken in the Hebrew language.

Their reason for visiting at that time, as we learnt, was political. Israel had been under threat of extermination since independence in 1948 and it was thought necessary to explore places of possible refugee domain for them in case it became needed. They sought first to visit 'their brothers' in other parts of the world and Ibo land was one of the first to be considered in Africa. The other possible place they considered visiting was, Uganda, and Zimbabwe (the Lemba tribe who are also thought as related to the ancient Israelites). But Lemba in Zimbabwe and Ankole in Uganda, regarded as of Jewish in origin were too small in size, land area and influence to be given serious consideration; so the most likely place for possible Jewish refugee habitation was to be Ibo land. Thus, they came to explore and survey the ground. It is on record that Uganda had been suggested as a possible land to be given to the Jews if Palestine failed but was rejected by the Zionist canvassers.

In October 1995 a two man delegation from Israel visited Iboland again. They were said to have come on a fact finding mission. Among the places they visited were historical sites in Aguleri and Agukwu Nri. They visited the Agbanabo-Ezu-na-Omobala- the confluence of the rivers Ezu and Omobala which form the Omombala (Anambra) river, a tributary of the River Niger (called in Ibo as Oshimiri Ogbaru). It was here that legend claims that Eri first landed before he moved to settle in Obugad (literally "the heart of Gad" i.e. "shrine of Gad") in Aguleri. They also visited the place called Obuga, literally OBU-GAD, regarded as Gad's Home, a royal palace Eri was said to have built in honour of his father, Gad. This particular place is regarded by some people as the cradle of the Ibo race and in fact some claim it is the cradle of most African tribes. They also visited Eri's burial spot which has apparently been revered for hundreds of years by the natives and Ibo community leaders from different parts of Ibo land. The delegates were said to have taken notes and made films of all that they saw. The films were said to have been later shown on Israeli television on several occasions.

In May 1997 another visit was made from Israel and elsewhere. This time the Ibos were accorded formal recognition as descendants of ancient Israelites by the King Solomon Sephardic Federation International (KSSFI). We were told that this recognition was announced at the annual Conference of the KSSFI held in Philadelphia, USA. The recognition was based on the research findings of the Israeli delegates. KSSFI is the official umbrella of organization representing the Ancient Sephardic Nations of Eastern Judeans, Hebrews and Israelites. Its primary purpose we were told is to identify, and assist the lost tribes of Israel and Jews in diaspora. It is a non-governmental, non-political, and non-religious cultural organization, with chapters in different parts of the world notably as we were told to include: Morocco, Ethiopia, Iran, Iraq, India, the USA, Ghana, Uganda, South Africa, Belgium, Jordan, Zimbabwe, Somalia, Mali, Yemen, Spain, Switzerland, Burundi, Rwanda, to mention just these. Eze A.E. Chukwuemeka Eri, said to be the then holder of the 'ofo Eri' which is regarded as the oldest symbol of authority among the Ibos was the recognized Leader of the Ibo Jews at that time. He Co-ordinated all the lost tribes of Israel in the West African region by the time I was in office.

This visit to announce the recognition of Ibo as part of the KSSFI occurred barely six months into our research effort; we learnt that some Israeli delegates had been visiting Nigeria and that some of them initially travelled through the West African coast for months claiming they were seeking to confirm historical information extant through archaeological discovery in Israel. They referred to a letter purported to have been sent from this part of the world, thousands of years ago, indicating among other information that a shrine was built by one of their travelling ancestors by name Eri. We were told that they emphatically claimed the name of the shrine was 'Obu Gad' translated as 'the heart of Gad.' I later confirmed from one of my students from Ora Eri that the people of Ora Eri in Anambra state (Ibo heartland) had retained such a legend. So the visitors at last were said to be able to identify the location of the shrine in a remote location of the village in Ora Eri by help of the older living members of the community. Ora Eri, I understand, literary means: 'the people of Eri' or 'the community of Eri' or 'Eri's children.' The visitors are said to have excavated the shrine in a very remote forest in the village and that became one of the main available relics so far known apart from the fact that he disembarked at the confluence of the Anambra (Omambala) River and the Niger River as stated above.

The discovery and announcement that the Ibo had been recognized as Shephardi Jews of the world, as I learnt, was greeted with celebrations and rallies including one rally held at the Israeli embassy in Lagos. The visitors were said to have visited some Ibo traditional rulers scattered all over Ibo land. The august visitors were subsequently referred to commonly as "our brothers from Israel." The visitors later claimed that scholars in Israel had been researching about this Ibo-Hebrew genealogical link "for at least thirty five years": we were told that they advised that all research about it should be stopped as it had been concluded; that they advised 'Ibos' to rather make themselves ready to enjoy the benefits of being discovered as others like the Falashas of Ethiopia were benefiting. It could be remembered that the Falashas were evacuated to Israel when their country was devastated by drought and famine. As I learnt they were recognized by the Israeli Knesset (the name for the parliament) as Jews as well as accorded status right to enter Israel and settle in 1975.

The visitors were said to have promised scholarships to young Ibos desiring to study specifically the Hebrew language, Agriculture and Engineering and spoke of possibility of interested Ibos relocating to Israel.

My observation was that to educated Ibos these promises sounded superfluous and unwarranted. While some people including the media hyped the visit and exaggerated the promises that were made. It was in National news and miscreants began to set up collating centres where people paid money to purchase application forms in preparation to emigrate to Israel. In spite of warnings many I learnt were swindled. Even some pastors began to use their church premises as registration centres for relocation to Israel.

However, some of us in the research project refused to accept the verdict of the visitors, and argued insistently that foreigners would not be the ones to tell us our genealogical linkage and expect us to accept without questions. We felt that we also needed to figure out if we are Hebrews or Jews, ourselves; moreover how would we be able to convince our people that they originated from elsewhere without presenting them our own evidence? Are Ibos the only children of Eri? Moreover, we already have some other Ibos claiming a different ancestral linkage though also of Hebrew origins. There were already professors, some in our midst, and from different sections of Igbo that had variously traced their root to Levi, Ephraim, Asher, Judah, and Benjamin clans. Already the Ora Eri people have indicated their root as Gadite clan. As stated above this claim was confirmed by a student from Ora Eri whose undergraduate final Essay was on 'Female Circumcision among the Ora Eri people'. According to her findings all the elders, men and women, in her village confirmed this legend as true. I supervised the writing of her Essay and her research findings are pertinent and useful to this study although female circumcision had been stopped in Ora Eri as she was not circumcised like her elder sister. According to her the practice was stopped when her people finally unanimously accepted that it was a foreign practice introduced to her people; Ibos generally did not have female circumcision as a custom, only males were circumcised on the eight day. She said she would have preferred to be circumcised for personal reasons; this was contrary to my own view.

Consequently we felt that our research had only begun. This is perhaps underscored by the extant verdict of Dr Olauda Equiano that the Ibo ancestors immigrated into Iboland during the time of the Exodus from Egypt. Ola Udah as someone reflected could mean "Judah's ornament," "Judah's gift," "Judah's offering" in Ibo language. I personally began to become convinced and accept that there was some truth in the claims and I began to muse that "it is likely that immigration into Iboland must have happened at various times by various Israelite tribes." The Gadite tribe might have eventually become dominant or perhaps the legend surrounding linkage to that clan became more popular than the other legends.

It was shortly after the announcement of recognition of the Ibos as Hebrews that we observed that some write ups on the genealogical linkage of the Ibo and Hebrews had already begun to emerge from every nook and cranny. Many of which, have been found to be not only a pack of lies but disgraceful to the Ibo race, to say the least. Also all sorts of rumours had begun to circulate. People who did not know the difference between Hebrew, Greek and Latin languages had begun to write rubbish. For example one very sad one interpreted the Old Testament book 'Genesis' as 'Ijenisisi' in Ibo language; which indeed is an insult to Ibo scholarship and a disgrace and shame to the

Ibo race. As one professor reacted, "some of these writers apparently did not complete primary education."

It was at this juncture that my friend Oscar pointed out to me that the need for me to do something could not be overemphasized or 'the whole issue would be trivialized and hijacked by charlatans'. I agreed with him but how do I begin; who would play part in the team. What about funding? I advertised for participants in the study but got no response. Apparently Ibo scholars who are specialists in Hebrew and other ancient near eastern studies were either very few indeed or not interested or lack the confidence to embark on such an elaborate study; or there is no other person. After waiting almost indefinitely I accepted I was alone in this task and would work alone.

A ray of hope did emerge when a colleague in the linguistic department introduced a European linguistics professor in a University in the Northern part of Nigeria, to me. Although a Jew by birth, a Jew whose parents survived the holocaust, it turned out that he had been "disowned" by his Jewish people because he and all his family had become Roman Catholics. So, according to him, he did not have the right or status to speak as a Jew. In my correspondence with him he contributed by pointing out that language similarity was not enough evidence to claim genealogical link. I agreed with him although I was aware that his opinion was debatable. Also he was not a specialist in the ancient Hebrew or Aramaic or in any of the ancient near eastern languages; nor was he a specialist in the Ibo grammar and culture. Consequently that hope faded away. I found myself alone in the task, yet the task must be carried out.

Apart from this there were other local and non local problems I identified might impede carrying out the task unless a means of circumventing them was identifiable. However the research challenges took me back to papers and researches I carried out as far back as 1983 that I find relevant and useful. This is why I rightly claim that the research began as far back as 1983.

Other Problems identified

Firstly we do not have an Ibo people; rather we can only talk of Ibo peoples with their different dialects, though they could be interrelated. However this situation eventually became an advantage.

Secondly, it is difficult to carry out any research among the Ibo peoples, the cost of travel and other expenses would be enormous and we had no funding of any sort. At least I was not told of any such funding and I have been in it alone.

Thirdly the ancient Ibo grammar and the modern Ibo grammar are both very difficult to handle and so though applying it might be useful, it might not provide strong basis for such investigation as the letters are Arabic and foreign. The native Ibo writing called insibidi had been killed and buried by colonial education and politics in addition to the hatred of the Roman Catholic against any association of Ibos with Hebrew ancestry. The thinking is also foreign imposition. Above all I am also not a specialist in Ibo grammar as I cannot claim to be a specialist in Hebrew grammar, though I have a working knowledge of the Classical Hebrew and Greek to be able to write and defend dissertations and theses and to be able to teach. The Ibo and Latin grammar I studied in the secondary school were considered as inadequate also the latin grammar I studied in higher Education was for a short time and not detailed enough.

Fourthly, the Hebrew language like Ibo languages has passed many stages in its development. It was also a palace determined grammar, just as the Ibo grammar has been foreign influenced, they are both far removed from what the lower level masses spoke. Yet this substructural level of the two languages should be expected to provide most relevant and useful material for comparing the similarities in the languages. Fortunately my doctorate research examined in detail the substructures of the culture and language of the Old Testament but not of the Ibo language. Yet still there has to be made a distinction between Ibo languages and grammar and Igbo language and grammar. We can speak of Igbo grammar but we cannot speak of Ibo grammar because of the many varieties of Ibo languages.

Fifthly, there will be need to differentiate between Modern Hebrew, Mishnaic Hebrew, and Aramaic from the Classical or Ancient Hebrew. Many expressions in the Bible are Aramaic. For example Yeshua/ Jesus Christ and his disciples spoke Aramaic. The native language of Yeshua/ Jesus Christ was Aramaic and this was translated into common Greek of the New Testament time.

Classical Hebrew, also called Ancient Hebrew is the Semitic language used by the Ancient Hebrews from approximately 1200 BC to about AD 60. It is the language of the Old Testament Text (Biblical Hebrew) whose vowels were inserted much later by the Masoretic School (1240 AD). However after the first destruction of Jerusalem and the evacuation of the people of the Southern Kingdom of Israel to Babylon, often dated about 586 BC; (we've already noted that the Northern Kingdom had been evacuated much earlier 721 BC to Assyria or scattered) - Classical Hebrew began to compete with an emerging Hebrew in which the Jewish text called Mishna was written and a dialect called Aramaic, a common language of the masses.

It was in the 20th century that Modern Hebrew began to be introduced. This is the spoken Hebrew in Israel today. (Lessons in Modern Hebrew were sent to me by the Israeli embassy in Lagos as I said earlier). We also have Yiddish, a version of Hebrew spoken by the European Jews most of whom are of the Ashkenazi (German) stock of Jews different from the Sephardi (Spanish) stock of Jews and others, some of whom are regarded as keeping the original ancient Hebrew vocabulary and practices.

The Sephardi derive their name from ancient Spain, then called 'Sepharad' in which many diaspora Jews had settled for many years including under the rule of the Moors until they were latter scattered when invading Christian army sought to exterminate them. They are also said to include the Black African Jews.

The Sephardi Jews have been united into a common federation called King Solomon Sephardic Federation as stated above. They are said to be of King Solomon because their beginning is traced back to the time of King Solomon, known originally as Jedidiah, when merchants were sent out to the world to represent King Solomon as emissaries and trading merchants. These merchants who settled in Sepharad (as Spain was called in those days) and all the other Hebrews who emigrated from Israel and settled elsewhere apart from Germany and East Europe are therefore referred as Sephardic Jews and today their descendants belong to the King Solomon Sephardic Federation. They have mostly retained the original Hebrew customs, names and practices though have various origins from Israel and places of habitation in the world today. They are today being fished out and identified. The Ibo are said to be one of such peoples as already stated above. This is why I think that Sepharad could be understood as people "afar off", and of Spanish stock, different from the Ashkenazi, the German stock. Nevertheless since there are Israelites-Hebrews from other places unconnected to Europe we can say that the common factor between all Sephardim are perhaps, their Babylonian root, their adherence to the Bible and their holistic attitude to philosophy as well as their accommodating features; for instance rather than depending on halakhic commentaries as Law as the Ashkenazic have tended to follow the Sephardim are all embracing and interprete the Tanakh and Halakha literally.

The Ashkenazi is derived from the ancient German called Ashkenazi. Thus the Jews, who settled in Germany and beyond, say Poland, were referred to as Ashkenazi Jews. These are said to have lost much of their ancient Jewish root including language and religious practices. They introduced an adulterated version of their language called 'Yiddish.' Above all is the suspicion that the Ashkenazi is made up of non-Hebrew Jews of a completely different ancestral descent, the Khazari Empire who were massively converted to Judaism. Some scholar describes them as the thirteenth tribe. Yet these have taken to shaping Judaism as a religion and have remained enthusiastic to decide the course Judaism and world Jewry should follow including parameter for Jewish identity. This situation adds to the difficulty encountered in any research of ancient Israelite Hebrew and the Ibo linkage. It appears that what is to be regarded as ancient Israelite Hebrew has been so adulterated and mixed up with foreign facts especially on matters of language, rituals, practices and beliefs, and perhas influenced adversely by politics of religion and ethnicity.

Also the time in history and the situation that might have forced Ibo ancestors to emigrate to this part of the world would need to be considered in terms of what language they spoke. Moreover the Ibo peoples could not have been a homogeneous people assuming that they are of the "lost tribes." They must have belonged to different "lost tribes" if they must be regarded as lost. It could be that rather than being lost they relocated to West Africa and perhaps concentrated in the Iboland as Ibos (Heeboes) with associated adaptations and modifications in culture including languages. And this raises the question what modifications existed among the tribes in language? Does this explain the various dialects we have today among the Ibo? This becomes more relevant to consider for the fact that it was only in about the thirteen century in the year of our Lord (anno domino AD) that the Masoretic School introduced vowels into the Hebrew letters. This means that no one can say exactly how the words were pronounced before this introduction, what more thousands of years before then when the Ibo ancestors were purported to have emigrated from there assuming there was such emigration. There is indication that the language spoken by our ancestors was far much earlier than all the most ancient of Hebrew languages.

It becomes obvious that to embark on a study such as this requires faith, courage and G-d's guidance; Courage to begin and faith to carry on. Guided by the belief that 'once there is a will there is a way,' I decided to take the bull by the horns, so to say.

Chapter 4
Hope and Triumph

An encouragement came in the form of an archaeological find in east of Jordan River of a huge shrine named as 'ala' (perhaps Elah, Aloah) shrine, in the Succoth area. Succoth was a territory of the Gadites, Benjamites and the Reubenites though it was said that the children of Gad built it.

Also Hosea 4: 13 mentions 'ala' translated as 'terebinth' in English. Much later Hosea's condemnation which occurred hundreds of years later reads as follows:

'On the tops of mountains they sacrificed; and on the hills burn incense under oak and poplar and terebinth (w'alah- literally 'and ala') for it has good shade...'

Reading an interesting historical account in Numbers chapter 32, I observed that the children of Gad, Benjamin and Reuben inhabited this part of the territory where the ala shrine was unearthed by the archaeologist. This perhaps is evidence that the children of Gad, Benjamin and Reuben must have worshiped the ala deity either as a syncretistic worship at this early time; or perhaps, this was before the worship of ayah asher ayah "I am that I am" (also called Yahweh) was fully established. It is also very likely that the children of Gad, Benjamin and Reuben never knew about the worship of the "I am", Yahweh and that ala (Aloah) was perhaps their sole deity by the time some of them left for Africa.

The children of Gad, Benjamin, Mannaseh and Reuben had made a special request to Moses to allow them inhabit that land rather than cross over to the west of the Jordan River as they found the east land favourable to their shepherding. Someone would notice evidence of 'I before Others' syndrome in the children of Gad, Benjamin, Manasseh, and Reuben said to be associated with the Ibo even today and for which sake they are said to be hated by their neighbours.

Moses had to get them to make a promise that they would first cross over to the other side of the Jordan, fight the battles alongside their brothers and then come back to inhabit the land before he agreed to grant their request to allocate the East of Jordan to them to inhabit. Moses warned them that if they failed in their promise they should be sure that they had sinned and that their sin would find them out (Numbers 32). It was during the time of Joshua that they fully inherited the territory after the battles were won. Joshua summoned the Reubenites, the Gadites, and the half tribe Manasseh and said to them: "you have done all that Moses the servant of the Lord commanded, and you have obeyed me in everything I commanded. For a long time now to this very day you have not deserted your brothers and have carried out the mission the Lord your G-d gave you. Now that the Lord your G-d has given your brothers rest as he promised, return to your homes in the land that Moses the servant of the LORD gave you on the other side of the Jordan. But be very careful to keep the commandment and the law that Moses the servant of the LORD gave you: to love the LORD your G-d, to walk in all his ways, to obey his commands, to hold fast to him and to serve him with all your heart and all your soul." Joshua blessed and sent them away. This perhaps underscores why Ibo ancestors would hold onto the Book of Joshua as explained by Eldad, the Ghanaian Danite historian.

Following this blessing and having fulfilled their promise, they (the children of Gad, Reuben and half tribe Mansseh) left their brothers at Shiloh in Canaan and returned to Gilead, their own land. When they came to Geliloth near the Jordan in the land of Canaan they collectively built an imposing altar there by the Jordan. When their brothers heard this they berated them and questioned why they should build the altar on their own territory and perhaps why they should so soon build such an altar in the first place. Their brothers prepared to go to war with them. They sent emissaries to hear from them including Phinehas, son of Eleazar, the priest, and ten of the chief men one from each tribe, each the head of a family division of the Israelite clans. They accused the Gadites, Reubenites and half tribe Manasseh of breaking faith with the G-d of Israel, "how could you break faith with the G-d of Israel like this, how could you turn away from the LORD and build yourselves an altar in rebellion against him now, was not the sin of Peor enough for us. Up to this day we have not cleansed ourselves from that sin, even though a plague fell on the community of the lord, and you are now turning away from the LORD?'', they asked. They went on to state if you rebel against the Lord today, tomorrow he will be angry with the whole community of Israel. If the land you possess is defiled, come over to the LORD's land, where the Lord's tabernacle stands and share the land with us. But do not rebel against the LORD or against us by building an altar for yourselves, other than the altar of the LORD our G-d,' they advised them. "When Achan son of Zerah acted unfaithfully regarding the devoted things did not wrath come upon the whole community of Israel? He was not the only one who died for his sin," they reminded them. This expresses corporate solidarity of the ancient Israelites like the Ibos – whereby one person's sin affects the whole community.

Then Reuben, Gad, and half tribe Manasseh replied to the emissaries: "The Mighty One, G-d, and the LORD: The Mighty One, G-d, the LORD, He knows. And let Israel know. If this has been in rebellion or disobedience to the LORD, do not spare us this day. If we have built our own altar to turn away from the LORD and to offer burnt offerings and grain offerings, or to sacrifice fellowship offerings on it, may the LORD himself call us to account. No we did it for fear that someday your descendants might say to ours: what do you have to do with the LORD, the God of Israel? The LORD has made the Jordan a boundary between us and you- you Reubenites and Gadites. You have no share in the LORD. So your descendants might cause ours to stop fearing the LORD... On the contrary it is to be a witness between us and you and the generations that follow, that we will worship the LORD at his sanctuary with our burnt offerings, sacrifices and fellowship offerings. Then in the future your descendants will not be able to say to ours, 'You have no share in the LORD. Therefore we said if they ever say this to our descendants, we will answer: 'Look at the replica of the LORD'S altar, which our fathers built, not for burnt offerings and sacrifices, but as a witness between us and you." This explanation pleased the elders, representatives of the families that made up Israel and they returned to Canaan. The people were satisfied with the report and peace reigned between the two parties (Joshua 22).

In fact it was this archaeological find of the alah shrine located in the same place near Jordan and the account of Joshua 22 and the

Obu Gad (heart of Gad) in Ora Eri in Iboland that first began to make me think again on my opposition to the whole idea of a lost tribe and the ancestral connect of Ibos with Israel. This is because 'ala' is known to be the universal deity among the Ibo and the description of the environment of the worship in the Bible fits very well with the location of alah (dialectal difference pronounce it as "ani") shrines in Iboland: oak tree, shade, hillside or on top hill, etc.

It is well known among Ibo scholars that other prominent deities in Ibo land perhaps emerged as a challenge to the singular "alah" universal presence. It is a known fact that the Ibos still revere the belief in this one deity, "alah", above all other deities and under it the other deities operate; in spite of later emergence of other deities. For example the Igwe ka alah (igwekala, literally, 'the heavens are greater than 'alah' earth, mother') is identified with the Umunoha people and it was also a much later invention claiming that the father heaven is greater than the mother, earth. "Ala" is metaphor for mother as "Heaven" is metaphor for "father." Also the Chi-ukwu (greater chi or deity in charge of destiny) deity is identified with the Aro Chukwu people and has been known to be also a much later invention. This people claim that the greatest of all is the great chi (ChiUkwu) because he is incharge of destiny; this means, that he is incharge of all of creation including ala and igwe. In spite of this contest, to the mind of the Ibo only Ala has remained the universal deity of the Ibo up till today and unearthing such a huge shrine of ala in the east of the Jordan where the children of Gad, Manasseh, and Reuben had lived in ancient time becomes significant to relating the two religions of the tribes of Gad, Manasseh, and Reuben; and the Ibo. This information sent shivers to my spine with some tremble, that I might be wrong afterall in opposing the possibility of any linkage between the Ibo and ancient Israelite-Hebrew peoples. I discovered this while casually flipping through an archaeological map I found in the University of Oxford library, UK. However though I noted this information down I still felt that it was insignificant to bother about as my mind was far from thinking of being involved in such a research to link Ibo and Israelites. It was when I began to think of the possibility of linkage many years later that various past fact discoveries began to link with one another going as far back as 1983 when I carried out my first research on Ibo Religion when I was a final year student in the Seminary.

Another encouraging experience was that I began to think through names of people around me from childhood that were not English words. For example one of my uncles was called papa 'Beni'. I began to ask how he got the name, Beni. I asked if he was baptized Bennedict or Benjamin. This question generated laughter as the elder person I was talking about never went to church and understood no English word. So he was not Christian Baptised. Beni is purely Hebrew name word that means "My Son."

My other uncle's name was papa 'Opera' which was also not English name and no one around me could say what language it was. My uncle had been called by that name from birth, according to him. He was born in early 1904 AD and was baptized with the name, Nicodemus. Among the Ibo we use the title 'papa' for an elder. It is used in place of "father," sometime in place of "uncle." The other word for uncle is "dede," "dod," for aunt is "dadah." Interestingly "opera" is a Hebrew word that is applied to describe being "in front."

Then I remembered my great grandfather's name Udum Adah. I asked one of my uncles, what Udum Adah meant and how His grandfather got that name? He said he did not know. I later asked my own biological father, who also did not know the meaning of the name; but said that the name of their grandfather's mother was Adah Adah. This was why my great grandfather was called Udum Adah. But that did not answer my question, except that it indicated matrilineal status as belief whereby a child attained ethnicity through the mother's line in those days.

In the first place these are ancient near eastern names as depicted in the Bible. As stated above 'Beni' in Hebrew means 'my son' literally; 'Opera' means 'to be in front' or 'be ahead of others'' 'progress ahead' or 'out-do others' and might be related to 'oparah' which is Ibo word reserved for the 'first son' as one ahead of his male siblings; just as 'Adah' is the designation, name or title traditionally given to the first born daughter and, like the 'oparah', confers on her certain rights.

'Adah' is a Hebrew name given to girls and means 'ornament', 'beautiful', 'adornment'. 'Udum' is ancient Hebrew sound of the name 'Adam.' This is to say that in ancient Hebrew the name 'Adam' was pronounced, 'Udum' when correctly pronounced. Thus 'Udum' is Hebrew equivalent of 'Adam'. Also from the names 'Udum Adah' one could deduce that in the times of my paternal great grandfather a child was named after the mother's name as 'Adah' was his mother's name that was used as his surname. Thus was he called Udum Adah as his full name as if he belonged to his mother's lineage and for a long time legally a Jew was a person born of a Jewish woman. We can also remember that the wives of Lamech and Esau were named Adah in the Christian Old Testament and Hebrew Bible. Further investigation indicated that Udum was an ancient Judean name.

Another fact that surprised me was the discovery that like the Ibos the ancient Israelites used euphemisms to express death- in fact same euphemisms were identified as common to the two groups. For example the Bible says that Solomon rested with his fathers and was buried in the city of David his father. The Ibos also used same euphemism to express the death of a King. Another euphemism is he 'went to the way of all the earth' as Joshua stated in Joshua 23:14 in reference to his death. Another common euphemism among the Ibo is "he breathed his last and was gathered to his fathers", this is usually followed by what happened next, "His sons... buried him". Among the Ibos this expression implies more than putting him in the grave. It also implies that he had sons who carried out their expected duty to honour the father by reuniting him with the ancestors. Thus it is stated that Abraham altogether lived a hundred and seventy five years. Then Abraham breathed his last and gave up the ghost, in good old age, an old man and full of years, and he was gathered to his people. His sons Isaac and Ishmael buried him in the cave near Mamre, in the field of Ephron son of Zohar, the Hittite, the field Abraham bought from the Hittites. There Abraham was buried with his wife Sarah (Genesis 25:7-10).

Thus from my little knowledge of the ancient Hebrew language and culture I began to see that there was something worth examining after all. I began to see that the research might be worth the effort and that it might not be as herculean a task as I was imagining it would be. I then began to think of strategy to adopt because as the motivation had kicked in, there was no going back.

How I approached the investigation:

I decided to revisit my Hebrew lessons including lessons from the Israeli embassy in Nigeria on Modern Hebrew sent to me. Hebrew lessons from the embassy were accompanied with cassettes. I also began to restudy the Hebrew grammar and to read the Old Testament Hebrew text from the point of view of the task at hand. It also meant my interest had to widen to include customs and language similarities. I was eclectic in choice of Hebrew words as I picked words from all available sources including Modern Hebrew, Classical Hebrew, Mishnaic Hebrew, Aramaic, etc. This approach suited the fact that the Ibo ancestors entered the land at different times, ages and of different tribes and dialects.

I was amazed at my discovery. Only a cursory look at the text provided me words that were not only spelt same way, pronounced same way, and found to mean the same or had similar meaning and usage among the Ibo and Hebrew languages. This was amazing bearing in mind the thousands of years and geographical demarcation and changes in use of words that must have taken place all these years among the two peoples.

Also I had decided that the convenient way would be to gather information from all sections of the Ibo and relate them to the Aramaic and /or Hebrew: Mishnaic, or Classical. The Ibo sections I have in mind are states of Rivers, Bayelsa, Delta, Kogi, Enugu, Imo, Abia, Ebonyi, Anambra- all around that is generally regarded as Ibo people in Nigeria so far, as well as relatives whose language is also derived from Ibo. I have in mind specifically the Akwa Ibom, Cross River states and the Beni Ephraimites in Ondo state considered as kith and kin of the Ibos. Within Imo, Abia, Anambra, Enugu, Rivers, Delta, Ebonyi, Akwa Ibom and Cross River alone there are many Ibo dialects to investigate words and they were very helpful. I observed that the Ibo sections that preserved the most ancient cultures also preserved useful vocabulary more than others. For example the Cross River, Ohafia, Ebonyi, Ikwere, Etche, Ibibio, Nkpa, and Owerre areas preserved more related words to the ancient Hebrew, though the most helpful was the Owere dialects. The implication of this approach reiterates the fact that the word Ibo, like the Israelite-Hebrew word, does not refer to a single people, rather it refers to a group of peoples who were collectively regarded as of the root of ibhri which came to be rendered as Heeboe, 'Ibo'. For example I see no reason why all the peoples that use the Hebrew word 'ba' 'bia', 'bra' as 'come' cannot be grouped together as belonging to this collectivity called Ibo. The other words include 'mama' 'ma' 'ima'' mma' 'papa' 'mi' 'mu' 'nmu' 'nmi' 'chi' 'chu' 'ani' 'anyi' to mention just these so long as the variations mean the same; people who use these should be regarded as belonging to the ancient Heeboe, Ibo stock.

I decided to begin by first investigating the Ibo as Hebrews rather than Jews in diaspora. This justifies that I include Aramaic and even other relevant ancient near eastern cognate words such as Ugaritic, Acadian, Summerian and other cognate languages related to the Bible if possible. The relevance of consulting a philologist can therefore not be over emphasized as I am also not a specialist in philology.

I decided to use the Bible, the primary source, more as a socio-anthropological book rather than just religious or theological book. This also means the study will also help throw better light on the understanding of each language and as religious text within the context of Ibo and Hebrew world and mind set. This is useful today for Christian ministration and fast growing Sabbath, Judaism and Messianic movements in Ibo land. It is today estimated that there are at least thirty thousand young Ibos said to have switched over to Judaism as they have started to claim it back as the religion of their fore fathers; complaining that Christianity and other foreign religions have made Ibo society worse than it would have been if true faith was brought to our people or if their people were allowed to continue to practice their pure religion, though many ancient fathers had included idolatry from their neighbours and their non Ibo wives. The core worship was still in place with the presence of Ibo prophets exhorting the people to come back to the true worship before the Europeans succeeded in entering and taking over the authority.

The young Ibos also argue that any religion that lacks the principle of justice (ofo), freedom and life is good for no one. The ofo is very revered; it is likened to the rod of authority in the hand of Moses given to him by Yahweh. It is regarded as a materialization of justice thereby its presence controls morality, and rules of conduct, and engenders equity and trust. It is believed to have been taken from a tree planted in G-d's compound and handed to the Nri priestly ancestors. Thus certain Nri families thought to originate from the Levitical priestly order of ancient Israel were said to have brought the ofo according to legend. This priestly class ensured the scarification of their males as priests as a puberty rite in preparation for handling the ofo later in life. They carried out circumcision and installed priests and titles among the Ibos.

 Thus according to those said to be reverting to the religion of their forefather, Christianity and Islam and indeed all foreign colonizing religions, lack the principle of justice, freedom and life embedded within the core of Ibo society. Some have argued that the foreign religions had achieved their purpose, which they claim is colonization and economic and political exploitation, they have had the cream of the fruit of Ibo land and should now give way to "allow us reestablish our own authenticity."

I must be quick to say that Judaism probably had not been developed as such by the time the Ibo forefathers migrated from ancient Israel, assuming that there was any such migration. Also people must not confuse being a Jew with being a Hebrew. A Hebrew is a person of the lineage of Abraham though it is impossible to separate being a Hebrew from being in Hebrew religion because it was a theocratic society in which G-d operated in different designations as "ayah asher ayah" "I am that I am" (usually said to be yhwh) as well as perhaps 'el, 'adonai', 'elohim', 'elah', 'eloah', Ha Shem etc and came to be owner of everything sacred and profane. There was nothing like secularity or secularism as we have today. This means that to be a Hebrew means to belong to G-d who was worshipped in different ways under different designations in spite of influences of picking and mixing from their neighbours. However a question remains did all Israel of this time know about "Yahweh" and is "Yahweh" actually the same as the ayah asher ayah, "I am that I am?" Perhaps some may not have heard of "Yahweh" worship but worshipped G-d in their own local understanding. Yet we could see that "Yahweh" began to be associated with a race during the time of Enosh, a descendant of Seth (Genesis 4). Perhaps the descendants of Seth through Enosh were called people of "Yahweh" to different them from the descendants of Cain who had killed his brother Abel and incurred a curse from

G-d. Also we can read that it was interaction including intermarriage between the descendants of Seth, known as "people of Yahweh" and the descendants of Cain that led to the destruction of the first creation with flood (Genesis 6).

Also a Jew is a follower of the tenets of Judaism as a religion. Judaism began after the return from exile in Babylon as a new religion aiming to preserve the moral and national values of the Hebrew religion before the exile, although it could be argued that the setting up of synagogues in the land of exile (Babylon) was the first step to ensure the religion and its values did not die out due to foreign influence. However this period introduced a backslidden and adulterated religion completely different from the religion of "I am that I am" handed over by Moses. Perhaps the book of first Chronicles seems to aim to correct shortfalls in the colonial religion that emerged following intermarriages with foreign women, hostilities, wars and deportations.

In actual fact it could be argued that only the children of Judah who came back as remnants from Babylon and rebuilt the temple in Jerusalem were the ones who laid the foundation for the invention of Judaism which was a further degeneration of the Mosaic religion of "the I am that I am." By the time of John the Baptist and Yashayah (also written as Yeshua) Christ, Judaism had many sects split by different beliefs and emphasis: Pharisees, Sadducees, and the Zealots; there were also the scribes, the God fearers, Jewish proselytes. The leadership of the religion was also different from the ancient Hebrew worship which was centred around the worship of G-d as Yahweh, 'el', 'Adonai', etc who acted as Lord and King over all national matters, through the guidance of priests and prophets. The prophets were made up of Pro-claimers of Justice (nabhi), Seers (roeh), Forth tellers (hoseh), and Yahweh related with the people directly and not through a council of elders as Judaism introduced in the name of the Sanhedrin and the rabbis and chief priests who interpreted the Hebrew Bible to suit themselves with compromises and alterations. They introduced the Talmud another Book which became authoritative and divided into Mishna and Gemara and later the halachic way as the only true way to Judaism and its practice, according to the orthodox faith.

Thus anyone speaking of going back to the religion of their forefathers should be clear as to which religion they are referring to: the religion of the tribes of Gadite, Benjamites, Manasseh, Reubenites and may be others ancestors to which Eri and others, the supposed progenetors of, perhaps, most of the Ibo peoples belonged and practiced, or the Old Testament Religion of King Solomon's time' that are not much different from the religion of our Ibo ancestors until the coming of foreign religions (Christianity, Islam, and Catholicism); or Judaism which replaced it, and which Yeshua, the Christ, and John the Baptist condemned the hypocrisy of the adherents. John the Baptist is often regarded as the last of the Old Testament Prophetic system by some Christian scholars, yet the Ibo religion had prophets before the advent of Christianity in Iboland and enacted mysteries not different from the mysteries involved in the Old Testament religion that endeared them to their neighbours including the people of the Benin Kingdom who sought their assistance. In order to offer this assistance the Ibo experts were said to have relocated to the Benin Kingdom where they and their descendants lived until they were eventually sent back to their original Ibo kith and kin.

Perhaps extreme syncretism obscured the religion of the Ibo ancestors making it inadequate for a peaceful relationship between the human, God and nature which is the desire of all religionists. The ala worship was supposed to ensure this harmony. Without this harmony there can be no justice and therefore any religion lacking justice is no use to the society. The question is will Judaism provide the peace and justice upon which the Ibo society was originally built and which the religion of our forefathers stood for, even if one argues that it should be accepted as the only representation of the Hebrew religion of old to which our forefathers belonged?

It is therefore important one appreciates the difficulty of this project and the fact that without good background in the languages of the Bible and the ancient near east the effort would be futile. Also in one of the meetings the chairperson gave us a history of how the task of embarking on the project came about. It turned out that it was a federal government challenge to Ibo scholars in Nigeria to 'unfold the origin of the Ibos which has been obscure if not an enigma, that had been existing only in rumours'. This was at least what the professor who was the chairman of the research team told us and that the challenge originated from the then director of research of the National Institute for policy and strategic studies (NIPSS) Kuru, near Jos.

Fear of reprisals against the Ibo

Meanwhile, as stated earlier some Ibo at that time, especially among the academia and Christianity were doubtful of any such linkage genealogically with Israel. Some scholars felt that it was a venture for Jewish political benefit and nothing more. Some even suspected colonial plans. Those that presented the most ferocious opposition against any talk of Hebrew linkage as stated earlier were Ibo Roman Catholic priests who would not want to be 'identified with those people who killed Christ, the son of God'. Some were my colleagues as lecturers in the same department of Religious Studies, Philosophy and Theology that included Islamic and Christian Studies. Others said that connecting with Israel was of no political advantage to the Ibo; that it might endanger the Ibo existence in Nigeria as some of those who already did not want Ibo peoples in Nigeria might use it as opportunity to persecute Ibo peoples once again. Others feared it might lead to genocide against the Ibo peoples again. I can remember one of these expressing the fear that the pogrom would spread worldwide, not just in Nigeria or Africa only. As the world did not come to protect the Ibo during the last killing pogrom against them what more now that it might be universal killing of the Ibo.

My own reason for refusing any talk of the linkage, as hinted earlier was that outsiders should not come to tell us we are a people, lost from our roots. The Ibo peoples should be left to feel lost and as far as I was concerned I was not lost and my forefathers did not teach me that we are a lost people; so, 'to hell with all this political nonsense'. That was how, I felt in those days of doubt before I embarked on the study.

It became apparent that the language dimension should be added to the study; this would be supported with further common cultural practices notably in agriculture and community life of the two peoples. As a way of making the language study credible I regarded as relevant to our task only those words and expressions similar or same in pronunciation and meaning in both Ibo and Hebrew languages. Perhaps the current study will enable opponents of this venture to change their mind. That the Ibos are Jews has been settled and concluded however there is also need to authenticate this fact through research study such as this. Although one of the objectives of the KSSFI Nigeria chapter is to encourage the Ibos to accept the Law of Return to Israel, promulgated in 1948 and to persuade the Israeli government to grant all members of the KSSFI right to enter and settle in Israel, including the Ibos, as stated earlier. However as stated earlier, it has been observed that not many Ibos are interested in going to settle in Israel, for the right to return as visitors by free entry for business, yes, they may ask for that, but not many are craving to enter and settle.

The Ibo Peoples' Jewish Identity

Perhaps an important issue surrounding the Hebrew origin of the Ibo is that it is difficult to identify them with any of the Jewish sub groups. Are we to accept we are actually Sepahardic? Or do we test if we are Ashkenazi, the Mizrachi, Yemenite, Ethiopian or oriental/Asian stock? It is even difficult to say if we could be regarded as one of the backslidden groups. Are we to be regarded as anusim, crypto Jews, Meshumad, or Min. Obviously we cannot be regarded as Min as the ancestors remained believers of the one true G-d though they were forced to practice it in syncretised or eclectic forms? We cannot be regarded as the Mashadi because the Ibos fought off the Islamic invaders and collectively rejected the Islamic religion up till date. Also the Ibos traditionally repudiate the 'Arab' in their collective unconsciousness. In fact the word "Arab" is used to derogatorily refer to someone worse than an 'osu' as stated above (see also osu section below), someone to be avoided, to not do business with and must not be associated with.

As stated earlier the Ashkenazim (plural) are descendants of Jews from France, Germany and Eastern European. They derive their name from "Ashkenaz" by which Germany was known. Most American Jews are of the Ashkenazi stock who emigrated from Germany and Eastern Europ from mid 1800s to early 1990s.

The Sephardi, as observed earlier are descendants of Jews from Spain, Portugal, North Africa and the Middle East and their descendants.

The adjective "sephardic" and corresponding nouns Sephardi (singular) and Sephardim (plural) are derived from the Hebrew word "Sepharad" which refers to Spain. Sephardic Jews are often subdivided into Sephardic from Spain and Portugal, and Mizrachim from Northern Africa and the Middle East. The word "Mizrachi" comes from the Hebrew word for "Eastern." There is much overlap between Sephardim and Mizrachim. Until the 1400s, the Iberian Peninsula, North Africa and Middle East were controlled by the Muslims, who generally allowed Jews to move freely throughout the region. It was under this relatively benevolent rule that Sephardim Judaism developed. When the Jews were expelled from Spain in 1492 many of them were absorbed into existing Mizrachi communities in North Africa and the Middle East. Most early Jewish settlers of North America were Sephardic. The first Jewish congregation in North America, "Shearith Israel", founded in what became New York in 1684 was Sephardic and are still active. Philadelphia's first Jewish congregation, "Mikveh Israel" founded in 1740, was a Sephardic one and also is still active. In Israel little more than half of all Jews are Mizrachim, and descended from Jews who have been in the land since ancient times or who were forced out of Arab countries after Israel was founded. Most of the rest are Ashkenazic, descended from Jews who came to the Holy Land controlled by Ottoman Turks or from the Holocaust survivors, or from other immigrants who came at various times. About 1% of the Israeli population is the black Ethiopian Jews who fled during the brutal famine of the late 1980s and early 1990s. There is an Ibo Jewish community in Tel Aviv, Israel today, who are Jews because they are said to have reconverted to Judaism faith as there are many such communities in the USA, and Nigeria. However majority are Messianic Jews.

Difference between the Sephardic and Ashkenazic Jews

The Sephardic and the Ashkenazics have same basic belief, However the Sephardic seem to be more orthodox with small difference in their interpretation of the Jewish Law (halakhah). The Ashkenazis are glued to the Halakha and depend on commentaries on it, while the Sephardics have a holistic approach to learning and philosophy. The Sepahardics adhere more to the whole Bible than commentaries on the halakha or Talmidic Laws. The Sephardics seem to be closer to the Babylonian tradition while the Ashkenazics are more Europea, prcisely more German.

There is also difference in Food. The Sephardic eat corn, rice, peanuts and beans during the celebration of Passover, while the Ashkenazic avod such foods.

The Sephardic do not have formal organized movements like the Ashkenazic.

The Sephardics integrate into non Jewish cultures, while the Ashkenazics tend to generate tension with non Jewish cultures.

The Sephardic's thought and culture are more influenced by Arabic and Greek philosophy and science and so are more holistic to learning.

A major difference also relevant to this study is that the Sephardic and the Ashkenazics pronounce Hebrew words differently, particularly of few vowels and consonants. However the Ashkenazics are learning to adapt to the Sephardic pronunciation because that is the pronunciation used in Israel

Both have different prayer services and sing with different melodies

They have different holiday customs and different traditional foods. For example the Sephardic eat Sufganiot (jelly doughnuts) to celebrate chanukkah while Ashkenazics eat latkes (potato pancakes) to celebrate chanukkah.

Sephardics speak Latino which is based on Spanish and Hebrew while the Ashkenazics speak Yiddish which is based on German and Hebrew.

The Yemenite Jews and Ethiopian Jews (also known as Beta Israel called Falashas) have some distinct customs and traditions.

The very many Jewish classifications so far identified include, the Italian Jews (Ebrei Italiani, Yehudim Italkim); the Jews of Asti, Fossano, Moncalvo (Appam) said to be of French stock of the time of Rashi; the Jews of San Nicandro said to descend from neofiti of San Nicandro Garganico; Iranian Jews living in Rome and Milan; Libyan Jews living in Rome and Livarno; Romaniotes; Mizrahim; Cochin-Malabar Jews said to be the oldest group of Jews in India dating back to the days of

King Solomon and most have immigrated to Israel others to Australia; Bene Israel, Beta Israel, called the Falashas that is interpreted as, "unwanted stranger"in the native language (please see above); Benei Anusim; Lemba; Crimean Kairaites; Krymchaks; Crypto Jews; Mosaic Arabs; Subbotniks and the Beta Abraham. We also have the Russian Jews, British Jews, etc. The classification may not be strictly classes of Jews but disparate communities; each following the practice of either the broad Ashkenazi or Sephardi culture. What we can notice readily is that there are fewer Jews of Africa mentioned above. This is perhaps because many of the Jews of Africa are yet to be recognized by official rabbinism as genuine Jews. Some of these African Jews have already been mentioned in this study. Prominently omitted is the Ibo Jews in spite of the fact that the history of the Ibo ancestors' migration to this part of Africa is to a remarkable extent tied up with the history of those called "Falashas" of Ethiopian and the Jews of Sao Thome, Jews of North Africa and the Black Jewish Empire of Ghana whose citizen were spread all over West Africa etc.

Also the differences among even the practicing Jews (Sephardim and Ashkenazim), who are closer to each other and of much later historical existence than the Ibo ancestors and perhaps other West African Jews that is characterized by very ancient Jewish experiences, become significant to this study. One implication is that much of the experiences of the Ibo must be far more different judging from the ancient times their ancestors left Israel and the Middle East. This is also significant because Africa was named by the descendants of Afer, who was a son of Abraham through Keturah. Certainly this extends to very remote past. What this remoteness implies is that the Jews of Africa are far more ancient than the Ashkenazi or any other Jewish group so far known. This also makes the question should Ibo Jews be aligned to any of these later versions of Jews or should they carve out their own existence as unique Jews in diaspora.

Also in the area of language study, it becomes difficult to expect the Ibo language to be same as the much later developed languages of the Ashkenazim and the Sepharadim. The Ibo language is therefore more likely to be more ancient and closer to the ancient Biblical Hebrew words and expressions than these present day Jewish/ Hebrew languages, especially that of the Ashkenazim that has been adulterated by European languages and called Yidish. In fact Yidish can be likened to pidgeon version of the ancient or main Hebrew language. This realization also means that Hebrew has many versions of as there are Jewish groups as local language vocabularies of the centres of location influence the language.

The dilemma of the Ibo within the world Jewry becomes more complicated if they are to be viewed as Jews. This is why I believe that the Ibo people should be regarded as Hebrews of the stock of Jacob, Moses, Ephraim, Aaron, Gad, Reuben, Manasseh, Benjamin, Levi, etc as the legends seem to indicate. Above all the Israelites in the Bible addressed themselves as Jews. For example in Judges 14 when Samson wanted to marry his parents questioned why the woman he wanted to get married to was not a Jew? According to the Bible... they objected strenuously. " why don't you marry a Jewish girl? Why must you go and get a wife from these heathen Philistines? Isn't there one girl among all the people of Israel you could marry?" (Judges 14: 1-3) This is almost a replica of the objection I received from my fellow Ibos when I wanted to marry a non Ibo as I stated above. The important point here is that all Israelites in ancient past regarded themselves to be Jews. This means that they remained Jews wherever their descendants might have emigrated to. Therefore the Ibos are Jews on this fact.   As I explained above, Judaism as a religion was developed in Babylon when the exiled Jews, having lost their Temple worship replaced it with the synagogue system. On return from exile the religion set up by Ezra and Nehemiah seemed to have followed the synagogue style. By the time of the Roman occupation the system had been developed into various sects each vying for a position of authority and believing in dissimilar doctrines and practices. Eventually the Pharisees dominated the scene and the rabbinic system of the Pharisee imposed strict religious dos and don'ts of which Yeshua, the Messiah, questioned their authority over the people because they were hypocritical in their sincerity and practice of justice and freedom to the people on which True Worship should be based according to the religion of Abraham. Yeshua called them "whited sepulchers." John the Baptist called them "brood of vipers." Many of them compromised the traditions of their ancestors and the religion Judaism was eventually corrupted to what we see them to be today. It was the same corrupted religious leaders that handed Yeshua over to the Romans to be crucified. The Sephardim are those who claim adherence to the original traditions and spirit of the fathers as founded in Babylon. What true Jewish worship requires is obedience to the rule of Justice and freedom to worship Yahweh in the way the fathers had taught them; not on the bais of belonging to genealogy of Abraham.

Many Ibos have become converted to Judaism today and are therefore Jews by virtue of their convertion. The common manners and customs of the Hebrew and the Ibo are to be emphasized as important in determining who they actually are and not the present day rabbinic Jewish practices, manners and customs, especially the Ashkenazic attitudes and rules. Therefore if by Jews is meant every descendant of Jacob and those who played major role in the religion of Abraham beginning from ancient days to the present then the Ibo are de facto Jews. But if by Jew is meant a member of the Judaism religion as defined by certain Ashkenazic teachings and practices today, then Ibo peoples had perhaps, existed before even that religion was founded (3000-2000BC) judging from the time the yam crop had been established in Iboland. Certainly Ibo ancestors had been settled in the land prior to the giving of the yam crops by G-d himself according to oral tradition.

Also if by Jew is meant anyone born of a Jewish woman in the sense defined by rabbinic Ashkenazic Jews then Ibo are Jews. Acceptable evidence is, perhaps, the fact that my great grandfather's identity like that of all Ibos of his era was matrilineal as he bore the name Udum Adah. Adah is a name given to a female Jew. These names as stated above, though Hebrew in origin, are traditional Ibo names. The next two chapters are dedicated to attempts at identifying Ibo words as Hebrew or Hebrew words as Ibo in which way and manner that may be viewed. My hope and prayer is that this investigation of similarities in these two languages will continue beyond this study.

OUR COMMON MANNERS AND CUSTOMS AS HEBREW PEOPLES

Chapter 5
Ibo and Hebrew Language Connection

In spite of the differences in language development of present day Jews from the ancient language of their ancestors, my experience shows that whenever any talk of Ibo Hebrew genealogical linkage is mentioned people's mind goes to language similarities. The question has been, "is there any connection in language between the Ibo and Hebrew peoples?" It is as if language connection is expected to seal the debate of linkage between the two peoples. In fact one professor of the linguistic department of the University of Jos told me that if there was no language connection or language similarity between the two peoples any research attempt on this subject would not be credible and would be a waste of time.

The pressure and desperation to provide this evidence perhaps explains why some people have made what can be described as hasty and uneducated attempt to connect the two languages. Consequently words were manufactured and "doctored" to mean what they were completely unconnected with. An example given earlier is Genesis that has been transcribed into Ibo i je n'isisi; which literally means: 'to begin from the starting point'. 'Eden' was transcribed as 'ide' which is Ibo word for 'pond' and 'Isaac' was transcribed as 'ishi-aku' which in Ibo stands for 'heir to wealth' or 'head of the father's inheritance.' But the Bible says Garden of Eden (גן עדן)

And we know that 'garden of Ide, "garden of pond" does not make any sense, or does it? We also know that the Bible states that Isaac means "Laughter" and not "heir to wealth" or "heir to riches" as these Igbo writiers claim. We also know that the Hebrew word transcribed "Eve" is "Hawwah" and therefore cannot be "Ifite" as these Igbo writiers claim.

Another Ibo writer who confessed being ignorant of the Hebrew language claimed that 'Netanyahu' is an Ibo word. According to him 'Netanyahu' is an Ibo word which means 'neta yahu', literally to look after them', 'oversee them'.   This writer who claims ignorant of the Hebrew language challenged Ibo scholars to delve into research on the much talked about Ibo-Hebrew linkage especially the two language similarities which perhaps attracted him (see article by Mbonu Okeke, 'Netanyahu' an Ibo man? In Champion Newspaper published in 1996. See also Max Elemuo et al, unpublished Manuscript, 1995). He is to be commended for being honest to admit that he was fabricating words to suit. This is unlike most other Igbo people, some of whom even claim to be "Professors" who dishonestly fabricated words to deceive.

There are other Ibo scholars who have shamefully carried out arbitrary connections of the two languages in such a manner that it would be too shameful and substandard academically to even highlight them in this work no matter how sincere they might have been in their intention.

The above mentioned unscholarly efforts at language connection are, perhaps, as a result of frustration, and in-patience which the enlightened Ibo faces for being told he is a Hebrew without convincing evidence. Worse still is the fact that those Ibo who have the tools to carry out such a research do not seem to be interested in such a research or lack the confidence to embark on it. It also shows how much obsessed people are with language connection as evidence of the Jewishness of the Ibo peoples. Langauge connection in this study is not aimed to as evidence that Ibos are Jews. It is included solely to buttress the fact that the Ibo and the Hebrew have comman manners and customs that include the use of language and consequently that both attach similar meaning to life. Thus with language similarity we can say the two peoples have similar philosophy to life that is to say similar thought pattern and conceptualization of reality.

The need for Caution

Although it is true that there is a dire need for researching into the Ibo-Hebrew language linkage caution must be taken in the approach to such a attempt. There must be need for the Ibo to 'make haste slowly' in this endeavour. Let the research be left to those who are tutored in the art of research including in the appropriate languages, to do so. As much as the efforts indicated above are commendable, the arbitrary connection of words from Hebrew to Ibo and vice versa will do no good to any attempt to examine the Ibo-Hebrew linkage. Words which have no Hebrew root have been wrongly regarded as being Hebrew. This is to say the least ridiculing the Ibo peoples. It in fact appears as stupidity in desperation. Only the LORD Himself should be left to raise the right people to embark on this task as it has been a continuous research and will continue to be so.

If the Hebrew and Ibo languages are to be in any way connected, the words concerned must not only be pronounced in similar ways but also must be similar in meaning. This is the guiding principle in the attempt made below. The writer is not a linguist though he believes that he knows enough Hebrew and Ancient Near Eastern Languages, Latin, Arabic and Greek to give him the tools to carry out the brief study outlined below. He also at least knows that Genesis is not a Hebrew word and that Netanyahu is not an Ibo word and that Isaac is not an Ibo word as he knows many arbitrarily quoted Ibo words as Hebrew are not anywhere near being Hebrew words. Words should be explored from the point of view of the language which owns it. There is therefore need for honesty and sincerity. This is essential to avoid being ridiculed or trivializing an important issue.

To do justice to a study such as this, the researcher(s) need to be aware that the two languages concerned have had modifications all through the thousands of years of their existence and usage and have interacted with and influenced by many other languages and cultures. Like any other branch of culture, a language is dynamic and changes with time, both in vocabulary and usage. This must be appreciated as connections are made of ancient languages in present day usage as the Ibo and Hebrew languages. Also the original vocabulary of these languages is perhaps lacking or missing as that has been lost through processes of enculturation de-acculturation, and acculturation. This is perhaps expected to have affected the Ibo language more because the original writing of the language seemed to have been lost, corrupted by colonial influence and religious bigotry. For example almost all Ibo names have been changed both in their written forms and pronunciation. What we have today is certainly not the original. 'Oma mbala' has been corrupted to 'Anambra,' 'Owu eri' has been corrupted to 'Owerri,' 'mbi eri' has been written as 'mberi' just to mention these. And as stated earlier many native Ibo name words have had their final 'h' dropped for one reason or the other, including, perhaps, for religious parochial reasons. It is as if the enemy invaded the Ibo land and did as it liked while the Ibo gazed helplessly. Syncretism also contributed to watering down Ibo words as foreign words infiltrated into Ibo vocabulary while the original Ibo words were dropped or modified.

Therefore all those who think that language similarities between the Ibo and Hebrew should be the yard stick for establishing the ancestral linkage between the two peoples may be over stating the relevance of language similarity for credible proof of such a linkage, as important, invaluable and vital as it is.

However in spite of the limitations of producing objective and reliable language study between the two peoples the writer must state that he was amazed by his discovery and sees the need for further research efforts in this area. He calls on those Ibo peoples who can remember the old Ibo words and expressions in proverbs, wise sayings, and cultic practices to please come and assist and help in carrying out this important research. Although the writer has been a student of the Hebrew language for at least thirty-four years and has had opportunity to teach the language overseas and in Africa, and he is an Ibo, this is not enough to claim expert knowledge of the languages. Moreover both languages are complex as there are very many dialects that could be categorized as Hebrew as well as Ibo. More so as stated above we cannot speak of an Ibo people, we can only speak of Ibo peoples which include all parts of the past eastern region which was formerly called Ibo country and beyond. Also we cannot speak of Hebrew people but rather the Hebrew peoples. So there are dialects and varied cultic terms which would be relevant in this study. Therefore our effort would be holistic as we gather words that project ancient usages of the two languages as well as present day usages among the various peoples related as Hebrews and Ibos.

Select Ibo Words and Phrases as evidence of common manners and customs with the Hebrew peoples

Words in Hebrew that have similar pronunciation and meaning in Ibo.

Ba- ba a: This is a Hebrew word (verb) which means 'come'. The Owerri Ibo use the word 'ba a' to mean 'come in'.The "You' is implied. Parts of Calabar also use the word 'ba' to mean 'come' The generic Ibo word for 'come' is pronounced 'bia', 'Bya'. We also have 'bata' to mean 'come in' and 'you' is implied; with the 'ta' referring to 'you' second person singular or plural just like the Owerri Ibo would say 'ba-a' in which the 'you' pronoun could be singular or plural. The Hebrew word 'ba 'itha' comes to mind and mean 'you come in'; the 'you' in the expression is also implied by the pronoun 'ta' in both languages. Thus we have 'batha', or 'bata' in Ibo language, and 'Ba'tha' in the Hebrew language not only pronounced in the same way but also mean or express the same thing. In Hebrew "baitha", "beth" 'baita' refers to "house." The Owerri 'ba-a' and the Hebrew 'ba a' are pronounced in the same way and mean the same.

Berishit: This is the Hebrew word translated "in the beginning" at the very first verse of the Genesis. "Be-rishi" reminds one of the Ibo word "Berishi", "benishi", and its dialectal dirivatives for emphasis "bedo nishi", "bedo rishi". The Ibo equivalent means the same as the Hebrew, "In the beginning," "starting from the beginning", "start at the beginning" (as an instruction or advice).

Bikko, bikkuo- This Ibo word is universal Ibo word and is similar to the Hebrew word 'biku'(plural: bikkurim) The English translation of 'biku' connotes 'please', 'I plead with you', 'I beg you'. It implies granting honour to the one from whom favour is sought. To understand its real meaning needs an understanding of the meaning of the Hebrew 'biku', 'first fruit'. The granting of the position of 'first fruit' to a person implies spiritual inferiority. Thus to offend a person is regarded as belittling oneself; making oneself inferior to the offended. The Ibo word 'bikko', 'bikkuo' is a reminder to the position of the first fruits given to Yahweh. Yeshua became the first fruit of all creation by the Cross event (death and resurrection) Thus Hebrew 'biku' objectifies

Ibo 'biko' and both connote plea before the superior from who favour is being sought.

Ga, gara- This Hebrew word means 'to live'. This word could remind one of the Ibo word "gara" which is often used to refer to someone who has gone to somewhere say journeyed to a place, another town or place. We also say O ga la, o gar a: He has gone to ... The important fact is that to go in Ibo in the sense of 'gara' implies going to somewhere else 'to live' for at least for some time. This is different from the word command 'ga' 'go' 'proceed'. Thus when the Ibo says Nkem gara London or Nkem a ga la London he means that Nkem has gone to London to live or to stay away for some time, in a far distant place. Thus the similarity between the Ibo and Hebrew use of the word ga gara is obvious in spite of the thousands of years of separation and historical experience. The dialectal difference between the North and the South produces the pronunciation gala, gara.

Oleh: This Hebrew word is used to ask for the cost of an item and to ask of the total count of an item in numbers. It is the same as the Ibo word 'oleh' in usage and in pronunciation. Oleh in Ibo means: 'how much', how many' as in Hebrew.

Dal: is a Hebrew word which is used to refer to the downtrodden i.e refers to one who has fallen from grace or from a height. In Ibo it reminds one of the saying da ala which means to fall down, to loose one's high position in life. Thus the statement 'Okonkwo a da la' in Ibo means that Okonkwo is no more as rich or highly placed as he was known to be. He has joined the downtrodden ones. To da ala also means to fall down literally to fall from a height. This is applied to social status also.

Dod- dodah: This Hebrew word 'dod' refers to 'uncle' while 'dodah' means 'aunt'. These words readily remind one of the Ibo equivalent 'dede' 'uncle' and 'dadah' for 'aunt'. They can also be shortened as 'de' and 'da' 'do' depending on the particular Ibo dialect being heard.

Lo: This is a Hebrew negative particle which means 'no', 'never', 'not'. It reminds one of the Ibo equivalent 'lo',' olo' also means 'no' 'never' 'not'. The 'O' in the Owerri version is an emphasis.

Gad- This Hebrew word means 'to enlarge' 'to progress', 'fortune'. It reminds one of the Ibo expression: 'i gadi' which means 'you will continue to be'. This is supposed to be understood as you will continue 'to progress', 'to enlarge your existence', 'to exist well', 'to prosper', to be fortunate, to have fortune

Shish: This word in Hebrew means six (6). The Ibo word for six is ishii. But reminds one of the past when the Ibo word for six pence was shishi. This perhaps shows that sometime in the past the Ibo must have used the word shish or its equivalent to refer to six or that the Hebrew modified their use of the word from ishii to shish. Whatever the case the connection of the two is obvious.

Asara: This Hebrew word means ten (10). This word reminds one of the Ibo word asaa. It is possible that an Ibo dialect pronounces it asara which means seven (7). The similarity is that the words are numbers and sound alike though they represent different numbers among the peoples. The question is which of the two languages interchanged the numbers. Does asara mean seven or ten in number count?

Ani: This Hebrew word means 'I' a first person singular in English. It readily calls to mind the Ibo word 'anyi' which itself means 'we' and is a first person plural. It is possible that a version of Ibo pronounce it as 'ani'. The word in the two languages is personal pronoun. The question to ask is how the singularity and plurality came about. Which of the two groups changed the use of the word? Who dropped or added the 'y' out of the two peoples? Or for the Ibo version who added the 'y'; whatever the answer, the connection between the two words is obvious. They certainly had the same root in its formation but perhaps acculturation and enculturation or de-acculturation modified it with time.

Brit: This is the Hebrew word pronounced 'berit'. The word means 'covenant' and is usually associated with the mark of the covenant "ot berit'. It reminds one of the Ibo word "gbritsi" which refers to special mark on the face of special Ibo priests of old who went about all Ibo land to carry out ritual sacrifices including male circumcisions. These marks and priest have been rendered in different forms by writers and include "mbrenche", "mgbirishi", etc depending on dialect and on who is writing for example an English writer may not be able to pronounce the word correctly as the native speakers. The connection is that in the two languages they represent 'a mark', a sign of an agreement to a duty.

We: This Hebrew particle is used to express particle as: 'to', 'and', 'so', 'then', 'but' etc and other conjunctions. It is used in the same way in Ibo expressions and the translation given to it in English depends on the context, just as it is in Hebrew. For example the Ibo would say: we ba, we bia, 'we bya', 'we da'la', 'nkem we si' or 'we shi' just to mention these. These mean 'so he or she or they, came' 'and he or she or they fell down', 'and nkem said'. The Hebrew would say we'omai' 'and he said'

Me: this Hebrew word 'me' can be rendered as particle for "from" "with" "through": It reminds one of the Ibo word me, applied to mean "from" in some Ibo dialects. For example we say meudum. With time it became umu, thus we say umu udum that mean from udum, from udum is to be understood as children of Udum, those who came from udum.

Nu. This Hebrew particle refers to "our" for example the Hebrew say "elohenu", "our God." In Ibo language it is "unu" means "your." How did the particle become plural third person in one but plural pronoun second person in the other? Though it is a personal pronoun particle in both languages.

Other words include Eri, abi, adah, udum, adama, abana, abba, asadu, ma'adu,

Ma'ad: This Hebrew word which means 'to be many', 'to increase', 'to add to'; also it means as 'to begin to grow'; 'to multiply' in the sense of 'adding to', 'multiplying'

The word is also related to 'ma'adu' which also means 'to be many', 'multiply', 'increase', 'to add to' Thus the meaning of the Ibo word 'madu'

(BDB: The New Brown Driver and Briggs – Gesenius Hebrew-English Lexicon 1979: 547) The word ma'ad is also related to 'me'od' as in 'tov me'od': meaning 'exceedingly good', 'exceedingly beautiful.'(Genesis 1:31).

'Ma'ad' and 'ma'adu' remind one of the Ibo word for 'mankind', 'a person', addressed as 'madu'. The exact understanding of the Ibo word 'madu' has been given various interpretations among Ibo scholars. Some regard it as referring to the beauty of mankind. According to this school of thought God expressed the word mma (beauty) du (has existed, has come)) which means 'there is beauty' or 'this is beauty'. The Hebrew version and understanding of ma'ad in ancient world can help our understanding of the meaning of the expression 'madu'. We can surmise from the Hebrew and other ancient near eastern peoples that it is an expression that describes the role of a new birth, the place of man on earth which is to perpetuate the lineage, the existence of mankind, to continue existence and increase and multiply. Madu is therefore that object through which mankind is to increase and multiply, and through which a family's continuity is guaranteed, through which means humanity continues to exist. Thus maadu in a sense means 'continuity of humanity' or 'humanity' in its full expression. Thus although there could be an element of beauty in mankind as a creature it is not necessarily the most beautiful creatures we see in the world of creation. What is beautiful about the human being is that ability to dominate, increase and multiply and perpetuate its existence through procreation of its kind and continue the lineage of its progenitor. Whenever a new child is born the world rejoices because giving birth is a way of saying the world, humanity, is to continue to exist.

Ma; mah: In Hebrew this is an interrogative particle. The Ibo also use ma; mah to express a question. The Ibo would ask: i ma Nkechi? i.e do you know Nkech?, 'ma ka gini', i.e because of what?

Miri: This is an Ibo word for water, drinking water. The Hebrew equivalent is 'mayim', being a plural word in Hebrew may be rendered as "waters". How the word "mayim" was turned to "miri" in Ibo is perhaps historical and may not be easy to decipher. How the word miri came to be used for water among the Ibo ancestors remains a mystery to us today.

An explanation has been suggested that it could be connected with Prophetess Miriam who played an important role in the prophetic fulfillment of God's promise to bring Israelites out of Egypt, and two of the biggest highlights involved water. She watched over the baby Moses as he floated among the bulrushes of Nile River in a basket. Miriam bravely intervened and offered her mother's services as a wet nurse when Pharaoh's daughter rescued Moses. Miriam led the singing of praises and dancing and rejoicing after God safely rescued the Israelites through the Red Sea on dry land while the Egyptian army perished.

The most interesting aspect of Miriam is that after the death of Miriam we read that the people thirsted for water and complained again against Moses:

"Why did you bring us out of Egypt to bring us to this terrible place, a seedless place without fig or a vine or a pomegranate, without even water to drink?" (Numbers 20: 5).

It is probable that the people were actually mourning the loss of Miriam, who was like a mother to the Israelites, especially women and children. This is underscored by the fact that a vine can represent a mother at home with her children, little shoots all around her table (cf Psalm 128: 3).

According to Jewish tradition a water-bearing rock followed the Israelites in the wilderness, but dried up and disappeared when Miriam died (cf 1 Cor 10:1-4). This rock is called "the Well of Miriam" because the water that flowed for the Israelites from it was based on her merit. A Jewish Midrash fills the gaps in the Miriam story:

Miriam died and the well was taken away so that Israel would recognize that it was through her merit that they had the well. Moses and Aaron were weeping inside, and the children of Israel were weeping outside and for six hours Moses did not know that the well was gone until the children of Israel entered and said to him: For how long will you sit and cry? Moses answered and said: Should I not cry for my sister who has died? They said to him: While you are crying for one person, cry for all of us! He said to them: Why? They said to him: We have no water to drink. He got up from the ground and went out and saw the well without a drop of water in it. He began to argue with them... (Otzar Midrashim)

God is said to provide them water miraculously. However Moses remained angry for the death of Miriam and said to the people, Listen, you rebels, shall we get water for you out of this rock? (Numbers 20:10)

We see a pun here. The Hebrew word for rebels is "morim" which is spelled the same as the name Miriam in Hebrew, mirim. This is so bearing in mind that the vowels of Hebrew were much later addition, perhaps well away from the ancient pronunciations. Perhaps Moses is thinking of his sister Miriam as he had not yet properly mourned her. He may have misdirected his anger about her death toward the people. In his anger and frustration Moses struck the rock twice and water gushed out and the people had drinking water and for their domestic use. Water is necessary for their survival.

But we read that God had told him to speak to the rock, not to strike it. Therefore the name of the water was called Meribah which means "to argue", "to strive" or "contend", "those were the waters of Meribah because the sons of Israel contended with the Lord, and He proved himself holy among them." We can also refer to this contention as bitterness because the people were not happy with Moses and God (Numbers 20:13). The word Meribah can also be connected to Miriam and so could be written as "miribah". It can be read as Miri-bah, which perhaps connotes miri (yam) "'miri' is in it'"- that is, Miriam is in the waters of contention. Although Miriam's name means "bitterness", it can be read Miri-yam (Miri of the sea), the sea (yam) could be regarded here as a place of contention, chaos, and bitterness. It could also reflect that it was because of the absence of Miriam that the waters dried and caused the bitterness of the people against God and Moses. So, in yet another way, this "woman of the sea" is connected to the waters flowing out of the rock after her death.

We see that the memory of Miriam after her death has remained irrepressible and there are indications that the Ibo ancestors carried on the tradition of connecting water with the name of Miriam. Thus the word miri is deeply rooted in the Miri yam (Miri of the sea) saga as explained above (Messianic Bible lectures, "The Bridge from Impurity to purity" 15 July 2016 emailed to the writer). The Hausa call the Ibo, ya miri. It is claimed that this name for the Ibos emerged when the first Ibo ancestors met the Hausas and asked for water. The Hausa people did not understand what they were asking for or what the Ibos were saying or who they were. However it is said that the Hausa people eventually gave the Ibos water. The communication must have been by way of using non verbal explanation such as pointing with the fingers at what they were asking for (water). But from then they began to identify the Ibos as ya miri. It is not clear what really happened and what the details are. However what can be deduced is that the Ibo ancestors continued the tradition of their forefathers by connecting Miriam with water. Thus till date the Ibo call water "miri". In the Ibo language "yem miri", or "miri yem" literally means "give me water". And in Ibo land water was revered. It was an abomination to sell water or refuse to give anybody water who asks for it. Also the first entertainment was to give a stranger or visitor water among the Ibo. All this perhaps reminds the Ibo of the fact that life became hard and difficult after the death of Miriam because of lack of water needed for the survival of the Israelites as a people.

Iba- This Ibo word is used to refer to a sever fever with high temperature, bitter taste and shivers. This is associated with what the colonial masters called Malaria (literally 'bad air'). The Ibo call it "Ibah". Ibah perhaps connotes the contending with ill health brought about by this fever exemplified by the bitter taste of the tongue the victim suffers. It is perhaps a reminder of the Hebrew word 'Miribah' (meribah), to contend, bitterness, unpleasant situation with life, "threat to life" and associated saga behind its origin in connection with God, Moses, Israelites and after Miriam's death (see Messianic Bible Lectures reaching me 15 July 2016).

Chapter 6
Ibo and Hebrew Language Connection Part 2

In the Part 1 above we began an attempt to examine the Ibo language as Hebrew (ibhri, ivri). The following Ibo words were among those examined: oleh, ga-adi, ga, bia, baa, gara, shishi, anyi, batha, dala, dede, dada, olo etc.

However before we continue this discussion the following key points need be noted:

Firstly, it must be noted that it was not the Ibo peoples who first began studying and writing the Ibo language(s). The Ibo peoples themselves were not allowed to develop their native language and writing by the colonial masters. So what is referred to as Ibo language today, especially the form of writing has little to do with the Ibo peoples rather it is a foreign representation of the original language spoken by our people. Let us not forget the "nsibidi" letters the colonial masters met but which they put aside as they could not understand it but replaced it with the current Arabic letters. Although the "insibidi" letters were pictorial in nature one could easily mistake some of them as similar to Hebrew letters or reversed Hebrew alphabets at best. Perhaps they were cultic in use by the time the colonial masters entered; so had not been publicly used by the common people to be taken seriously. However one can also argue that like every developing language, the Hebrew language was cultic in the same sense as it was only after many centuries that the language became universally coded and used among the peoples. Above all Hebrew was a dialect of other major languages of the time. Hebrew pronunciation was not settled until much later by the Masoretic School of Moses Maimonides (Rambam as he came tyo be called). This makes the two languages difficult to decipher both in morphology and phonetics.

Secondly some scholars claim to categorise the Ibo language as of the kwa or Niger-Congo group of languages. Our contention is that the Ibo language is Semitic. These scholars, some of whom are Ibo, who only copied the colonial masters theories need to think again. The world has come of age. Today is no longer the age in which peoples' minds are colonized by foreign and hastily drawn conclusions about any peoples from pretended research or studies.

Thirdly as Ibo language has Hebrew roots and vice versa, the implication is that experts in Ibo studies and Ibo language must allow academic justice to be done. There is therefore need for more objective restudying of facts including a people's language.

Fourthly, the Ibo peoples themselves must begin to rediscover their roots as Semitic and begin to think and live as such for the benefit of posterity and natural self fulfillment of the creator's intentions. This is also essential for the development of the full potential of the Ibo as a people in this universe.

Fifthly, it would be unfair and myopic to regard the language similarity as mere accident. It is true that there are also observable and documented similarities in folk experiences between the two peoples who are in fact one people separated by historical accidents, the language connection could still be considered enough evidence to convince the doubters to recognize and declare the two peoples as brothers, same kith and kin. This is in addition to the visit of our Jewish brothers in 1997 as stated earlier during which the Ibo peoples were confirmed Hebrews and also made it a national and international issue.

Sixthly whether sceptics accept it or not the Ibo peoples as stated earlier are already incorporated into the King Solomon Separdic Federation International (KSSI). As stated earlier, this is a federation of Sephardic Jews, separate from the white Ashkenazi Jews. They have a permanent representative at the United Nations. Thus investigations into the linkage is to strengthen this membership as it will help to convince people that Ibo peoples are not just being led the goat, so to say; and to check against the menace of charlatans. The research thus remains an ongoing task.

Finally we must appreciate the fact that people of the lost tribes so called have interacted widely and culturally syncretised and modified their ways and manners, customs and philosophy, as well as mix up religious rituals and beliefs. Language variations should therefore not be an issue in identifying who a people are originally. Historical accidents will continue to occur and modify people's native ways and customs. Many Sephardic peoples must have lost their identity as such and this underscores the need and necessity to search them out and reintegrate them. In all fairness it is obvious that the Ibo language closeness to ancient Hebrew despite thousands of years of separation should commend the Ibo peoples for retaining their Hebrew /Jewish identity to the ancient Hebrew/Jewish world rather than repulse them.

Our current words of interest include:

Eze: This Ibo word has come to acquire the meaning 'ruler' 'king'. When one realizes that the Ibo does not recognize kingship...in fact it has been proved that Ibo peoples do not know kingship in the same way as their neighbours recognize kingship as a monarch, questions begin to be raised as to how the Ibo word 'eze' came to mean king and in what sense is it king. The saying,' the Ibo has no king'- 'Ibo amaghi eze' could be contradictory if no explanation is given. In other words, if the Ibo do not know 'kingship' how did the word 'eze' come into their vocabulary?

In answer to the question we can state that the interpretation given to the Ibo word 'eze' as 'king' is wrong and needs to be understood within the original cultural milieu of the usage of the word. It was a much later interpretation of the word's original meaning. We must not forget that the Ibo had what was regarded as 'eze ji' which if translated means 'king of yam', a crop that was domesticated in Igboland (sic) around 3000-2000B.C. (Obiechina 1994: 20). Yet we say the Ibo do not recognize kingship. Yes it is true that the Ibo place no importance to the king's seat. We therefore contend that the Ibo 'eze' has its root in the Hebrew word 'ezer' which means 'help', 'supporter'. Therefore when the Ibo said 'eze ji' they meant the one who was not only blessed with wealth especially yam tubers that was regarded as the king of crops, the king of agricultural produces, he was also what was expected of him in nature and generosity- he was to use his wealth especially yam tubers to support the needy, to assist the community in various ways. Having been blessed by the gods the person was expected to see himself as privileged to be the helper of the people with his wealth especially of yams which was the means to riches at that age. He provided yam seedlings for the young who go to him for such assistance and support and new entrants into the farming work and most often family life also, and he was expected to provide food for the needy, the orphan, the widow, and the invalid. He willingly supported the community projects with his wealth above others and must be "a man with clean hands." Consequently he was entrusted with leadership, settling of disputes etc. Thus his rulership was in the sense of service and generosity to the people. This explains why some of them declined ruling the people alongside the colonial masters who wanted to rule by imposition, human authority, divide and rule and in fact as a monarch. His position as eze was earned and he was seen to deserve that title. Thus it was ignorance of the root of the word 'eze' that made the colonial masters and their scholars to drop the final 'r' as in the Hebrew equivalent word 'ezer'. This Hebrew word ezer is same word G-d used to describe Eve when he promised Adam he was going to get him an 'ezer', the support suitable for Adam. Perhaps the Ibo ancestors in their attempt to glorify Yahweh in all things including titles came to end the spelling of the word with an 'h' as in some other names, when the 'r' was replaced with 'h'. Thus we have 'ezeh' not for the title but for the period when they began to give the name to their male children. In Ibo only males are named 'Ezeh'.

Perhaps the Ibo ancestors that left behind the legacy of not recognizing Kingship/monarchy emigrated from Israel before the Israelites appointed kings to rule over them in ancient times or they must have remained opposed to the idea of human kingship over the rule by Yahweh. They were possibly a remnant of the ancient Israelite priestly class who rejected human rule that retained the concept. It is perhaps noteworthy here to state that the writer's great grand father was the ezer of his people and ruled a vast territory befor the foreign European invasion. He was appointed to continue ruling with the White colonial representative and he accepted doing so. However he after a while abdicated the throne when he discovered he was being enthroned as a monarch over his people. According to one his daughters their father called the whole district, with water in a big calabash, he washed his hands off the rulership with the white man because the white man placed him high above everyone else with the aim to use him against his people; a method of leadership foreign to the way and manner he was ruling our people before the white man came. The irony of it all was that the white man concerned was "the suitor to our eldest sister," my aunt stated.

Iyi: This Ibo word means 'stream', 'Spring' like its Hebrew equivalent. The Hebrew equivalent is written as 'iyin' which also means "stream," "spring". Some Ibo dialects pronounce it in the same way as the Hebrew, 'iyin' and it means same as 'spring', 'stream'. Again ignorance of the root of the word 'iyi' or its pronunciation has led to the dropping of the final 'n' or perhaps it was a dialectal difference. The two words are pronounced the same way and mean the same. Therefore their root must be the same. Their users must be same people. Historical modifications can explain the slight difference in spelling of the word. The word 'iyin'- in Ibo is also used to describe that which is 'dirty' in some dialects; that which needs to be washed because it has been dirtied by the environment, by dust or long usage. In the Ibo language the context differentiates 'iyin' from 'iyi' (stream, spring) The Igbo says oru ola iyin: 'It has became dirty' implying need for washing or cleaning. 'Ka mu ga iyin': 'I am going to the stream or spring,' "let me go to the stream"- usually to wash or fetch water; 'O gara iyin', he/she went to the stream or spring.

Ki tha, kita - This is an Ibo word for 'now', 'immediately'. It is supposed to be understood as 'verily now'. The Hebrew equivalent is 'ki atta' which means 'surely now'.

Ozara- This is Ibo word which means 'an open field ', 'wildernesses, 'a place of trees,' 'the wooded land.' The near Hebrew equivalent is 'zara' which means 'enclosure'. Due to long separation the usage of this word might have been interchanged in its meaning. The question is deciphering which of the two peoples is correct. However there is a sense in which a wilderness could imply an 'enclosure' especially of wood, trees, forests or grass.

Ene, i ne- This Ibo word reminds one of 'to look', 'to see', 'to perceive'. Its Hebrew similarity is 'ene' which means 'eye', 'see'

Mbritshi- This is perhaps the most wrongly spelt Ibo word so far.

The difficulty in writing the exact form of this word is because of its ancient root. The colonial attempt to represent what they heard is commendable. However, again perhaps ignorance of the root word has led to problems. The Ibo renditions of the word by the colonial masters are mgburichi, embrenche, breeche. Thus we read an account of Equiano, the Ibo who was taken into slavery at the age of eleven years in the 17th century. He wrote when he was about age forty his memoirs about his people. According to him, his people were of the Hebrew stock. Quoting from one of his write ups (Narative 2) we read:

My father was of these elders or chiefs. I have spoken of and was styled Embrenche, a term as I remember importing the highest distinction and a mark of grandeur. The mark is conferred on the person entitled to it...most of the judges and senators were thus marked, my father had long borne it. I had seen it conferred on one of my brothers and I was also destined to receive it by my parents. The Embrenche or marked titled men decided disputes and punished crimes for which purpose they always assembled together...

Dr Catherine Acholonu in attempt to trace the Ibo homeland of Equiano, found that three members of his family in Isieke still bore the ichi mark on their faces (Acholonu 1989) and John Adams confirmed that the Igbo word for gentleman was 'Breeche' (Adams 1822:41-42). Also James Africanus Beale Horton, son of an Ibo parents in Sierra Leone described the face scarification of Isuama Ibo as Itshi and that people bearing the marks were referred to as mbritshi (Horton 1868:178).

Bir, bie, is Ibo word for 'to cut'. Thus 'berichi, or bierichi' would refer to people with a cut mark on their faces usually for special identification of function or title.

It is the belief of the writer that the mark referred to here also remind one of the ancient Hebrew covenant mark which the ancestors came with from ancient Palestine, although Obiechina has linked it to the scarification as representing the mythic sacrificed children who emerged as the yam crops (Obiechina 1994: 20) among the Ibos. Thus the Ibo word rendered as 'britshi' originally should read as the Hebrew berit 'ish which means 'covenant man'. In Hebrew the berit means to cut a covenant. Thus we have 'ot berit' which means literally 'the sign of the covenant' in reference to Abrahamic circumcision covenant with El Shaddai (Genesis 17). Thus the Ibo gentlemen and judges with these marks on their faces were men who lived their lives according to the covenant having had the mark of the covenant cut on him. Thus he was referred to as berit ishi, 'mbirishi', 'brenche', 'the covenant man'. This covenant can be said to refer to the covenant Yahweh made with the Ibo ancestors and their descendants thousands of years ago (Genesis 15). In the Old Testament the mark of the covenant was referred to as 'ot berit as stated earlier. The Hebrew b'rit is translated 'covenant' short form of 'to cut a covenant'. A full account of this myth of the covenant circulates among the Ibo Nri myth of origin and life practices which this short paper cannot delve into here. Only to state that these covenant men were said to have travelled around and among the Ibo people to carry out certain covenant rituals including male circumcision, and identity marks on faces of titled men.

Berishit: This Hebrew statement means 'in the beginning'. It is the first phrase of the Hebrew Bible and Christian Old Testament text. The Ibo word for the same expression would read bedo rishi', rishi, berishi. We should not be surprised to see an added particle 'de' 'do' as modification do occur in languages as the people move around among other tribes and peoples. However if the 'be' is removed in the Hebrew form, we have rishit which is same with the Ibo equivalent rishi that also means 'in the beginning' or 'from the beginning' or 'beginning, 'si rishi' m'rishi literally 'from the beginning.' Again the ending letter 't' found in the Hebrew version must have been dropped in the Ibo version as the years passed. It could still be that the transcribers of the Ibo language dropped or spelt it differently or wrongly. Perhaps there is an Ibo dialect that pronounces the 't' at the end.

Natha, nata: This word means to 'collect', 'receive', 'get'. It reminds one of the Hebrew 'nathan' which means 'he has given'. Nathan also means 'to give'. Thus the name 'Nathanyahu' means 'Yahweh has given' and metanyahu means 'gift of Yahweh'.

The difference is that while one means "collect", 'receive', 'get', the other means 'give' 'gift'. There is in fact not much significant difference in the two because ' getting' , ' receiving' , 'collecting' imply 'giving' and 'giving' implies 'receiving' and 'collecting'.

Anyia: This is an Ibo word which refers to the 'eye' and implies 'ene' (see). The Hebrew equivalent reads 'ayin'. These two words are similar. Again, perhaps dialectal differences could account for the slight difference in spelling. The Ibo word 'ayin' could also refer to the Hebrew word ayin' or ani. Anyi in Igbo means 'we' collective first person, pronoun plural, while the Ibo word 'nu means you people plural. These are similar to the Hebrew equivalents, In Hebrew 'ani' refers to 'I' first person singular as ayin (anyi) means Ibo 'we' first person plural. Both are pronouns except that while one is singular the other is plural.

Kara: this Ibo word is understood as 'to vocalise" "to call out", "to emphatically state". It reminds one of the Hebrew word 'qra' which is used to mean "call", to 'vocalise'.

Ariri: This is an Ibo word for 'contempt', 'derision', In the Hebrew it means 'childlessness', ' barrenness'. In the two communities the barren woman is held in derision, and often in the Ibo community such a woman would refer to herself as one in derision, ' i ri' ariri' literally 'to eat derision'

Arar: This Hebrew word means "curse". It also means to blaspheme, to treat with contempt or disdain, to dispise, and even to be treated lightly or without proper regard. The word fits well with the Ibo word for 'madness'. In the Ibo language "Ara" refers to "madness." It can also refer to excessive action, dangerous wrecklessness, and unnecessary risk. The word is pronounced in the same way as the Hebrew equivalent. It also implies being cursed, and behaving like a cursed person. The curse cast on the person, as believed by the Ibo, makes the person behave as a mad person. A mad person blasphemes. The person is treated with disdain, dispised and related with contempt and without proper regard. Such a person is said to have been struck with 'ara'- a curse put upon him /her.

Apari: This is an Ibo word, also of the Owerri dialect that means foolish or stupid behavior. It is used to humiliate a person who behaves below expectation as human. The Hebrew equivalent as recorde in BDB p 68 " 'apar' " refers to ashes of humiliation and contrition, loathsome, worthless and ignominous behavior 2 Samuel 13, Num 19.

Binah: This name word spoken more in the Bayelsa area means "understanding". In Hebrew it also means "understanding and it is also a feminine name word. It is spelt the same and pronounced in the same way as the Bayelsa Binah.

Aru, alu: This is an Ibo word that means "abomination". The word is perhaps reminder of the Hebrew word " 'alah' ". In the niphil it means to be morally corrupt (BDB p 47). Though not pronounced in similar way, the two words refer to the same corruption in attitude and seem close enough to be connected.

Ibari: Owerri, Etche and Ikwerre dialects nwa Ibari is a common designation given to a female. In Hebrew we have " 'ibar " means "fortress", "strong." Therefore nwa Ibari means 'a strong child" in these Ibo languages

Mbari: This word common among the Owerri and Rivers Ibo languages is a reminder of the Hebrew "bari" whose root is "birah" which refers to fortress, castle, palace. However when personified it becomes bari. Thus the Ibo mbari which is usually referred to as history in art shrine could also refer to personified fortress represented in art. The "m" letter in the Ibo version is perhaps a particle of emphasis.

Kama: this is an Ibo word that is used to say "in other words", "rather", "instead" depending on context. The Hebrew equivalent is "ki 'amar" "Camar". Amar means "to say" speak. Kiamar is used to turn around from what was said earlier BDB 485 and means "but lets say", "instead lets say".

Otobo: this Ibo word is similar to what the English language calls bedroom. The Hebrew equivalent has it's root in the word "tob", "Tov" and means pleasant, good, delightful in the Qal, It is also used as of the tents of Jacob Num 24: 5, of Caresses, pleasant to the higher nature, giving pleasure, happiness, pleasing; it is used to refer to the best part of a woman's house (Esther 2:9) The 'o' in the Ibo version is also a particle of emphasis. Otobo in Ibo should be best interpreted from the Hebrew equivalent to be fully appreciated as the inner most pleasant part of a woman's house that the English people refer to as "bedroom."

Lama, lawah: These Ibo words mean the same: "go home"as implied but literally "to join home", "to join home at home". The Hebrew equivalent is "lawah" and means literally, "be joined to". In the Qal it means "attend", "to join oneself; in the niphal it means "to be joined unto". The common inference here is "to join others", 'to go away from here and go to where you belong and have your rest". That place to join is home by implication.

La ba: This Ibo word means in English "go have rest", "go to bed", "go to sleep." The root of the Hebrew equivalent is "Lab", "lev". The Hebrew lev lab means spirit, mind soul, inner man, will, " or "going out of mind or consciousness" is to go and have rest or "to go to sleep" Psalm 31: 13. Thus the word laba in Ibo language that is common understood in English as "to go to bed" actually means "to go and rest your soul"

Dibia, diber: these Ibo words refer to what the English people have called "native doctor," "witch doctor" or even "soothsayer." The Hebrew equivalent is perhaps "deber." This Hebrew word is used for "pronouncement", "Speech" and is noun-masculine. In Ibo the dibia makes pronouncements, He speaks out the mind of the spirits. They are both noun and masculine. The Ibo emphasizes the role. The honorific village/ community/town title is "eze dibia" or "eze diber." It is also literally used as the title of the village or town chief priest. Eze dibia is different from the Eze Ala that refers to the high priest of Ala deity. There is also dibia afa that refers to a diviner; this same title is used for an oracle or spokesperson of the deity. The oracles that move from community to community are refered to in English as prophets.

Regel: This is an ancient Hebrew word for 'foot', 'leg'. It reminds one of the Ibo word 'rege' 'rege'; an expression used to refer to a toddler as they learn to use their legs characterized by standing, stumbling, repeatedly on the wobbly legs. The Igbo expression 'rege rege' is perhaps a reference to the folk Hebrew 'regel'.

Kuru ume, Kurume: We can perhaps address an expression said to have been made by Yeshua the Christ in the New Testament text of

Matthew where in healing a young girl Yeshua, the Christ was said to have stated in his native Aramaic dialect: 'talitha cum' which is interpreted as 'young girl arise'. The Ibo equivalent of the statement would be 'ta litha cume' which could be literally rendered as: 'today or now, rise up and take a breath of life'. Or "today arise and breath." A version of Ibo uses 'telitha Kurume' literally meaning 'arise and take a breath', 'rise up and breathe'.

Lewit: is Hebrew word anglicized as Levite. The Ibo equivalent is variously Ivite, ifite, Ihite depending on the part of Iboland and the dialect being used. One significant observation is that there are communities bearing the term ivite, ifite, ihite, either as suffix or prefix to their names, scattered all over Ibo land or standing alone. Some examples are: Ihite in Ngor Okpala local Government Area; IfiteUkpo, Oralfite etc. Also significant is the fact that these ihite, ifite, ivite, communities are responsible for the spirituality, understanding and using the benefits of the numerous dynamic forces in nature, and teaching of the same, as well as correct interpretation of omenala: this means the traditions including ritual purification, and customary boundaries allowed human; of communities under their custodianship wherever they live. Some possess powers to control weather among other abilities that they claim are learned and passed down from their fathers. This perhaps shows that there are Levite descendants all over Iboland.

Naga: this Hebrew word means to reach. The Ibo equivalent is also pronounced "naga" and is used to address a person "to continue going until you reach your destination."

Ahab: This Hebrew word has its root in Love "aheb". The Ibo equivalent is Ahabah which is the name of a community.

Shema: This Hebrew word means "hear", "listen". The Ibo equivalent is perhaps the expression found among the Owere people "shimu," "Shemu" which means "said to me" "reported to me that..."; implies that I am expected to hear what is being said, an important warning most often.

Apari: an Ibo word of the Owere dialect that connotes to present as "foolish", "humiliating," "loathsome", as worthless with ignominy.

The word is perhaps rooted in the Hebrew word 'aper. In Numbers 19: 9-10 the word is used as loathsome, filthy, worthless and behaving ignobly (see BDB p.68). In 2Samuel 13: 19 the word is used to refer to ashes on the head of a heifer as a sign of humiliation and contrition.

Beraka: This Hebrew word means 'blessing." Its Ibo equivalent is perhaps Abaraka. Abaraka is a statement used to impress gloating over a blessing or favour a person has received. This is also commonly used among the Owere people.

Re'eh: This Hebrew word means 'see,' "behold". It reminds one of the Ibo version "le'eh", (dialectal difference "re'eh") that also means a call to "see", "observe", "behold".

'Arelah: This Hebrew word is used to refer to the detested uncircumcised state. It reminds of the Ibo "Arualah", "iru ala" that means committing an abomination, polluting the land. Failur to be circumcised before engaging in sexual intercourse with a lady is regarded as detestable, and most ladies abhor it. It is unheard of in Iboland that a lady marries an uncircumcised male such a person will usually not be Ibo. This is one of the many reasons why Ibo girls are encouraged to only marry Ibo men.

Amad: This Hebrew word "Amad" perhaps has its Ibo equivalent as "Amadi." "Amadi" is a common name among the Imo and Rivers State peoples especially among the Owere and Ikwere, Eche, and Obite peoples. "Amad" is presented to be a name among the children of Asher in the Hebrew Bible as found in Joshua 19: 26 genealogy listing. Does this indicate that the Owere and Ibos of Rivers state are descendants of the tribe of Asher? Perhaps when one takes the study further in regard to the blessing upon Asher by Moses in Deuteronomy 33:24 we find that Asher is said to "dip his feet in oil." Oil is found among the Owere and Ikwere Eche and Obite parts of Iboland in abundance and more exploration is being carried out today. The use of the expression Ashim; shim, shi, is also common among them.

Aphiah: This name found in 1 Samuel 9: 1 belonged to the Benjamite tribe. He is said to have been a father of Kish "a Benjamite of rank" who was the father of Saul described as the handsom and above his fellows. Saul was to become the first king of Israel. Now there is an Ibo equivalent to the name Aphiah. It is rendered as "Afia". Thus we have an Ibo community called "Oha Afia" which literally means people of Afia, the dwelling of AFIA people or the gathering of Afia people.

Abi-Etam: This Hebrew name word means "my father Etam" (see 1Chron 4: 2-4). The closest Ibo equivalent is perhaps Item, Itam. We have a community in in Iboland referred to as Item people. We also have Itam in Akwa Ibom state. Abi-Etam is of the tribe of Judah. Does this imply that the Item and Itam people descendants of the tribe of Judah?

Amon: In Matthew 1:10 genealogy of Christ, Amon is a name mentioned where the author writes that Hezekiah fathered Manasseh, Manasseh fathered Amon, Amon fathered Josiah, and Josiah fathered Jeconiah and his brothers. The deportation to Babylon took place. It can be observed that today we have an Amon community in Abiriba in Abia state. Does this imply that the people of Amon in Abia state are descendants of David?

Archi, Archites: In Joshua 16: 2 the Archites are mentioned as descendants of Joseph through the tribe of Ephraim and Manasseh. Among the Ibo the name of Archi is common and relates to communities. Thus we have Achi in Enugu state, also Umun-achi, Ezi-nachi. Does this imply that these are descendants of Ephriam and Manasseh who were children of Joseph?

Abiyah: This Hebrew name means "my father is Yahweh" The Ibo equivalent is perhaps "Abiah" a very common word used among the Ibos to express relevant emphasis usually acceptable agreement or pleasantry. It has been used to name a state in Ibo country. Can this Ibo Abia genuinely be related to Abiyah in the Hebrew Bible? I personally doubt this very much for reasons stated in the Appendix below. "Abiah" is not a name word. Perhaps it served as such in the past among the Ibo: a particle used to express delight. It could perhaps mean "G-d has done it; I am delighted". This word is not connected to the present Abia state that said to be derived from the abreviation of groups of people making up the state.

Uzzi: 1 Chron 7: 2; is a name word. Its equivalent in Ibo is also spelt and pronounced in the same manner. There are communities in Ibo land bearing the same name. Uzzi's descendands belonged to the tribe of Isaachar in the Hebrew Bible. Does it imply that the Uzzi communities are descendants of the Uzzi's descendants and are of the Isaachar tribe?

Kalika: is a Hebrew word that connotes "waiting." The closest Ibo words to it are Akrika, kalika which do not mean "waiting" but could be used to connote an object for shelter and superiority. We find the words Abakalika (Abakelike), Umukalika, Umuakirika, Umuakilika, as Ibo communities.

Abida: is found in Gen 25: 4 as one of the sons of Keturah, Abraham's wife. The closest Ibo equivalent to this name is Obida, Obuda, and perhaps Obudu (in the Cross River state)

Abi'ama- This is an Ibo word that is used to refer to "the fathers' of the people" and eventually to imply "G-d of our people's, father". It is usually used when a person seeks to invoke justice. Like the Hebrew the word 'abh' refers to 'father' and 'am in Hebrew refers to 'people'. Thus the word "abi ama" in Ibo expresses 'father of the people': literally 'my father people." Abi ama is perhaps the title that universally identifies 'Abraham' as our people's father" among all Ibos. According to the Hebrew Bible Abram knew El SHADAI who later revealed himself as Yahweh. The Ibo communities being descendants of Abraham through Jacob (Israel) also identified themselves with Seth through Enosh, and Canem, who were sons of Seth and their descendants who inhabited the lands within the desserts of Seth as briefly explained above were first to begin to be identified "as people of Yahweh." The Chi concept is perhaps helenistic influence at a time in the History of some of the Ibo ancestors before they immigrated to Iboland. This was probably when they were in Babylon and the Greek, Alexander "the Great" universlised Greek culture. The term was infiltrated into Ibo worship by the Greek Xi written as Chi. In Ibo it refers to the spirit force in charge of all creation and destiny and later referred to as God of destiny. The other significant Greek term like Chi is "Eke", the creating force or power that never stops creating. Thus we have a combination of Chi na Eke; Chi and Eke (generally shortened as Chineke) are the forces or power perhaps the Ruach Yahweh, the Spirit of Yahweh, responsible for life as we see it physically. Yahweh,

El Shadai of Abram is regarded as the name that is above all names and the Power and source of all creation and life physical, visible and invisible. It is believed among the Owere people, that after the world was created the creator sent Eke to complete creation: fashion it and give it the final shape it should take, while chi, as perhaps the same as the Ruach Yahweh, determined its destiny.

However, later the concept of the great Chi emerged as "Chi-ukwu," CHUKWU. The Ibo began to call Yahweh El Shaddai as "Chukwu Abi 'ama", which refers to "Chukwu, the God of the father of our people"; Chukwu the God of the father of our people "Abiama" (Abram/ Abraham is "Abi 'ama"). His God became the God of our people. Thus we have Him as the G-d of Abram/Abraham. The name of the God of the father of our people is not to be mentioned as He is too holy to be uttered by sinful mortal man. Rather Chi na Eke are known names by which Yahweh's activities and presence among the people is known and expressed. This is how the God of the Ibos was expressed as Yahweh/ El Shaddai. However the concept of "alah" remained universal being the native original deity of the people just as was the case with the ancient Israelites who revered Yahweh, as God of the Fathers, as well as recognizing the operation of other deities including 'el, 'elah, 'eloah to mention just these.

During an "Eshe" dance in my village, a ritual dance to celebrate the life of all the righteous elders, who died morally righteous (Ibo All saints festival), I asked one of the popular organizers why there was a white flag flying over the venue of the dance and what it represented. I was shocked to hear that it was representing the Highest Deity. I asked if that was Chiukwu, he exclaimed, "No!"; then I asked what then the name of this highest deity was and was told that no one knew the name and that he was not designated any name. I left musing in my mind how then should people worship a deity that has no name. In all honesty I concluded it was fetish because of the answer I got from the organizers. The Eshe dance used to be common among the Owere Ibo area where I partly lived as a child. So also is the display of masquerade during festivities reminiscent of the Jewish celebration of Purim during which masquerades are displayed in commemoration of the story of Esther and Mordecai who strove successfully to preserve the memory of the Jewish ancestors by saving the Israelites from extinction. The Ibo will tell you that masquerades are displayed to remember and honour the ancestors.

Some local groups used Chi-ukwu, and others dialectically use Chukwu, referring to the native name for "G-d of destiny" that was, perhaps, borrowed from the natives of the land as emphasis. Some other groups use the designation "Chineke" emphsising the designation as creator though some others regard the designation to be a compound word Chi na Eke (G-d of destiny and G-d of creation). Others use "Igweka ala" or "Igwe" emphasizing his supremeness over all of creation. There are universal names like Ala which perhaps was universally used among the people at one time as the universal name for G-d.

Thus the Ibo calls on Chukwu Abiama, 'G-d of our fathers' for justice. This is an appeal to the 'Highest Other', 'the G-d of our ancestors'. 'Abi' in Hebrew literally means 'my father' while ama probably connects '"am" the Hebrew word for 'people' or 'Community'. Thus the Hebrew root of Abi ama is perhaps apparent. The implication is perhaps that in the remote past the Ibo did not use any name for the creator and referred to the creator as "G-d of our fathers" showing that local names emerged much later among different peoples as they mixed with other nations. The designation "ala" is similar to the Hebrew name 'el, 'elah which could also be used for sanctuary rather than names of the creator. This remind of the commandment that G-d must not be named or likened to anything on earth that the Ibos ancestors sought to obey before intermarriages and mixing with other nations they met around the Niger delta syncretized their worship.

Ether, Eter: in Joshua 15: 42 brings to mind Ibo communities called Akwaethe (Akwete), Obithe (Obite), Ogbethe (Ogbete), to mention just these. The Hebrew letters Tau, ("th") and Teth ('t') could be interchangeable in tracsription of words). This name is mentioned among places owned by Judah in the Hebrew Bible.

The Israelite town "Nazareth" should perhaps bring to mind the Ibo town of "Naze" in Owerre Imo Sate.

It is perhaps also important to add that like the ancient Hebrews, the Ibo are split in the dialectal use of words and letters. For example some Ibo, mostly those of the northern part use the letter 'S' while the southern group use 'Sh'(see Judges 12); 'L' is commonly used in the south, the Northern Ibo use 'R' or pronounce 'L' as if it were 'R' and 'R' as if it were 'L'. Among the Hebrew this distinctive use of 'shin' and 'sin' Hebrew letters is also observable. For example the south would say "ishi gini"/ I shi nini what did you say?; the north saying same thing would say "isi gini" what did you say? The southern Ibo would say "miri" for water; the north would say "mili"; mili yam. This dialectal difference in pronouncing words is also observed in among the Jews. The Ephraimites pronounced "Shibboleth" as "Sibboleth" (Judges 12).

In 1997 an Ibo rabbi presented a list of words, mostly name words claimed to have Hebrew roots. I examined these words but had my doubts about the claim. As time went on further examination raised more doubts about these words and many more as being of Hebrew in origin. Finally I decided to exclude them from the words I considered as likely to have Hebrew roots, at least until further expert checks. The following words were therefore excluded: Agu (as Agur), Boni (as Bani), Amakiri (as Machri), Ide (as Eden), Ife (as Eve), Ifite (as 'Ivrit', Ibrit'). Others are ije nisisi (as Genesis). Although I later reconsidered my stand on some of these words there were those that are not even Hebrew words. These were excluded in this study. What is pertinent to note is perhaps, that there are Canaanite names that have become Hebrew through cultural diffusion; in fact some scholars think that Hebrew is a dialect of the Canaanite language, Ugarit. I also do agree that Aramaic names, words, and expressions are found among Ibo languages and it appears to me that Aramaic and Ugarit have influenced much of Ibo language and culture. That does not mean that the Ibo ancestors were Canaanites. What we know is that perhaps the first Ibo ancestors did not inhabit the land of the Canaanites as they might have left Egypt long before the Moses led Exodus. However those that joined them later must have imbibed some non Hebrew influences that have lived with us till today. I also admit that there must have been cultural diffusion between Ibo and the natives the Ibo ancestors met. However this does not justify arbitrary connection of words as Hebrew or Aramaic. Some of the words suggested to me above are not even Hebrew, Aramaic nor Ugaritic as state earlier. Those Ibo scholars and rabbis who recommend these words they claim to have been found in the Bible as identifying Hebrew origin of the Ibo, are confusing Latin and Greek words as Hebrew and Aramaic language. This mistake reiterates the need for caution in the use of language connection as basis to prove genealogical linkage. The Hebrew word translated 'Eve' by the English translators of the Old Testament is Ishah (woman- as against 'ish or Adham, man Genesis 2) and Hawwah (Genesis 3: 20) translated as 'Eve'... 'And the man ('adham) called the name of his wife, Hawwah (translated as Eve: "hauwa" in the Hausa language said to be a dialect of Arabic): because she became the mother (em) of all living' (translated from the Hebrew Bible Text). So Eve is not a Hebrew word. Also Genesis is not a Hebrew word; Isaac does not mean 'ishi aku', an 'inheritor of riches' or 'head of wealth' as the Ibo meaning reflects. Rather it means 'laughter', in Hebrew. Eden is a Hebrew word but it does not mean 'ide' which in Ibo means 'pond', neither is it pronounced as 'ide'. Eden is a garden, though might have been beautifully watered by rivers and minerals implying paradise, it is not a 'pond' as is claimed is reflected by the Ibo word 'ide'.

Also I have not seen any Hebrew word written as 'Ibrit, or 'ivrit' except the Ibo word mgbritshi might impress. "Levite " (Hebrew 'lewit') could be related to 'ifite, 'ivite, ihite in Ibo; this may be acceptable because of the priestly role such communities are associated with universally among Ibo peoples. Also I have seen b'rit (berit) which as stated earlier means 'covenant'. There is no doubt that the levites in the ancient Hebrew world were strongly tied to ensuring the keeping of the covenant by the Hebrew people, thus could be said to have included teaching in ritual practices and observance. There is also no doubt that these ifite, ivite, ihite communities in Iboland are associated with special powers and maintenance of morality and omenala, agreed traditions/ there is no reason why they cannot be identified as Ibo replica of the Levitical order even though that status is not emphasized today. There names seem to identify them as descendants of the lineage of the Levites. Also like the Levites of the Hebrew Bible they are scattered among almost all Ibo communities and are not necessarily found in a geographical location like their brothers. As stated above some professors claimed their community in Abia state of Nigeria, one of the Ibo states, was of the Levitical order in origin, "not Cohanite order," he claimed. Perhaps the name

KANU among the Ibos reflects Cohanite, priestly origin.

Nevertheless I can go on and on to show why zealous arbitrary connection of words must not be allowed. It will serve no useful purpose. If any words should be connected as Hebrew or Ibo equivalent, those words must be pronounced in a similar way, spelt in similar way and have similar meaning, as well as play similar role among the two peoples. This principle should apply to name words also. For example as stated earlier the name 'Adah' is common to the two peoples as female names and mean the same. So also is the name 'Udum' which is an ancient manner in which the word 'Adham' was written and pronounced among the ancient Judeans and mean the same "red earth" that could also be translated as "mankind".

Perhaps equally important is to point out that unlike the English language the Hebrew and Ibo languages place the Adjective after the noun. Thus Ibo would say "nwoke oma," "nwanyi mma", "Adah mma" literally "man handsome", "woman beautiful", "Adah beautiful." The adjective reverses in the English version. Thus in Hebrew and Ibo also we say "yom ehad": day one; in Ibo we say, "Ubochi mbu": day one.

To sum up, once again an attempt has been made to relate Ibo words and Hebrew words. This amazing find should be food for thought especially for those who think Ibo and Hebrew have no linkage in terms of manners and customs.

However, this investigation into this language similarity should continue to ensure that words are not arbitrarily connected with Hebrew language and that relevant words are fished out among the many Ibo languages; which are very many indeed. It is important to note that there are words, just as there will be rituals, practices and beliefs that are original to the natives of the land who the Ibo ancestors met when they entered and which have formed part of the vocabulary of the Ibo language. Prominent are perhaps, the names of some deities, names of days, ritual and cult practices. Some examples are perhaps, attitude to the Osu, the killing of twins, human sacrifice and the rearing and eating of pigs to mention just these. We also have this watering down of Ibo culture, morality, beliefs and ritual practices, by western colonial influences that have continued till this day. This has remained a serious concern to those Ibo peoples who are patriotic to the values bequeathed by the Ibo ancestors. It is not surprising that same is the experience of the present day Israelite especially the Ashkenazi who have even corrupted the language, religion and customs of their ancestors by interaction with the European colonial world where they migrated to live for such a long period. Obviously the present day Yiddish and other versions spoken among the Ashkenazim and elsewhere as Jewish, is not the language of their ancestors and fathers.

It is perhaps important to observe that the reader would have thus far come across names of peoples of some Hebrew tribes and clans refelected among the Ibo communities; in fact identifying such communities as representative of the Israelite clans of the past. We can humbly state here that first of all it does not mean that identifying such names as reflecting Ibo communities may not necessarily automatically grant such communities Israelite status or descendants of such Israelite clans. However the fact that there are overwhelming number of these names and clans with their unique similarities should make the reader purse to think aloud. Why would these communities not be the remnants of the so called lost tribes? Also that there are so many of these clans scattered all over Iboland should be evidence that the Ibos are descended from different Israelite ancestors and not just from one ancestor. The fact that there are just very many dialects of the same language should call attention to the fact that there is something useful in this phenomenon. Also as it appears that almost all the tribes and clans of ancient Israel seem to be represented in Iboland might indicate that there may be no need to look far outside Ibo land for the so called lost tribes of Israel, as arrogant as this statement might sound. However I have to accept the fact that this research has only just begun.

The next section of this study is focused on the customs, practices, beliefs and manners of the Hebrew and Ibos that evidence their commonality. This should lead us into examining the implication of this for individual and collective re-invention of all the backslidden surviving children of the ancient Israelites as required by all the covenants and laws handed down by Chukwu ABI 'AMA, the G-D of Abraham in whatever name he might be identified: Yahweh, El Shaddai, 'EL, 'ALA', 'ELOHIM. The Ibos know him simply as the God of their father Abraham: CHUKWU ABIAMA.

The materials used in the next section will be all inclusive to reflect what has wrongly or rightly considered Jewish among Israelites of today. This includes use of some Judaism and Ibo concepts through the ages. There is need for reinvention because many of these so called Jewish communities are nothing short of "Synagogues of Satan" and people claiming to be Jews and are not (Revelation 2: 8-9). It is still the desire of Yeshua to rescue his people from their backslidden state.

SECTION TWO

OUR COMMON MANNERS AND CUSTOMS:

A CALL FOR REINVENTION

Chapter 7
Pregnancy, Birth and child upbringing in Ancient Israel and among the Ibo

In every society a child is seen as the source whereby the society is made to perpetuate. This is perhaps, why every society endeavors to ensure that a child is brought up in such a way that the child learns that his or her duty to the community is to perpetuate it. It is a joy and a cause for rejoicing whenever a child is delivered.

To understand the philosophy of a people there is need to know how that people takes seriously this issue of child upbringing for the child as the saying goes, "the child is father of the man." It is therefore important to examine child upbringing in ancient Israel in order to compare it with what obtains among the Ibos today and what it was among the Ibo ancestors. The aim is to enable the Ibos to readjust to the noble values of their ancestors for the well being of the Ibo society. Pregnance, birth and Child upbringing are one major and important aspect of our common manners and customs with the ancient Israelites.

We shall begin with pregnancy, then go on to examine birth and upbringing of the child. It is to be noted that not everything on this subject can be treated in this short study, so only what is considered as salient will be treated here.

The Christian Old Testament shall be our basic text although references shall be made to extra biblical materials where necessary. Oral interviews will provide information for the Ibo section of our investigation as has been usual in this study.

Pregnancy, birth and child upbringing among the Israelites

Pregnancy

The word 'hara' means to conceive, to become preganant. The imperfect, "wettahar" expresses the onset of pregnancy which is usually understood as "conceive"(BDB 247, Theological Dictionary of the Old Testament TDOT: 3: 458)' The word "yabam" is another word for "conceive" but it is used more for animals (Psalm 51: 7, see also "heron" Genesis 3: 16, "herayon" in Ruth 4: 13, Hosea 9: 11) Thus in 1 Chronicles 4: 17 we read, "wettahar et Miriam we et- Yared ..." and she conceived Miriam and Jared...).

In the story of the fall in Genesis 3: 16f pregnancy is presented as part of the divine punishment inflicted on the woman.... Among the Ibo a female child is referred to as "nwa nyi' literally a child of burden because of the punishment or burden she will carry upon herself including pregnancy.

Genesis 30:1 shows that to become pregnant was viewed as a social event. It might bring about envy among the women folk and a baren woman was looked upon with contempt. In fact one of the words for childlessness, 'ariri', means 'contempt', 'derision.' Ancient Israel recognized the possibility of man being barren although it is the woman that was often blamed for any infertile union between a man and the woman.

The word 'aqar', 'be barren' occurs in connection with a male subject in Deuteronomy 7: 14 although this is perhaps, the only mention of barrenness in connection with the male gender.

Pregnancy was also regarded as determined by Yahweh, the G-d of the fathers. Yahweh also shapes and forms the foetus (Job 3: 3-11, 31:18; Psalm 139: 13; Jeremiah 1: 5).

Yahweh also brings the child forth from the womb (Psalm 22:9; Hebrews 10; Isaiah 46: 3).

Yahweh superintends the life of the foetus from earliest monments (Psalm 71:6; Isaiah 49: 1).

The fruit of the womb is Yahweh's reward (Psalm 127: 3; Deut 7: 13, 28: 4, 11; 30: 9). The wicked go astray 'from the womb', 'merahem', and 'speak lies' from birth, 'mibbeten' (Psalm 58: 3).

And Yahweh curses the womb of the adulteress (Numbers 5:21). This shows that barrenness is a curse from Yahweh as was generally believed. The phrase, 'withhold the fruit of the womb' in Genesis 30: 2 may indicate failure of birth while the phrase, 'close the womb' in Genensis 16: 2; Genesis 20:18, I Samuel 1: 5f indicates total barrenness.

The intervention of Yahweh in barrenness is referred to as 'open the womb' Genesis 29:31f, Genesis 30: 22 or 'visit'. The word translated 'visit' in Genesis 21: 1f, 1 Samuel 2: 21 is 'paqadh', and can be understood in the sense of 'sleep with' Paqadh here refers to a special divine intervention different from other ways of deity relating with the queen to produce a 'royal child' as was believes among Israelite neighbours and most ancient world belief.

Death during child birth was later to be regarded by the Rabbis as an indication of neglect of family purity by the woman (Shab 2:6).

Judges 3: 11 seem to indicate restrictions for the pregnant woman. Manoah's wife was admonished to avoid drinking wine and eating any unclean thing.

We also read about indications of seemingly magical practices and use of charms (cf Genesis 30: 14ff 2Mac 12: 40). In Genesis 30: 14ff mandrakes (dudha'im) were believed to enhance pregnancy.

Other rituals practiced during pregnancy in ancient times could be seen from Jewish folklores and practices. The rabbis are said to have included a woman in child birth among the classes of people who must be carefully watched in order to guard her against evil spirits (Berakot 54b cf 2Mac 12. 40). These evil spirits are perhaps same as the seven evil spirits mentioned in the Universal Jewish Encyclopedia which prevented pregnancy. In order to prevent the evil attacks of these spirits, it was customary to strew the bridal couple at a wedding with hops, wheat, barley, at the time the bride was veiled and hen was placed in front of the couple (UJE 8 1948: 629f, Kraus, 'Childbirth' in Jewish Encyclopedia 4: 1903: 28-31.) Perhaps the most prominent diabolical forces of the Jewish world were Lilith, Satan and Azazel. Lilith in rabbinic literature is presented as female with long flowing hair and wing. Lilith was believed to attack any man whom she found sleeping alone. Satan is regarded as superhuman being but created by God, so is a dependent being. He was said to have been on same day as Eve. An alternative legend claims that he was created an angel but fell because he objected to the creation of man and after the creation of man he sought to deceive man in form of a serpent. He is portrayed as the enemy of man in rabbinic literature. It can be implied that the concept of Satan arose to explain the presence of sin and evil in man and the world. Satan taught man to sin and corrupted man. Azazel is mentioned in Leviticus 16 as a desert demon. This is in connection with the atonement rite. This rite demanded the presentation of two he-goats. The casting of lots decided which of the two goats, he-goats, were to be used as sin-offering. The one was brought before Yahweh and killed. The second he-goat served atonement purposes. It was not killed but left alive. The priest layed hands upon it and confesses the sins of the whole community over it. So to say, the sins of all the people were laid on this goat. It was then taken into the desert. It was given over to Azazel who was supposed to inhabit the desert. This ritual is believed to be an attempt to pacify the demon Azazel (cf Anijielo: 1984: 123-129).

It was also a Sephardic custom to recite the following Biblical selections for a woman in labour: Psalm 20; 1Samuel 7; or Genesis 21: 1-8(see also "Birth Customs and Folklore" in Encyclopedia Judaica 4: 1971: 1050f).

Also in the Talmudic times a magic circle was drawn with chalk or charcoal on the floor of the room of a pregnant woman who was in labour to guard against evil spirits. If her travail was difficult, the keys of the synagogue were placed in her hand, and she was girded with the band of a Torah scroll and prayers were recited at the gravesite of pious relatives. At times the circumference of the synagogue was measured and according to the length the number of candles was donated to the synagogue.

To prevent barrenness the woman was told to take the skin of a fox, burn it, take the ashes, mix it with water and drink of the water for three days, three times each day. This was said to be the instruction given to Manoah's wife by her fellow women in Judges 13(see M Gaster, "Birth: Biblical Notions and Practices Surrounding child Birth" Encyclopedia of Religion and Ethics 2: 654. Cf Mishna 3: 2, 246, Genesis Rabba 36:1; Tosefta Kelim, Baba Bathra 7: 12). However, the

Bible tells us that Manoah was advised that: " be sure that your wife follows the instructions I gave her. She must not eat grapes or raisins, or drink any wine or beer or eat anything that is not kosher" (Judges 13:13-14). At the end of the encounter Manoah took a young goat and a grain offering and offered it as a sacrifice to the Lord; and the angel did a strange thing, for as the flames from the altar were leaping up toward the sky, and as Manoah and his wife watched, the Angel ascended in the fire. Manoah and his wife fell face downward to the ground, and that was the last they saw him. It was then that Manoah finally realized it had been the Angel of the Lord. Manoah cried out, "we will die... for we have seen God." (See Judges 13: 13-22 –The Catholic Living Bible).

It was also believed that whatever a pregnant woman saw influenced the shape and features of the child in the womb. The Superhuman beauty of the priest Ishmael was thought to have been due to the fact that his mother has returned to bath, time after time after meeting a pig, a dog, and an ass. Each time after such animal met her she returned to the bath until at last Metatron, the angel of the face came and met her on her way home, she then conceived and bore a son as beautiful as the countenance of that angel (Mishna Niddah 3: 2) The countenance of a dog could make the child look like a dog, that of an ass could make the child stupid, that of a pig could make the child have unclean habits. As a proof of such influence is the experiment of Jacob with the sheep (Genesis 30: 39 Gaster ERE: 654 also citing Chronicle of Jerahmeel).

There was also the notion in Talmudic times that a special angel called 'Lailah' presided at the beginning of conception and through his intermediation the embryo was brought before the divine throne where the embryo's future was decided upon, its station in life was determined and whom it was going to marry. At the bidding of God, a spirit was said to enter the sperm, and then it was returned to the womb of the mother. In the womb, the child was folded up with its head between its knees. Two angels watched over it. A light burned over its head by which it saw from one end of the world to the other. In the morning an angel carried it into paradise and showed it all the righteous who had lived a good life in this world; and in the evening he takes it to hell; shows it the torments of the wicked. Finally, the angel ordered the child to come forth, and he strikes it, thereby extinguishing the light and causing it to forget whatever it had seen whilst in the womb of its mother.

Birth and Upbringing

The words used in the Tanakh (Hebrew Bible) in relation to the birth process, include 'yaladh', which is understood as, "bring forth" or 'bear'.

There is indication that prayers were made to Yahweh to provide male offspring in preference to female. The birth of a boy was accompanied with rejoicing (Jeremiah 20: 15; 1 Samuel 4: 20f). Since Yahweh was regarded as the bestowal of fertility, the child when born naturally becomes Yahweh's property (Exodus 34: 19). This was especially the case with the first born who is described as the 'bekor' (Exodus 13:2 etc).

When a special child was conceived, the pregnancy was announced to the parents. For example in Genesis 16: 1 we read: 'hinnakh hara we yoldadht ben weqara'th shema...'

And in Genesis 17: 19 we read: 'abhal sarah 'ishtekha yoledheth lekha ben

We kara'th a 'eth shema...'

Also in Judges 13: 5 we read: 'Ki hinnakh hara we yoladht ben...

And Isaiah 7: 14 reads: 'hinneh ha'almah hara we yoledheth ben weqara'th shema...' (in Ugaritic it reads hl glmt tld bn)

It is however, not clear whether this is a birth oracle known in ancient sacral style or a form of expression drawn from everyday speech. What is clear is that the formula is concerned with special children and all of them are boys. This type of birth is announced in Genesis 16:11 and Judges 13: 5 by the angel of Yahweh. In Isaiah 7:14 it was announced by the prophet through divine inspiration and in Genesis 17: 19 Yahweh Himself did the announcing. In Isaiah 7 and Genesis 17, men were addressed, while in the other passages woman were addressed.

In the Old Testament times a son was perhaps literally born to the father (Genesis 21: 3, 50: 23) who probably received him on his knees. However De Vaux observes that the father was absent during child birth implying that to 'receive onto his knees' might be expression of joy with which the birth of a boy was greeted by the father of the child (De Vaux, R. Ancient Israel: Its Life and Institutions London: 1965: 143ff, 4ff, 72ff, 43, cf Baab, O Birth International Dictionary of the Bible 1962: 440) The words "upon thee was I cast from my birth" may suggest the act of receiving the child on the father's knees when it came from the mothers womb during birth(Psalm 22:10). Rachel, on the other hand, hoped that Bilhah, her maid, bore a child upon her knees (Genesis 30:3). Job cursing the day of his birth, bewails that he found two knees to receive him (Job 3: 12). Exodus 1: 16 indicates that stool was used to assist women in childbearing and midwives were perhaps, a later introduction in child bearing (Genesis 35: 17, Genesis 38: 38; Exodus 1: 15)

A birth was the occasion of rejoicing and ceremonial activities, especially the birth of a son (Ruth 4: 14; Jeremiah 20: 15).

After cutting off the afterbirth the child was washed, rubbed with salt, which was believed made the child strong (De Vaux 1965: 43). The child was wrapped in swaddling clothes (Ezekiel 16: 4, Job 38: 8-9). The mother nursed the child (Genesis 24: 59, 35: 8; Exodus 2: 79; Numbers 11:12 2Samuel 4: 4; 2Kings 11: 2)

The afterbirth must not be buried at a cross road or hung upon a tree. The afterbirth was preserved for curing certain childhood illnesses. The child was made to wear magical amulets as protection against demons such as Lilith, Agrath, or roof demons, daughter of illness, Shimdon or Ashmadon or destruction (Hul 4: 7, Shab F 129b. According to Gaster these charms protected the mother and child and give strength of limbs, length of life, and blessing of health to the child. He mentions especially the demon Ummes Subyan, 'she who does harm to children' and Lilith (Gaster ERE citing Gnensis Rabba 36:1, Erubin 100b, Midrash Rabba to Numbers 16)

The birth of a child made the mother unclean, in the first place for seven days, and then if it was a son, thirty-three days; if a female sixty-six days. At the end of the period of uncleanness, lustration or purification took place and the woman brought offering to the temple (Leviticus 12: 2ff). In Hebrew, the concept of clean and unclean, or pure (tahor) and impure (tamei) showed that only those who were 'tahor' could enter the dwelling place of God's presence and anything object or person considered to represent God. Those who were deemed 'tamei' would be kept outside and if not purified would be cut off from Israel. To effect purity from defilement a red heifer (para adumah), a young female cow that has not yet borne a calf was to be without blemish and defect free. It must never have been a yoke. It would be killed under the supervision of the priest who would then sprinkle its blood seven times towards the tabernacle. Its body would be burned outside the camp and its ashes used to create the waters of purification. The waters of purification are necessary to ritually cleanse those who had been contaminated by death through contact with corpse, bone, or grave. Once purified, they could enter the Tabernacle to draw near to the living God (Numbers 19: 1-22; Judges 11: 1- 33; Hebrews 9: 1-28 see also Lessons on Chukat (Statute or Decree) Online Messianic Bible Class 15 July 2016)

The sacrifice of a sin offering was also known to have been practiced among the Falashas at the close of the forty-day period of uncleanness and the purification of the mother took place (cf Morgenstern J Rites of Birth, Marriage, Death and Kindred Occasion Among the Semites, 1966: 28 n 37).

Niddah 316 states that sin offering of the mother was offered for swearing any future relations with her husband at pain of labour which swearing she would later regret she made.

The first born of any womb was to be consecrated to God. In Patriarchal times the first born enjoyed special privileges and had the right of leadership within the family. He had preference in inheritance above other members of the family. In the last disposition of Jacob (Genesis 49), Reuben was deprived of his privileges of primogeniture for the reason that he lay with his father's concubine and although not stated, the double portion which according to Mosaic legislation was given to the first born was, instead of Reuben, given to Joseph. This is made evident in 1 Chronicles 5: 1. The male first born was in ancient times the priest of the family. Since the Levites later took over the place of first born, the first born had to be redeemed at the completion of thirty-days after birth (Numbers 18: 16, Leviticus 22: 27, Exodus 22:29). According to Morgenstern, the first born was redeemed in order to avert and free the child from the power of the threatening spirit or of the deity who had bestowed the gift of life to it and who would claim this life back. During the danger period which lasted three to forty days, the new born child was actually under the power of supernatural beings, supposedly hostile. The child was only redeemed after the rites were performed. According to Morgenstern it was only then that the child began to live as an ordinary mortal (Morgenstern 1966: 29).

If Morgenstern is correct in his explanation, it will then mean that the redemption of the first born recorded in the Tanakh must be a reinterpretation of an already known ancient practice and ritual.

According to Numbers 3: 47; 18: 16, the father redeemed his first born son in ancient times by giving to the priest thirty silver shekels presented to the sanctuary. The priest could reduce the cost if the child was sickly. The priest had to come to the house, as the mother could not appear with the infant in the sanctuary because her days of purification according to the laws (Leviticus 12: 2-4) were not yet accomplished. When she was ritually purified, the mother brought the baby to the priest into the temple to be presented publicly to the Lord (cf Luke 2: 22). Among the ancient Jews when the first born male was thirty days old, the Cohen (a descendant of Aaron) was invited to the house of the parents for a repast. After the Cohen had prayed, the priest looked at the child and redemption price was given to him. The father was asked by the priest to choose which one he preferred, the child or the money. Upon the father's reply that he would rather pay the price of redemption, the priest took the money and swung it round the infant's head in token of his vicarious authority, saying: "this is for the first born, this is in lieu of it, this redeems it and let this son be spared for life, for the law of God and for the fear of heaven. May it please thee that he be spared for the law, for matrimony and for good works. Amen"

The priest then laid his hand upon the child's head, and blessed it as follows:" the Lord make thee as Ephraim and Manasseh" (cf 1 Peter

1:18).

Another important ritual following birth was naming. The aim was to incorporate the child into the community of the living. There is no prescribed age at which a child was named in the Old Testament. However there are indications that a child was named immediately following birth (Morgenstern 1966: 43ff D Jacobson Child Care" UJE 3 1948: 149). The custom of postponing naming to time of circumcision is perhaps, deducible from Luke 1: 59; Luke 2: 21. Perhaps the mother or the father could chose the name of the child (Genesis 29: 31-Genesis 30:24, Genesis 35: 18; 1 Samuel 1: 20, cf Genesis 16: 15; 17: 19; Exodus 2: 22 cf Genesis 35: 18)

The various stages of a child's life from its birth to manhood were given different expressions (see C D Ginsberg Bible Educator 1 London: Cassell Peter and Galpin nd 29-251).

These nine words by which a child was denoted show the tender care with which a Hebrew community watched and marked every period in the child's growth and development. It also shows that the child's upbringing was the responsibility of all. There is the word 'ben', son, with the feminine equivalent as 'bath' for daughter. These were the general terms for every child of any age. Then the characteristic and specific 'yeledh' newly born child (Exodus 2: 3, 6, 8) indicating by its name the fact that it has arrived. Next is 'yonek', suckling (Psalm 8: 2, Jeremiah 44: 7, Lamentations 4: 4, Joel 2: 16); this expresses nursing period. The age when the child is about to be weaned the child is called "'olel" (Lamentations 2:20). 'Gamul' refers to 'the weaned' as in Psalm 131: 2; Isaiah 11: 8 and marks the period when the child becomes independent of its mother. The other terms are 'taph', "the quick stepping"; shows the child is achieving some independence of the mother and now makes short and quick strides to keep up with the pace of his parents as in Jeremiah 40:7; Esther 3: 13. 'Elem', the strong, almah (the virgin Isaiah 7: 14) describes the child when it is ready to assist the parents in their labours (1 Samuel 20: 20) Naar, the free (from na'ar, to "shake off", to "become free" describes him as the youth, grown up who though still assisted by his parents, is no more at their side but has attained to that age when he can walk about freely and defend himself(Genesis 37: 2; Judges 8: 20;

1 Samuel 20 : 38). Then we have the term "bachur" which means "the matured", "the ripe" and describes the time the child attains majority, is marriageable and fit for military services (Isaiah 31: 8; 42: 5; Jeremiah 18: 21)

These expressions show that the injunctions, "Train up a child in the way he should go and when he is old he will not depart from it" (Proverbs 22: 6) was taken seriously in ancient times. This injunction must have concerned the whole community and not only the efforts of the child's parents. This type of community training provided the child acquisition of practical wisdom (hokma) fear of God, and service to the community.

The period during which the child is a 'yonek' and became an "olel", or ready to be weaned is not mentioned in the Tanakh. The Talmud however gives us the information which enables us both to determine it and to explain the expression, describinbg the child at this age. This authority informs us that it was incumbent upon every mother to nurse the child to at least two years of age (Keth 59b). The book of Maccabees informs that children were nursed up to three years (2Maccabbees 7: 27). This explains such passages as Jeremiah 9: 21, Lamentations 4: 4; where the "'olalim" are described as playing in the streets and are represented in great famine as asking for bread. In the same way we can understand the Proverb in 1 Samuel 15: 3, 22: 19 which reads: "infants and suckling" (Authorized Version) thereby bringing out the difference between "yonek" and "'olel" but also rather inconsistently "children and sucklings" which translation obliterated the difference. The phrase described the period of infancy intervening between the birth and weaning of the child or the stage of its existence in which it is utterly dependent upon its mother for nutriment (Lamentations 2: 11, Psalm 8: 2, Jeremiah 44: 7) The 'gamul' or weaned child commenced its independent life by a feast which the parents gave to their friends and relations on the day of the weaning (Genesis 21: 8). We see that this took place when the child was about three years of age. Hence we find that Samuel was weaned and his mother took him up to the Tabernacle to appear before the Lord; he was old enough to be left with Eli to be initiated in the service of the sanctuary (1 Smauel 1: 24- 28). This will also explain why no provision was made for the children of the Levites before they were three years old (2Chronicles 31: 16); since up to this age they were still dependent upon their mothers for nutriment.

The "taph" or "little trotter" as the Bible designates the weaned child appears often in the Tanakh and is rendered in Authorized Version as "little one" or "little children". From the fact that they always held to and throttle after their mother in walking, they are often coupled together with the women, so that "the little ones" and the women" is a common technical term or expression in the Bible (Numbers 14: 3; 31: 9; Deuteronomy 2: 34,; 20: 14; Joshua 8: 35, Judges 21: 10; Esther 3: 13; Judges 8: 11).

As their age extends from three to about twelve years, they were considered old enough to have formed certain habits and to be able to attend to instructions. Hence under certain circumstances they were not spared (Numbers 31: 17, 18; Judges 21: 10). The expression "taph" is also included while describing the three classess of human beings who came under the operation of specific laws or regulations (Deuteronomy 3: 6; 3: 12; Jeremiah 40: 7; 43: 6). It was at this stage of life that the child was dressed in the fringed or more correctly the tasseled garment in accordance with the injunction contained in Numbers 15: 38-41 and Deuteronomy 22: 12. The Tasseled garment reminded the child the commandments and need to keep them. On putting on the tasseled garment the following prayer was said: "Blessed art thou O Lord King of the Universe, who hast sanctified us with thy commandments and enjoined us to array ourselves with tassels"(Chobin 89, Shabbath 118b, Matthew 9: 20; 14: 30).

It was likely that a child's education began at the stage of "taph". The 'elem' occurs in 1 Samuel 17: 56; 20: 22. The AV translates it "the stripping" and "the young man".

The stage perhaps marked the transition from irresponsibility to responsibility. Up to the age of twelve the parents were regarded as answerable for the boy's conduct, and they had the absolute control of his ritual performances. But after age twelve the parents presented him to the Lord (Luke 2: 42). He was inducted into adulthood. At this induction the boy wore the religious dressings which included the phylacteries or tephilim and an elaborate religious ritual followed.

The 'elem' was also responsible to the law and to the deeds of the law which totals 613. These included the honouring of the father and the mother, charity, early attendance at the sanctuary, morning and evening, entertaining strangers; visiting the sick, giving outfits to brides, following the dead to the grave, devotion at prayers; making peace between a man and his neighbour and studying of scripture (see J Kiddushin1:7; Mishna Snahedrin 8: 1-4; Nedarin 1: 4; 3:2; B Bathra 10, Mishna Pea 8: 7).

According to the Mosaic instructions the early education of a child devolved upon the father. Of course the mother offered the first training (Deuteronomy 11:19)

The exact age at which education commenced is not mentioned in the Old Testament. However it is likely that it began early enough through the religious features around. It is likely that as the child became old enough to become aware of their presence in the community, his education commenced. This is probably earlier than age five- long before the child could speak: notably the family prayers, the shema, the Sabbath observances, the feasts etc.

The 'musar' literature helped immensely in the child's education. The meaning of 'musar' both in the earlier and later Biblical sources is those educational practices by which every generation initiates the generation following it into the rules and particulars of the Torah-centred life system. Musar is first of all the ways in which parents teach their children to acquire behavior patterns. Authoritative corrective measures verbal or by action for proper recompense for good and bad of rules and norms passed from generation to generation. The child learns societal norms and responsibilities (Exodus 12: 26; 13: 8; Deut 4: 9-10, 6: 7, 20; 11; 19; 31; 3; Psalm 78: 5,6 see Schweid E "The Authority Principle in Biblical Morality" Journal of Religion and Ethics 8, 2 Fall 1980: 180-203; Joseph M "Education" Encyclopedia of Religion and Ethics 5: 1912: 194-198 cf Kenneth R Ancient Hebrew Social Life and Custom As indicated in Law Narrative and Metaphor 1933: 9f).

In conclusion the child in the Old Testament became important from the time of conception and remains important all life. Rites were carried out to initiate him from one stage of life to the next and for protection against evil forces around. The community as a whole contributed to its growth and well being. More responsibilities were expected of the child progressively in degrees. It was expected to live like everyone else in the community-meeting up with the moral requirements expected of him or her as a human being. Important responsibilities perhaps began from ages 10-13. The child in the Hebrew community was conceived religiously, carried in womb religiously, born religiously, lived religiously and must die religiously. Life to the child is a linkage between cult, kin and the afterlife in a kinship relationship. The kith and kin included the ancestors, the living and yet to be born in kinship solidarity.

Pregnancy, birth and Child Upbringing among the Ibo

Any Ibo person brought up in an Ibo village will easily connect with the above description of attitudes to pregnancy, birth and child upbringing of a typical ancient Hebrew society as captured from the Old Testament and other sources.

Life of a person born and brought up in an Ibo village is conceived to be a linkage between kin, cult and the afterlife. An ancestor is expected to come back in his descendants and the birth of a child is the fulfillment of every person's ambition and a means to perpetuate the name of the father, the ancestors; it is a means to enliven the life of the fathers in the afterlife. It is a religious duty to procreate. Failure to procreate is regarded as a great calamity to say the least. Barrenness is regarded as a curse, so also is failure to deliver a baby (still birth). Mmadu (mmanu) means 'posterity is to continue to exist'. A new baby is therefore a blessing that ensures the existence of the human species. In this sense 'mmadu' 'mmanu' means "what has come is a blessing", "beauty and well being, therein".

Once a woman shows signs of being pregnant everyone plays a role to ensure a safe delivery. The key protectors of the pregnancy against the envious are the mother of the pregnant woman, the mother of her husband, her husband, her husband's brothers and sisters and the father of her husband in the first instance and then extending to the rest of the umunna (father's people) and wider compound and then the wider community and clan. This also includes her sisters who have been married in other places. This responsibility reflects the feature of an Ibo family and how the Ibo society operates as an individualized entity whereby problems are handled collectively yet the closest relatives to the individual takes the bulk of the responsibility in the first instance. The Ibo society does not operate through any hierarchy of political leaders or priests, although these are present. Life circles around the individual, yet the respect is accorded to the spirit world, elders and the ancestors. A child in the womb has as much right as the highest titled member of the community in matters of existence and governance. It is important and must be given its own right to exist. This is because the baby in the womb like any other person is linked to the ancestors and moreover one of the ancestors is about to come back to the family as a child. Sometimes protection of the baby includes consulting an oracle to determine which of the ancestors is coming back and what the destiny of the child might be. The oracle might recommend some ritual performance to enhance the baby's protection from enemies of the family. Enemies are not unusual to exist because the birth of a child is regarded as a major achievement, a possible progress, possible the coming of a great person that might enrich the family. In most polygamous families where there is rivalry among the wives enmity was likely to increase.

The pregnant woman herself must observe known precautions. Some of these include never allowing anybody to step across her legs and never to step across anybody's legs or body especially strangers; to avoid eating certain animals including snail, dog meat, snake, lizard, and to avoid staring at deformed and disabled persons. She is to avoid contact with people who are unhealthy and physically and mentally ill. She must be cautious of the sort of animals and things she stares at. Amulets are also worn to protect the baby and the mother.

She is encouraged to eat 'good' food full of vegetables, fruits, and mushrooms and must have regular bath; keeping clean and hygienically acceptable. As the pregnancy progresses she must avoid over straining herself with work and must not be found walking about late in the dark. Her husband, mother and close relatives collectively supervise this.

The birth of baby usually took place behind the mother's hut or inside her hut. Wives are usually heard saying that I have put a son to his knees (thighs) and it is the desire of every wife to achieve this for her husbands; by 'husbands' here is meant her husband and his relatives. It is usual practice that the wife sets up her chi omumu (fertility shrine) on entering her new home. It is here that she prays to her husband's ancestors for fertility. This means that she gives herself fully to her husband's clan on marriage including their deities and their omenala (traditions of the land). Male children are preferred because they immortalize the name of the ancestors; consequently a man who has only daughters is expected to keep one of the daughters to procreate while unmarried in order to "give lease to the man's life in the afterlife".

During labour women of the compound gathered to assist in the delivery and sometimes traditional midwife or midwives are present. The birth of child is announced by the cry of the baby at birth and the women chorus a traditional song usually sung during such occasion with rejoicing. The afterbirth (placenta) of the baby is planted as close to the homestead as possible and the point of planting it is marked by planting an ogirishi plant. This spot remains closely watched to make sure that an enemy does not "come and take it for some nefarious medicine." Following birth of a baby, the mother goes into a period of seclusion called "omu-gwo". She and the baby are moved to a seclusion demarcated as such by the use of a sacred leaf called omu-nkwu (fresh palm fronds usually yellow in colour). Omu nkwu (also called simply 'omu') is used to depict sacredness, specialness (no longer ordinary) which implies seclusion: sacred sites and places or objects that are no longer profane. For example, a dead body, a shrine, a sanctuary, an osu house, a priest's house, a holy person, mbari (a type of shrine showing the history of the community in ritual art), a secluded farm land, a forbidden land, a traditional place of learning (usually learning the secrets of the land); these and many other such sacred places, persons and objects are all marked out by the use of omu (taken from nkwu (palm tree) so referred to as "palm fronds" by the English people). There are also heroes, sacred dancers, war dancers, war musicians, and instruments for sacred music that must also be identified with the use of "omu".

In the case of a woman in seclusion due to child birth the omu may be tied around the hut or just made to act as curtain to the door and window of the hut. She remains impure and ritual purification is carried out from one stage of the seclusion period to the following stage until the period of seclusion is concluded. Meanwhile she must not carry out any domestic chores including cooking. She may bath the baby and take her bath. Visitors including the little children who visit the baby are encouraged to give him gifts and salute him and the mother. They are given 'nzu' specially garnished kaolin bake. The domestic chores are carried out by a close relative who is summoned immediately following birth. This close relative is usually her mother, aunt or sister.

The first stage of purification ritual is made at the end of the first one week (izu) as she is considered impure for the first week as during menstruation; she is then allowed the visit of children. Usually white chalk is rubbed on the children as symbol of oneness with the new baby. The seclusion period lasts for a while and the number of days depends on the gender of the child. The woman remains impure for a longer period if the child is female (usually izu iri at least 10 weeks) than if male (izu asaa 7 weeks at least). The end of the seclusion period was celebrated with great feast and the woman is showered with gifts from every relation. One significant observation is that the woman is fed very well following birth; she is fed with most nutritious food of her choice as her husband and relatives are expected to have saved enough money and food items for the responsibilities and challenges of birth. This is especially the case if the baby is a first born son. Also before the feasting the woman is ushered into the profane life firstly by visiting the village stream (iyin) in the company of maidens. At the stream she takes her ritual bath or lustration. She may wash part of her body, say feet, face and hands if the weather does not permit full bath. The village stream is chosen because it provides the right condition for such a rite, which must be done in a flowing stream (iyin).

While in the omugwo the child's naming ceremony may take place if the parents so wish to postpone the naming ceremony beyond first days following birth. However, it is usual practice that the child is named a few days after birth before circumcision. Naming involves a simple ceremony of roasting yam or maize or both. If yam is used it must be carefully chosen species and be the very best and most loved yam. Usually, "nwanyi eri" yam which is literally the species naturally made for female consumption because of its attractiveness and taste is chosen. It is eaten with well garnished palm oil. Naming ceremony is usually chaired by the eldest member of the close family who is regarded as occupying the position of the ancestors and of the family head and by virtue of this position is regarded as holding the ofo of the family and compound at that level. He is also regarded as the priest of the family at that level. Ofo is the sacred symbol of justice; therefore the holder must be seen to be living a righteous life and fair to all in his relationships within the family. Ofo could likened to the "rod in the hands of Moses."

Naming took place at the family Obiri (Obi) where the shrine of the ancestors was located and the venue for all family worships and gatherings. The Obiri is also a meeting place for all family discussions that include all members of the fathers' people (umunna).

Another evidence of free from seclusion is the presentation, dedication and redemption of the child during which the child is taken before Chukwu through the village deity (Ala) as intermediary. The mother and her entourage dance to the deity sanctuary while the father is seen following behind with a gift of a goat or ram or whatever livestock gift they are able to afford. This marks the end of the omu gwo. "Omu gwo", literally means seclusion with "omu", the palm frond marking the hut as as sacred spot in the sense of impurity, because of the debt, or offering owed to the deity. If a first born is being dedicated the animal must be tender and must not have given birth. The Ibo call it "a gba ra" (tender). It must not be a he goat (cf Leviticus 12). It is perhaps to reiterate here that the Ibo have no dealings with pigs. I do not know of any specific colour required of an animal for such an offering. What I know is that there is absolute meticulous care in selecting the animal and in everything about this offering. Also explanation as to why this takes place is not known to me, perhaps it reminds one of the Hebrew practice of purification after birth whereby a red heifer (para adumah) was used as substitute for the first baby son. It might interest the reader to know that the Ibo refer to the first born son as "opara" of the family. Perhaps this designation reflects the Hebrew redemption ritual practice. Opara might have signified a "child of redemption" among the ancient Ibo ancestors. Opara later came to be title for the first son of a household and the redemption aspect forgotten. Opara can also reflect the Hebrew opera which means "front" connoting first to "be in front';' to come first before others. The first daughter is "Adah" which in Hebrew means "adornment", "the beautiful one" (Adah mma in Ibo). Adah later became used to refer to the first female child of a family and kindred.

It is perhaps significant to state here that any baby born in Iboland is automatically regarded as Ibo. It is unacceptable that any foreigner living among the Ibos would take away the placenta of their new born baby to anywhere else to bury. Every child born in Iboland is regarded as belonging to the Ibo ancestors and must not be regarded otherwise. That baby is Ibo by birth and belongs to Ibo ancestors. Also Ibos living anywhere in the world are expected to take the placenta home to bury on the family compound because every Ibo baby has a linkage with Chukwu through the Ala deity, ancestors his kith and kin. This is ritually practicalised by the burying of the placenta in the family compound and the spot must be well marked out. This spot is shown to the boy anytime the child visits home and is old enough to understand. This shows a strong blood solidarity that is inviolable among the Ibo no matter where they are in the world.

Following the removal of the taboo on the mother, attention diverts to the child's upbringing. Bringing up a child is the responsibility of the whole household, compound and community. Naming the child ushers the child formally into the community to begin "living as one of us" and the expectations of him reflected in the names he was given. The child straddles around the mother, learns to walk and run and participate in communal work as he grows up. The child is taught the traditions "ome nala" literally "ways of the land" as he interacts with all and sundry beginning with his close parents. Beginning from his own close father, mother, uncles, kith and kin, and age groups expectations the child learns to adapt to the ways of his people. He is made to understand the republican and egalitarian nature of the Ibo society. He learns that even his father and mother do not expect him to prostrate or worship any human being; his opinions are important on matters that affect him. He/she learns that the Ibo do not recognize kingship and that hard work and good moral life is what marks out a person as an individual; that hard work is the only legacy by which a person is remembered after death. He learns that the Ibo are a proud people who refuse to beg for food, and would not succumb to humiliation nor allow his brother Ibo to suffer for want. He observes worship at family level through his father and married life through his parents. As he interacts with other ethnic groups he begins to appreciate that the Ibos are different in a number of ways. Many of these lessons are acquired through daily interactions, songs, legend and moon light stories. An Ibo girl learns to be a wife and mother from childhood till she gets married and even while married the mother and women of her husband's compound collectively educate her. These also includes the taboos of marriage and how to ensure that she makes her marriage a success as the Ibo believe that such success of marriage is the responsibility of the wife to ensure. A proud wife leaves an enviable legacy of discipline, respect, hard work and decency into her children. Above all she is expected to be a woman of strength spiritually as this grants her the virtue to be the successful woman. "Beauty", the Ibo say, "is in a woman's character, not in her physical appearance or in her material wealth" (cf Proverbs 31). In Proverbs 31 verse 10 we read:

Eschet-chayil mi yimetsa' werachok miphninim mikrah: "An able woman who can find and far above all gems is her value". The capable wife is the able woman. Such a woman is a woman of strength of character, hard work and manners.

Among the Ibo she is expected to cover her head at all times except when situation does not allow it. She must not serve her husband without covering her head and must not cook or serve her husband food when menstruating. Most often she sits by him while he eats in normal situations. There are also traditionally allowed ways to welcome visitors and with her spiritual intuit she is expected to identify and enemy in the midst of her husband's visitors and even relatives.

Divorce is rare and when it happens, the whole umunna (father's people) which includes the ancestors must endorse it; this is usually very difficult to achieve. There are unacceptable behaviours from a wife or her husband. For example it is an abomination for a woman or man to drive away her husband or wife out of the family home without the umunna endorsing it.

There are ways and manner of divorcing a recalcitrant woman. During divorce the woman is sent back to her parents and "to her people" in the same way and manner she was married. Her people here include her ancestors. The most disgraceful way is perhaps when the women of her husband's village or compound drive her away. When such method is used the woman was followed by the crowd who sweep her footsteps along as she departs until she leaves the vicinity of the village. Women who are treated in this manner must have been guilty of abominable offences such as prostrating naked before a deity or in a public place, denying her husband access to enter the house, blatant adultery, and stealing; others are theft, murder, feuding, and witchcraft, to mention just these. A wife who discovers her husband is infertile must keep this condition secret between and her husband and if possible her husband's relatives. As it is the duty of the wife to procreate for the family usually she is expected to get pregnant "in her own way'. The husband and his people more often than not must know the true biological father of the children, although this is to be kept secret and in order to sustain this secret most women adhere to her husband's brother or closest husband's relative. There is no bastard in Ibo community so long as the father of the children is known. The children become regarded as bastards if their biological father is not known. Thus the Ibo community allows the practice of concubinage and in some places wife husbandry is practiced. In wife husbandry the barren wife marries another woman for her husband. When this occurs it is the first wife of the man that is the husband of the newly married and the newly married must respect her as such.

At puberty the young woman undergoes education of the deeper 'secrets' of community including fertility and infertility issues and how to deal with infertility problems. She is also taught what makes the Ibo woman and man proud as a people and is encouraged to participate in dance groups as means of capturing the admiration of a suitor. Ibo men chose wives during dance entertainments especially in dance competitions. Women from other villages move around in dance groups to neighbouring villages and towns. It was during such dance visits that they market themselves by putting on the best show of themselves to attract potential suitors. Women testify to getting their husbands during dance festivals.

Also their war strategies, land demarcations and boundaries become better appreciated by the boy child. He is initiated into the Masquerade society, and must undergo circumcision if he had not been circumcised earlier.

If female, in addition to the above so called deeper 'secrets' she undergoes the iru mgbe, mbari, how to be a wife and mother, making a success of a marriage, cooking and feeding the family, skills in traditional diets, and presentation of food, dressing, trading, mixed farming techniques, to mention just these. She also learns how to comport herself as a woman and worship including the priestly position of her husband and her roles and why "the beauty of a woman is in her husband, children and home". Many of these are learned by observing her mother and other women. She also learns ritual commensality meals (nshi oriko) for reconciliation and rituals for dissociations, divorce, banishment, and purification etc. Failure to achieve success in her marriage is announced to her by her fellow women in the community who tell her this by mocking her. This is what every woman dreads to happen to her. That is why the Ibo say that it is the woman that makes the home, "it is the woman that owns the home", "it is the woman that builds the home". A woman who fails in this responsibility has failed in all of life and faces disgrace before other women.

At marriage he/she fulfills the eternal requirement of a man and a woman and begins to raise his or her own family. In all this the key to success is respect for traditional values of his people including worship, collective assistance and mutual cooperation as Ibo peoples.

Comparing the Ibo belief and practice and expectations about pregnancy and child upbringing with the Old Testament we can see that the two are similar. The next chapters will hopefully help to throw more light on this fact.

Chapter 8

Kinship Solidarity among the ancient Hebrew and the Ibo Peoples

Kinship occupied a central role in social interactions in ancient Israel. Beginning with the family to clan kinship determined a person's entire attitude to life. An adult male left his mother and father and cleaved to his wife, both founded what was called the' House;' they form a smaller family unit in the company of their children. The children became of one blood. The community they founded became the House (bayith) who collectively worked together for the well being of 'the house' as blood brothers and these constitute the breeding group (Genesis 12:1).

According to Genesis 46:8-26, they also constitute the one flesh concept. Genesis 12:1 explains this principle clearer. Yahweh instructs Abram to leave his immediate kindred and clan (mispaha). He was to leave his father's house (moledeth) to found another house, kindred and clan different from his father's lineage. This means that the source of unity of the clan is the kinship bond. It kept the father's house together and united the mispaha, the clan. The strength of the tribe (sebet) was also a function of the kinship bond.

In ancient Israelite community the clan was made up of several families while the tribe was made up of a collection of clans. This kinship relationship extended to the world of the departed relations. This is explained by the reverence of corpse of a deceased relative and attachment to the ancestors (2 Samuel 21. 13-14). It was after the bones of Saul and his son Jonathan were put in the right place that peace came into the land; Yahweh heard their supplication.

We also find that this kinship bond continued even when a son founded his own house. For example the married sons of Noah are said to constitute Noah's house and Jacob's house is said to be made up of three generations which the biblical writer took time to list (Gen 46: 8-26).

The bayith was named after the first ancestral father whose blood and flesh was believed to be in all his descendants. This was the beth abh, the house of the ancestral father (cf J. Pedersen, Israel: Its Life and Culture. Oxford: OUP 1940: 53).This is perhaps why the descendants of a lineage were referred to as sons of the ancestor. An example is the statement that Cush begot Nimrod while in actual fact Nimrod was a descendant of Cush.

The family was also the beth abheth, literally,' the house of the fathers'. A man who acted as the beth abh was expected to be responsible to maintain the kinship relationship spirit in the children. He was accountable to his fathers who were the progenitors of the beth abheth. When the father of the beth abh was about to die, he was expected to keep his house in order. According to Isaiah 38: 1-2 Isaiah instructed Hezekiah that the Lord had instructed that he should keep his house in order because he was not going to recover from the ill health that had befallen him. The will of the man who was about to die was dependent on his earlier fathers who constituted the beth abheth. He only handed it over to posterity and so maintained the continuity of 'the house of the fathers.' This means that a common ancestor begins the bayith and it was the person who started it that stamps his personality on the bayith and became the bearer of the unity and all those who joined him were regarded as his sons. This is perhaps, why we read of 'the house of the evil doers' (Isaiah 31:1), and 'the sons of the wise' (Isaiah 19:11), 'the sons of the needy' (Psalm 72: 4), 'the sons of the stranger' (Psalm 18: 45). This shows that the various traits and abilities of every individual made him a part of the wider group and determined the ethical image left behind by the fathers by which they could be remembered (Pedersen 1940: 54). Also people could come together who are not blood relations to agree to live together under one leader who became the founder of that group.

The belief in remembrance calls attention to the importance of 'name' (shem). In the Book of Ruth the word 'shem' refers to the family line which is comparable to the same force as 'bayith', 'house'. The expression 'leqra shem' in Ruth is equivalent to 'lehaqim hammed' in Ruth 4.5 and 'wehakem zerya' in Genesis 38.8. The expression 'qra shem' in this context would simply stand for continue, perpetuate the family line. This is the Akkadian parallel for 'qra shem', beget, produce. To grant a name thus means procreation of a son, 'insuring the continuity of the line', 'ensure posterity'. Thus we have the intermediate cognate of 'shem', 'remember the name'. The Septuagint renders it 'weyiqra shemo' in Ruth 4. 14: 'proclaim' or 'call his name', in the sense of 'make him somebody', 'grant him honour', thereby strengthening the meaning further (H. Brichto, 1973: 'Kin, cult, land and the afterlife: A Biblical Complex' in HUCA 44:22ff, see also The New Brown, Driver and Briggs-Gesenius, Hebrew and English Lexicon 1979: 1028 BDB).

Failure to continue the line of the father of a house in this way meant extirpation. In 2 Samuel: 24. 22 Saul asked David to guarantee that he would not eliminate his offspring after his death, and in the oracle of Isaiah 14.4-23, the prophet pictures the kings descent into 'sheol' and gloats over the tyrant not having received proper sepulture 'as the evil doing line' will continue no longer in the expression: 'lo yiqra' le olam zer' mere'im'. He went on to declare: Prepare the slaughter block for his sons for their father's crimes that they not rise to possess the earth and fill earth's surface with ruins (verses 18-21 see also Brichto 1973: 24).

Also the expression 'yi qre tah hanepheet hahi me' meyeha': 'that person shall be cut off from his kin', that appears frequently in the Pentateuch is perhaps antithesis of the expression 'ne'asaph al 'ammyu' i.e 'be gathered to ones kin'(or people). To be cut off from ones kin means the extirpation of a lineage or the rooting out of his name which expresses the danger of ending the continuity of a community or race (Brichto 1973: 67, 97 see N. de Coulanges, 1873: The Ancient City. New York: Garden Press: 19-100).

This type of kinship relationship carries along known advantages. Firstly it ensures unity of purpose among children of the same father or household. Secondly, it ensures strength of the family as unity is strength. It motivates individuals to sacrifice for the existence and survival of one another. The enemy was fought willingly. The sounding of the trumpet was willingly responded to by every able bodied male to war. Thirdly no one needed to be told to work hard towards the well being of the community. Although the poor were provided for, this was in exceptional cases as poverty was regarded as punishment from God. In fact the phrase which indicates begging, 'to put out ones hand to solicit arms' or 'to beg' is rare in the Hebrew scriptures. It only occurs twice: Psalm 37: 25 and Psalm 109: 10. The intrusion of the enemies introduced poverty and begging as previously provision was made to ensure that nobody begged. These provisions included the introduction of collections into a common stock, the 'tamchu' (literally 'alms for the dish') which was distributed every morning and 'the kuppa', 'alms for the box' which was distributed once a week. Every Jew was bound to contribute to these collections. Abiding in a city for thirty days qualified one to contribute to the alms for the dish. If he resided for three months in the same place he must contribute to the alms for the box (Pedersen: 1940: 54).

In addition was special collections made secretly for good families who were ashamed to be known. These collections were kept at the Temple chamber (B. Bathra 10). It was better that the Jew threw himself into the lime oven than to put his brother Jew into humiliation (Kethuboth 67). Everyone was exhorted to work no matter how low than to beg (Dessachin 112, B. Bathra 110). Provision for the needy led to the law of gleaning after harvest which instructs that the gleaning be left for the needy who would come secretly to collect them for his household (Prov 31.20, Ezekiel 18.17, Isaiah 58.6).

Kinship Relationship among the Ibo

The community among the Ibo consists of houses that form compounds and compounds form small family units; small family units is the nucleus of life and makes up the kindred (obiri, obi, obu). A group of kindred makes up a hamlet; a group of hamlets make up a village, a group of villages make up a town and a group of towns make up a clan. The whole Ibo land is a collection of small family units, hamlets, villages, towns and clans. The name of each of these may be derived from a totem which may be an animal, a plant, or an ancestral founder. These include towns like Owu eri (Owerri), mbi eri, Agulu eri, Ora eri, Abba, Abam, Item, Ngwa, Ohafia, Ora ifite, to mention just these. The name Imerienwe reflects a people who abhor the eating of Monkey. The name 'Mba ise' (five communities or towns), 'Mba ino' (four communities or towns), 'Mba ishii' (six communities or towns) reflects the coming together of a group of people under one leader or commune. Mba could therefore be interpreted to mean 'people'. They are a people of Chiukwu Abi-ama (God of Our fathers). This type of collectivity might attain a strong political entity. As each house has its head usually the man, so each compound, has its head. The eldest at each level is regarded as the head and the person closest to the ancestors at that level: house, compound, family unit, kindred, hamlet, village, town, clan respectively. He acts as the priest in community matters at that level. The eldest male in a village, town, and clan holds the 'ofo ndicie', a staff of ancestral authority acting as a symbol of moral authority, equality and justice and handed down to him from the previous ancestral head. Today the ofo remains the symbol of moral authority with which rules and regulations are made and enforced. It has such a strong influence on the people that a mere mention of it sends fear into peoples' minds. No one dared go contrary to the principles of justice and rules instituted by the use of the ofo. It is like the rod in the hands of Moses and Aaron and the elders rule the people with its authority. The ofo is actually a stick of the plant deuterium senegalense that has been ritualized and sanctified for religious purpose.

The Ibo believe the ofo is a sacred plant that is planted in the compound of Chiukwu (G-d), and has been ritualized and handed over to the first Ibo ancestor to serve as a bond of kinship among the Ibo peoples. Thus it is believed to link everyone to the Ibo ancestors directly and to God as well as to one another; wherever the Ibo people are found in this world, is expected to be the ofo and kept in the custody of the oldest man who is regarded as having a close and direct link to the ancestors (ndi ichie, 'ndi iche': literally 'revered people of old'). Thus it effects the brotherhood and blood solidarity among the Ibo peoples. Anyone who willingly accepts the authority of the ofo over them is a brother to the rest of the Ibo and to all Ibo no matter where that person comes from; race or colour is no barrier to becoming an Ibo person. Accepting the authority of the ofo means you have agreed to abide by the rules and regulations of the ndicie, the G-d of the Ibo and all ways of life of the Ibo. This acceptance of brotherhood is symbolized by the burying of the umbilical cord of the new born baby within the compound, usually under a well marked tree. This ritual links the new born child to the ancestors through the ala deity.

The ala deity is venerated as the earth deity who is believed to have everything as she is believed to give birth to everything and thereby a mother to everyone. She is believed to ensure procreation, fertility of soil, human and animals; and also the general well being of everyone and the community which includes protection and safeguarding of property.

A person bound by this cord of brotherhood is regarded as belonging to the umunna, 'father's people', 'children of one father'. Consequently the offence of such a person affects the whole community. Everyone was therefore brought up to work towards ensuring that peace is attained between 'ala', nature and Chiukwu, though the idea of Chiukwu came later into the theology of the Ibo peoples. In fact it was believed that the sin of one person could endanger the existence of the whole community if God was to unleash his anger on the people. In such situation a ritual purification is carried out. This is usually by means of the eldest in each compound carrying out a sacrifice of purification to protect the compound from such a wrath. The blood of the sacrificed animal was spilled on the main entrance door post of each compound referred to as 'obiri', 'obu', 'obi', 'ogba' as the case may be. In some cases the blood of the sacrificed animal was sprinkled on each inhabitant of the compound. This is a type of Passover as the Jews of old had practiced. This blood solidarity is extended to the wife's home if she was a foreigner. Thus when a woman marries to an Ibo she was expected to accept the Gods of her husband as her God just as she has accepted his people as her people. Her husband's ancestors became her ancestors and she practices the rituals of her husband's people having become subjected to the rules and regulation of the 'ofo'. However, the syncretistic effect of marrying non-Hebrew women cannot be overemphasized. And in fact might account for backsliding of the Ibo peoples from the religion of their fathers, as we find them today.

The elders as representatives of the ancestors were highly respected and as priests were highly revered. They were addressed as fathers before their name. Thus we hear an Ibo addressing an uncle as 'papa' or 'nna' before mentioning the first name. The wives also accord their husbands same respect by addressing them as 'Di m' which literally means 'my master', 'my lord' and never by their first names. As priest of the house she must not prepare food while in her menstruation period, nor serve him at such periods. She presented food to him with the utmost respect and worked hard to provide for him the best food while the husbands also gave her the utmost place in his life and possessions. She owned him and protected him from potential enemies with her feminine gifts of intuition and insights. She supported him to ensure he is successful in life. The blood solidarity between husband and wife is at a much stronger level than with others. This is necessary so that the children would appreciate what blood solidarity actually involves at the home level before they could exercise it fully well in the wider community.

The senior adults in the community are addressed as uncles with the term 'dede', 'de' (short form); the female seniors are addressed as 'dada', 'da' (short form). The belief is that by respecting the elder and the seniors the ancestors are being respected and revered. Thus blood solidarity is extended to the ancestors in this way. This respect of the ancestors is essential for them to willingly reincarnate into the family and repopulate. Repopulating the family is also a way of continuing their existence by immortalizing their names in the world. Keeping their names alive is believed to give the ancestors lease in the afterlife. This means that blood solidarity and kinship relationship among the Ibo also extends to the unborn who is potentially to be born into the family (kindred). A new born is regarded as the fulfiller and the fulfillment of the hope of the ancestors in the afterlife. Therefore starting from pregnancy the baby is carefully nursed to ensure that this role is achieved. It was a tragedy to have a still birth though ignorance made the community always blame the mother of the still born as an ill luck to the family and so such a woman was disgraced. When born the child was the responsibility of everyone to help bring up and integrate into the community. Care was taken that the child was raised in the ways of the ancestors. Each stage of the life crises of development the child was assisted and enabled to get into the next phase until the child enters to maturity and even in death the child is collectively gradated into the ancestral world. Thus in all initiations the child is supported: at birth to ensure that the umbilical cord was rightly placed as the ancestors required; in naming ceremony to ensure that it was carried out on the eighth day and ritually appropriate and by the specialist who must use the right tools to carry it out; puberty to ensure that the child is given the right knowledge and protection needed to help him prepare for adult life; marriage to ensure that the right person, right knowledge, and right tools were given him, and death to ensure that he was rightly gradated into the afterlife as he joins the ancestors. Each phase of life and its roles must be communicated to the child and the child must be well ushered into it. The Ibo society is thus a religious society whereby every aspect of a person's life involves a ritual, yes life to the Ibo is a religious ritual and each phase must be rightly carried out. Even matters of sexual intercourse and relationship to nature are not left out. The Ibo believe that foolishness is in the young person and if left on their own they might destroy 'themselves' and the whole community. So he or she must be carefully brought up. This is why in every life crisis his or her kith and kin must identify with him or her to encourage them, to support them, and to initiate them. The ancestors are also believed to be present when these initiations are taking place though they are not visible to the naked eye. It is all geared towards keeping their 'lamp' of life glowing (cf E. Obiechina: 1994: 'Ncheteka: the story, memory and continuity of Igbo culture, Ahiajoku lecture: 35 quoting Olaudah Equianos remembrance Narrative written in the 17thcentury). This kinship solidarity made it easy to gather to fight an enemy. Whenever threatened, the trumpet calls the people to war and every able bodied person gather to face the enemy for offence or defense. Also whenever there was need for communal work everyone gathered willingly to do their part at the call of the town crier; and anyone that failed to do their own part was made to pay a fine which might be in form of a livestock. The fine was usually collected by the person's age mates, sometimes forcefully if defiant.

It was shameful to beg or to see a brother begging. There was usually a common stock whereby food was collected just in case there might be someone in need. The person was expected to collect it secretly and even if seen by anyone must not be spoken about. Nevertheless laziness had no place and the lazy person was rebuked by their age mates and made to work harder. It was as if the age groups were in competition in ensuring that no member of their group brought shame to their age grade.

Agriculture was the main occupation and members of an age group supported one another in farm work. So also were there other occupations such as hunting, fishing, knitting, palm wine tapping, mat making, hat making, music making, bed making, metal carving, wood carving, livestock keeping, and weaving to mention just these. Rearing of pigs was rare and if reared they were sold to foreigners. Pork was never eaten. These occupations are additional to agriculture which is the main employment. Of significant position is the eze ji. The eze ji refers to the richest in crops and farm produce. Such a person supported all the others in need of food or crops for farming. They are usually the one the beginner young man went to humbly request seed crops to begin a farm. He is regarded as blessed by God and he saw himself as gifted by God so as to give to others. He is often the one regarded as the leader of the people and gives advice and counsel in times of crises. It is for this reason that he was called king of yam ('eze ji'). The word for king is 'eze'. This underscores the fact that the meaning of the Ibo word 'eze' is not as a monarchical seat rather it is as 'the chief or leading helper or supporter of the people'. It is universally known that 'Ibo amaghi eze': 'Ibo do not know kingship'. This fits into the Hebrew meaning of the word 'ezer' as it refers to the wife of Adam, 'a help meet for him'. Thus Adam was not given a help mate but a suitable supporter to help, the right kind of support he deserved (cf Gen 2: 18ff, Prov 31)

To assist the needy in Ibo agricultural society there is also the law of gleaning whereby the harvester was expected to leave behind gleanings for the needy to go and collect at the time convenient to them.

Thus Equiano was right when he stated:

'... agriculture is our chief employment; and everyone contributed something to the common stock; and as we are unacquainted with idleness, we have no beggars(Narrative 7) when he wrote about his Igbo peoples manners and customs long ago (quoted in E. Obiechina: 1994:35 see also extracts from Equiano's Interesting Narrative...)

So Ibo kinship relationship was the type that lived together, ate together, worked together, fought battles together, protected one another's back together etc; it also included the ancestors and those yet to be born; all were believed to be under the watchful eye of the gods. It was the type of kinship relationship that gave strength to a people to survive the test of time and made the inhabitants unwilling to cheat or deceive for personal gain. It ensures a pride of race. A family head bequeathed family estates to his children and he would be accountable to the fathers if they were misused.

Conclusion

In sum one could easily see that the Ibo and Hebrew kinship is not just similar, they are the same. The languages may be dissimilar the spirit is the same. It was based on strong blood solidarity guided by a common faith, common father, and common purpose- a close knit between kin, cult and the afterlife indeed. Every father was expected to keep his house in order before dying and bequeathed the family estate to the first son. First sons were regarded as priests at each level of kinship, family, compound, hamlet, village, town, and clan; they were accountable to the ancestors who were the custodian of morality and conduct and proper worship. A father wakes up in the morning goes out to the front door facing the rising sun and prays for the well being of all including protection and prosperity and above all fertility. Whatever affected oneself affected everyone else including the ancestors and those yet to be born.

Chapter 9

The Dignity of the Human Person among the Ancient Israelites and the Ibo

Introduction

Did the ancient Hebrew as represented in history place any dignity on mankind?

This is a question that can be given various answers. The answer given may be

determined by how one looks at the historical facts including the Old Testament

evidence on the ancient Hebrews attitude to man especially to the so called gentile, the non Hebrew nations. Some scholars claim that the ancient Hebrew psyche was

centred on the existence of the Hebrew relegating other peoples as nobody. There

are some others who claim that the Hebrew woke up to first thank Yahweh for not

making him a gentile among other things.

This short chapter is an attempt to bring to the fore that the Hebrew highly

dignifies the human species. This could be readily seen in the abhorrence of human

sacrifice and in other aspects of their history and beliefs such as in creation,

worship, and community life.

Man's dignity in creation

A study of creation of man as found in the Old Testament so connects man and the

creator that one would think that the existence of man naturally points to the

existence of the creator. In the Hebrew economy, Yahweh created all things

including man. It is true that Yahweh is understood as the all powerful, ever

present, all knowing, demanding the highest honour and worship, greatly to be

feared and reverenced by man in the created order, the Hebrew realized that

Yahweh made man in such a way that creator is imperative in the heart of man.

Yahweh has his imprint in man so that man should imperatively acknowledge his

existence in order to worship him. It is only the fool who can say in their heart

that there is no G-d (Psalm 63).

The Hebrew also recognize that the complexity of creation called 'adham' and

translated as 'mankind' includes mankind's numerous capabilities, namely to produce,

to build, to destroy or preserve. This is man originated and sustained by the

creator. The 'ruach' translated as the breath of G-d can therefore be regarded as that part of man which seals man as G-d's highest creation. Isaiah 61 declares that

it was through the 'ruach' that the anointed servant fulfilled his destiny. Through

the ruach man can have fellowship with G-d as well as interact with him. This

fellowship and interaction is ritually maintained and in this way profane man

acquires a sacred status. In fact the fact that man was fashioned by G-d renders

man sacred. This is, perhaps, why the biblical writer used the word 'yasar' to

express the special creating of man in Genesis 2: 7 because it denotes fashioning

man as an image already conceived in G-d's mind prior to effecting its

materialization. The other word 'bara' is not used in the making of man but in the

making of animals(Genesis 1:21) and in general creation, perhaps, as a way

expressing the bringing into being as if initiation of something anew (cf Theological

Word Book of the Old Testament 127; Isa 27:11, 43:1, 45:9-11, 64:7, 44:2,24; Ps

94:9,45:18). This, perhaps, why man's blood must not be shed as stated in Genesis

9: 6. The Hebrew also believe that man was created in the image and likeness of

God expressed in Hebrew language as 'betselem and kidemut 'elohim'. This expression not only denotes man's sacredness but also indicates that only man is

capable of enjoying support, love and fellowship with God. This status also exalts

man above all other creatures and makes him able to have dominion over the non

human world as G-d instructed him to have in Genesis 1: 28.

Man's dignity in creation is also expressed by the belief of the Hebrews that G-d

made man a little lower than the highest of the created beings('elohim Psalm 8:5)

The word dilumin Psalm 8.5 is translated variously as 'angels' (RSV), gods (KJV),

yourself (Good News Bible). The Hebrew also believe that man is so highly placed

that man would judge the angels on the last day. Even after mans fall by disobeying

G-d still found him special and made provision for him to continue to exist, rather

than discarding him for another species or object. However G-d gave man the

status of dependency upon G-d by making man a nephesh; consequently man must

not be worshipped, worship is reserved for G-d and G-d alone.

In sum G-d designed man's dignity by making him in his image and likeness, what

Karl Barth described as the I-thou relationship between man and G-d and between

man and fellow man (Barth K 1956: Church Dogmatics vol 3. Edinburgh: T & T Clark.

Sawyer J F A: 1974: 'The Meaning of Beselem Elohim in Genesis I-XI in Journal of

Theological Studies 25: 418-426. See also Clines D 1968: 'The image of G-d in Man'

Tyndale Bulletin 19: 53-103 esp 88). God calls all creatures to respect humanity

Gen 9.6, 5:1-3, Prov 17.5. Sharing a commonality with G-d in fellowship and in Spirit is the highest honour, dignity and respect man can be accorded.

The dignity of man expressed in privilege to worship

Man's dignity is also expressed by the ancient Hebrew in man's worship. Throughout

the old testament we see man given the status of an ever worshiping creature. It

is as if man should never cease from worshipping. The spiritual dimension of man

assists him in his ever worshipping mood. He is a personality created to worship.

According to the Old Testament G-d revealed himself first as the G-d of the

fathers to the Hebrew peoples. G-d was real and not abstract. G-d's relationship

with the community was identified through the first person he revealed himself to;

call him the leader, chief, founder, or ancestor of the community. This cult founder

would establish a strong relationship with the deity and then passed it on to his

descendants. This is why we read of 'the G-d of Abraham' (Genesis 15:1, 28:13,

31:42, 53); 'the fear of Isaac' (Gen 31:42, 53), 'the mighty one of Jacob' (Gen 49:24) and such like expressions.

This is why the patriarchal deity is presented as a family G-d rather than bound to

a special locality. The family also moved about taking their family G-d along

wherever they went and believed that this God protected them and upheld the

family in their historical pilgrimage so to say. This effects a strong linkage

between cult, land, and the ancestral realm (afterlife) and even extends to those

potentially to be born into such a family. Thus the preservation and worship of this

family G-d becomes imperative and a duty owed to one another including the

ancestors and those yet to be born.

As time went on this family G-d became conceived as a clan or tribal G-d. He became referred to as 'Yahweh'. The Yahweh concept has been traced to time of

Enosh (Gen 4: 26) far before the time of Moses. Genesis 4: 26 expresses 'nosh' as

meaning 'man'. However we read that G-d introduced himself to Moses as 'Yahweh'

as well as reiterating that he was the G-d of Abraham, Isaac, and Jacob as well as

introduced himself as 'el shaddai in Genesis 17:1; 28:3, 35:1. Thus the same G-d

that revealed himself as El Shaddai is the 'Yahweh'. Yet we read of the name

'elohim used long before the time of Moses as we find in Genesis 1:1 describing

himself as the G-d of all peoples, God of all human, G-d of all the earth. He is the

creator and owner of all life. He first revealed himself as the 'Yahweh' to Moses as

we read in Exodus 3:6, 9:14. One thing is certain in all these names; the same G-d

was being worshipped. The G-d of the fathers was the same as the G-d of the

descendants. The G-d of the fathers who was central in family units continued as

the G-d of a people as well as worshipped by families and individuals. G-d remained

the G-d of the oppressed, the rescuer of the oppressed (cf Clements R E 1979:

The Old Testament Theology London: John Knox Press: 61; Amos 2:1).

The same

God was worshipped at the monarchical period and after. The Ark at Shiloh had

been the religious rallying place of the tribal confederacy. However, at the time of

monarchy the place of worship was expanded; places of religious pilgrimage were

established. These included sanctuaries at Gilgal, Bethel, Gibeon, Ophrah, Mizpah,

and Dan. Peace offering, burnt offering and cereal offering were made while human

sacrifice was strongly abhorrent (Judges 11: 34-40). Religious festivals were not

left out. These include the feast of unleavened bread, the feast of weeks and the

feast of ingathering (tabernacle or booths). Everyman was expected to participate

as self exclusion was regarded as abominable. Every child was brought up to be God

fearing. The laws of G-d were to be memorized by everyone. The Shema was

recited by everyone and bands on the fringes of dresses reminded one of their

servanthood to God. The Passover festival was never to be neglected. All of life

was worship to the Hebrew.

The high point in man's dignity is perhaps expressed by the Hebrew in their belief

of the future suffering servant Messiah who was to come as man to lead mankind

to blissful life through a vicarious sacrifice of expiation. Christians identify him as

Jesus, the Christ.

Man's dignity in community life

The ancient Hebrew peoples recognize man's dignity in man's origin, and nature, and

in his expression of worship. It is perhaps in the community life that the dignity of

the human person has its greatest expression among the Hebrews. Although

individual rights and expressions are recognized among the Hebrews, man is

regarded as complete firstly in community. Man must belong to his kith and kin,

parents, brothers, sisters, uncles, who are immediate and to a wider relationship

within the extended down to the fathers who have passed on and to the unborn

relations also. The consciousness of this belonging becomes very vital to man's

existence and to collective survival as a people. The centre of a Man's social life is

in his kinship('am).

The immediate family of a young man called the moledeth (Gen. 12:1) formed the Breeding group (Gen 46:8-26) and the kinship bond kept the fathers house together and unites the mispaha (clan). It constitutes the strength of the sebet (tribe). A clan consisted of several families while the tribe consisted of a collection of clans. This kinship relationship extended into the world of the dead as certain passages seem to indicate (1 Sam 31: 12-14f)

The family is not only the beth 'abh ('av), the father's house, it was also the beth

'abheth, 'the house of the fathers'. A man who was about to die set his house in

order (Isa 38:2). His will was determined by the earlier fathers and now he is

expected to hand it over to posterity thereby maintaining the continuity of the

father's house. It is perhaps why the new born was sometimes described as

(ma'adu) that which has come to ensure continuity of the lineage. No family land or

estate was to be sold away, as it was bequeathed by the family by common ancestor

who bore the unity of the family.

The name of such an ancestor must be continued on the family land (Ruth 4),

through procreation and family reverence.

To be driven out of the family or community or to be disowned by ones family was

opposite of 'to be joined to his ancestors at death. Thus an ancestor was said to be 'gathered to his kinsmen'. Through Levirate marriage the kin was expected to

produce progeny for a person who died without such within the kin group ('am).

Those who belonged to the same kin group called each other by such terms as, 'ah,

'brother', 'amith, kinsman, or re'a, 'fellow or 'neighbour'. Living in such a community

meant sharing ones life, having common objectives with others with whom one lived.

Sharing life crises, sorrows and joys made life easier for one another. Also the

upbringing of a child was not the sole duty of the biological parents but that of the

whole community. Pregnancy, birth, naming, circumcision, marriage, death rituals

were community responsibilities.

To belong to the 'am was also to belong to G-d of the kinsmen. This religion

connected the individual to his ancestors (the 'am olam', 'the people of old').

It was also the desire of every family head to leave sons who would continue this

religious duty after his death. He also maintained the family morals, through

teaching his children right morality with the help of the community at large. The

musar literature is thus first of all the way in which parents taught their children to acquire right behavior patterns through the authoritative corrective measures

which. It may be verbal or by actions of proper recompense for good and bad. It

was also those rules and norms passed from generation to generation within the

community. Through this careful upbringing, every individual learned what the

spirit was all about, and endeavored to continue the brotherhood spirit. He also

ensured that it same was inculcated into his own children. A young girl must be a

virgin on her wedding day. Adultery was punished by stoning to death, thus

disobedience to G-d might lead to the death of the whole household as one man's

sin against G-d could lead to the punishment of a whole family and even the whole

community. The rule of Jubilee was compulsorily obeyed and gleanings after havest

must be left for the needy to harvest. The stranger, the widow, and the orphan

must not be oppressed and must be provided for whenever they were in need.

Thus the high dignity placed on man can be seen from the strong family

connectedness of everyone and community spirit. Care was taken to ensure that the traumas of a man's life were collectively shared, resolved and settled. It was

this feeling of brotherhood that held communities together and that enable

members share their joys, and sorrows. It strengthens a people and makes lives

difficulties easy to handle. It also ensures longer life span, the essence of G-d's

reason for creating mankind. It is also perhaps this strong brotherhood spirit that

brought about the practice of blood revenge and cities of refuge to ensure that an

innocent blood was not shed.

Conclusion

Man as conceived by the ancient Hebrew is a special creature among the world of

creation. He has very high dignity placed upon him by virtue of being specially

created. He is created to ensure continuity of humanity. Although he may be

imperfect he still has special place in God's 'heart' who made provision for his

restoration after fall and continued fellowshipping with him in worship, and in

community life. This made man morally responsible and so gives him dignity. Man's place in the community dignified him and exalted him above all else as provision was

made for dealing with life's traumas, corporately. It also made one man responsible

for the well being of others as one man's sin could lead to the punishment of the

community including possible obliteration of a community. This is contrary today's

individualism, and inhumanity of man to his fellow man and disintegration of

community life leading to oppression, competition, wars, hunger, and fear of self

destruction.

The dignity of the human Person in Ibo belief

Any Ibo who was raised in Iboland and by a good Ibo would have readily realized

what a similarity of culture and belief between the Ibo and the ancient

Hebrew. Every aspect of the Hebrew belief and practice is same as the Ibo belief

on the dignity of Man. This is same as in the origin of man as being a special

creation of the maker of the all things the creator. When a child is born there is

enormous rejoicing because humanity (ma'adu) has come to the earth. The birth of

person is regarded as a miracle, a blessing to the community. Humanity to the Ibo is the high point of G-d's creative act and it is around the human person that the

physical and spiritual dimensions of existence cohere.

Man is the creature that has worship with G-d and so is the only creature

regarded as having contact with G-d and this contact continues in spite of man's

shortcomings. This contact with G-d gives man moral responsibility and makes him

accountable to his fellow human being as well as to G-d. Thus man lives in a moral

society made by G-d who demands morality from man because G-d is the one who

directs that morality. G-d has to be reverenced as well as the ancestors who

bequeathed the worship of G-d to his children. The head of the family introduces

the worship to his children who in turn does same to his own children. This worship

pattern must be followed from generation to generation. Worship is thus regarded

as imperative, no one is expected to worship, it is assumed that everyone has

worship in him. There is no spiritual vacuum must in mankind Failure to worship

means such a person is subhuman.

Belonging to a community and working as a community person is also imperative and failure to be what is expected of a man is almost an abomination. Community is the

existence of everyone and links into the ancestral world as well as includes the

unborn members of the community. The community is made of father's house, who

belongs to the fathers' compound, These make up hamlets and hamlets make up

villages. All constitute the close community referred to as umunna, father's people.

This means children of one parent. These come together to settle quarrels, share

in joys and sorrows. This strong brotherhood spirit connects everyone to the kit

and kin and the cult (religion). The offence of one person could lead to the whole

community suffering unless the God is appeased. The Ibo do not believe that

anything happens due to western understanding of luck, rather they believe that

one's destiny (chi) has been determined by God and it is expected of man to

cooperate with God with the help of the wider community to ensure that such a

destiny is achieved. This also impinges on how morally responsible the person has

been. An immoral person could be separated from his kit and kin forever and it is

believed that this separation continues even in the world of the dead whereby the

person is ever separated from his ancestors. This is regarded as a calamity. Selling

of the family estate or land was one major sin as well as refusal to worship God,

incest, murder, especially homicide (i. e murdering of a fellow Ibo), removal of land

marks, refusal to observe the rule of gleaning, neglecting the widow and the orphan

and those in need.

The delicate nature of life requires collective upbringing of the child and the

gradation from childhood to adulthood and into the ancestral world. Thus

upbringing of a child remains the collective responsibility of the community.

Circumcision is carried out on the eighth day following the birth of a boy. There is

ritual purification time for a woman to be observed following birth at the end of

which period there is the woman and child are incorporated into the community

with feasting. Through the age group system the child learns the rules of Collective Existence in addition to the parental guidance at home.

What about the Osu caste institution?

As has been known with regard to the human frailty to offend even when such offending will be disadvantageous to him, the boundary between the profane and the sacred was not kept sacro-sanct. The result was the beginning of the osu, a caste institution which has been near impossible to bring to an end in Iboland and has become a scandal to the morality of a people who claim to be descendants of Abraham the worshipper of the Yahweh, the God of Justice; Yahweh who has created mankind in His own image and likeness.

Origin of the Practice

Details on how this boundary crossing started have been lost in antiquity. However, a number of oral information has been given.

One such oral tradition claims that there was a time in the remote past when sacrifices could no longer appease the angry deities. Human beings were therefore used as replacement of lower animals for sacrifice. The human beings were not killed but were given to the deities for a life of servitude that will affect their descendants.

One other account of its origin claims that intertribal wars introduced osu. On such occasions communities promised their deities gifts of human servants if they emerged victorious in battles. War captives became the usual victims of such gifts to these deities.

Yet, other information claims that sometimes the deities themselves began to request that some chosen people should be given to them to adopt. Messages of the deities were conveyed through the oracles and diviners dedicated to the service of the deities.

Couples who had difficult in childbearing would promise to dedicate any offspring they happen to get through the help of any deity to the deity who they believe had assisted them.

The villages or communities could come together to agree to hand over any criminal to the deity to avert the wrath of the deity.

Another claim is that sometimes people who were guilty of offences considered abominable voluntarily ran into the shrine of a deity for protection. When this occurred no one dared interfere as the offender is regarded as safe and had surrendered to the protection of the deity and consequently an indication of self dedication for servitude to the deity with its consequences on his descendant. The individual thus was expected to dwell within the surrounding land belonging to the deity and becomes custodian of the property of the deity as an adopted child. Thus fleeing into shrines of deities provided protection from a hostile and oppressive community or individual.

Anyone who has been dedicated to servitude to a deity lost to their free born relatives and 'diala' (freeborn) status. This process is finalized through an elaborate ritual observance which involved the whole community. The aim of this ritual is to openly declare the individual an adopted child of the deity and the ritual of crossing the boundary confers certain rights to the individual and his descendants forever. Social status does not exempt anyone from entering the osu. However the rich bought their freedom by purchasing a substitute human or cow. A woman stripping naked incurred the wrath of the deity. The offence is worse if the woman stripped naked in front of a shrine or inside the shrine of a deity. Whenever was considered abominable must call for the appeasing of the gods. And the deity must be appeased and seen to have been appeased by being offered a reasonable sacrifice and the correct rituals must be carried out.

Dedication into the osu and its privileges

The dedication took place before the representatives of the village and once completed the person is declared a property of the deity. This ritual included cutting part of the ear (not cutting off), total shaving of the hair. The hair must never be cut again all life and the osu and his descendants inhabited the vicinity of the shrine and owns the property of the deity including its life stock, and landed property. There was usually boundary marking the crossing over from life as diala to life with the particular deity to whom the human osu has been ritually dedicate. The osu, be it human or animal, had the right to enter into any compound or farm and take anything without being challenged. It was only the osu who could eat with the spirit and they alone had the right to take and eat whatever was offered to the deity. Any non osu who violated this rule automatically became osu. The osu must not have sexual intercourse with non osu (diala), otherwise the diala became osu. The osus's blood must not be shed or be caused to be shed so as not to incur the wrath of the deity that owns them.

Social stigma against the osu

The osu must not be married by the diala (free born). They must not attend the same stream, farm on the same area of land, etc. They had no right to traditional title or leadership position. They were never to be accorded burial rites; consequently they could not join the retinue of the ancestors. They were rather thrown into the evil forest instead of burial.

Identifying an osu

It is becoming more difficult to identify an osu as the villages are today enlarged into towns and cities with wide mix of peoples. Also the conspicuous marks identifying them have also disappeared and the prohibition of cutting their hair and the opening of ear lobe is so insignificant or missing. The descendants of an original osu are not forced to open the ears nor to leave the hair uncut and in fact they no longer live within the confines of the shrine of the deity that owns them. Above all most of them are known to be the richest and most educated in their communities as they have been known to be more progressive than even the diala. However some diala still claim they are capable of identifying an osu even in cities when they walk by them though they claim they could not explain how it happens. Some allege that it is the mystery of the osu system.

Putting an end to the osu institution-recommendations

Perhaps because of the psychological effect of the osu institution and beliefs on the Ibo, it appears near impossible to imagine an end to the osu system. Even in these days of modernity, social integration, Christian influence and secularization of people the institution is still strongly felt. Thus many educated and Christian free born (diala) still adhere to this old belief. A love relationship will readily come to an end once one of the partners is discovered to be osu. Even when couples decide to continue in such relationship, societal pressure forces them to part ways.

However it is only in the area of love relationships that the fear of the osu is most paramount. Some osu have been known to have bought their freedom, some are said to have bought traditional titles. Some others have participated in politics and defeated their diala opponents. This perhaps shows how pragmatic the Ibos are as a people.

Unlike in the past when the diala Christians dissociated themselves from Churches that accepted osu, both castes are well integrated into churches. Many osu people are pastors as well as bosses to diala in offices. Both castes belong to same family meetings in cities and even in the village communities that once ostracized them.

The influence of the osu belief on marriage and love affair is psychological and must be treated as such if any end to the discrimination can be put. Perhaps because the effect is psychological could account for its sustenance. However because the effect is only felt today when it comes to marriage shows that much of the effort today has been to prevent the children born in such a marriage becoming osu. Marrying an osu automatically makes the children of such a marriage to became osu without any fresh ritual of dedication. This is perhaps the worst form of injustice that can be meted on the innocent for the sins of their fathers. This practice is of course contrary to the Hebrew attitude to the human person in the Old Testament and seems to indicate the extent to which the Ibo has backslidden from the faith of their fathers.

A possible solution might be to gather all the traditional rulers, priests, and church leaders to carry out a final rite that would absolve the osu of the offence of their forefathers and ritually reclaim them from the ownership of the deities. Carrying out such a rite might make the people to believe that the deity have disclaimed the osu, this could be enhanced by elaborate teaching and emphasis on this cleansing. Also the rite could be carried out on any individual person and baby born of a marriage between the osu and the diala. A similar rite is performed to absolve a woman from the effects of her association with her dead husband and vice versa.

The effecting of this rededication to the diala status should be simple and effective because the osus living in same village as those who purchased their ancestors regards themselves as possessions of the family and respects as such. In fact some introduce themselves and remind these owners of their ancestors that they 'should not forget that we are your relatives'. These present day relatives of the osu who actually never participated in this ritual btu know about it from stories told them by their fathers and uncles should be humane enough to play a major role in rededicating these osus to the diala status. Failing to reverse this ritual means that the descendants are sharing in the sins of their fathers. The osu practice and consequent stigmatization of a human being must be seen as another abomination ignorantly practiced. This is more so because the Ibo believe that it is the humans that invented deities and it is the human that relinquishes a deity that is not seen to be effective in providing help and succor when needed. The osu deities are effective only in the minds of those who believe in them. They are today irrelevant and should be discarded.

In fact there is a sense in which every human being is osu as long as they belong to God. Every human being is in servitude to the devil but Jesus Christ has paid the price that set us all free from the bondage of the devil.

Also since the osu is a national issue, the governments at both state and federal levels , must participate in the rite and the reclaiming ritual should be made a national issue and information spread all over the country. Attempts to eradicate the osu in the past failed because they were only legislative steps (Nwaiwu 1987: 16) which showed that the authorities perhaps underestimated the extent of the psychological effect it had on the people. Osu is not a legislative issue. It is psychological, and the spiritual import enhances the effect and the grip upon the people. Thus any attempt at providing solution to it must be approached from this angle. For example a bishop of a well known denomination is said to have been asked by his congregation to set an example by giving his daughter away in marriage to an osu. He is said to have refused to do so. Politicians are said to have campaigned against their opponents by using the osu factor. One such politician is quoted to have referred to his opponent as an osu. These show that the osu issue cannot be easily eradicated through just legislative process. It is deep seated in the psyche of the people no matter how educated they might be. Even those who are supposed to protect the legislation disobey it before anyone else. The osu phobia is passed from parent to children and from generation to generation. This is in spite of the federal government of Nigeria constitution section 39 sub section 2 of chapter iv on fundamental human rights which bans the osu institution. In 1956 a law abolishing osu failed to achieve any positive effect. The people neglected the law although it declared the osu and their children free from the stigma. Also although Christian ministers condemn the belief and practice of osu they do not adhere to the Biblical injunction of equality and practice same ostracisation they preach against. There has been no new osu dedication ritual for centuries and even during my great grandfather's time there were people who refused give human beings as osu to any deity including himself and he taught his children never to do it. My own father followed his example so that when one of the women committed some abominable acts that required the appeasing of the deity he offered cows.

The osu institution remains a scandal to the morality of the Ibo who claim special relationship with the Abraham who is the God of Justice. Continuing the social stigmatization of so called osu is a desecration of the ofo, the symbol of Justice among the Ibos. The Ibo say 'omeni jide ofo'- whatever actions you may carry out

ensure Justice is on all side.

Chapter 10
On Circumcision

It is important to note that the practice of circumcision did not begin with Abraham. As far back as 4000 BC circumcision of boys took place as a rite of passage to manhood. This is seen in the carvings in ancient Egyptian tombs. However El Shaddai still saw it needful to make this ancient rite of passage into a rite of passage to belong to him when G-d wanted to enter into a special relationship with Abraham and his descendants (Genesis17).

My aim here is to examine the role circumcision played in ancient society by using ancient Israel and the Ibo belief and practice of circumcision. The focus for the Israelite section will be on examining what I consider the three major texts on circumcision: Joshua 5: 2-12, Genesis 17 and Exodus 4.

In view of the variety of interpretations partly due to antiquity of the topic I shall include Biblical exegesis to assist in clarifying seemingly difficult expressions and words. Redaction criticism will also be included as well as the opinion of renowned scholars in Biblical Studies, Anthropology, Philosophy and Theology. Yet try to make it simple enough to be understood by the non initiate in this typr of study.

Genesis 17

 Genesis 17:1ff states that El Shaddai made a covenant with Abraham, the great ancestral forefather of the Hebrew. The account implies that El Shaddai found Abram and changed his name to Abraham (father of many nations) following this covenant. The covenant was that every male in his household should be circumcised. Obeying Abraham began with circumcising himself at old age ninety years old; and then his first son Ishmael who was aged thirteen years age was circumcised next. He also circumcised his entire household. According to the passage anyone not circumcised was cut off from his people in all generations of Abraham's descendants. Even servants, strangers, slaves etc were not excluded in this covenant. We could gather from the passage, at least by implication, that no other tribe known to El Shaddai was practicing circumcision or had practiced circumcision before this covenant was made. Abraham's children would possess Canaan and Kings shall emerge from them. The circumcision was to be observed as early as the eighth day of birth. In Genesis 21:4 we read that Abraham got a son in his old age called him Isaac who became the first person to be circumcised at the age of eight days as El Shaddai had commanded Abraham. This perhaps, by implication at least, qualified him to become the child of the covenant. One other interesting observation on the account of circumcision in this passage is that it is the only passage on circumcision which makes the rite binding on all descendants of Abraham in all ages (cf Exodus 4: 25-27, Joshua 5: 2-8).

In the light of other passages we realize that circumcision has been known to exist in several tribes of Abrahamic lineages apart from Isaac's descendants. These were Edom, Amon, Moab, Tema, Dedan, and Kedar (see Fox' "The sign of the covenant- circumcision in the light of the priestly 'ot etiologies' RB 81 1974: 589f.) Tema (Jeremiah 9: 24f, 25: 23) and Kedar (Jeremiah 49: 28, 32) are Ishmaelite tribes (Genesis 25: 13f), and Dedan was descended from Abraham through Keturah (Gen 25: 3) and as indicated earlier among the Africans. The formula found in Genesis 17: 2-6 is also found in Genesis 17: 16, Genesis 28: 3, Genesis 35: 11; Genesis 48: 3f; Exodus 6: 2-8; although with slight variations.

The phrase "El Shaddai" which belongs to these passages is an expression which belongs to the religious tradition of the religio ethnic group of Hebrew sons of Eber of which Israel was a part (see M. Haran "The Religion of the Patriarchs" ASTI 4 1965: 42).

The title is perhaps derived from the idea of "G-d the Sufficient", known to be an old Jewish interpretation (see The Broadman Bible Commentary vol 1 1969: 182). The title could be derived from the Akkadian word for 'Mountain". "God of Mountain" is also a Mesopotamian name (see The Jerome Bible Commentary vol1 Raymond Brown et als eds 1968: 20)

We also see a promise similar to Genesis 17: 1-4 in Genesis 15: 1-20. Also Genesis 17: 15ff corresponds to the announcement of Isaac's birth in Genesis 18:1-15. Both passages agree in basic facts, but Genesis 17 materials seem to be modified and more updated than Genesis 15. Genesis 15 represents God of Israel as "Yahweh", while Genesis 17 has "El Shaddai" included.

We also find that there are at least three promises made at different times in Israelite history in the passage. The promise of land belonged originally to the patriarchal religion where it assured the semi normadic tribes on their way toward the civilized territory that they would succeed in achieving their goal (see G Von Rad, "The Problem of the Hexateuch" in The Problem of the Hexateuch and other Essays E W Trueman Dickens -translator (1966: 61).

The promise of posterity and the promise of Land had been united long before Genesis 17 and they form the nucleus of one of the redactors of the passage.

The promise of progeny is probably the oldest of the three promises found in the passage because it originally applied to all the Abrahamic tribes, whereas the promise of land and Yahweh's Godship promise belonged only to the traditions of the sons of Jacob (Fox 590f).

The fusion of these passages into one covenant is not only perculiar but shows that there must have been some deliberate aim in the way the passage is rendered. It is likely a reinterpretation of an old and well known tradition. It can be observed that the promises in the introduction of the passage are introduced syndetically and asyndetically.

Syndetically it is introduced with the finite verbs:

We 'arbe oteka bim'od meod (v2)

Wehayita le'ab ha mongoyim (vss 4, 5-6)

Asyndetically, the promises are introduced with an infinitive

Lihyot leka le'lohim

The syndetic clause in Genesis 17: 2b, 4b-6 and 8 are not promises additional to the covenant " I will establish my covenant with you and increase you ..." but that they rather defined its content. We can surmise that vss 2-6 must have been an ancient posterity promise which was communicated orally and common to the Abrahamic tribes.

In addition Genesis 17 witness to El Shaddai becomes a point in hand to buttress the proposition of a common oral tradition. This is because of the common practice of Genesis to give a picture of many Els such as El Elyon (Genesis 14: 18-20), el pachadh Gen 31: 42; el Shaddai Gen 31; 13 and El Bethel Genesis 31: 13, 'elah,' 'eloah.' 'This corresponds to the polytheistic religion of Canaan as shown in the tablets of Ras Shamra (see the Broadman Commentary: 182 for this argument) Genesis 17 witness to El Shaddai must therefore be a preservation of an early and maybe reliable tradition. We can in fact go further to say that the whole account of circumcision in the Bible is a reinterpretation of this oral tradition.

The above observation if acceptable raises the question of what the content of the oral tradition is and at what stage in Israelite history was the Genesis 17 account recorded.

In order to respond to the first question we need to look at Exodus 4: 24ff account of circumcision and Joshua 5: 2ff account of circumcision also. This is necessary because the age at which the circumcision recorded in these passages took place must be very ancient- as early as the Stone Age as evidenced by the use of the flint knife. Some scholars claim that circumcision originated from the Kenites from whom they claim Moses borrowed it and introduced it into Israel (see Morgenstern: 1966:70ff). The account of Exodus 4: 24ff circumcision took place in Median, a Kenite territory. According to Morgenstern, Exodus 4: 24 -26 was part of the Kenite code, the oldest document of the Hexateuch, coming from the southern kingdom and dates from 899BC (Morgenstern, " The Bloody Husband... once again HUCA 34: 1963: 38f). This date shows that the Ibo ancestors were already in Ibo land and must have preserved this oral tradition and practice.

This date is also certainly far earlier than the date the account of Genesis 17 occurred (generally taken as c 600-500BC among scholars). The cultic nature of Genesis 17 makes it a possible priestly redaction or authorship. This also places it within the palace traditions. Thus we can surmise that the Kenites had known Yahwehism before the Israelites. Their Yahwehism probably predates Abrahamic being descendant of Cain. Therefore there must have been an oral tradition that was circulating commonly among the Semites. Enoch, the name of Cain's city, is a Medianite name (Genesis 25:4). Can we then conclude that the source of this oral tradition is Median or among the Kenites.

Concerning the content of the oral tradition, Morgenstern relates it to the ritual sacrifice in which the sacrificing of a part redeemed the whole. The sacrifice of a part removes the taboo on the object (Morgenstern: 1966: 48). Some other scholars would regard the content of the tradition to be connected with initiation into adulthood which is performed at the advent of puberty so as to prepare the boy for marriage and for the responsibilities of a man with the privileges of kinship with every member of the tribe and with the deity of the tribe or clan. This kinship or blood of union was established primarily by virtue of the blood that was shed during the rite whereby an enduring covenant was established between the circumcised boy and the deity of his fellow tribesmen.

WOE Oesterley and Robinson (Hebrew Religion 1949: 136) would trace the oral tradition to Africa from where they claim it spread to Arabia and among the tribes of the Steppe Land. Their view is that circumcision possibly denoted the consecration of the reproductive organs to the deity in order to ensure offspring. The penis itself is revered among the Jews because the penis and the semen discharged might have been regarded as the seat of life. Some sanctity was accorded to the penis in its use for oaths and kindred practices (Morgenstern: 1966: 224) In Arabian countries mothers and young maidens visited married women to kiss with a kind of devotion the hammam (sexual organ) of the male children.

In Palestine, the oath "my hand below thy girdle" is indicative of male organ reverence (Morgenstern 1966: 237, 261: citing "the Immovable East" by Baldensperger PEF 1910 and Doughty Arabia Deserta 1)

Noteworthy also is the formula " I cause you to swear by your girdle and your genitals, by your children, which you already have or can have, by your relatives and by your posterity" (Genensis 24: 2, 47: 29) that indicates traditional Hebrew reverence of the penis (Frazer IR 1904 204FF, The Golden Bough and H. Spencer Principles of Sociology 11: 67)

Genesis 15 covenant

After leaving Mesopotamia, Abraham migrated to Canaan where G-d gave him the assurance of future grandeur and prosperity of his descendants. In order to confirm this promise, the deity entered into a covenant with Abraham. The procedure and significance of this covenant would not have been different from the known practice of such covenant in Abraham's time. Abraham was told to kill a heifer of three years old, a she goat of three years, a ram of three years old. A turtle and a young pigeon were to be allowed to fly away. Abraham cut each animal into two pieces. He laid each half of the animal over the other and made sure that he drove away the birds that came to prey on the carcasses. At sundown we read that Abraham went into a deep slumber, and a horror of great darkness fell upon him. When it was dark a smoking furnace and flaming torch passed between the pieces of the victims, and G-d proclaimed his covenant with Abraham. We can surmise that an already well known procedure was being described here, a formality required by ancient Hebrew law at the ratification of a covenant. The horror of great darkness was an indication of the presence of G-d who passed in the likeness of a smoking furnace and a flaming torch. If we read Jeremiah 34: 18 we see this picture clearer:

"I will give the hands of their enemies the men that have transgressed against my covenant, which have not performed the words, of the covenant which they made before me when they cut the calf in twain and passed between the parts thereof"

This passage indicates that the procedure of Genesis 15 followed along the regular ancient Hebrew form of cutting a covenant. The ancient Hebrew phrase for making a covenant is literally to "cut a covenant" (Gen 21: 27, 32; 26: 28; Exodus 23: 32; 34: 10; Deut 5: 2; 7: 2; Joshua 9: 6). The same expression appears in a cuneiform document from ancient Qatna in Syria of the fourteenth century BC (see T. H Gaster Myth, Legend, and Custom in the Old Testament 1969: 41 citing J

Botero in RA 44 1950: 112f W Albright BASOR 144: 1951: 22; E Vogt in Biblica 36: 1956: 566). Among the Ibos "i cha aboshi" means to cut "aboshi"; aboshi is a sacred ritual leaf used to severe a relationship through a covenant before witnesses. The two people held the leaf at each of its ends and pull apart. The leaf is cut in the middle, thereby ending that relationship. So Ibos also "cut" a covenant. Cutting of Aboshi can also be used to cut a covenant relationship anew before witnesses and declaring of oaths was included. In certain situations e. g to purify a compound of sin of murder (ipu ala in igbu ochu) and reconcile them with the victim's family, compound, village, clan and town, animal sacrifice might be used.

Other Nations

The Greeks also speak of cutting an oath in the sense of swearing them (Odyssey 24 483; Herodotus 7: 132 cited in Gaster 1969: 41).

The Masai of East Africa settled disputes by oath. In such a situation each disputant took hold of a goat or sheep which was then cut in two. This was done in the presence of witnesses, and the matter was settled and never to be reopened again (J Macdonald in JRAL 1899 cited by Gaster 1969: 233).

A chief among the Barolong tribe in South Africa made peace with another chief with who he had been at war and who had surrendered to him with an Ox. A hole was bored through the Ox and two chiefs crawled through the hole, one after the other in order to intimate by this ceremony that their tribes would henceforth be at peace (Gaster 1969: 278 citing R Moffat, Missionary labours and Scenes in Southern Africa 1842).

Covenant theories and Genesis 17

We have two theories that explain why making a covenant involved cutting of flesh and blood. One is the retributive theory that states that the killing and cutting up of the victim symbolises the retribution that will overtake the perjurer of the oath. An example of this is represented by the oath of fealty taken by Mati'ilu King of Arpad (751 BC) to Ashur-narari, king of Assyria (see ANET 350f). The perjurer of this oath was said to be capable of bringing a curse on his children up to his great grand children. Similar rites are identified among the Babylonians and the Hittites.

The other theory is the sacramental theory which was propounded by Robertson Smith (Smith: 1927: 481). Smith is of the view that the procedure of passing between severed pieces of the animal in covenant was indicative of protective rather than retributive intention. The flesh and the blood of the victim are thought to present an obstacle to the power of evil on the person.

The Arabs of Moab who observed such rites during calamities such as drought or epidemic explained them as intended to deliver the people from the evil which afflicts or threatens them (Gaster: 1969: 148) In such situations the Sheikh stood up in the camp to cry out "redeem yourselves' people redeem yourselves". Thereupon every family was expected to sacrifice a sheep, divide it into two and hang the pieces under the tent, and all the members of the family passed between the pieces (Gaster 1969:148). Since the Arabs and Hebrews are both Semites, speaking kindred languages and influencing each other or perhaps having a common ancestral lineage (Abraham) with whom G-d covenanted, we can infer, with Gaster, that the ancient Hebrews and the Arabs rite and by extention, the Ibos, are derived from a common Semitic origin, the purification or protective intention of which is still borne in mind by the Arabs of Moab and the Ibos in Africa. It is very likely that there was a common belief and tradition of this covenant with Abraham, the record of which must have been kept and passed on among the Hebrew children. It is very likely that a situation arose in which the Bible authors had to put them down in record. Different versions appeared in each section. The composer of Genesis 17 must have been a much later composer who reinterpreted the tradition to make a special claim of the ownership and favour of El Shaddai making G-d and G-d's favours and blessing solely that of Israel.

What we are saying is that the source of Genesis 17 account of circumcision had no connection with circumcision as sign of the covenant originally. Genesis 17 becomes a theological interpretation of an already existing tradition on covenant making which God made with the ancient forefathers of which Israel was a descendant. The ancient tradition must have been preserved by the Kenites and from them passed on from generation to generation among the peoples of the ancient East. Perhaps it was this over spiritualization of the rite of circumcision that has led to the loss of the purpose and meaning of circumcision as observed by Professor Hans Mallau in a verbal conversation with me. It can also account for the politicization of the rite in the history of the Jews especially during the Maccabean times. The true meaning of the rite of circumcision can therefore only be preserved by those whose tradition remained unadulterated by happenstance in the Middle East. Ancient Ibo ancestors are among those who have preserved the true meaning of this rite.

However we shall next examine the Joshua 5 passage closely and relate it to the account of the Ibo practice of circumcision.

Circumcision account in Joshua 5: 2- 12

In this translation we shall attempt to be as literal as possible to this rather difficult Hebrew Text

At that time Yahweh said to Joshua, make you knives of flint and return, circumcise the sons of Israel for the second time (v.2). And Joshua made for himself knives of flint and circumcised the sons of Israel at the hill of the foreskins (v.3). And this (is) the reason (for) which Joshua circumcised all the people that came out of Egypt (v.4). All the males, the men of war, had died in the wilderness on the way as they came out of Egypt, for all the people were circumcised (v.5). For the sons of Israel had walked forty years in the wilderness, until all the nations of war who had come out of Egypt, who did not listen to the voice of Yahweh to whom Yahweh swore to the fathers to give to us a land flowing with milk and honey, were consumed (v6). And he raised their sons in the place; Joshua circumcised them for (v7). And it came to pass when all the nations had finished being circumcised that they remained in their places in the camp until they recovered (v8). And Yahweh said to Joshua. Today I have rolled the reproach of Egypt off you, therefore the name of that place (is) called Gilgal to this day (v9)... (taken from the Hebrew text)

Opinion of some scholars on the above passage:

According to Matthew Henry circumcision rolled away the reproach of Egypt on the Israelite. By this he meant that the Israelites having been tainted with the idolatry of Egypt needed circumcision to put an end to the reproach caused by this idolatrous life style. And having successfully entered Canaan, the Promised Land, the Israelites, he said, were exonerated of the suggestion of the Egyptians that they had been shut off in the wilderness because of their mischief. In other words that their God had forsaken them in the wilderness (Matthew Henry's Commentary: 217). According to Matthew Henry's Commentary, circumcision was also needed to restore Israel back to the fellowship of God and as a living sacrifice to God who alone delivered the Israelites and also owned them. Achieving this status once again made room for other institutions such as Passover to be revived. Thus we have Passover celebrated following their circumcision (Matthew Henry's Commentary: 1975: 216 - 217).

The Jerusalem Bible commentary regards the reproach of Egypt as reference to the uncircumcised nature of the Egyptians.

Blair is of the opinion that the whole exercise was to qualify the Israelites to carry out the Passover, a repeat of the feast which marked the first miracle of deliverance in Egypt from death of their first born during the time of Moses (Blair The New Bible Commentary: 1977: 238).

The NIV indicates that the role of circumcision and Passover were two significant preparations for the conquest of the Promised Land. Circumcision, it says, marked every male as a son of Abraham (referring to Genesis 17:10-11) bound to the services of the Lord and that it was a prerequisite for Passover (referring to Exodus 12: 48) which celebrated deliverance from judgment (Barber et al NIV Study Bible: 1985: 294). The implication is perhaps that Israel's wandering in the wilderness symbolized judgment of God and that circumcision rolled away the reproach Egypt would have cast on them if they had perished in the desert as they had reached safety in the promised Land (referring to Exodus 32:12, Numbers 14: 3, Deuteronomy 9: 28, Numbers 14: 21- 23, 29-33, Numbers 9: 1-5).

Etymology of the word "mul"

The Hebrew word for circumcise is 'mul'. Ordinarily "mul" means "to be in front of" or " front". In Hebrew economy, however, "mul" later came to mean "to cut off" as in cutting grass (Briggs Driver and Brown BDB: 557). In the Hiphal the word means "to ward off". In 4 Maccabees 1: 29 mul occurs in the sense of "to cut off" as in cutting a plant. In the LXX (Septuagint text), we find the word "peritemno" as representing the Hebrew word, "mul". Ordinarily, the verb peritemno means "to cut around", "to make incision round ones arm" as a mourning sign (BDB 557 cf Gen 17 10-14, 23-27; Exod 4: 25; 12:44, 48; Lev 12: 3: Joshua 5: 2-8, 21- 42; 24: 31a; Esther 8: 17;) The verb also occurs exclusively as a ritual in the LXX (Meyer Theological Dictionary of the New Testament (Kittel ed.) 1968:74)

The LXX of Psalm 119: 10ff that gives us the word "amno" seems to present us with a clearer and more acceptable meaning of 'circumcision'. "Amno" has the dual meaning of " to ward off and keep off anything from someone", or " to keep off anyone from oneself". It also means "to defend oneself against anyone" (2Maccbees 10: 17; LXX Joshua 10: 13. See Thayer: The New Thayers Greek English Lexicon of the New Testament 1979: 33; Josephus Antiquities 9:9:1:2)

Josephus Antiquities explains it to mean "to take vengeance on anyone" (Ant 9:9:1:2). There is however a slight deviation in the meaning given by LXX of Deuteronomy 30: 6 where it uses "perikatharizein" for Hebrew root "mul" and in Joshua 5:4 Symmachus, a Jewish Christian of the second century used "Katharizein" for Deuteronomy 30: of LXX.(see Tergum Onkelos and the Vulgate).

The noun 'peritemi' is also used in a ritual sense for circumcision.

'aral zakor

Also noteworthy is perhaps the word 'aral zakor' which refers to verb 'uncircumcised" (Judges 14: 3; 15: 18) In the LXX 'rl is translated "aperitmetos" which is also "uncircumcised". Usage here is also in the ritual sense (Gen 17:14).

By rendering peritemno and periteme in ritual sense the LXX has helped us to understand what mul could represent in the Hebrew sense. The ordinary usage of mul originally as "front" or "in front of" could refer to its local primitive usage. Its usage as "to cut off" as in cutting a grass or plant, though has not any ritual implication, its hiphil which means " to ward off" and better explained by the LXX amno brings out the ritual implication of Hebrew "mul". Amno has therefore given us possible original meaning of the word "circumcise". This is as a protective rite which "wards off" something or someone from oneself.

The vocabulary of the circumcision ritual in Leviticus 19: 23f which must have been derived from sacrificial ceremonial in which a fruit less than four years old is regarded as not circumcised which also means "not matured for food" connects circumcision with maturation for harvest or reproduction. Just as a fruit needed a time limit to be matured for food, perhaps, the human species had time (age) limit to be matured for reproduction. Circumcision rite, perhaps was a sign of this maturity (cf Exodus 4: 24- 26, Gen 17) in ancient world, a prerequisite rite for the important function of sexual activity and reproduction as well as protecting the one from certain dangers.

Joshua passage presents a motivation and purpose for the practice of circumcision. This is as the conditio sine qua non of the celebration of the festival of Passover in ancient Israel. We are told that Joshua was commanded to circumcise the Israelites the second time. The phrase "the second time" perhaps indicates that Joshua was carrying out a rite already well known to the people. It also perhaps indicates that it was to follow the one carried out by Moses on the children of Israel, slaves, and strangers during the Exodus from Egypt at which time the Passover was first celebrated. Circumcision thus has been made to be a cleansing or purification rite for the celebration of the Passover in ancient Israel. The passage further, states that it was necessary because a generation of Israelites, all who left Egypt in the Exodus and who were circumcised in order to participate in the first Passover celebration had all died. Their children and grand children were at this occasion to celebrate another Passover. So it became vitally necessary for them to be purified enough to participate in it. One implication of this could be that the Israelites of Joshua's time waited until it was time for Passover celebration before they were circumcised. Passover celebration was therefore presented as the only motivation for circumcision as if all males remained uncircumcised until the celebration of Passover came. However, if we accept this circumcision practice here to be ad hoc then we can surmise that circumcision on a more general level was what was meant here as the second time indicates, rather than circumcision as a traditional practice among the ancient Israelites. This is explainable by the fact that Abraham's circumcision was not during any Passover, and ancient Israelites like the Ibos must have practiced the rite at individual family levels. Perhaps only later on did it become carried out only during the Passover celebration that a general circumcision was declared on all the uncircumcised for making them ready for the festival. What then was the traditional belief about circumcision in ancient Israel judging from glimpses from Joshua 5:2-12 account? There are glimpses of the aim for the practice of circumcision in ancient Israel from this passage; different from what the theology of Joshua 5 seems to present.

A closer look at Joshua 5: 2-12, we can see that it is a composite passage; we can also see that some statements pointing to some other explanations which can be said to be unconnected with the Passover. For example how does the rolling away (Galah) of reproach of Egypt from Israel connect the incident being talked about. We are told that this rolling away of the reproach gave the place where the circumcision took place the name Gilgal. This expression gives room for different interpretation of the passage.

The composite nature of the passage Joshua 5:2-12, in addition to what has been said above reveals some deliberate theologizing by the author or authors of the passage. We see that part of the passage which describes the Passover celebration (vss 10-12) does not make any mention of circumcision. The earlier verses make mention of circumcision without mentioning the Passover. It has been suggested that verse 10-12 came from a different author or redactor from the other section that came from at least two different authors or redactors (cf J. Morgenstern: Rites of Birth, Marriage, Death and Kindred Occasion among the Semites)

The fact that there are at least three deducible reasons given for this ad hoc circumcision practice attests to a possible composite nature and deliberate theological interpretation of the traditional circumcision among the ancient Israelites of Joshua's time. Moreover despite the ancient use of flint knife, which suggests it to be a very ancient rite, the passage presents multiple motives for the practice of the rite. This further raises questions concerning the unity of the passage. It is therefore very likely that the practice of circumcision in ancient Israel was originally not associated with covenant relationship, or with any Passover. Joshua 5: 2, 8f must have been based on a different ancient oral traditional which was popular among the people. This is further attestable by the discovery of a hill of foreskins (geb'ot ha'aroloth) at the pre-Israelite sanctuary of Gilgal near Jericho. This place has been identified as an ancient place of circumcision for the circumcision of people as a puberty rite or so. This oral tradition, perhaps, belongs to the Benjamite cycle and is perhaps historicized in Joshua 5: 2, 8f (Myer: 1968: 76). In historicizing the tradition it came to be associated with Joshua, the hero of the Ephraimites (Myer: 1968: 76). In this Joshua 5 passage it has been extended to include all Israel.

What we can say therefore is that the Israelites needed to renew their covenant with Yahweh before settling in Canaan. This renewal required circumcision. However, the theology as presented in Joshua 5 was so in order to achieve the above stated aim. The original role of circumcision was thus restated to suit official Yahwehism.

The above assertion could be better appreciated when one looks at Joshua passage from the point of view of yet another difficult passage, Exodus 4: 24-26. We shall follow the NIV translation just to avoid confusing the readers with intricaciy of Hebrew text and translations. The NIV reads:

At a lodging place on the way, the Lord met Moses and was about to kill him. But Zipporah took a flint knife, cut off her son's foreskin and touched Moses feet with it. "Surely you are a bridegroom of blood to me," she said. So the Lord let him alone. At that time she said "bridegroom of blood" because of the circumcision (lemuloth).

Literally the passage is difficult to translate and interprete because it is not clear who was circumcised, Moses or his son although the passage states that Zipporah cut off her son's foreskins and deposited it at "his feet". The passage does not explicitly state whose feet the foreskin was deposited. We can only presume that it was Moses feet. Again what is the symbolism of feet? Is it a euphemism referring to

Moses' private part or literally Moses feet? Again why did Adonai seek to kill him and who did Adonai seek to kill, was it Moses or his son Gershom? The passage is not clear on all these questions. Again we can only presume that Adonai sought to kill the boy because Moses perhaps failed to circumcise him, perhaps, an indication that Moses was not used to the ritual of circumcision and must have learned about it through Zipporah's family in Median. Again how old this boy was at this time is not easy to decipher; we can only deduce that he must have been long matured for circumcision, most likely the boy was in his puberty. This is a possible indication that deity in Median claimed right on the first born boys, perhaps the foreskin and blood of circumcision of all first boys.

The phrase "hatan damim atah li": "You are bridegroom of blood to me" becomes a most significant statement in the passage. The phrase "hatan damim" is translated, "bridegroom of blood" by most translations including NIV. Whatever the passage means of which we cannot go into elaborate exegesis here, we can gather that the time of the incident was very ancient times as indicated by the use of flint (stone) as knife. Also we can deduce that circumcision rite spared life, either of Moses or their son from the vengeance of an angry deity. We therefore deduce that the deity sought to kill because the right was not carried out as was expected by the custom of the land. Also we can see another connection of a possible common oral tradition with Adonai, the reverenced Lord of the Semites.

Finally it is important to state that circumcision is so vital in the life of the Jew that later Judaism placed the practice far above every other ritual. The Talmud (Jewish oral law) considers the milah (from the verb la'mul meaning to circumcise) to be equal to all the 612 commands. This is expressd mathematically in the Jewish gematria, numerical symbolism. Since the Hebrew letters are also numbers, the Hebrew word 'brit', meaning 'covenant', has a numerical value of 612 as follows: bet(b)=2; reish(r)=200; yud(')=10; taw(t)= 400: totalling 612. Thus BRIT = 612. When 'brit' is combined with the singular commandment of 'milah' in 'Brit Milah', it equals 613 which is the full number of the commandments in the Torah (email from weekly Hebrew Messianic Bible translation group to me).

The implication of this, perhaps, is that fulfilling the command to circumcise is equal to fulfilling the whole commandments of Yahweh; and failure to fulfil the command is equal to failing in all the commandments of Yahweh. Today preparation for the circumcision covenant observation includes the following items: a clamp, scissors, a sharp knife, Kiddush cup, sweet wine, a prayer book and a chair of Elijah on which the man holding the baby boy will sit while the circumciser called the mohel performs the circumcision.

An examination of Ibo belief and practice of circumcision will perhaps help clarify the role of circumcision in ancient Israelite community.

Circumcision as Practiced among the Ibo

As I stated above circumcision had been practiced in Africa long before the time of Abraham. Also being descendants of Seth through Enosh when people began to regard themselves as "People of Yahweh", Ibos should be regarded as part and parcel of the descendants of that generation of the descendants of Enosh who inherited all that it takes to belong to Yahweh. Thus Abraham a descendant of Enosh also belonged to the People of Yahweh. However what is special is that G-d is said to have entered into a relationship with Abraham through a special rite of passage called circumcision. However what is perhaps essential to note is that circumcision did not make Abraham and his descendants including the Ibo descendants a People of Yahweh. They were already a People of Yahweh by being descendants of Enosh. However to belong as a descendant of Abraham and be in a special relationship with Yahweh, chosen apart from all other peoples, circumcision acts as a seal of this special relationship with Yahweh.

There is a general Ibo belief that a human being comes to this world through the collective sanction of the ancestors and the Supreme Being. In fact the world of the ancestors is believed to be populated with people awaiting their turn to reincarnate into the family of their relatives in this physical world. Man, therefore exists originally as spirit who comes to earth in a different form (human).

A new born baby is regarded as a spirit and still belongs to the spirit world. Consequently, he is taboo and must be ritually rendered profane if he must participate in any important affairs of the profane world. The Ibo also believe that the life of everyone is in a structure of roles and functions within the society. One role must be successfully completed before the next phase is successfully entered into. The roles may not be all equal in magnitude in terms of responsibilities expected by the community, however each phase and role are as important as the others for the well being of the community. To enter a new phase with its roles, rituals are carried out to render the one being introduced into the new phase first of all profane and then sacred as he or she enters into the new phase.

Generally and ordinarily, circumcision among the Ibo is one of the means by which a person is introduced ritually into the adulthood phase and its responsibilities and expectations. Circumcision as a practice is deeply rooted in the belief that a male to be able to participate in the sacred act of procreation, the one must be purified from the childhood taboo. An uncircumcised male adult is therefore regarded to be of same status as a child. He is too immature to copulate with any female. Such a person faces social stigma and ridicule. He is referred to as "apingolongo" which means "one with the foreskin still protruding" among the Ibo. The Efiks refer to such a man as "esurisu". As an uncircumcised adult male is not accepted by the community of the living, so he is rejected by the ancestors, the spirits, and the deities. Consequently, no sensible lady would accept him for marriage.

The circumcision rite among the Ibo

A brief example of circumcision rite is that performed among the Ngor Okpala people of Owerri. Among this people circumcision is called "i bi ugwu" which literally means "cutting short of the ugwu". Ugwu here means "the foreskin" a symbol of indignity/ dishonour. This severing of the foreskin grants the boy honour, dignity and maturity and serves as an everlasting sign of the covenant the God of the fathers made with our ancestors. It serves as a reminder of this covenant to every male Ibo. It is an important link between kin, cult and the afterlife.

In the past, at about the age of twelve (10-12), the parents of a boy were expected to invite an "obi i ugwu", the professional circumciser, who was usually of the Levitical order (ihite people). The professional circumciser was invited to circumcise their son or sons as the case may be. Sometimes, in the past collective compound or village circumcise their boys collectively as a rite of initiation into adulthood. All the males who were considered ripe to be circumcised were gathered and the rite was performed. However, the more popular practice was that circumcision took place in front of the hut of the boy's mother at family levels; this implies link with maturity for procreation. The family fertility shrine is usually located inside the mother's hut. In most cases the representative of the Eze Ala, King Priest of the Ibo peoples, must be present to authenticate the rite as accepted by the Supreme Deity. This is the role of the Levites (referred to as the "people of Ihite" who also trained people in circumcision ritual practice)

On the morning of the appointed day, the mother brought the boy to the front of her hut after thoroughly bathing him. The professional circumciser, who had been earlier invited, dug a hole in front of the mother's hut and placed the boy to stand with his two feet placed each at the sides of the hole. The elders and members of the compound as well as the boys 'agu' a type of God father usually gathered to watch, observe and to encourage the boy to endure the pain. The boy was expected to endure the pain no matter what. By so doing he was expected to prove that he was capable of the roles of an adult and their associated grief and pains by not showing any sign of being in pain when the foreskin was being cut away; for this would indicate weakness which was reserved for children. However, most communities carry out ritual circumcision at the family level only. In this case circumcision took place mostly on the eighth day after birth while the mother was still in the "Omu ugwo" stage of purification (please see pregnancy and birth above)

The items brought for the circumcision included in every case include: a razor blade (aguba), egg yoke (odo), four ogirishi sticks (neubauldia laevis), yam tubers or cocoyams. The baby's agu (a type of Godfather) carries the baby or presents the boy to be circumcised before the circumciser.

The circumciser then places the boy in the appropriate position, and first cuts the yams or cocoyams into pieces and invoked the ancestors and Ala (the deity of fertility) to accept the yam or cocoyam pieces as the offering of the boy's family. The deity was then called upon to protect the boy at all times and to grant him fertility and procreation.

The foreskin of the boy's or baby's penis was then piled off and thrown into the hole. The blood from the cut was allowed to drip into the hole and the resulting sore was treated with sap from special herbs. The hole was next covered with the heap of sand dug out from the hole. The 'odo' was sprinkled on the top of the mound. The 'ogirishi' sticks were then planted by the site to mark the circle of the hole.

Having been circumcised, the boy if it was circumcision at puberty was instructed to stop associating with children since he had from then become a respectable grown up male. The father of the boy showed him the family estates which were bequeathed to them by their ancestors. He was allocated his portion of the estates. He was also taught how to offer prayers and perform rites as well as conduct family worship. At this stage he was ripe to join societies where he was taught secrets of his people and secrets of life generally. This is similar to the Hebrew bar Mitzvah as the boys were circumcised in a place close to the shrine of the Ala deity where they were all gathered away from females. They however went home to be nursed by their parents although in some villages they remained in the secluded hut for some days before going to their family.

Symbolic representations in the ritual practice

The products of circumcision were buried in a hole in front of his mother's hut also for protective reasons. This is so that "no enemy will come and dig out the foreskin and use it for mischievous 'medicine'".

The 'ogirishi' plant represents everlasting nature of the sign of circumcision. It also marks the burial site of the foreskin forever. It symbolizes continuous fertility and the ever presence of the ancestors. The 'ogirishi' plant is believes to survive every weather condition.

The blood that is shed at circumcision and allowed to spill into the hole binds the boy to the community which is made up of the living, the ancestors, and those yet to be born as well as to the earth deity, alah, who is regarded as being solely in charge fertility and reproduction. The "agu" (godfather) of the boy is similar to the Hebrew practice whereby a 'shalliach' (godfather) is committed to supervise the upbringing of the child. The child's agu is introduced to him early in his life and usually the child naturally becomes attached to his agu all life. I knew my own agu and he has remained a very special person to me up till today, although he passed on a long time ago. The attachment to him was very special indeed.

The endurance of the pain of cutting of the foreskin symbolizes the transition from childhood and getting ready for adulthood. The discarded foreskin symbolizes the previous childhood status and its associated non sexuality and childish behaviours.

The rite of circumcision is usually a condition sine qua non for initiation into higher societies of the boy's clan as well as for sexual activities. Above all circumcision is regarded as an introduction to the religious life of the immediate family, compound, hamlet, village, town, clan and tribe. It is as if the child's first shed blood was dedicated to the family deity as a right the deity expects from the family.

Following the thinking of Van Gennep, circumcision to the African is therefore a rite which separates a male from the taboo of infantile asexual status and incorporates him into the status of sexuality expected of an adult male in readiness for the sacred duty of procreation and community worship (Van Gennep 1960: The Rites of Passage M Vizedom, translator Chicago: University of Chicago Press)

The aim of the duty of procreation is to help strengthen the life force of the boy's family and clan. Procreation is a vital necessity among the Ibo; through it the living and the ancestral worlds are populated. As stated earlier sometimes collective circumcision is carried out among age mates. In such a situation boys shed the blood together and none would want to be left behind.

The blood of circumcision is believed to be sacrificed to Chiukwu Abi 'ama (literally: Great chi, father of my people) through the deity, alah, which as is believed owns everyone and has the blessing of procreation in his hands. All sexual sins are regarded as sin against the ancestors and the alah deity. Such offence is greeted with public shame and purification of the land is carried out called "ipu ala" (see Edmund Ilogu 1983: "I ro mmuo and Ikpu ala" in Traditional Religion in West Africa E. A Adegbola ed Ibadan: Daystar Press: 138f). Any pregnancy resulting from premarital intercourse, especially if with an uncircumcised male, was also regarded as abominable act that must require purifying the land; and remaining uncircumcised was unacceptable and an invitation for the wrath of the malevolent spirit in charge of disciplining such offenders. These spirits are given permission by alah to punish the uncircumcised male. Thus so long as the sign of circumcision remains on the boy, the boy remains under protection from the malevolent spirit called "arusi".

Circumcision on the eighth day following Birth among the Ibo

Just as it was with the ancient Hebrews, in addition to circumcision being a puberty rite, the Ibos carried out circumcision of a male child on the eighth day after birth. This practice has continued to the present day. In fact it seems that circumcision on the eight day of birth overshadowed circumcision as a puberty rite. The method adopted perhaps depends on the tradition that has the greatest influence on a community or family. The implication of two versions of circumcision among the Ibo is perhaps that some Ibo ancestors might not have come under the influence of Genesis 17 injunction to Abraham or that the injunction was not known universally among the ancient Hebrews as the only method of implementing the covenant made between El Shaddai and Abraham. However there are circumstances that might make circumcision on the eigth day impossible. It will then be carried out in puberty.

Deductions

Circumcision accounts in both Hebrew and Ibo traditions and practice show that circumcision is a very ancient practice. Joshua and Exodus passages show that its practice is far into the Stone Age when flint knife was used. This is confirmed by practice among the Ibos.

The accounts point to the use of circumcision as sacrifice to the goddess of fertility. "Yahweh" in the passages of Joshua probably refers to an original belief in this fertility goddess. This becomes clearer when the Joshua passage is compared with the events in Exodus 4: 24-26 and the observed Ibo ritual.

The sacrifice of the foreskin was a removal of a taboo which rested upon the uncircumcised child. In order to get involved in the sacred duty of worship and procreation this taboo was removed.

Failure to be circumcised carried with it some derogation as depicted by the words, "arelah" (iru ala in Ibo) "apingolongo", "esurisu". Male Circumcision is taken as given, imperative, among the Ibo. In fact it is regarded as an abomination for a boy to live uncircumcision. It is abhorrent to see an uncircumcised male. Seeing an uncircumcised person sends shivers throught the spine of any Ibo person. No success is recognized of a male who is uncircumcised. Such a person is treated as not existing. Such a person cannot offer any sacrifice or participate in any religious ritual or socially interact with other boys. Failing to be circumcised is tantamount to ostracizing oneness from the community. This is also reflected in the place of importance of the rite in ancient Israel as a sign of the covenant between Abraham and El Shaddai.

Circumcision originally provided a protection upon the circumcised as well as a purification rite for any important religious function. Among the Hebrews it was interpreted as having purified them for observance of the Passover festival and other cult life while in Canaan. Among the Ibos it made a boy ready for cult life as well as for entering into any sexual activity. Thus, that it served as a puberty rite in both Joshua 5 and the Ibo cultural milieu shows that it perhaps served the same purposes in the ancient world of the two peoples; at least at a time in the history of the people. The Joshua account as presented in the Bible is a possible reinterpretation of a known ancient rite to suit emergent official Yahwehism. However what still mattered is the belief and practice of the common people. Moreover circumcision has often been connected with marriage and fertility among peoples (cf Genesis 34:1-24; Exodus 4: 24-26; I Samuel 18: 24-27; Smith 1994; ANET 543:4; Old Babylonian Text BM 78296, CT. XLVIII, No 50; Barton: 1902: 98ff; ERE vol 3: 1901:679ff; Lodds: 1948: 197ff).

Chapter 11
The Sacrificial Systems and Festivals

Priesthood and the sacrificial system of ancient Israelites

Much of the Old Testament seems filled up with information on the sacrificial system of ancient Israel. The Tanakh in particular presents ancient Israelites as a worshiping community whose worship was foundationally sacrificial. The Book of Leviticus seems to be mainly instructions on types and methods of sacrificing while the other Books in addition include the occasion people sacrificed and why the scarifices were necessary. The Book of Leviticus states that without the shedding of blood there cannot be remission of sin. So this means that the purpose of sacrifice according to Leviticus is for purification of the land when polluted by sin. Sacrifice becomes a means of calming down the anger of the deity. Thus we find that the gravity of the offence and the extent of its effect on the nation of Israel determined what animal was used for the sacrifice. An individual's sin affected the whole nation and this must be addressed as such. There are some sins or offences that relate to person to person (civil) while those offences specific to the deity were addressed as such. Thus we find the following offences: domestic offences, personal states, person to person, tribe, clan, community, tribe and national offences. The sacrifice demanded at each level must be appropriate to the instructions given on how to address such. States of impurity demand specific treatment. Such states include a menstruating woman, child birth, child dedication, entering adulthood; ritual state of a man also demanded specific sacrificial attention (e.g spilling semen, making contact with an impure person, touching a corpse, and other wrongful associations etc); every infringement of the instructions of purity had a prescribed offering and sacrifice to make in order to appease the deity.

In the earlier stages of Israelite religious experience as a religious community, the sacrifices and offerings were either carried out by the individual adult or by the designated person who acted as priest at that level of relationship. Individuals set up their personal altars; there were also family, clan, tribal and national shrines and sanctuaries for sacrifices. The Old Testament especially the Tanakh contains very many of such sites, including groves, and what is called high places. Some of these were close to households some were far off. An indiviual honours their encounter with the deity by setting up places as shrines or sanctuaries and went their regularly to offer sacrifices.

Sacrifice and offering could be for various purposes: for cleansing from impure state or sinful act, thanksgiving, and harvest (please see below on Levitical instructions for more on this).

What is important here is to note that ancient Israel was a religious community in which kin, cult and the afterlife were strongly knit together; consequently the sin of one person was believed to affect the whole including threatening the existence and survival of the nation. This means that every individual was brought up to appreciate the key to survival as a people; was to collectively live righteously according to the Laws of the Land. The Laws of the land focus on living in harmony with humanity, spirits-deity and the ancestors. Sacrifice and offering maintain harmony with the deity while respecting the dignity of the human person, the natural environment and self, is crucial to ensuring harmony among humanity. Sacrifice for collective national sin was carried out in the Temple which was operated by a priestly class trained specifically to lead in Temple worship.

The Book of Exodus contains information on preparations for consecrating Aaron and his sons for service unto Yahweh including all manner of instructions for sacrificing unto Yahweh (please see especially Exodus 20-40). In the same passage we also find prohibitions, types, and methods of ritual sacrificing. By ritual I mean the processes and pattern that must be followed rigidly for the expected results to be achieved. Also we find warnings against offering sacrifice to idols and the fate of a sorcerer among the ancient Israelites was highlighted.

An outline in the book of Leviticus detailing instructions of the sacrificial system is as follows (see Leviticus 1:1-15:33):

the great day of atonement for the sins of the nation (Leviticus 16:1 1-35), Regulations and instructions on sacrifice 17: 1- 20: 27,

Rules for priests 21: 1-22:33,

Rules concerning festivals 23:1-25:55, and

Specifications on matters of obedience, vows and tithes 26: 1-27:34.

Among the types of offerings carried out are:

Burnt offering (korban olah), usually of sheep or goat, turtle dove or young pigeons: Levitivus 1: 1- 3 commands (tzav), "the Lord now spoke to Moses from the Tabernacle and commanded him to give the following instructions to the people of Israel: When you sacrife to the Lord, use animals from your herds and flocks. If your sacrifice is to be an ox given as a burnt offering, use only a bull with no physical defects. Bring the animal to the entrance of the Tabernacle where the priest will accept your gift for the Lord. The person bringing it is to lay his hand upon its head, and it then becomes his substitute: the death of the animal will be accepted by G-d instead of the death of the man who brings it as the penalty for his sins. The man shall then kill the animal there before the Lord, and Aaron's sons, the priests, will present the Blood before the Lord, sprinkling it upon all sides of the altar at the entrance of the Tabernacle. Then the priest will skin the animal and quarter it, and build a wood fire upon the altar, and put the sections of the animal and its head and fat upon the wood. The internal organs and the legs are to be washed, then the priests will burn them upon the altar, and they will be an acceptable burnt offering with which the Lord is pleased"(Catholic Living Bible, CLB)

If the animal used as burnt offering is a sheep or a goat, it too must be a male, and without blemishes... for burnt offerings give much pleasure to the Lord. A turtle dove and young pigeons are recommended if a bird must be used.

Grain offering (minchah) of fine flour with olive oil and incense poured on it and seasoned with salt because the salt is a reminder of G-d's covenant: In the case of grain offering the priest burn a fistful (kometz) of this offering on the altar and eat the rest. Honey or leaven is to be avoided in any mix to ensure it is a sweet smelling offering.

Honey gives unpleasant smell while leaven changes the grain. Salt is included in the incense offered as salt preserves. Leaven is associated with sin, pride, hypocricy, false teaching, worldliness(1 Cor 5: 6-8, Luke 12: 1, Gal 5: 9, Mark 8: 15) Animals and vegetables could also be given in the Mincha offering (Gen 5: 6-8, 1 Samuel 2: 15-17). Both Cain and Abel offered a Mincha but Cains offering was not accepted while Abel's fat portion of his first fruits of his stock was accepted. The Bible does not state that Cain brought the first fruits of his produce. It just states that he brought the fuit of the ground, perhaps indicating an inferior offering, not from his choice stock, so sub standard. Also perhaps indicating that his mincha was not offered in faith, not with good attitude (Heb 11: 2-4, 1 John 3: 12). Cain was unrepentant of anger and envy and is said to have killed his brother Abel (Gen 4: 7).

Thanksgiving offering of bull or a cow, goat, sheep, lamb without defect and male or female, nanny or billy goat, ram or ewe;

Sin offering (chatat), most holy offering for guilt: This is offered for unintentional sins (Leviticus 4: 1-4). By this is meant sins of carelessness or inadvertence. However if the offender is a leader, such as a king, a male goat is to be used otherwise a female sheep or goat is used. The priests eat the offerings within the Tabernacle grounds. Chatat is also offered for withholding witness, becoming impure due to an interval of forgetfulness, and violating an oath unintentionally.

Peace offerings (shelamim): This is a voluntary offering used to express a sense of well being, praise and thanksgiving. This occurred when Jacob and Laban made a treaty with each other (Gen 31: 54). This offering is similar to burnt offering; however birds were not to be used and the animals were to be completely burned; only specific portions of fat and internal organs were placed on the altar. Also a portion of the shelamim without the blood is to be eaten.

Guilt offering (Asham): Leviticus 6: 5-7 gives detailed account of guilt offering of a ram for the following:

Unintentionally using sanctuary property for personal interest

Forestalling punishment for one's sin when uncertain the one has sinned or for unknown sin

Living under oath or defrauding a person in regard to a found article, a deposit loan and such like

It does not suffice to simply offer a sacrifice in carrying out guilt offering; the offender must restitute and this includes an additional one fifth of the value.

An observed practice among the Jews is the practice of kaparah-atonement whereby the sin of a young person is cleansed by waving a live chicken around the head of the person. The chicken must be held with the right hand and a circular motion three times round the head is carried out while reciting prayers as follows:

This is my substitute, my vicarious offering, my atonement (kaparah).

"This rooster (hen) shall meet its death, but I shall find a long and pleasant life of peace". The chicken is later killed and given to the poor. The aim is that the ceremony will ensure repentance (teshuvah).

Other ways of effecting penitence is by giving tzedakah (charity alms). The other is by mild lashes of belt strap on the young offender by some religious rabbis while the penitent recites prayers of repentance from their sins. Also instead of waving chicken round the head some wave coins. The coins are given to charity (Messianic Bible letters to the writer)

Also included in Leviticus are:

Instructions that the thigh and breast of animal sacrificed for peace and thanksgiving offerings belong to Aaron and his sons throughout all generations.

The Israelites must not eat blood and fat from any animal that died of disease.

Also a ceremonially unclean priest must not eat the thanksgiving offering so also must no one unclean or touched anything unclean eat a thanksgiving offering.

The following animals must not be eaten: the camel, the coney, rock badger, the hare, the swine, only fish taken from rivers or sea that have fins and scales, eagles, the métier, the osprey, the falcon, the raven, the nighthawk, the seagull, all kinds of hawk, the owl, the cormorant, the ibis, the marsh hen, the pelican, the vulture, the stork, all kinds of heron, the hoopoe, the bat;

all insects with four legs must not be eaten; only the following insects may be eaten because they jump: locusts, crickets, and grasshoppers.

They are to avoid any animal that has semi-parted hoofs, does not chew the cud, or walks on paws. Therefore the following animals must not be eaten: the mole, the rat, the great lizard, the gecko, the mouse, the lizard, the snail, the chameleon (please see Leviticus 11 for these instructions).

Leviticus Chapter 12 is particularly devoted to ritual purification of a woman who has given birth.

Perhaps of particular interest to this chapter is also that according to the Holy Scriptures God commanded Moses to anoint his brother Aaron as the first High Priest and his sons and descendants as his assistants acting as the levites. Aaron was to become the first person to perform sacred service unto the Lord in the Tabernacle. Aaron and his descendants would occupy this privilege as high priests and priest for ever: literally Exodus 40: 12- 16 reads:

And you shall bring Aaron and his sons near the door of the meeting of tent (Tabernacle of the congregation); and you shall wash them with water, bemayim (literally in water).

And you shall clothe Aaron (with) the holy garments (binda hakadosh) or "garment of holiness" and you shall anoint him and sanctify him (wekidashetha) and he shall serve as priest for me (verse 13)

And you shall bring his sons near and you shall clothe them (with) tunics (verse 14)

And you shall anoint them, as you anointed their father. And they shall serve as priests to me and shall be as priests to me for them forever; their anointing as priesthood shall be everlasting for their generations (ledrotham) verse 15

And Moses did so according to all that Yahweh had commanded him so he did verse 16

These commands of Yahweh were given after He had anointed the tabernacle and made it ready for use through Moses.

And Jeremiah 33: 21-24 seem to reiterate the everlastingness of Yahweh's covenant with David and the multiplication of the number of the Levites.

The duty of the Levites was to assist Aaron in the service of the Temple of the Lord, including being in charge of the courtyards, the side rooms, the purification of all sacred things and the performance of other duties at Temple. According to 1 Chronicles 23 the number of the Levites had increased to include those who were not descendants of Aaron. However, the duty remains the same as stipulated in the passage, assisting in worship and sacrificial duties. The Levites also sang psalms during services, maintained the temple and served as guards among other duties including maintaining the tabernacle, dismantling and reassembling the structure and its furnishings as the Israelites moved from place to place in the wilderness. The Tabernacle was believed to house God's presence and provided a place for the sacrificial system. The sacrificial system was totally under the direction of the Cohanim, the priestly class.

The sacrifices were designed to temporarily cover or appease for the sins of the Cohanim and the sins of the whole nation of Israel, to cleanse each member of the community from their iniquities before God and man. People also brought their own sacrifice for their own individual transgressions. But once a year, on the day of Yom Kippur, Day of Atonement, the Cohen Ha Gadol (High or King Priest) entered into God's presence inside the Holy of Holies and made atonement for the entire nation of Israel. In spite of this privilege God gave no right of land ownership to the Levites. They were to receive agricualtural and monetary tithes from the people as their inheritance. The most prominent was the "Maasar Rishon", or the first tithe, which was ten percent- Numbers 18: 20 reads:

And Yahweh said to Aaron, "you shall have no inheritance in their land, nor shall you have any portion among them. I am your portion and your inheritance among the sons of Israel" (verse 20)

"And behold I have given all the tithe in Israel to the sons of Levi for an inheritance, in return for their service which they are serving, the service of the tabernacle of the congregation" (verse 21)

"And the sons of Israel shall not come any more to the tabernacle of the congregation lest they bear sin and die" (verse 22; see also Num 10: 38, 18: 24).

Thus we see that the Levites and the Cohanim lived among the people on pasture land allotted to them by the Israelites outside the city, a location that perhaps, makes it easy to raise cattle and minister to the people on the Torah (see Nehemiah 8: 7-8).

However by the time of Yeshua the Levitical priesthood had become religious aristocracy and a political priestly cast. For example the Chief Priests in the Sanhedrin court were holding powerful political positions. Although they still gave scripture a more important position to oral tradition, political matters held stronger sway on them. Consequently many judicial decisions were made in order to please the Roman colonial power instead of God's law, thus Yeshua was condemned and turned over to the Romans to be executed. Following the destruction of the Temple in 70 AD, and the dispersal of the Jewish people to foreign lands the authority of the Priests including the Sanhedrin waned and eventually was dissolved. In the vacuum created, Phariseeism took over.

The Pharisees were of multiple tribes and worked in the marketplace among the people. They formed a council and rose to power. They continued to thrive, developed traditional Judaism into a religious organization as we have it today. The worship and sacrificial system was replaced by prayer, charity and repentance. However the religious Jew seems to still crave for the return of the old traditional sacrificial system even today. Exodus 28: 1-42 not only reiterates that the priesthood of Aaron and his sons and descendants shall be everlasting; the passage also gives details of the arrangements including elements and specifications of the regalia and holiness of the position.

The question is how the lineage of the Levites can be traced and determined today. According to tradition the Cohen line must be patrilineal and moves from father to son. This has been the case for 3300 years. In addition to the use of DNA test, family tree, oral tradition, possession of common priestly surnames such as Cohen, Kahn, Katz (kohen tzedek-righteous priest) possibly Kanu, and Kohn, may be included. Since the separation of the Jews into the Ashkenazi and Sephardic (c AD 1000) Cohanim have adopted various skin colours, eye collour, and hair colour. Yet some scholars think there should be a common Cohen Modal Haplotype (CMH) that should determine the genetic marks traced from Aaron HaCohen (Aaron the Priest). However tribal identity is derived through one's father but Jewishness (religious Jewishness) is derived through one's mother. This means that a Cohen without a Jewish mother is not accepted and converting to Judaism does not make a person eligible either (chabad). Also markers for non-priestly Levites have been identified in surnames such as Levy, Levin, and Lewis. Yet genetic markers of the Cohanim are said to be helping scientist hunt for Jewish genes and dispel myths throughout the world as to who is or is not Jewish by descent especially in relation to the lost tribes.

Divination and Diviners in Ancient Israel

Divination can be defined as a means of ascertaining hidden facts that are not physically determined.

In ancient Israel the methods of divination as presented in the Bible include: prophecy, which applied for national and individual interest;

dreams as divine disclosures of his will and intents (Jer 23: 28, 32, Gen 41, Gen 37:19),

priests through the use of Ephod in form of garments and/or sacred statues (1 Samuel 23: 10, Deut 33: 8-10, 1Kings 3: 6),

also the use of Urim and Thummim by priests which some identify to be the twelve precious stones installed on the breastplate of the priest (1 Samuel 14: 41-42)

and consultation of the dead (1 Samuel 28: 1-25)

Other methods of divination in ancient Israel are crystal gazing, gazing into cups of water, accidental citation of Bible passages to mention just these.

Thus we find that in spite of condemnations of some of these practices ancient Israelites still got involved with them (see Leviticus 19: 31; Lev 20: 6; Deut 18: 11). The specialist diviners were called priests though we also have non priest specialist diviners. There is every evidence that the belief in these practices is aligned with the belief and fear of evil forces believed to be militating against the Israelites progress and survival as a nation. However, the prophets spoke against equating Yahweh's power with these forces. Allegiance should be only to Yahweh the God of their ancestors.

In sum sacrificial system served the purpose of ensuring the necessary harmony to exist between the human, spirits, nature, and the afterlife. This ensures the survival of the nation of Israel and sustaining the worship of Yahweh. Divination provided a means to reassure the individual of the presence of the spirit world that may not be as unfriendly as conceived. The diviners, who perhaps were many, varied and operated in various ways, revealed the mind and will of the deity to the people. Aaron and his descendants were later anointed to be the priestly class in all generations and enjoyed certain privileges. They supervised the sacrificial systems among the people with Aaron as the first King-Priest. The priestly class seem to have become institutionalized and politically corrupted by colonial invasion and rule whereby the Laws of the colonial rulers were given preeminence over the Laws of Yahweh that was based on His justice and ensuring harmony with His creation. Thus the close knit between kin, cult and the afterlife which the sacrificial system maintained fell apart. The question is how can this harmony be reactivated among the people today especially among the Diaspora Jews? Can DNA tests be relied upon to be able to validate the Aaronic line of descent (Levitical priestly class)?

Ibo Priesthood and the Sacrificial System

Precolonial Priesthood

By the time the colonial masters and Christianity entered the Ibo land priesthood followed the social structure of the Ibos. Thus at the family level was the family head (opara), who was the first born of every family, followed by the oldest male of a compound which was made of families and referred to as the Umu nna (literally "from the fathers" "begotten of the fathers" in the sense of ancestral cohesion) and the living father's children. At the hamlet level, made of a number of compounds, the priest was the oldest male at that level. This role continues at the level of village; a village is made up of hamlets; towns, a town is made up of villages; and clans; a clan is made up of a number of towns. At the clan level the oldest person presides over other priests. Thus the oldest male at every level carries out the role of a priest. The role of a priest is acting as the bridge builder between the people and God (Chukwu). However the function is not as direct and simple as that. Sacrifice and offering are used to appease the deity offended at each level. The bridging of the gap depends on the deity offended and the level affected.

As there are multiple deities and divinities believed to control every aspect of life, any of these could be offended necessitating appeasement. Appeasement is usually through sacrifice carried out through the leadership of the priest. The Ibo in general believe that enemies could act to impede a person's progress, cause barrenness, and even end life of an individual prematurely; this was regarded as a calamity, a tragedy because it threatens the life of the ancestors and those yet to be born. The agents of such mischievous acts are the arushi, numerous goddlings. This belief gave rise to other specialists diviners (dibia afa), medicine men (dibia ogwu). Both dibias are called healers and they combine the art of physical healing with herbs, psychotherapy, and spiritual healing. The dibia are usually easily accessible to the people and are at the service of the people at all times. The diviners reveal the enemy and the means they are operating to harm their victim. Some dibia are prophetic in foretelling the future and the mind of the deity on matters of appeasement. Like the ancient Israelites all are considered to be working as a team with the chief deity to ensure harmony between the spirit world, nature and humans.

Ibo Priesthood

Apart from the family priest who leads in worship, keeps the symbol of authority and justice (ofo), and leads in sacrifices to appease the ancestors, we also have larger level priests. These so called larger level priests are the priests of the Spirit cults, cults of deities such as Ala (earth deity), Anyanwu (sun deity), Igwe (sky heaven's deity), Amadioha (storm deity), Agwu (medicine, divination deity) and deities of other elements. The priests of these cults are given different designations or titles depending on the community or clan. Some of the titles are: atama, isi, eze. The Eze Nri claims the highest title among the Ibo priesthood class and is so highly respected to the extent of almost revered. He is regarded as the Eze Ala (King Priest of Ala deity) of the whole Ibo land and exercises this role across Ibo land through the operation of his representative priests. The role is such that he and his priest class are referred to as the Aaronic King-priest and Levites of Ibo land. They made laws, and created prohibitions and the means to purify these prohibitions if infringed upon. They also created Ibo titles such as the Ozo, Nze, Duru, etc; they also trained ritual performers and were invited to install priests in all parts of the communities, including ritual circumcisers; they are expected to be present during ritual circumcision and during any purification rites called "ipu ala"). Special facial marks mark them out as belonging to this special priestly class (CA3/035/7 Niger Mission, Pastor Onitsha, 1872-1880. Report pf Rev. Soloman S. Perry, Native Pastor cited in Metuh 1985: 174). These are the Levites of the Ibo communities and are almost universally found among communities living in separate quarters designated as ihite, ifite, ivite depending on dialect) They are custodians of the rules and laws which the Hebrew Bible regard as covenant of Yahweh with the people. As the Levites reminded the people of Israel the need to keep the covenant so the priests scattered all over Ibo communities reminded the people of the need to keep Omenala of the people so as to ensure peace and harmony between the creation and the creator.

It has been claimed that the Ibo believe that G-d created the deities but that the spirit forces (arushi, arusi) were created by humanbeings and the ancestors. The practice of worshipping the Arusi is an abomination to the Ibo sensibility. Arusi also metaphorically and literally means that which is an "abominable practice." Any one practicing it was to be killed or exiled. It was the coming of Christianity that put an end to killing and exiling offenders. Usually such offenders had the choice to run into the protection of a deity by running into its shrine as refuge. If such a person refuses to leave and choses to belong to the deity they were ritually dedicated to the deity or spirit and their descendants became Osu. I have also been informed that these deities and their arushis were imported from neighbouring communities including from the native riverine neighbours who were not Ibos originally. Divination, sorcery and witch craft were also said to have been imported as Ibos went far off to learn the art; they still travel to distant lands to consult diviners today.

Like the ancient Israelites Sacrifices offered by the Ibo include thanksgiving, peace offering, sacrifice of atonement, sacrifice for purification to mention these.

The following acts require purificatory sacrifice:

A woman pushing her husband down

Having sexual intercourse with a girl before her first menstruation,

Sexual intercourse with an uncircumcised male

Selling a family land without permission

Adultery by a wife, not involving incest, is believed to threaten the life of the husband and the children

Every compound is considered unclean before a festival and must be ritually cleansed before the celebration

A bed is unclean if a woman urinates on it

A house is considered as unclean if there is birth of child, a menstruating woman and if a woman cries in it, and pounding food, cooking at unholy hours

Eating a forbidden animal or food e.g pork, human flesh, any totem to a family, village or clan or being in contact with anybody who has eaten such

Sexual offences of women are believed to threaten the existence of a family as it is believed to cause difficulty at child birth, serious illness and frequent death in the family; therefore confessions are encouraged and sometimes demanded. A newly married woman must confess all sexual offences on arrival at her husband's home, before child birth, and sometimes during husband's illhealth. There is obligation to cleanse anyone who has been in contact with ritually polluted places and with people considered as impure; failure to do so is believed to results in misfortunes because of the anger of the Ala deity and the ancestors.

Sexual intercourse on a farm land

Incest of certain degree

Walking naked before a shrine

The 'ipu ala,' purification, involves purifying the land of its sin. In the past a human being could be sacrificed to purify the land among some Ibo communities. This is a result of zeal and desire to ensure to give the choicest of sacrificial gifts to the deity. The use of human being was an exception and not the rule and was not universal Ibo practice.The sacrificial victim who might have volunteered himself was made to carry the sin and guilt of everbody. However, most other places sacrifice rams or cows. The process involved victim being dragged along every nook and crannies of the village with a rope tied to the neck alive. The dead body was thrown away in the evil forest or thrown into the sea if there was any nearby. Later cows or rams were compulsorily used as the only object for "ipu ala." For incest the guilty is made to crawl around the village or town.

In place of cows and ram, a calf, chicken and some yams was used (i. e. crop or grain offering).

As was observed and recorded by an early colonial missionary to Iboland Mr Basden states that in the case of murder or homicide the murderer was required to hang themselves and their property burnt immediately while his living brothers offered sacrifice of yams and chicken. If the murderer fled, his kindred must flee with him and their properties must be burnt. They might return after the bereaved family had accepted their settlement terms. Then a ritual cleansing of their compound would take place. This is called 'izafu ntu ochu'. This was considered very vital before they could go back to live in it. Included in the ritual process, Mr Basden observes is that the Adah of both kindreds walked around the compound with a cock and a hen tied together, pleading with Ala deity not to allow such to happen again. They finally collected the sweepings of the compound and threw them into the "bad bush" (Basden 1938:61; Metuh 1985:98). It is noteworthy that sacrifice for purification of abomination is not eaten as in other joyless sacrifices.

In some minor forbidden acts, commensal meals were eaten. This is called "nshi oriko." This symbolizes restored communion with the deity and with the worship community.

Offences against the arushi, arusi, such as theft of yam, must be cleansed before the shrine of Ajoku ji; the person who kills in a war and who commited incest with a far relative must be cleansed before the shrine of Ekwensu. In all purification sacrifices the priest of Nri or his representative must be present as stated above. An offence against an ancestor must be purified in addition to a public confession.

As it is with ancient Israel, to the Ibo sin is death and every breaching of any prohibition is sin, it is a dirty act that defiles and the sin of one person affects the whole land (corporate personhood). So the land must be cleansed. This means that purification sacrifices are also aimed to drive away evil spirits refered to as "ichufu agbara ojoo".

The "i gba ndu" ritual

The phrase "i gba ndu" literally means, "to join", "to mend"; "to rejoin", "to reunite," "to save", "to atone a life." This ritual is used primarily to amend a serious breach of bloodline, kinship and broken blood solidarity pact. Such an offence is taken to as very grievious and is believed to be capable of ending a family line or the bloodline of the contending parties. In order to restore or mend the situation a special ritual is performed and the ritual specialist supervised that every necessary ritual step was carefully followed. The process usually involved the drawing of blood from the parties, mixing them together and the contestants ate specially consecrated kola nuts with the mixture. This ritual was believed to restore the broken bloodline. It thus guaranteed trust, security, mutual protection, and well being among the parties. I gba ndu, in precolonial times, was also applied to cement various other types of relationships apart from blood solidarity. These included marriage, business, friendships, mutual protection pacts and peace among neighbours and states, for mutual cooperation and coexistence. Through i gba ndu the Ibo states became joined together as an entity, a tribe, a clan, one people forming a federation. This federation extended to other peoples and neighbours for mutual defence and other socio-economic and political purposes. When applied it signified an eternal covenant between families, communities, clans, states and tribes. I gba ndu involving states is called "ogbugba ndu". It is an eternal social contract.

Ogbugba ndu process might include staging a sports competition by the communities seeking to be united to seal the covenant. Usually the spot where the sport took place was marked with an evergreen tree that acted as a reminder of the eternal covenant or bondage to one another. It ensures a good conscience toward one another and toward the deity.

As an eternal social contract, i gba ndu was effectively applied in business to ensure the Ibo partners were protected as they travelled far into the hinterlands for business. And to enhance this business ambition they often entered into marrying the women from their trading partner states, communities, towns and clans. As they believe that the marriage contract if everlasting, I gba ndu is applied in the marriage contract ensuring safety and trust of their business partners wherever they travelled for business. This also involved the use of guilds based on known oracles such as U bini Ukpabi of the Aro people, Igwe ka ala, Ojukwu Diobu, Onojo Oboni of Oguruguru, the Agbala of Akwa. The minor ones include Agwu, Ozuzu, Ogbunka, Eha-Amufu. These play the same function as the guild or School of prophets among ancient Israelites.

Igba ndu was also applied among diplomatic circles. The three main diplomatic circles were the age grades determined by birth and age;

the titled groups as guilds of noble men determined by partly birth and partly wealth; and the secret societies in which membership was determined by wealth and to some extent by birth. The title lodges that applied the igba ndu ritual included the duru, ozo, nze, di ji, ogbu inyinya while notable secret societies included the mmanwu, ekpe, okonko, akang (Adiele Afigbo 2005: Nigerian History, Politics and Affairs: The Collected Essays: African World Press).

An individual could use the igb ndu ritual to reclaim their life from an angry deity if the oracle determined that his misfortune or bad fate was from the wrath of such an angry deity. It is unclear what the details were but it also operated on giving life in exchange for the individual's life thereby reclaiming the lost fortune having been reunited in fellowship with the deity.

One common observation among the Ibos was same as what the ancient Israelites called kaparah practice whereby a chicken is waved round the head of a young person with prayers of atonement and other forms of penitence including waving of coins and giving gifts for charity. The coins and gift were given to the priest of the deity to deliver. Also the chicken involved in ritual of atonement is usually eaten; sometimes it was given away, shared among the relatives, villagers or eaten by the priest alone.

Thus we find at least four types of rituals involved, "ichu aja" (sacrifice to drive away evil spirits), "imeri mmuo" (sacrifice of prohibition), "ipu ala" (sacrifice of purification) and "i gba ndu' also refered to as "iri arusi" (joining or mending groups for kinship relations, also reclaiming one's life from an angry deity).

Thus we see that the Ibo sacrificial offerings correspond to the Jewish offerings of korban olah (burnt offering), mincha (grain /produce offering), shelamim (peace offering), chatat (sin offering), asham (guilt offering) and kaparah (atonement). I personally did not know the rituals had ancient Israelite roots. I, like most of the younger and Christian influenced Ibos, regarded them as devilish and relegated them to "paganic" and of idol worship.

The aim of sacrificial offerings among the Ibo is to maintain the status of harmony that should exist between the three dimensions of life:

the Spirit world, the natural world including the human beings, and the world of the ancestors (afterlife). This harmony is needed to ensure peace and well being. This is not different from the role of the sacrificial system among the ancient Israelites as taught in the Old Testament, especially the Tanakh (the first five books). In fact reading through the Old Testament especially the Levitical instructions and practices and comparing it with the sacrificial system among the Ibos, as with most other customs and manners one would readily think the two peoples have same root of origin. This is the case in spite of thousands of years that have passed by and in spite of the different environments and influences involved. We already observed that olaudah perhaps, means "Judah's sacrifice;" 'ola' is Hebrew word for sacrifice. This is pointing to Judean root of some of the Ibos.

Feasts and Festivals

Perhaps it would be very correct to say that the Ibo peoples are truly the same people we read about in the Hebrew Bible as reflected in the following festivals:

I gba Nkwa: The Festival of Promise

This feast comes up by the first three months of the year. Nkwa in Ibo rfers to agreement, promise. Achicha was eaten and is unleavened bread, roasted goat head and legs and bitter leaf. As stated earlier while the Ibo word "nkwa" means literally that which has been promised i gba is Ibo word for "to celebrate", "to feast," "to observe." This means that in i gba nkwa the Ibos celebrate the feast of the Promise just like the Hebrew children of old and today celebrate the pascal feast (feast of the Passover Exodus 12: 25-27) that is also a festival of promise: when I see the blood I will pass over you, implies protection promised to the ancient Israelites while in Egypt. During the celebration the Jewish children will ask, what does this celebration mean? their parents were to explain to them the promise of protection and possession that their forefathers were promised by the God of their fathers and that began with the successful removal and departure from the bondage of Paroah of Egypt. Although details of the origin of this festival is missing among the Ibos as no one seems to care to ask, the observance of this festival is crucial to an understanding of who actually the Ibos are and their origin as of the same root as the ancient Israelites. The festival is celebrated among the Jews within the first trimester (3-4 months) of the year just like the Ibos.

Onu mkpuru okuku (akuku)

The Ibos celebrated the "onu mkpuru okuku." This phrase, literally means the beginning of the first harvested fruit or crops. "Onu" means literally mouth, entrance; "mkpuru" means literally "fruit, seed of, produce, crops." Thus the festival of "onu mkpuru okuku" could be translated as "festival of the first fruits, produce, seed, crops." Thus "onu" could also mean "beginning or entrance into." Thus we have first or beginning fruits of harvest. This feast was celebrated in the 3rd or 4th month of the year depending on the calendar. Ibo year has 13 lunar months and one izu (week) is 4 sacred days doubled as 8 days. This period of celebration coincides with the same period the same feast is celebrated among the ancient Hebrews.

Ahiajoku festival

Ibos celebrated the "iwa ji", "ahajoku" feast generally referred to as the new yam festival. Iwa ji literally the cutting of the yam, this festival celebrates the harvest of yams regarded as the king of all crops and farm produces. It is also called ahiajoku festival as it is believed that the deity that deputises for the Ala deity is Ahia joku. So some people regard it as reverencing the ahajoku deity. However it is a thanks giving festival marking the blessings of yam by Chiukwu, the supreme God.

Onwa Asato Festival

Then we have what was called the "onwa asato" feast, literally the feast of the 8th month. This feast lasts a week, equivalent to 8 days of Ibo week, and coincides with the 7th month of the Hebrew calendar. This is the feast of Tabernacle of the Hebrew children. However some Ibo communites for convenience of today's world have moved this feast to December when most Ibo in diaspora from the Iboland come home. Some southern Ibo communities also merge the ahiajoku and the onwa asato festivals as marking Ibo New year. This is usually a very elaborate festival and up till today Ahajoku regarded as the most important festival in Ibo calendar.

CHAPTER 12
Death and Burial among the Ibo and Ancient Israelites

Firstly we can see from above that the Ibo and the ancient Israelites is closely a community based people. They believe that life is to be lived as a community. The community welcomes everyone, prepares every one for life stages, and sees to it that everybody lives an expected standard of moral life. This morality includes respect for the individual and this respect for individual is enhanced and ensured by blood solidarity. This solidarity extends to the the sick and dying and respect is accorded the sich by enabling the sick have an honourable and dignifying exit to begin another life in the afterlife. Both peoples describe this exit in euphemistic language. This includes 'joining the ancestors', 'resting with the Kings', 'gathered to his kingsmen'. Thus we read that 'Abraham breathed his last and gave up the ghost, his sons Ishmael and Isaac buried him'. 'Buried him' in this statement is far more involving than putting him into the ground and covering with sand of the earth. It connotes all the trappings of funeral and respect accorded the dead following the injunction, honour thy father and thy mother in the land that your days may be long in the land. We also have the same use of euphemisms to express the transition into the life beyond among the Ibo. Thus we also hear expressions like the 'mighty Iroko has fallen', 'he/she has refused food', 'he/she'has crossed over'', he/she has begun the journey', he /she has embarked on the journey'. When a child dies the expression "the water has been spilled" is often heard. Euphemisms are used not only to accord the person respect and dignity but also to show teach that is not the end as to say that a person 'has died' is more or less regarded to connote annihilation which no Ibo or Israelite would associate with their loved one. The use of euphemism also implies that both peoples prefer life to death; both fear death as an enemy.

Perhaps of particular note is the expression, "gathered to his kinsmen", "gathered to his fathers or people. "This expression points to the belief that the righteous dead are in heaven, a kind of bliss while the unrighteous dead though also gathered to the community perhaps close to their ancestors and could see them are not in the same place. They are somewhere closeby like the righteous dead are expecting or waiting the judgement time when Chukwu Abiama will judge everyone. We see this expression in connection with Abraham in Genesis 15: 15; 25:17, Isaac in Genesis 35:29, Jacob in Genesis 35: 29; 49:33; Ishmael, Josiah 2Kings 22:20; Aaron Numbers 20:24; Moses Deuteronomy 33: 50. We can also refer to the story of Lazarus and the richman in Luke 16: 19 that indicates the separation between the two although both of them were gathered to their fathers or kinsmen following death. The fact that in Genesis chapter 50 we read that the Egyptian physicians took forty days to embalm the remains of Jacob after he was said to have been gathered to his people is a clear proof that gathered to his people has no connection with his burial as he had been gathered to his people long before his remains were transported to Canaan where he was buried. Thus we read, " When Jacob had finished giving instructions to his sons, he drew his feet up into the bed, breathed his last and was gathered to his people." Another proof that burial has nothing to do with the joining of the righteous ancestors is perhaps the case of Moses in Deuteronomy 32: 50. We read that G-d told Moses that there on the mountain he had climbed he will die "and be gathered to your people...". Two chapters later we read, "And Moses the servant of the Lord died there in Moab, as the Lord had said. He buried him in Moab, in the valley opposite Beth Peor, but to this day no one knows where his grave is" Deuteronomy 34: 5-6. So Moses was "gathered to his people" long before he was buried by God. Perhaps it is the same expression of joining the righteous dead in heaven that New Testament writers expressed as the angels carried him to "Abraham's bossom", which could mean to Abraham's side, wherever Abraham was, the abode of bliss, happiness; may be paradise. The same could be said of expressions as "rested with the Kings" and such like expression. It means joining G-d in his abode which of course is what we today call heaven (1Kings8: 22, 27-30 NIV). This also means that the ancient Israelites who came to this part of the world and begot Ibo as their descendants must have retained their very early understanding of joining the righteous at death and these righteous were believed to be where ever G-d of their fathers dwelt. As history has it their ancestors left Egypt either at the Exodus or before the Exodus experience to this part of the world. This also means this group perhaps did not undergo the revivals and encounters of the journey in the wilderness, not being part of the company that Moses led to the Promised Land. It could also mean that some may have encountered the experiences but turned back to join the group that eventually entered what became Ibo land. This may explain why even among the Ibos today ancient Israelite customs and manners are expressed in various ways yet depicting the same meaning and significance to the people. Some might have left during or after the time of Joshua.

Also among the Ibo it is not unusual to watch over the sick being on the verge of dying. In other words relations would remain close to such a sick person. Such a sick person must not be left to begin their journey to the beyond without anyone by their side as this is regarded a serious neglect, an abuse of negligence. Firstly the last words of the dying are very important. This last word may reveal the cause of their death and who was responsible for their death. The person who is sick unto death may also have sins to confess to their people. This also is very important.

Secondly among both peoples just as the sick is noticed to be gasping for breath, all mirrors and photographs are quickly removed.

Thirdly death is greeted with mourning and mourning is started with wailing, and expression of very serious grief and with all signs of mourning like neglect of personal hygiene, stripping naked, rolling in sand and dust etc. Consequently the close relations who start the mourning are joined by the wider compound, hamlet, and village and even the town and clan if the dead was a title man or a respectable elder and ruler. Mourning could last as many as thirty days among the Ibos and the ancient Israelite. The widow of the deceased may continue mourning for as long as one year before she and the children of the deceased would be ritually separated from the man.

Burial of the dead in both cultures was as soon as possible. The corpse does not remain unburied for more than a day. In fact if the person died in the morning the burial could take place before sundown; delay to bury the dead could also occur if the death occured on any festival that is sacred to the people. No dead is buried after sundown because the Ibos do not bury the dead at night. Such dead is buried the next day. Burial took place after there was ritual bathing usually carried out by the Umu adah under the leadership of the Adah (eldest daughter) of the family.

Fourthly it is significant that digging the spot for burial is also ritually significant. For example a tired digger must not hand over the instrument for digging to the next person to relieve him. The tool is dropped on the ground for the next digger to pick up and take over. Also the people who dug the hole were revered and remained impure until they had had bath. They must not come near anybody or touch any body before purifying themselves by bathing.

Prayer is offered by the eldest family member or eldest member of the village. Holding the ofo stick he ofers prayers for the dead that G-d may enable him/her to go on a smooth journey. This is same as the Jewish Kadish recited on the 12th year and believed to cleanse the soul of the dead and assisting in transferring him into heaven.

Also among the Ibo the bereaved family was provided everything. These included every need they may have and everything needed for the burial; these include food, water to drink and bath, care of the homes, their personal care, care of their children, and even farms. They spent nothing. Every arrangement was made and provided by their kith and kin which included the whole villagers and even may include the town and clan. It is regarded as abominable to violate these customs as it is regarded as insulting and dishonourable to the fathers and ancestors (See Isaiah 25:7 Gen 46:4, Gen 23, Gen 25: 9, Gen 50: 25, Gen 47: 29-30, see also Shulhan Arukh for later practice in Judaism). Usually after the first thirty days or so (izu asa) the larger community vists to join in the mourning at the end of which the mourning period was ended. However the bereaved are observed to remain distressed in such a way that they hadly participated in any festivities. In some communities there is what is called strengthening rituals. These rituals involved the sacrificing of a dog and a goat. The blood of the dog was poured over the eyes of the dead while the heart of the goat was torn off and placed upon the chest of the dead. It is possible that these are symbolically carried out again during the year memorial funeral celebration. It is explained that the blood of the dog sprayed on the eyes was expected to give the dead wisdom to see far into the future, to see far beyond the ordinary and bravery to face eventualities while on the journey to the beyond. The heart of the goat grants the dead ability to rmeber and conceptualise without being told what to do. It is believed to give good memory and understanding. It is a question among the Ibo to say, 'are you sure the ewu obi ritual was performed on you in your previous existence.' This is a question normally asked when a person fails to produce expected results commensurate with their age. It literally means 'why do you forget things so easily? These rituals and statement perhaps connote belief in reincarnation among the Sephardi Ibos. The statement regarding Abraham being gathered to his kinsmen connotes a belief in joining his ancestors as is believed by the Ibos. What seems to be lacking is the absence of a time of resurrection of the dead among the Ibos as we seem to find among the ancient Israelites as expressed in Job and Isaiah. However the idea of a possible resurrection among the ancient Israelites seems to contradict their belief that life is only valid when lived on earth; thus death is the enemy in both peoples' beliefs. Perhaps the concept of resurrection of the dead was a much later theology that evolved among the ancient Israelites very much after the Ibo ancestors had left, perhaps it was a product of official Palacial Yahwehism of later generations teaching that Yahweh's dead will not be defeated by death. Yahweh is strong enough to rescue his dead from the grip of the final enemy, death.

CHAPTER 13
SUMMARY AND DEDUCTIONS

The HEEBOES have been variously referred to as Ibo, Igbo, Eber, Eboe, Ibu etc. The Heeboe could be said to be a conglomerate of Hebrew peoples who inhabit the present day West Africa, especially made up of the ethnic groups that made up the former colonial Ibo country and beyond. They became members of the King Solomon Shepardic Federation International (KSSFI) in 1997 and have been given the responsibility of gathering all Jews of Africa starting with the Jews of West Africa. The KSSFI is an international federation of Sephardic Jews who regard themselves as maintaining the line of Jews of the Old Testament tradition. They however regard the Ashkenazi Jews (European Jewish immigrants) as their kith and kin although the two have slight differences in their philosophies, practices and traditions. This means that the Ibo peoples of Nigeria are accepted to the world Jewry as Jews. However the Heeboes do not need to identify themselves as belonging to any Jewish branch. As stated in several places the word Ibo is a derivation of the word eber, ibhri, ivri that came to be rendered in various similar forms by early writers (heebo, heebro, ebo (e), Ibo (e) and currently 'Igbo'). The Hebrew or Jewish origins are embedded in legends pointing to the same genealogy and ancestry that connects them with ancient Israelites ancestors, specifically the children of Jacob. However there are indications that other Hebrew clans inhabit same community and have been absorbed into the current Ibo stock as one people. The "Igbo" version is claimed to be a name change of Eri according to the ERI legends, who in turn gave same name to one of his sons that providentially became more famous than his brothers; so the name eventually became the most common name of some of the dominant Ibo peoples. Thus we have some Ibos as a people made up of a group that descended from Igbo according to another legend (the Uturu or most popular legend in southern Iboland). It is therefore needful to understand that not all Ibos who inhabit the present southeastern states of Anambra, Enugu, Ebonyi, Abia, Imo, Delta, Rivers, Kogi and

Benue states are Igbo; Ibos also inhabit parts of Equatorial Guinea, Gabon, Sao Thome and Principe, and parts of Cameroons; not all these are the descendants of the ancestor Igbo. I was recently completing an application form for a position in an oversea country and realized for the first time that the European people had all the while known the difference between Ibo language and Igbo language. A section of the application process listed among the languages of the world, Igbo language and Ibo language separately among other world languages including German, French, English, Spanish, Italian, Arabic, Hebrew, Hausa, Yoruba, Greek, Rusia, etc. When I was asked at the interview I answered that my language was Ibo. Thus the information being spread that all Ibos are Igbo has been an incorrect conception for perhaps too long. The descendants of Igbo proper know themselves and could be figured out by the names of their communities, towns, and names given to their children and perhaps through the dominant Eri legend (common among the Anambra Ibos). Thus we have towns called Amaigbo, Umuigbo, and such like town and community names in these states. There has been so much integration that this distinction seemed to have been forgotten. The non Ibos and to some extent even the Ibos of Anambra, Imo, Abia, Enugu, Ebonyi have thought that everyone originally inhabiting these states is of Igbo descendant. It has also not been proved that the colonial teachers who could not pronounce gb reduced the name of the people to Ibo for their convenient pronunciation. A visit to the UK proves that the English and other Europeans have words containing gb and have no difficulty pronouncing them appropriately.

Perhaps among the issues surrounding the Jewishness of the Ibo peoples is the question: "if the Ibo peoples should be regarded as Jews in what sense are they Jews?" This study sought to respond to this issue by pointing out that apart from well known legends and testimonies of historical figures, the Ibo peoples could be regarded as Jews just as the Israelites in the Old Testament world and other people identified today as such and are referred to as Jews. A Jew in this sense is therefore a descendant of Abraham through Jacob; and inhabitants of the ancient Judea who considered themselves as descendants of Jacob and Abraham who claim to worship the G-D of their father Abraham in truth. Because the Ibo peoples have legends that connect them as descendants of ancient Israelites, and not any where else, they are therefore genuinely Jews in this sense. This claim cannot be controverted as very many evidences point to this fact in spite of present day Ashkenazi legalisms, political hostilities and religious parochialism. Consequently those who teach and propagate the idea that Ibo peoples are only to be regarded as Hebrew need to think again although they could be said to be made up of the only original Hebrews of today. This reaction is an attempt to dissociate Ibo peoples from the backslidden and highly politicized Judaism of yesteryears and today. In fact these propagators of this idea may be right in their claim that Ibos are the only true Hebrew people of today. Earlier in this work it was stated that not every Hebrew is a Jew and that every Jew is a Hebrew. In the book of Revelation the Angel of the Lord who spoke through John the Apostle at the island of Patmos giving a message to the churches of Asia pointed out a congregation that claim to be Jewish, but was described to be "a synagogue of Satan." This passage implies that a Jew is a true worshipper of Yahweh, one who has no dealings with Satan and his agents; one who serves Yahweh in Spirit and Truth. Certainly we cannot claim that every Ibo person is a true worshipper of Yahweh today. In fact they could be counted as the backslidden Jew and consequently have no right to claim to be any better than the rest of the world they are trying to disscociate themselves from. The Ibo peoples are Jews as well as Hebrews seeking to meet the demands of the Holy and majestic Yahweh, the G-d of the Fathers, the father of the People, "Chukwu Abi 'ama" as He is literally referred to among the Ibos everywhere. However it is not clear if "Abi ama" refers to Abraham as "Abram" or literally means "the G-d of the fathers of my people." The Hebrew word for father is "Ab" and the Hebrew word for people is 'am (thus we have Abiama). Perhaps we could say that when prefixed with Chukwu, Abiam refers to the G-D of the fathers of the people. Thus the Ibo says Chukwu Abiama when refering to the Almighty G-d of Abraham: the AYAH ASHER AYAH" -"The I am that I am" who appeared to Moses in the burning bush.

The study also brought to the fore that Ibo ancestors entered into the Ibo land from different directions: north, south, west, east, and at different times in history as all roads led the wandering Hebrew immigrants beginning from Judea, Palestine and Egypt at different times to the Niger River confluence. Perhaps from Babylon, through the East, through the Red Sea (yam suph: "Sea of Reeds") to Egypt and finally to the same River Niger valley and area; even as the Book of Esdras seem to teach in a prophecy that they were to cover a far distance to at least 3000 miles. Other Israelite ancestors also later entered as emigrants from Spain, Portugal etc entering through the northern African axis, Ethiopia and Egypt; through the ancient Middle East axis; then from Sao Thome, Morocco through Timbuktu and from the Black Jewish Empire of Ghana that existed in West Africa. Of course we must not forget that the children of Seth had settled in this part of the world in remote ancient times. His descendants through Enosh were the first to be called "the People of Yahweh." The time of much later entry into Africa, attracted by the presence of brethren, and perhaps also to join their kith and Kin was traced as far back as the time of Abraham. His descendants through his wife Keturah as recorded by Flavius Josephus Antiquities also populated the area. Abraham and his descendants must have therefore been of dark colour or a mixture of colour but not so called white; Keturah and Abraham begot, perhaps, some Africans through their descendant Aphir (Afer) and others. We also concluded that the Jewish ancestors of the Middle East who must have been dark in skin colour naturally moved into Africa where they would be safely mixed with their kith and kin while fleeing from their persecutors. This should be especially the case with the immigrants from Spain and Portugal. This study also observed that colour differentiation was later introduced by racists as a ploy to denigrate the Africans and the black race as inferior to the so called white race. And we know that there is no such thing as white or black race in creation. We are each white, black, red and even of all colours from the creation of Adham and Eve whose genetic make up we all carry.

The study made efforts to bring to the fore the attempts of certain people to deny the Ibo peoples of their Jewish privilege because of parochial, political, and personal reasons. These are explained as the reason that the religious bodies that influenced not just religious education among the Ibos, but education in general made efforts to deny the expression of worship of Yahweh in Ibo names by dropping the final "h" in Ibo names that end in vowels, a tradition that was known many years into the colonialist leadership and education. An example is the name "Olaudah" spelt with the final 'h' which readily connects him with the tribe of Judah and the worship of 'Yahweh', "the father of the people" ABI-AMA. The same religious organizations sought to hamper the continuous technological development of the Ibos by making sure they "were not taught technical subjects". They were to be taught the three Rs: religion, rithmetic, riting. The religious organizations sought to change the Ibo technical mind set by diverting their traditional orientation away from their cultural technological roots. On the political front, the Ibos were subjected to negative mind control and vices formerly unknown to them and their traditional morality and culture were relegated to the background. In the modern times the fear of massive immigration to Israel and its feared and suspected economic consequences have lead to the politicians in the Knesset refusing to recognize the Ibo making aliyah to Israel. This is in spite of the fact that there has been no proof that Ibos are even interested in making such aliyah.

The second section of the study brings to the fore the fact that apart from legends and testimonies there are unquestionable practices, customs, and manners common to ancient Israelites and Ibos. This includes language similarities, beliefs and rituals in pregnancy, birth and child upbringing, circumcision, sacrificial system, community life, worship and beliefs and other doctrines; also meaning of life and its interpretation, as well as common philosophies that are unique to the two groups were brought to the fore. One such philosophy worthy to be mentioned again here is the concept of justice, truth and freedom. Where there is no justice, there can be no freedom and where there is no freedom and justice there can be no truth. Where Truth is lacking there can be no justice and no freedom. This explains why the Ibos are not given to diplomacy; not recognizing kinship; and not willing to live a life without freedom and justice that characterizes the history of the two groups of peoples, the Ibos and the ancient Israelites. This philosophy in addition to the common practices as found among the Ibos and ancient Israelites indicate a common source and from same background and origination. This calls for individual and collective re-invention of a people who have rapidly lost their ethical roots of "the G-d of their Fathers."

The study also acknowledges the fact that the Ibo peoples might have forgotten or relinguished many ancient customs and manners or modified them thereby mixing their original ancient customs and practices with those of their neighbours to such an extent that it became difficult to separate them as well as difficult to separate the true Ibo of Israelite origin from their non Israelite neighbours. Some of these practices might have been accepted by the Ibo peoples under duress due to persecution and influence of colonial experience. Some of these neighbours' influences include, perhaps natives of the land whom the Ibo Israelite ancestors met.Above all it would be wrong and unfair to judge the Ibo beliefs and practices as Jewish by present day Jewish practices introduced by rabbinic Ashkenazi Judaism. Present day Rabinnic Ashkenazi teachings and practices are way different from what the ancient Israelites actually believed and practiced. In spite of all the influences there are many Ibo customs and manners that relate to ancient times. For example we still have Ibo names and words that reflect ancient Israelite origination (like Udum Adah, Adah, iyin, iba, miri, anyi, maadu, be, etc). Some other name words that could be related to the Hebrew Bible include Asha, Abia, Ubulu, Abba, Nice, Ihite, ivite, ifite, to mention just these although it is not certain if these names of towns have similar meaning as their Biblical equivalent in ancient times. Perhaps this relatedness may confirm my opinion that the Israelite ancestors are spread all over the Iboland (former Eastern Region) and beyond and the opinion that the Ibo Sephardi Jews should not depend on one legend to conclude their origin. The diversity of dialects and accents seem to justify my observation and should lend some credence to this school of thought.

The later ancient Israelite ancestors of the Ibos must have started emigrating from ancient Israel as far back as 1305 to 2000 BC and immigrated into the Ibo territory. This time points close to the Exodus period as recorded in the Exodus account. This may indicate that some of the Israelites of the time of the Exodus experience diverted to Africa rather than follow Moses to Canaan. Thus these early immigrants into Ibo land could not have experienced the accounts of the wilderness migrations under Moses. It could still possibly be that some who began the wilderness migrations never followed through to the end but rather turned back into Africa. Yet still some others might have truned back from Babylon to join their brethren who had already crossed over the sea (possibly the Red Sea). This immigration into Ibo land continued to about the eighteenth century AD. Therefore the worship and practices of the Ibo peoples must be seen as a mixture of very ancient and "newer" Jewish ways. By "newer" here I do not mean Ashkenazic rabbinic Judaism. I mean the ancient versions as described in the Old Testament. This is why the Ibo language, ways and manners are very similar to the Hebrew Bible ways and manners, including as found in the Books of Leviticus, Numbers and Judges as represented in the Hebrew Biblical text. The similarities in Ibo Sacrificial system and the Ibo understanding of circumcision, pregnancy, birth, child upbringing, kith and kin solidarity, blood solidarity, community life, marriage, and the vocabulary and expression in language testify to this fact. It is therefore very probable that to understand the true meaning of the ancient Hebrew religion the Ibo traditional belief system should be explored once again. By this I mean the substructures of the Hebrew text different from palace interpretations that seem to have influenced today's Biblical understanding of some western scholars who have been aped by so called African academics. These substructures of the Biblical as understood and practiced by the masses constitute the true worship of Yahweh. The Ibo peoples were already Jews before Judaism was organized as a religion as we see it today. It is vital to put this fact into perspective while interpreting the ways and manners of the Ibo peoples in this light; yet there is need to avoid arbitrary connections especially in the area of language and meanings. The importance of language as a tool for genealogical linkage of peoples should also not be emphasized as words do criss cross boundaries and their usage and meaning is dynamic and changes with time and age.

The colour of the present day Jews presents as if the majority of them are of the so called "white" complexion. This is only because the dark skinned ones have been with us all the time while the so called white Jews emigrated from the European nations and had assumed the colour of the descendants of Japhet whose dark colour had been transformed from dark to "white". Japhet was not originally "white" neither were Noah and Abraham "white". They were all dark skinned colour originally. As has been observed the Israelites left to the Caucasians with their natural and native dark skin but came back with white coloured skin. A feature that has given their Arab and Persian neighbours much concern.

The large population of the Ibo nation does not annul their Israelite connection. Yahweh's promise to Abraham and then Jacob is that their descendants shall be multitudinal. Moreover most of their descendants live outside the Israel of today and majority does not belong to Judaism. Many do not even believe in the existence of a creator called Yahweh or Adonai (G-d), yet they are apparently accepted by Orthodox and other fanatical members of Judaism as genuine Jews while many genuine believers in Yahweh who have traced their origin to Israel are being denied Jewishness. There is nothing special about being a Jew over and against being a non Jew. Jewishness is only an ethnic identity and nothing more. Above all as the next chapter shows an individual Ibo seeking to reinvent themself will realise that Jewishness by ancestral claim to Abraham is no more the issue as Yeshua ha Maschiach has clearly taught the world. Many Jews are at present realizing this fact and surrendering to Yeshua the expected Messiah of the Jews and of the world.

CHAPTER 14

THE CALL FOR PERSONAL AND COLLECTIVE RE-INVENTION

As stated earlier in this study there is no doubt that the scriptures state that Yahweh chose the Israelites as His own. According to Deuteronomy 7: 6: "For you are a people holy to your G-d. The Lord your G-d has chosen you out of all the peoples on the face of the earth to be His people, His treasured possession".

For a people to be referred to as a "treasured" by a fellow human person is highly elating what more being referred to as such by the Almighty, the creator of all that is in existence. This should indeed be regarded as "exaltation per excellon". Also as stated earlier a position so highly exalting could lead to smug elitism as the chosen will be tempted to self delusion by believing and even acting as one specially favoured and preferred by Yahweh over and against other peoples.

The prophet Isaiah repeats the same chosenness of Israel by referring to them as "my servant", "Jacob whom I have chosen", you "descendants of Abraham, my friend" (see Isaiah 41:8).

Also in Psalm 135:4 we read: For the Lord has chosen Jacob (i. e Israel) to Himself, and Israel (i. e Jacob) for His perculiar treasure. Also we read again "You His servants, the descendants, His chosen ones, the children of Jacob (1 Chronicles 16:13, cf Psalm 105: 6).

Yet take a little time to examine this claim and so called privilege granted to the people of Israel, one will readily realize that there is nothing so special about it. Firstly it is the right of anybody and every body to join the privileged position. This could be by converting to Judaism and claiming the promises granted to Abraham by faith.

Secondly a closer examination shows that to belong to G-d, who is infinite is invitation to, perhaps, overwhelming responsibility. It is easy to arrogate the position of exaltation if one belongs to a human political office. But to arrogate such position cannot be associated with someone belonging to the Almighty G-d, the creator of everything and the owner of all. Thirdly it is far more tasking to fit into the demands of the Almighty who is Holy and exalted above all creation. Meeting G-d's standards of Holiness will be most difficult. This is more difficult because G-d is unfathomable and incomprehensible by mortal human.what I am saying here is that there is nothing so special in being referred to as the chosen of G-d as to warrant smug elitism or claim special favouritism or privileged position. Belonging to G-d as specially chosen of Him demands constant self examination, introspection, self-improvement rather than arrogance or smugness. Abraham was required to bring up his children and his household, with him and after him to keep the way of the Lord. What is right and just in G-d's sight and according to G-d's standards is a herculean task. Yet the scriptures seem to indicate that observing this rule was the condition for fulfilling the promises to Abraham. After the flood which destroyed the first world due to continual sin of disobedience and immorality in the sight of G-d, the world did not get any better in expected obedience to G-d's expectation for a good life. So it seems that G-d decided to have another plan and Abraham presented as the person willing to exercise faith in God. So G-d chose to introduce righteousness into the world through him and his descendants if he obeyed G-d. Let us not forget that Abraham was called out of a world of idolatry for a land he did not know with promises and blessings. Praise be to Yahweh Abraham exercised that faith expected of him and the blessings of G-d became effected by G-d in him and his descendants after him. In addition it was through Abraham that the nations of the world would be blessed because his descendants would work with G-d to achieve G-d's intention for the nations. As one can realize the emphasis remains on carrying out the responsibilities given by G-d to whom Abraham and his descendants are to account to. This is of course not a privilege or a special favour. The scripture enumerates instruments by which G-d has given same responsibilities. These include Moses, the Torah, the Prophets, Judges, etc.

However in the fullness of time G-d sent His son Yeshua, the Messiah. According to Jewish tradition, a possible Messiah is born in every generation-someone who could rebuild the Lord's Temple, restore Jerusalem, bring back the dispersed exiles to the land of Israel and set up a just and righteous government to judge between the nations (Isaiah 11:11-12, Jeremiah 23:8, Jeremiah 30:3, Isaiah 2: 2-4, Isaiah 11: 10, Isaiah 42: Messianic Bible Group letters)

Thus we read "for unto us a child is born, to us a son is given, and the government shall be upon his shoulders. And he shall be called Wonderful Counsellor, Mighty

G-d, Everlasting Father, Prince of Peace (Isaiah 9:6). Yeshua claimed this refers to him by relating the Isaiah 61:1-2 passage to himself and his ministry (Luke 4: 18-19, Math 15: 24, Mark 16: 15,16, Isaiah 53, Rev 1:5, Micah 5:2)

Yet we can also see from scripture that G-d has not abandoned his covenant with the Israelites. He remains a covenant keeping G-d and his promises to Israel remain unconditional (Leviticus 26: 44-45 Exodus 19: 5-6.) This has remained so in spite of all the efforts, in many cases using fabricated excuses of lies against them, the agent of destruction has made to frustrate Israelite participating fully in achieving this plan of God. Israelites everywhere have faced gruesome persecutions, torture and murder. The Ibos have been subjected to continual gruesome persecutions for very many decades beginning from persecutions their original Israelite ancestors faced when they were on their journey to settle in the land. Persecution of the Ibos in Nigeria is also traceable to as far the 1920s, 1930s, 1940s, 1950s, and the 1960s and has continued. When the other parts of Nigeria use the word Ibo they mean all peoples of the former Ibo country understood to include the inhabitants of all the eastern states including states of the Niger Delta, parts Benue State, East of the Niger River.

In the 1960s inhabitants of these states were massacred; so they made efforts to create their own independent nation called Biafra. That this desire did not materialize is additional evidence of hatred the Ibos are still facing today. The only reason for being persecuted, murdered and denied their rights is because they are Ibos. As a teenage boy living in the Jos, Plateau State Nigeria in the 1970s I was told I was hated because I am Ibo. A very beautiful, kind and adorable lady friend, a native of Du village near Jos, one day pointing at a man approaching told me to "avoid that particular man". I asked her reasons. She told me, "He hates the Ibos and does not hide it. He just stated that to me, so please do not go near him". When I asked why he hated the Ibos, my friend answered, "He just has no reason, He says he just hates Ibos". Yes I was told that we are hated because we are progressive and too enterprising for our neighbours. Imagine a boy of eleven years old being told he was hated because of his ethnicity. At that time I could not understand as I do now understand and appreciate the degree of this hatred of the Jew.

The persecutions of all Jews can be explained by the fact that it has been aimed at stopping the Jews everywhere from being a blessing to the nations wherever they are settled and stopping them from ensuring justice and peace among nations through the worship of the true God: "I will bless those who bless you and curse those who curse you; and the entire world will be blessed because of you" (Gen 12: 3, Isaiah 62: 6-7 Catholic Living Bible CLB). Hosea 6: 3 gives assurance that G-d cannot turn away from his chosen people and is ready with open arms to receive his people back.

Leviticus states, "But despite all they have done, I will not utterly destroy them and my covenant with them, for I am Yahweh their God. For their sakes I will remember my promises to their ancestors, to be their God. For I brought their forefathers out of Egypt as all the nations watched in wonder, I am Yahweh."(Lev 26:44-45 CLB)

What all this means is that every Jew who deserves that ethnic origination must reinvent self and live as the God of their fathers has destined them. They must go back to promoting justice, fairness, equity and dignity. They must join the fight to bring orderliness and well being to reign among all peoples beginning with their community. They must eschew cheating, theft, immorality, witchcraft, slavery, and backwardness. They must go back to the fear of God and exercise faith in the G-d of their forefathers so that former blessings of the exalted position would be restored. They must begin to repent of their wrong ways and trace their life back to fit the demands of right living. In the past every Ibo was careful to avoid doing the wrong and immoral acts other nations were practicing.They were a religious community and saw themselves as role model for their neighbours. Hard work was promoted and everyone saw themselves as a role model to other ethnic groups. Ibos were so cautious that an Ibo boy or girl never had boy friend or girl friend that was of other ethnic group. They married endogamously and had a close knit family solidarity. The Ibo were highly respected as a people and unlike today they 'were their "brother's keeper". This religious consciousness perhaps contributed to their innovativeness and achievements. However that it was the Ibo who betrayed and sold Olaudah Equiano and his sister into slavery, began to sell lands, began to change land boundaries, deny the widow and orphans their rights, oppress the strangers in their midst, and commit all the forbidden abominations contrary to the advice of their ancestors including thieving, stealing idol worship of previously unknown proportions, and even some are denying their identity and are now so disunited, calls for concern. This perhaps justified their suffering in the land the G-d of their fathers has given them and if they fail to repent and turn around might incur more suffering and damnation.

Therefore all the Ibo peoples must as a matter of urgency first repent of denial of who they are; identify with their kith and kin and with the right people, their brother Jews in other parts of the world and emulate their push for inventions. They are to do business with their brethren, they are the ones to do business with today and the future if the Ibos must achieve their natural ambition to develop themselves and be a blessing to others. The present governors in all the Ibo states mentioned above must as a matter of urgency come together to reinvent themselves and educate their peoples to do the same. The governors must unite and forge a common front to fight for their rights and to ensure moral uprightness and patriotism to the Ibo nation is realized, maintained and sustained. In order to operate as a nation the Ibo peoples must come together. They have a common enemy and any attempt to live in denial of this is playing the ostrich. They have no choice but get united rather than fighting one another.

The native philosophy of the Ibo must be reinstated. The Ibo believes that life is freedom; there is no life without freedom. Freedom is core of The Truth and the truth cannot dissolve in the blood of a person. This perhaps explains why they are described as recalcitrant and full of uppity and unyielding. This truth is symbolized by the ritual staff called ofo which they believe "grows in the compound of the the creator of this world." According to the Ibo "Truth is life": "ezi okwu bu ndu." Truth gives freedom. There can be no freedom without truth and there can be no truth where there is no freedom. This explains why the Ibo are said not to recognize kingship or monarchy/ supreme ruler. However this philosophy seems to have been waned since colonials introduced western politics into the Ibo peoples and everything falls apart as Truth became politicized and Freedom became diluted and diplomaticised. In fact to the Ibo Diplomacy is nothing else than legalized system of telling lies and nationally and internationally justifying it. This negates Ibo philosophy that there can be no grey area in Truth and Freedom. This philosophy of the Ibo explains why group of Ibo slaves would rather collectively drown than be taken into slavery and why many of them worked hard to purchase their freedom when granted that opportunity during the slave trade. Our hero General Philip Effiong was aware of this philosophy when he timely warned the Nigerian government officials, represented by General Olusegun Obasanjo while offering the surrender of Biafra that TREAT THE SURRENDERING BIAFRANS WELL OR RISK THEIR CHILDREN RISING AGAIN. Is there any wonder why some Biafran youth are today rising massively against the system that has been oppressing them especially since the end of that phase of oppression of our fathers by the same generals that our hero General Philip Effiong advised? There at present exist at least forty agitating reactionary groups including The Movement for the Actualisation of the Sovereign State of Biafra (MASSOB), The Indigenous Peoples of Biafra (IPOB) and the Billie Human Rights Initiative (BHRI) to mention just these. Rather than heed the intelligent Biafran hero General Effiong's advice as a much senior and far better trained, educated and disciplined soldier than all of them they have rather perfected the system of oppressing the Biafrans. They have in addition taken over our natural resources, denied us education and well deserved development and taken away our right to self development and national leadership position; now they want to take possession of the land of our fathers. As if that is not enough they have resorted to seeking to cause disunity among us in order to be able to exploit us the more. The call of every Ibo is to reinvent and live out this Philosophy of Truth and Freedom handed down by Chukwu Abiama through our common ancestor. This reinvention is very vital for individual self improvement and national development of the Ibo nation.

This could be achieved by remaining within the territory called Nigeria in whatever structure she might take. Moreover the solution of our problem may not be achieved in a structure that Nigeria might take. Rather it will be achieved in repentance through personal and collective re-invention of who we are as a people. That the rising of the Ibo youth has achieved the popularizing of the need for Restructuring Nigeria within a very short time is perhaps an indication that the Ibo peoples will excel more if they remain within the polity called Nigerian than breaking away to form an independent nation. The Ibo youth have all to gain and win so long as they reinvent. Any breaking away without first personal reinvention as stated above may be a risk too dangerous to take at this time. The average Ibo person is still struggling with the problem of identity. Who am I realy? This explains why present leadership of the Ibo is slippery and inconsistent, self-serving and sometimes hostile and inhumane. So long as the Ibo person has allegiance to their political party rather than to the Ibo nation this untrustworthy perception of the Ibo leader will continue. It is also this situation that has created division within the Ibo society. While some say, 'I am for Zik (nationalist)" Others say,"I am for Emeka Ojukwu" (separation)." Others say "I am for Aka Ikenga," others say, "I am for Ohaneze Ndigbo;" others claim "I am for indigineous Peoples of Biafra IPOB." The core native values of the Ibo person is not emphasized perhaps relegated as irrelevant usually for political convenience or they are unknown to these factionizers and their followers. What makes a people is the value system guiding their aspiration and cohesion as a people. Where this is lacking or found wanting, the centre cannot hold and everything else will fall apart and such a society falls into disarray. This perhaps describes the current state of things among the Ibos. Some of these now deny their Ibo nationhood in spite of the fact that they answer Ibo names, speak Ibo languages and are naturally Ibo in all ramifications. Others are into kidnapping, selling and betrayingtheir fellow Ibos- a practice that was never heard of among Ibos of the past. A realization of our unique position as the chosen of Yhwh like our ancestors lived should ginger us to re-invent ourselves and seek to being Ibo again rather than living just like the enemies of the Ibo nation have planned to make us live.

The necessity for separate existence is underscored by the current subjugation of the Ibo nationalities to a prison yard, under lock and key by the enforcement of a constitution that was promulgated by military decree 24 of 1999, not signed into law by the national assembly or by any president; not subjected to referendum; written by a handpicked few Nigerians; does not provide for state constitutions to create true federation; kept a secret till after all inaugurations in 1999; not printed by the government printer in 1999; takes care of one religionin sections 275-279 and neglects all others; over centralized governance; centralized the whole judiciary; gaives the national assembly power over concurrent items; created a unitary government, not federal government; falsely claims Nigerians willingly handed over their lands and resources to the federal government, thus pauperizing states and Nigerians; sections 275-179 negates section 10 regarding non-state religion; calls state governors chief security officers but does not give them security outfits or power over police; a civilian government can never meet section 8 requirements for the creation of new states and local governments; says married girls less than 18 years old are adults who can sue, be sued, vote, and be voted for, for no clear reason; the military land use decree, later Act, were embedded in the constitution so not easy to amend for no stated reason; provided for only one police force unlike other federations; section 6 frees government from liability regarding citizen rights provided in chapter 2 thus, these rights are not justiceable. Nonetheless only a liar, charlatan, or the self deluded lunatic would be under this high security prison yard called country and begin to talk of setting up their own nation instead of fighting as hard as possible to be released from the prison first of all, then there will be a clearer understanding and in the right state of mind to begin to contemplate the type of country to set up and why. The wise step should be to first extricate themselves from this bondage called Nigeria Constitution carefully planned to enslave the masses of Nigeria to the advantage of the ruling nationality. This requires cooperation with other nationalities who are victims of this enslavement. Bringing down the constitution will naturally set every nationality free from the contrapment called Nigeria and will be free to think for themselves who and how to realign themselves.

Consequently, if the Ibo must seek separate national existence, it should not go along the present corrupted approach. It should rather be indigenous, original and express the pride of race and industry for which the Ibos are known. The current Biafra is obviously foreign and not indigenous to the Ibo. This is because the flag, the anthem, the name, are all foreign and even the lyrics of the Biafra national anthem is under legal battle due to accusation of plagiarism by the composer against the leadership of Biafra. The design of the flag is Jamaican Marcus Garvey's pan-african flag, the tune is Finish (Finland), and the name Biafra is foreign. Although the father of Pan Africanism (19th century), Edward Blyden, was Ibo by descent this does not justify the use of Pan-African flag to represent the Ibo Nation. This is a message to the current agitators of Biafra to take note of and begin to fight corruption rather than agitating for Biafra that is not even indigenous to the Ibo peoples. The area to be Ibo nation should also be well defined. Current Biafra is also ambiguous in boundary whereby unwilling peoples are being forced to answer Biafra through coarsion and manipulation and even threat as propagated by the current leadership of IPOB. This is why currently the agitation for Biafra while under the enslavement of the Nigerian Constitution is an unnecessary diversion that has tended to frustrate the fight to bring down the enslaving constitution. The fight to bring to end this apartheid constitution is so vital that nothing should be allowed to trivialize or divert attention from the struggle. All indigenous nationalities in Nigerian have come together to seek self determination by fighting to bring down this 1999 constitution. NINAS is the right action to take at the present time. The Nigerian Indigenous nationalities Alliance for Self determination NINAS, is a coalition of the whole Middle Belt, South West, South South, South East states, this means so far the whole of Nigerian except the Sharia territory made of 12 Sharia states of the far North that technically have actually seceded from the rest of Nigeria by adopting the Sharia and declaring themselves as Sharia states in a secular state that Nigeria is since the year 2000 under the presidency of Obasanjo, a supposedly christian president. The same Obasanjo was responsible for setting into the process of Islamisation and current fulanisation and Arabisation of the whole of the country. He did this by decreeing 17 exclusive lists into the 1979 constitution. It is to be noted that the foundation of this prcess was set by Murtala Mohammed in 1975 when he overthrew the regime of Yakubu Gowon and took over the governing Nigeria without giving any reason why Gowon was to be overthrown. Sadly he also invited two so called

Christian barristers, Rotimi Williams and Ben Nwabueze to draft him a constitution that ended up removing the federalism of the country. It was this constitution that was endorsed by Abdulsalam's government in 1999 and has subsequently been endorsed by all governments since they swore to uphold it. If the constitution continues to direct affairs in Nigeria it means that leaderships will continue to swear to uphold and defend it to the continuing destruction of the people.

This singular action of the far North Sharia states that has been tolerated by the Nigerian Government is indeed a proof that Nigeria has ceased to exist as an entity to be considered valid as a country. Accepting one section to self determination has given automatic permission to other nationalities making up Nigeria freedom to declare their own self determination and take action. The implication is that the entity called Nigeria ceases to exist. A new phase therefore has to been entered whereby other nationalities should decide their fate. The issue Nigeria as a country is facing is herculean and could be traced to as far back as the early 1920s when the Arab nations and later the Islamic Brotherhood proposed to islamise the rest of the world and Africa in particular, including South Africa and Nigeria. This agenda took stage with the regime of Murtala Mohammed and his boys in the army in 1975/1976 who are at present continuing his legacy and explains why Gowon was overthrown in the first place, and why the whole Arab world joined hands with Nigeria to fight Biafra. This means that any attempt to draft another constitution for Nigeria is unnecessary and dangerous because the whole issue is an ocestrated plan to take over Nigeria completely by the enemies of Christianity and the Jews everywhere, who histories identify, are vicious killers and occupiers of Jewish and Christian lands. Sadly, the enemies have been using so called Christians to achieve their aims in Nigeria. Meanwhile we need to remind ourselves that after independence in 1960, Ahmadu Bello went to the Arab world and promised to deliver Nigeria into the Arab nation as an Islamic country. And in 1988 under Babaganda, Nigeria was declared an Isalmic nation by regiatering as a member of the Organisation of Islamic Countries OIC, and today the 1999 constitution has entrenched Islam as a state religion with some section of the country implementing the Sharia as their constitution. Babagida, Abiola, and others actions resulted in the resignation of his Ibo Christian Vice President, Ebitu Ukiwe, for not consulting his opinion on this matter. In addition to all this the Mohammed Marwa, Maitatsine and Bokoharam, ISIS in the West Africa etc Islamic revolts as well as the current attempt at fulanisation and islamisation through the so called herdsmen killings and possession of Christian lands have all been continuation of the agenda to own Nigeria and Africa completely to themselves.

The point being made here is that all talk of setting up a separate Biafra at the moment is premature and diversionary, as well as trivializing such a serious matter especially as the killings have already begun right under our noses. They should join NINAS in their effort to bring down the 1999 constitution first of all then individual nation building will follow, if God so wills it. The question is: can Christians, Jews and other self appointed freedom fighters be able to unite to fight as one in order to avert this iminent danger threatening us all? Yes, the different indigenous nationalities have come together and have been fighting but can the various disparate organisations join them?

Chapter 15
CONCLUSION

That the Ibos are Jews being descendants of ancient Israelite nation has been settled as true. They inhabit the territory known as the Deserts of Seth that existed within the district called Biafara. Seth who was the son of Adam and Eve and during the time of his descendant Enosh, Yahweh made himself known to them as the G-d of their fathers and they began to be known as "the people of Yahweh."

The Ibo of Biafara became registered as one of the Sephardi Jewish nations and peoples of the world in 1997; into the King Solomon Sephardi Federation International (KSSFI). Above all the consciousness to this fact and the common customs and manners shared with the Jews of today and ancient Israelites serve as proof to this fact even as Olaudah Equiano testifies in his narrative.

Although at present there is no massive genetic proof of the Jewishness of the Ibo except the haplo group of e1b1a1 to which the writer belongs, there is no evidence that genetics can prove or disprove the Jewishness of the Ibo generally; neither is there any evidence that the Ibo are the oldest ethnic group on the earth as some scholars tend to argue, claiming that the Igbo are older than Adam.

The Ibo peoples originated from different Jewish clans who immigrated into the area at different times and from different routes: south through Sao Thome, north through Ethiopian and Egypt, west through the Black Jewish Ghana Empire, and elsewhere. The Eri origin is today the more popular legend and perhaps more influencial legend that is extant about the origin of the Igbo peoples. This legend has been popularized perhaps due to the influence of Eri's descendant called Igbo and is known to be dominant among the Anambra, Enugu, Ebonyi, Delta, Kogi, and parts of Benue states. Other popular claims of origin include Ephraim, Manasseh, Asher, and Benjamin (known among the Ohafia, Owere, Ngwa, Etche, Ikwere, Mbaise, Akwa Ibom and Cross River areas), Zebulon is associated with the Ijaw (Izhon), some Imo, Anambra, and Enugu areas, and other Riverine peoples; and Levi also associated with the Ohafia, Owere, Mbaise, Ebonyi and parts of Anambra and Enugu states. Asher, Isaacher (Rivers, part of Imo, Akwa Ibom). The descendants of Levi are believed to be most spread among the Ibo populace because they are priest of the communities they inhabit. They seem to be found among every community in Iboland.

Many customs and manners of the Ibos and those of the ancient Israelites are similar including their philosophy of life which is embedded in their religious concepts centred on the worship of the Monotheistic G-d, Yahweh generally referred to as "The G-d of the fathers" whose name is so sacred that "it is not to be mentioned because it is not known." He is simply the "I AM" The Ibo represent his presence with a white flag that is strapped between two tall bamboo sticks.

Some practices common to both include the following beliefs and practices:

Appeasing the G-d of the fathers through sacrifices when obedience to His laws is infringed upon; these practices are similar in both peoples, and include period of seclusion for the mother after the birth of a child, and secluding a woman when she is menstruating; such a woman is said to be in her "forbidden period" (nso). Also purification rituals are carried out when the following have occurred: murder, incest, and any offence against the use of the land, theft, refusal to obey the levirate law, breaching the law of cohabitation, killing and or eating of forbiden animal or food, wrongly mixing of crops or food items etc

Deliberately eating an animal killed in the inappropriate manner such as strangling or already dead

Similar laws for the Priesthood such as right to specific parts of a sacrifice, marriage to only a virgin for the high priest, and the high priest must not marry a widow or the divorced woman, while a priest was allowed to marry a widow

Forbiden to touch a dead animal including a dead human being.

Compulsory practice of circumcision of males by law on the 8ᵗʰ day following birth: while female circumcision was not known among the Ibos. Those who practiced it got the idea from non Ibo communities. So also was the practice of circumcision at puberty not common among the Ibos unless the child was sick or there was a known reason why it was deferred. Naming also took place most often during circumcision but not as a rule among the people.

Strong brotherhood solidarity

Having a place of refuge for the offender involved with certain specific offences

Strongly linking kin, cult, land and the afterlife in which the sin of one person affects the whole community that includes the living descendants, the ancestors and those yet to be born

Worshipping of false deities called "Arushi". "Arusi" in Ibo means "abomination" and such worshippers were killed in the past. They were called "Amosu." Amosu is also synonymous with witchcraft. Ibo has no place for witchcraft, witches, soothsayers, and clairvoyants. However the coming of Christianity banned such killing so this was replaced by ostracizing such spiritual adulterers.

Practising what used to be called "the dance of promise"

Period of dance was time to choose wives.

Marital laws whereby the elder must first get married before the younger ones. In this situation the older girl should be given away to marriage before the younger sisters unless the elder does nto intend to get married which was also rare.

Eating of bitter herbs; this is popularly eaten with roasted goat head (nkwo obi)

Collective bringing up of a child

Life as a gradation of stages whereby each stage ushered into by use of known rituals

The use of similar euphemisms for describing death and certain parts of the body

Others manners and customs common to both peoples are:

The fear and avoidance of the sea

Sacredness of the land: belief that the land belongs to G-d and so must not be sold and the boundaries must not be altered

Obligatory Care of the widow, the orphan and the stranger, and the poor

The same agricultural rules including the law of gleaning, jubilee, avoiding the mixing of certain elements and crops; avoiding the eating of pork, not dealing on pigs, avoiding of eating of certain animals; following same agricultural festivals, having same calendar including following the moon and start of end of the day

Use of the three-stroke back-hand greeting

Levirate marriage

Upholding the dignity of the human person

Belief that community life as vital for a happy existence here on earth and following death

Reverence for water

Perhaps it is in the area of language similarities that one is most amazed of the sameness of these two peoples. In spite of the thousands of years of separation and the variation in the use of the ancient Hebrew language this study was able to uncover words that are not only pronounced in the same way and manner but also have same or similar meaning. This is also in spite of the fact that vowels were introduced into the Hebrew language much later by the Masoretic School of Moses Maimonides (as late as 1240 AD).

One other amazing find is the connection of water to Miriam regarded as the Prophet of Water in the wilderness by the Israelites and according to Judaism lore. Thus the Ibo word for water is "miri" and the Ibo say "ym miri" or "miri ym" for give me water. This has given them the Hausa name "Yamiri". The Ibos also revere water as water must not be sold and nobody must be denied water. Water is also the first gift offered to a visitor.

Also belief in the sacredness of the marriage institution is the same. This begins with similar way of finding a wife, say, during dance festivals. The Ibo female is to be groomed to be a mother and wife. She is to honour her husband as the priest of the home and must observe known practices to make this effective. She marries while still a virgin and a bethrotal is regarded as de facto marriage. The husband is addressed as "my lord" (Di m) by the wife and she must not cook or serve him food while in her menstrual period. Food is also served with her kneeling and head covered. She does not cook or serve her food when in her period of purifying following birth of a child (Omu ugwo sacred seclusion period) and at the end of the seclusion for puficiation a gift is taken to the deity usually a goat without blemish carried by the husband while the maidens take the woman to the village stream to wash. The occasion is ended with feasting and celebration. The child is named on the eight day of birth as circumcision in some cases. However, sometimes the name of the child is known before birth. Children visit the newly delivered woman and she offered them gifts.

Similar business strategy including the use of guilds and marriages for business alliances

The Need for Personal and Collective Re-invention

However, the question is what next? Now that both Israelites and the Ibo people they know they are of this stock what challenges lay ahead for Sephardi Ibos? How can they appropriate the blessings and meet the challenges associated with this status? The writer believes that this discovery calls for personal reinvention both individually and as a community wherever the Ibo people may live in the world. It is estimated that very many Ibos constitute the population of the United States of America, as much as eighty percent of some of the states. This is because of the removal to that part of the world during the slave trade to the Americas. There are also very many of them in Asia, and the Oceania, all over the world such that it is said that anywhere the Ibo man is not found is an indication that such a place is too dangerous for any human habitation.

My opinion is that on a more serious note, the Ibo Jews need to decide how to reinvent themselves. This could be done collectively as a people through posing a united front to educating the Ibos what it means to be a Jew and what it means to be an Ibo Jew in the midst of some hostile Ashkenazic Jews and hostile Christianity. It is not enough to call on the Ibos to collectively abandon Christianity. The advocates of this call claim that western Christendom has been a canker worm to the Ibo peoples and should be cast out of the psyche of the people. They claim that western Christendom has been too much of a burden to the Ibos and should be abandoned. This call for re-invention will involve personal religious reinvention and collective political reinvention.

In doing this they have two options to choose from:

1.   By carving out their own pattern of worship as Jews although some think the niche can easily be achieved if Ibos see themselves more as Hebrews than Jews and reinvent a type of Christianity that has roots in the Hebrew Old Testament life pattern rather then following sheepishly the present version of Christendom that does not seem to give direction to the worship of YHWH. The claim here is that you cannot reinvent yourself as a Jew without reinventing yourself as a Hebrew, a genuine Hebrew. It is not possible to be a true Jew without reinventing oneself as a faithful Hebrew. The emphasis can only be on the faith of our father Abraham "father of the people" ABI'AMA(literally in Hebrew "my father, our people")
Yes, the rites of our ancestors that were misunderstood as idol worship could be reformed by pruning those aspects of them that were borrowed from their non Jewish neighbours and then creating their own Jewish ways and manners as suits the worship of AYAH ASHER AYAH, the God of the fathers. This means that they must realize that the God of the fathers is Yhwh, the G-D of Abraham and Moses. They would need to follow the already laid down foundations by our forefathers before the western style of religion distorted their religious practices and dismissed them as of the devil. This option may pose difficulty to achieve the needed religious reinvention because Christianity especially Roman Catholicism has been embedded into their fabric. This influence will be very difficult to eradicate or replace.
2.   The second option is to completely retrace the true worship

of Yahweh as taught by Yeshua ha Machiach, Jesus, The Messiah who has been shown to be the expected Messiah of the Jews. The sacrifice of Yeshua as the final offering for all sin and offences against Yahweh must be recognized and accepted for what it is. Yeshua declared that he is the gate through which anyone can go to Yahweh, His father who is also "the God of the fathers" of the Ibo Jews who revealed himself to Enosh and his descendants who inhabited the deserts of Seth. The "deserts of Seth" was replaced by the area that came to be called BIAFARA (B'Ephra). All the fathers including Abraham looked forward to the Messiah, who is Yeshua. Yeshua has been the focus of the worship of Yahweh. Without Yeshua as the focus and object of worship, the congregation remains the synagogue of Satan- a religion without peace is a religion without Yeshua. It is a synagogue of Satan. Yeshua did not abrogate the Law which constitutes the religion of the fathers. Ananias in the Acts of the Apostles is described as "a devout man according to the Law" though he was a disciple of Christ (Act 22: 12). Ibo race is suffering today because they have neglected the omenala of their fathers and have been made directionless by western version of Christendom. There is therefore the need for redirection to the right ways- a Christianity that is rrooted in the Law handed down by our ancestors of which Yeshua is the Lord and Master in all aspects of life.

According to traditional Jewish belief of today the Yom Kippur is regarded as the period when the gate to Yahweh is widest open for everyone to enter. After the Yom Kippur the gate closes (nillah). However Yeshua declares that He has opened the gate to Yahweh forever and that any one who is willing to be among his flock can get strait to Yahweh (John 10:9). In the ancient Israelite times Sacrifice was relevant to fulfill the law that states that without the shedding of blood there can be no remission for sin. However, in the sacrifice of Yeshua, all the sacrifices and sacrificial systems of the past are therefore no longer relevant: be it "korban olah", "mincha", "shelamim", "chatat", "asham", "kaparot" etc including all their Ibo equivalent sacrifices and sacrificial systems. Yeshua's death on the cross has paid it all and he has his arms wide open to receive the repentant Ibos, all Jews and whosoever wills. However this is a call to true repentance in order to have a direct individual relationship with Yahweh. It is not a call to join a religious body, undergo the rite of baptism or Jewish

Bar Mitsvah or bath Mitsvah or any rite of passage in order to claim to belong to Yahweh or to Yeshua. The reinvention of the Ibo must open their eyes to understanding the difference between being in religion and belonging to Yahweh through Yeshua, the Messiah for which reason Yahweh has chosen them in Abraham in the first place. Yeshua has given the Ibos fresh access to Yahweh for true worship of Him (John 11: 25-26). Yeshua has provided a fresh way through the barrier to Yahweh that was created by sin and ignorance; that blighted their vision and understanding of their true identity in the first place (John 14: 6). Yeshua determines the person who will enter into this relationship with Yahweh.

Yeshua as the only Messiah is in total control of everything that patterns to salvation (Rev 22: 14-15, John 10: 1, John 3: 17, Matt 18: 14, Luke 23: 43).

Strictly speaking the approach of totally reverting to the old ways would certainly be cumbersome and almost impossible to achieve in view of the fact that the minds of the Ibo peoples have been disconnected with their past history for perhaps too long to imagine reconnecting them with the past without adverse mental stress and its consequences. Also reinstituting these practices may be unacceptable to very many people. Above all for the Ibo to follow the line of the present system of Judaism that is regarded as way off from their ancestors' faith will mean another colonization of their minds with falsehood of another type. Instead of aligning themselves with Judaism of today, that has been dominated and determined by Separdic and Ashkenazic rabbinic systems, the Ibo had rather form their own system of Hebrew worship. I think the second option will serve the Ibo Jews better. This Ibo type of worship will be Christianity from the Biblical background based on the foundations laid by Yeshua in the New Testament (berit chadasha). It will be the Christianity as Yeshua and the Apostles meant it to be; the true faith of Yeshua devoid of Judaizing and European Helenistic principles, philosophies, practices and ethos. The current system of Christianity has failed the Ibo and the world in general for many obvious reasons. Yeshua himself was Jewish but he repudiated the hypocricy of the Judaism of his time. Unfortunately this type of Judaism has prevailed among the Jews and has been perfected in its hypocricy and human manipulations just as the present day European determined, interpreted and directed church followed the same pattern of hypocrisy and deceit with economic and social exploitation of the people. Christianity turns the blind eye away from the murdering of the Ibo peoples. Even fellow Christians participated in various pogrom against the Ibos, even championed the genocide against the Ibos. Thus Ibo peoples have every reason to repudiate western version of Christendom. Moreover the present Christianity is not rooted in Yeshua the Messiah of the Jews.

Accepting Yeshua, the Messiah, as the expected Jewish Messiah along with his teachings, his practical examples and the grace he offers to live out the life he gives, is the solution and best way for the Ibo peoples and all Jews to reinvent themselves in the proper biblical way.The Ibo must repudiate all blasphemies of rabbinic Judaism against the Messiah. Experience and facts of history have proven the rabbinic Judaism fabricated accusations against Yeshua, the Christ. Some Western Christian theologians and leaders have also followed this line of fabrication to discredit the only Messiah, the Son of God. Consequently they have presented an ugly fragmented image of the Messiah to the world. The Ibo Jews must look back onto their humble beginnings and must accept their Messiah, Yeshua with whom their forefathers covenanted now as they reinvent themselves and become a means to win over other Jews to their Messiah. There is need for unadulterated Biblical faith.

In carrying this task out there will be need to re-educate the Ibo peoples on the fact that the G-d of their fathers is the G-d who is the father of our Lord and savior Yeshua, the expected Messiah and that He has not abandoned us. In fact he states through Prophet Jeremiah that he would make a New Covenant (Jeremiah 31: 31). The people will need to be taught that helenistic faith of the current western Christianity needs to be replaced with a good understanding of the intention of the Yeshua. Christianity should be taught to reflect the Jewish principles by which Yeshua first intended it before western Christianity distorted and removed the Jewish emphasis. This distortion was done through Roman Catholicism and even European Reformers. Both movements teach that the Church had replaced the Jews in God's plan of salvation. The result of this teaching is the form of Christianity that has failed all adherents as adherents have been made to read the Bible devoid of Jewish roots. This has limited the fear of G-d and consequently presented a shallow worship of the G-d. This also explains the emergence of such doctrines as predeterminism and predestination and the wars between Calvinism and other Protestants in England that claimed so many lives as well as the massacring of subjects by their Kings in Europe and England and elsewhere Iboland included. The politicisation of the church has led to very many inhumanities and paved the way to the shape of the world as we have it today including the hatred of the Jews and compromises to the word of God including the practice of infant baptism and associated nominalism of Europe due to the teaching that children could become born again through the faith of their parents when they are baptized as infants.

Jeremiah 31:31 is the clearest prophecy in the Tenach that God would one day make a New Covenant based on individual's faith rather than on belonging to a nation or group. Apparently the teachers of salvation by baptism by proxy did not heed this prophecy. The faith in the finished work of Christ was ignored by these teachers. Perhaps prominent effect of this teaching is waring against one another and hatred of the Jews by frontline theologians and politicians.

The Puritan Presbyterian wars also come to mind. During these wars the so called "G-d ordained" groups were known to unmercifully slaughter each other even though they were Calvinists. The wars of Cromwell and Owen as holy wars could be said to be likened to Islamic Jihads of Muslims slaughtering each other and the so called infidels.

The status of women was deplorable under the Calvinist as under Islam. As Dr Prasch puts it: "...The status of women under Calvinistic Puritanism and in Islam is likewise identical; philosophically the two are the same. Jesus said we know them by their fruits and from Calvin's Geneva, to the Salem witch hunts, to slavery and apartheid we have seen the fruits of what Calvinists call "predestination" and what Moslems call "Insha'Allah" (all that transpires is the perfect divine will). As Muslims read the Judeo-Christian Scriptures through the prism of the Quran which combine elements of Judaism, Christianity, and Zoroastrianism with a recycled Arabian paganism and then re-interpret the Quran in light of the Hadith in a religion based on The Five Pillars. Calvinists read it through the prism of Calvin's Institutes which are a recycled Patristic theology of Augustine, an African, who laid the doctrinal foundation of Roman Catholicism, and then reinterpret that along the lines of the five acronym terms of their "TULIP". All of this tragedy, treachery, madness and hypocrisy stems from the mal-definition of "Undeserved Grace" as "Unconditional Election" in the philosophical and moral sense. Calvinism could be likened to nothing more than Islam pretending to be Christianity".

Prasch notes, "The final problem is that the primary New Testament definition of "election" has to do with a corporate identity such as Israel being an elect nation or the collective Body of true believers. Calvinism distorts Romans 9-11 out of context to misapply election to individuals." It is needful to remind everyone that the Islamic and Calvinistic doctrine of predeterminism and fatalism produced Islamic Triumphalism and western colonialism and oppression of the weak. This also implies that any connection with such doctrinal belief whether it is as expressed in Calvinism or Islamism, with peace is a delusion. Anyone who opposes this assertion here should reflect on historical experience of the Church and perhaps also read Sura 3: 83. Also the Ayatolla Khomeini in Iran in 1979 clearly injuncted Muslims to "conquer Britain and the nations of the world with Islam" as a duty. In Nigeria in particular I remember that in the 1960s a certain politician stated that to deep the Qur'an into the Atlantic was a duty to be achieved. By this he meant the conquering of the Ibo nation was a duty for the Muslims to accomplish. We also know that the major motivation to fight the Ibos was to achieve this aim. As is the present causing division among the Ibo peoples of the coastal regions and the other Ibos especially the Igbos. The purpose is to skim their way into the so called south south carve them out of the union with their brother Igbos and then take over the affairs of the people very easily. This is why the people have been told that the rest of the Ibo peoples are their enemies. Unfortunately some Ibos seem to have bought this idea wholly for selfish purposes. Also we can see that experience so far has shown that Islam has remained hostile and aggressive to Jews, just like the so called Christians in the past and present. Today hostility of the Chrisitan leaders to the Jews has been incited by the desire to win votes for political positions during elections (political correctness).

Jews have suffered in the hands of some Christian leaders in history some of which have been highlighted already. I have in mind here people like the German Martin Luther regarded as father of the Protestant Faith. He wrote referring to the Jews:

"Whoever would like to cherish such adders and puny devils—who are the worst enemies of Christ and us all—to befriend them and to do them honor simply in order to be cheated, plundered, robbed, disgraced, and forced to howl and curse and suffer every kind of evil, to him I would commend the Jews.

"And if this is not enough, let him tell the Jews to use his mouth as a privy, or else crawl into the Jew's hind parts, and there worship the holy thing, so as afterwards to be able to boast of having been merciful, and of having helped the Devil and his progeny to blaspheme our dear Lord." (quoted in Martin Luther: Hitler's Spiritual Ancestor www.moriel.org)

In his book On the Jews and Their Lies, Martin Luther wrote:

"Therefore be on your guard against the Jews, knowing that wherever they have their synagogues, nothing is found but a den of devils in which sheer self-glory, conceit, lies, blasphemy, and defaming of God and men are practiced most maliciously and veheming his eyes on them."

In this same book, he advised that Jewish homes be destroyed and that safe-conduct on the highways be abolished completely for the Jewish People.

He also wrote that Jewish prayer books and Talmudic writing (Rabbinic commentaries and oral laws) should be taken away from the Jews, that rabbis should be forbidden to teach, and that synagogues should be burned and buried.

However, Christian anti-Semitism didn't begin with Martin Luther. In fact the history of western Christianity is full of Violence against the Jews.

It cannot be forgotten that Hitler carried out his evil plan against the Jews based in part upon the words of Martin Luther and other anti-Semitic decrees and actions of the early Church Fathers and Councils.

Over 20 anti-Jewish measures instituted to persecute and eventually attempt to exterminate the Jews by the Nazis were derived from Roman Catholic canonical law.

Also the yellow Star of David that Hitler forced Jews to wear as a badge of shame to mark them for abuse and execution actually evolved out of the Fourth Lateran Council in AD 1214.

This Council met in Rome to reaffirm and to institute several canons of religious law. With regard to the Jews, they enacted the following: Canon 67 states: Jews who charge «excessive» interest are to be restricted from commercial lending with Christians, especially since such interest prohibits Christians from tithing to the Church. Canon 68 states: Jews must wear dress that distinguishes them from Christians, and they cannot appear in public from Good Friday through Easter Sunday.

In 1227, the Synod of Narbonne enacted its own Canon 3: «That Jews may be distinguished from others, we decree and emphatically command that in the center of the breast (of their garments) they shall wear an oval badge, the measure of one finger in width and one half of a Palm in height." It also forbids Jews from appearing in public on Sundays, festivals, and throughout Holy Week. Canon 69 states: Jews cannot hold public office and Christian officials cannot interact with Jews. Canon 70 states: Jews who have been baptized should be restrained from returning to their "former rite."

As history progressed, so did the censures and restrictions progress and seems to have continued to be so.

This is the Coat of arms for the Tribunal of the Holy Office of the Inquisition in Spain. The text in Latin reads: "Rise up, O God, and judge thy own cause." (Psalm 74:22; Psalm 73 in the Latin Vulgate translation)

As stated earlier during the Spanish Inquisition of AD 1491, throughout Spain, hundreds of thousands of Jews were tortured and burned at the stake for refusing to accept the official system of Christian religion as their own.

In Russian pogroms (mob attacks) from 1881–1921, the Jews were persecuted with the formal approval of the Church. Jewish men were beaten, Jewish women raped, and Jewish villages were razed.

The Nazis used canons issued in the Fourth Lateran Council and others to dismiss every Jew in Germany from civil service positions and, ultimately, all rights endowed to them by their Creator.

Also as stated earlier in Nigeria the Ibo Sephardi Jews have at different times in history been unmercifully massacred in different parts of the country in the 1920s, 1940s, 1950s, and in the 1960s to 1970, and are still being murdered; claiming at least three hundred thousand innocent lives for the the only reason that they are Ibo. On each occasion the British turned the blind eye because they know Ibo are Jews who must be punished for their uppityness. In ancient times many Ibo fathers denounced their identity as Jews and adopted the ways and manners of their gentile neighbours. The result was the extent of the loss of Jewish identity as we find today. They lost their Biblical text of the Book of Joshua and other practices that identified them as Jews. This threat of killing has not stopped even today in Nigeria; this is such that some of them have begun to deny their identity as Jews, even as Ibos for political reasons.

Perhaps historical persecutions could explain why we find in rabbinic literature, such as in the Talmud, increased opposition to and arguments against the idea that Messiah could be Yeshua. This reaction increased especially since the 11th century AD and explains why the Ibo need to forge their own pattern of true worship and service to Yahweh through Yeshua.

Is it any wonder then that the Jewish people, who have been persecuted, maligned, beaten, tortured and murdered over the centuries by the very people who professed to follow Yeshua (Jesus), are resistant to hearing anything about Him or believing in Him as their Messiah?

In addition the plethora of titles associated with western version of Christianity raises questions in the mind of honest believers. Some call themselves Pope, Patriarch, Holy Patrarch, Eminent, His Eminence, Pre Eminent, His Holiness, His Lordship, and Lordship. Others are called Bishop, Pastor, Apostle, Holy Apostle, Man of God, Most Holy Apostle, Reverend, Right Reverend, Most Reverend, and Venerable. Yet others call themselves Evangelist, Holy Evangelist, Prophet, Prophetess, Holy Prophet, Holy Prophetess, Deacon, Deaconess, and elder . This is in spite of their lies and hypocricies associated with these posts. How guillible the human being could be. The least common title is "Disciple" like Ananias who was described simply as "a certain disciple" though he was to anoint Saul as Paul who was the Apostle to the nations. They would not want to be addressed as "disciple" because none wants to be identified with Yeshua. Identifying with Yeshua requires being the role model he is and living an exemplary life that he taught and still teaches. As there are these honorific titles so there are expensive and high flowing regalia and staff of authority all of which are man made and world-inspired materialistic mind set. Nobody wants to be of the status of Jews like Simeon, Hannah, and Ananias, Paul, Peter and many other Jews who laid the foundation of Christian teaching and life. This mind set is far removed from the humble, sober, and meek and spirit filled attitude of the Disciples of Christ whose examples should be model for all believers. Even some of those who claim to be miracle working are so flamboyant and desperate for positive results that doubts and questions are raised in the minds of observers. Some have equated themselves to Christ and G-d on the basis of the authority of their words and statements. They command by word of their mouth for results to be achieved such that questions are raised about the difference between their methods and that of a magician. There are also very many versions and doctrines of western version of Christendom. Is Yahweh, the G-d of Abraham, involved in all these, is the begging question? It is essential to state that true Christianity built on the fear of G-d and selfless service to humanity in addition to the humility and meekness the adherent gains has helped in developing the psyche of the Ibos and may have in fact strengthened their faith and trust in Yahweh in spite of present charlatanism that has bedeviled the faith. This charlatanism includes the current epidemic of exploitation of the guillible Ibos through wrong teaching about paying tithes and giving to the church. As highlighted above the original faith of the Ibos encourages sharing and generosity to those who are lacking, orphans and widows while current version of Christianity rather exploits the weak ones.

May I add that from this type of Christianity the Ibo Jews must, I repeat, extricate themselves. The Ibos should be emboldened by the well known fact that Christianity existed in Africa, precisely among their brothers, the Ethiopians about a thousand years before the western colonizers entered Africa and began to enslave the minds of the Ibos with their wrong version of Chrisitanity and as stated earlier

Yahweh had been known to the ancestors even before Abraham's promise was made through the lineage of Seth and Enosh (Genesis 4). The first set of Ibo ancestors must have pledged allegiance to the religion that existed before Abraham and that Abraham must have embraced and perhaps modified as El Shaddai, Yahweh, had directed him: The allegiance to the Spirit of Yahweh (ruach Yahweh) and the traditional religion that was later incorporated into what is regarded as "Old Testament religion", perhaps, finally very much later to the New Testament covenant. These perhaps constituted the religion of the Ibo ancestors some of whom came from Ethiopia through Egypt and else where in phases. Perhaps the Ibos can share views with the deep rooted religion of the fathers as expressed by the Ethiopian Christians today and pre Abrahamic faith in Yahweh. This will be more profitable than still being enslaved by western ideologies called "Christianity." This reinvention will go along way liberating the Ibos from the present clutches of hydra headed backwardness. The Ibo must admit that they had gone far from the true religion of their fathers. For example during Jacob's encounter with Laban, his uncle, they made a pact and sealed it with building a pillar, exchanging vows, and a meal just like the Ibos do today (Genesis 31). However there is indication that Jacob insisted that his God was different from the god of Laban. Laban called to God to "judge between us." However the expression seems to imply plurality of Gods ishpetu beineinu referring to, perhaps God of Abraham and God of Nahor (as two separate gods). Jacob resists and rather swears by the fear of his father Isaac, thus avoiding the use of the generic term, 'elohim for God of his fathers. He therefore resists equating his God with that of Nahor that Laban refers to. The Ibos don't seem to adhere to the Chukwu okike Abiama of their fathers any more and the society has been turned upside down, morally and practically in worship. Some use the holy name yet in the next moment swear by other gods, tell lies, manipulate and deceive. Many of the youth have joined cults from foreign lands and mix the religion of their Fathers with foreign ideas; there has been massive backslidding. Our fathers woke up in the morning and before proceeding on the day's duties, presented outstretched open hands to the sun (direction of the east) prolclaiming their innocence/holiness before Chukwu okike Abiama. Many Ibos fail to do this today because they lack good conscience toward God; they have soiled their hands with immorality: murder, hatred, adultery, betrayals, kidnapping, witchcraft, fornication, theft, embezzlement, incest, and other abominable acts. In the words of one Ibo traditional rulers: "we have lost our young people; evidently this 1999 constitution of this country that has removed us from participating in the governance of this country has contributed immensely."

They Ibos must admit the fact that this backsliding is inevitable in view of the various pressures to which they have been subjected and for the fact that they joined together at different times in history and consequently had different historical experiences of the religion of Yahweh. The influence of the religion of their native neighbours their fathers met must have been tremendous on them leading them to pick and mix contrary to the warning of Yahweh that these practices must not be embraced. According to Eldad the Danite the Ibo fathers lost all scriptures and traditional practices because of persecutions from the colonizing Western Christians and Arab Muslims. They even lost the Book of Joshua as stated earlier which he said they had retained and which practices and belief informed their faith for a while. Eldad the Danite view is a further view that the Ibo fathers came from different traditions and influences in history. As we have tried to explain above the first set of the fathers must have entered strait from Egypt before and during the Exodus event and never followed Moses to embark on the journey into Canaan, the Promised Land. This is apart from those that dwelt in the Dessert of Seth as descendants of Enosh when they first began to be called "people of Yahweh." The batch from Egypt in the pre exodus exodus went into Africa instead of the Middle East. They did not cross the Red Sea but went towards the Nile River and later to the Niger River confluence where they settled eventually. Our forefathers came to this territory at different times of history and from different directions. The Ibos need to put all these historical events and experiences into perspective in order to have a genuine religious or political reinvention. Achieving both reinventions should lead to new alignments and renewed vision and mission as the chosen People of Yahweh.

On Political Reinvention

Just like they need Religious reinvention the Ibos need political reinvention. The aim of this political reinvention should not be directed towards making Aliyah to Israel or for aligning with present day secularized Israel, for this is not necessary. The aim should be directed towards carving out a political niche for themselves as the people of G-d that they are. They need to use it to position themselves back into respectable world position. This calls for intellectual, moral and ethical reorientation and underscores the fact that the indigenous peoples of the territory known as Ibo country (some identify it as Biafara) should not be a metaphor for restructuring Nigeria as some people tend to say; it is not just a poetic or historical idea. It is a real and factual struggle for survival, a cry for freedom and justice to be allowed to uphold and express their G-d endowed value system for self determination and self development. Freedom is a human right and human right is real, factual and attainable. As stated earlier the Ibo philosophy is: Life is worthless without freedom and freedom is informed in Truth. This includes freedom to exist and develop; freedom to actualise a person's chi (God given destiny), the gift endowed to individual by the ruach Yahweh, the Spirit of "the God of the fathers." And self determination is not actualized by mere sentiment; it needs action and self realization as one indigenous people seeking the same purpose in unity of purpose and determination to actualise it.

Religious reinvention without political reinvention leaves the Ibo vulnerable to continual blackmail, misinformation, misdirection and continuing economic exploitation. The Biafran slogan that was echoed very loudly and unequivocally by the Honourable Oko Okon Ndem, "they want your prosperity and not your progress" has remained true to this day and this must be brought to 'a full final stop.' The identity of all the Ibo needs to be solidified by reinventing themselves politically and religiously led by the governors of the states of the Ibo country. 'Man is a political animal' is a well known old saying and a people without political emancipation remain tied to the aprons of their oppressors. If there is any time in their history for political rethink, it is now. The political atmosphere in the world today is compartmentalized into groups for survival. Also it is a well known fact that the leaders of the Ibos throughout recent generations have not succeeded to integrate their views for collective benefits. All efforts they made following Independence of Nigeria have been stifled by the colonial power Britain with the assistance of their puppets in other parts of Nigeria. Apart from ensuring that Industrialisation, innovations, personal and collective, were stopped and discouraged, the centralization of all potentials for such innovations and entrepreneurship through policies in the present confused federal system/ yay unitary system, has made it almost impossible. The policies of the Federal government helped to dismantle the growth of indigenous Ibo industries through targeted national economic policies. This was exacerbated by lack of funds or controlled inflow of funds to the Ibo territories. Thus there has been no infrastructural investment in the Ibo country apart from the Niger Bridge that was commissioned in 1966. Even the current attempt to build a second Niger Bridge is being embarked upon reluctantly. Thus in spite of the fact that the Ibo country in the days of regionalization had the highest depth of investment in rural, cottage industries geared towards achieving industrial and technologically selfsustaining economic culture ahead of any country in Africa and perhaps outside the then western world. As people have continued to lament, what has happened to impetus that generated the old PRODA, where are the Chemical and biological laboratories that used to be in the Ibo country? Not to talk of the motor parts manufacturing industry, the Salt molding industry at Uburu, locally made refineries and Oil milling industries? What has become the fate of the Eastern Nigerian Gas Masterplan made ready by 1966; the Waterprojecs of past Mbakwe Government; the proposed Imo Rural Electrification Project, the Block industry, the Paint and Resins industry etc of former Imo state government before 1983. Why were all these projects abandoned? Why was the University of Technology Proposed for Port Harcourt in 1967 abandoned? And immediately after the Biafra war the Very honourable and well respected Dr Nnanna Ukaegbu conceived ofTechnical Educational Development Mission TEDEM for the Ibo country in particular and for Nigeria in general. Much earlier in 1966 Shell Company is said to have been compelled to set up Petroleum Technology Training Institute in Port-Harcourt, rather than seting up a second training Institute in the territory of those who conceived the idea in the first place. The university of Technology was not actualized rather it was set up as University of Nigeria Nsukka UNN with a totally different mission for Technological development. Even further efforts made by Ibo leaders, Mbakwe and Jim Nwobodo, in seting up centres for research in Technology were stifled by inadequate funding and finally frustrated by the military intervention of 1983 and its aftermat. Thus ASUTECH and IMOSU have remained a shadow of the original intentions as centres of research and innovations as were past visions for technological emancipation of the Ibos from white controlled and dominated technological culture become beclouded. The actualization of this vision for Technological development was stifled by the political might that was misguided.

Why are there no major sea Port and no major international Air Port in the Biafara area of the country? Port Harcourt and Calabar used to have international AirPorts and sea Ports; why were they closed down?These infrastructures could have led to industrial revolution as was experienced in Europe sometime ago. The colonial masters must have noticed this potential in the Ibos that early in their education of the people they warned the white teachers in Ibo land to "teach them the 3 Rs, but never teach them technical subjects". This instruction was given as early as 1868 when there were only twelve pupils in a class in Onitsha diocese most of whom were girls. The story has not changed today as evidenced by attempts to frustrate the motor industry in Iboland.

In addition efforts by the leaders of the Ibo country for cooperation and collective planning for the development of their people have been frustrated by the same politicl and military might of the centre all in the name of checking against any calls they might make for confederation. It is on record that Olusegun Obasanjo in particular threatened these leaders in 1999 when they met and unanimously agreed for a confederation of states in response to the Sharia advocated in the Northern part of the Ngeria. Also their efforts to set up secretariat for a common purpose were stopped with threats from then General Obasanjo. Thus the common partnership of the Easterners is made to appear threatening while that of the Northern leadership is allowed and encouraged.

It is perhaps more disheartening to see that the leaders of the states making up the former Eastern states (then known as the Ibo Country) that constitute what we regard as only a small part of the land of Ibo Jews have allowed themselves to be intimidated and seem to have abandoned this spirit of cooperation that had existed. The situation today is perhaps more critical than ever as there are even signs of rivalry and betrayal among them. Yes, some argue and say that the late Biafran leader's political ambitions exacerbated this political divide and unhealthy competition. However, the current paucity of development that is making the Ibo country to lag behind the other leaders: the Northern Governors who constitute Governors of the Hausa Country and those of the Western States who constitute the Yoruba Country (Yaariba country) should be seen as a call to the governors of the Ibo Jews (Ibo country) to urgently unite and forge a common plan for development as brothers with a common destiny, and not any more as people of the old Eastern Region. The creation of states and misinformation on true identity of peoples accompanying it is only aimed at disuniting Ibo blood solidarity that characterizes as Ibo Jews. This call for reuniting cannot be achieved under the current atmosphere of confusion and lack of appropriate self identity. A people who were united by a common ancestry has allowed themselves be made to appear as people of disparate ethnic groups and of cultural divide by outsiders who are using it for their own economic and political advantage. This should not be. The Ibo Jews in Nigeria are today being martyred in their own land by the same oligarchy/mafia that attempted to exterminate them in the past. This situation means they have no other means to escape from oppression and perhaps annihilation of their peoples, than mutual cooperation. Any political leader encouraging the ravaging of the land of the Ibo Jews should be treated as an enemy of the people, a betrayer of the people and the G-ds of our fathers will not spare him and his lineage unpunished.

In the attempt for political reinvention Ibo Jews have the following options:

1. Remain within the present status quo whereby the same corrupt institutions that have denied them their natural rights and stifled their natural capabilities prevail. Remain within the political environment that has created divisions among them. As some people have argued this division is traceable to have begun majorly when the former Biafran leader joined the enemies of the progress of the Ibos to fight against his own brother politicians. Some even refer to him as a war lord

that succeeded in introducing a politics of division among the Ibos. These opponents claim that it was his "politically misguided actions" that also introduced suspicion among the Ibo South and North even during that war that came to be referred to as "political sabotage." Sadly, the same Biafran war leader, they claim joined the enemies of the Ibo country (later called eastern region), and introduced political thuggery and openly insulted Ibo elder statesmen especially Dr Nnamdi Azikiwe and Jim Nwobodo, the former was said to have been influenced by an old family animocity against the elder statesman; he also called some of his fellow Ibo politicians unacceptable names in public. They claim he did all these for self centred political ambition ignoring the fact of "our obvious common struggles." Since the introduction of this political divide and rule, in addition to the actions and influences of the enemies of our progress, the whole eastern region (then known Ibo country) has not been able to cohese as they previously were. The disharmony they claim has eaten the fabric of the Ibo community with the result of Ibo not only expelling one and the other from fellow Ibo states, but also callously exploiting one another; the blood solidarity that had existed and that characterized the Ibo cultural and political ethos has continued to wane.

However I do not think the disintegration of the Ibos can be blamed on one person's actions and ambition. I do agree that we today have an Ibo community that has lost its spirit as a people, following the loss of its identity; an Ibo society that has fallen apart once again since after the colonial unslaught on the Ibo: courtesy of the late very honourable Professor Chinua Achebe's 'Things Fall Apart'. I do remember that the very honourable Dr Nnamdi Azikiwe mistakenly alienated the fellow indigenes of the Ibo country, people of Akwa Ibom and Cross River States at a time by a rash reaction to his earlier rejection by the Yorubas through the instigation of chief Awolowo. Dr Nnamdi Azikiwe was said to have vented his frustration on Very honourable Eyo Ita, the first head of government of eastern region (then Ibo country) by sending him away from Enugu. I understand that Dr Nnamdi Azikiwe did realize he over reacted and made peace. The other accusation of the Igbo by other Ibos was that Igbo politicians denied other Ibos scholarships and favoured only their fellow Igbos. Firstly this information is true but the politicians will always favour their close relatives anywhere they are. I was a victim of that fraud. I lost my first school leaving certificate to fraudulent politicians in the Igbo land. I also lost an international scholarship awarded to me by an overseas country. The position was sold out to a close relative of a poilitician. This young man later confessed this to me. Also a senior secretary in the ministry of education in the first republic confessed to me how they fraudulently diverted scholarships to their relatives at that time. So the accusation that Igbo politicians denied others scholarships and other benefits is correct but it was the product of corruption and nepotism that characterized the first republic and left a legacy of corrupt political class among the Igbos till today. They denied benefits to their fellow Igbos as they denied benefits to other Ibos. Is it not sad to know that this so much needed reconciliation talk seems not to have been fully cemented among these brothers? Over ambitious politicians still make reference to past corruption and nepotism to score political point when situation suits them, solely to accummulate votes from ignorant and gullible electorate for self serving purposes. The mischievous misinformation and disinformation that has been used to fuel suspicion and division has continued and there seems to be no attempt at addressing this issue by those present governors and elder statesmen in the concerned Ibo areas. This has been the case in spite of all the support collectively given to people of the area and continued cooperation among them. This continued animosity among the Ibo brothers has only been serving the interest of these corrupt politicians.

Also the attempt to carve out a separate identity for the people of Rivers and Bayelsa Sates by foreigners seems to be yielding negative fruits. This is disheartening and beckons for action to remedy the situation. The young ones of these states need to be educated about the political and cultural implication of this divide with loss of their original identity. Many of these young ones do not know the history of the distortion of their native names as attempt to manipulate their psyche against their true brothers.

I believe that the Ibo political community can be reinvented again. And now is the opportunity to reinvent it with their native status and self awareness as people of Yahweh (Ibo Jews). They also lost this status as 'people of Yahweh' by falling allegiant to foreign colonizers and their antics in addition to mixing their religious and cultural practices for so long.

2. The other option is the Ibos collectively carving out a political niche for themselves by going back to the drawing board, evaluating their present political stance, restrategising and collectively presenting a united front under the banner of who they really are: 'the People of Yahweh.' They would need to reinvent the appropriate political allies to join forces with in world political affairs. The Jews of the world are there as ready natural associates and allies, being their brothers also, children of one father. The Jews of the world are nearer to the Ibos than they may think. All that is needed is to make the right contacts. This is needful today that there is a realigning of political interests. The enemies of the Ibo country (Ibo Jews) have encroached into their land and with political power always in their grip could dislodge the very territorial integrity of the land and forever exterminate or emasculate the people of the Ibo country (Ibo Jews). A look at the map of the Ibo country will readily show those who are to be accepted as Jews. A look at the world will readily identify the Jews of the world with whom to politically align. Also political alignment will mean economic alignment for economic survival in a hostile world. The Jews of the world will need to come together to do business for economic and political survival and continued existence. It is first essential to acknowledge there is a problem before a right solution is sought. The sooner the people that constitute the Ibos realize and acknowledge there is a political and economic problem to grapple with; these are staring them on the face, the safer it is for their collective survival as collective solution will be urgently sought. It is certain that the present political order in

the country they now belong is a recipe for disaster if ignored or playing the Ostrich in it. The Ibos are today far more unsure of their survival as a people than in any time in history. However because they are among the chosen People of G-d as promised by Yahweh, they have G-d's favour with them and will overcome any threat to their existence and progress in life. The People of Yahweh have overcome the world and its threats. All they need is to became aware of this favour and act appropriately. Yes achieving this may appear difficult but with the favour of G-d they will be able to educate, disabuse the minds of the Ibo politicians and traditional leaders most of whom have perhaps forgotten their roots and history that G-d is the only King the Ibos know and recognize. This is why it is said that the Ibo do not recognise any kingship (monarchical leadership) and reject all forms of oligarchy. This belief of the Ibo also reflects the time of history some of their first ancestors, perhaps, left Israel and entered into the Niger River area: as early as before kings were introduced in Israel. This would be perhaps by the time of Samuel, the priest. The present kingship system was either forced on the people by circunstances or imbibed and does not seem to be of any effect in politically mobilizing the people. This situation is worsened because the imposed traditional ruling system is regarded as corrupt and misleading and tends to assumming the resented monarchical structure. They are also suspected of encouraging present day kidnappings and human ritual killings and colluding with the so called fraudsters. All these were unknown to core Ibo morality and values. Above all most of these traditional rulers seem to lack an understanding and appreciation of the historical experience of the Ibo peoples and are aligning themselves with other traditional rulers in other parts of the country Nigeria.

3. The former Ibo country (Ibo Jews' territory) can become a nation through cooperation as they are motivated and inspired by what they have in common with other Jews, 'the People of G-d'. At present as in the past they are a disparate group though they have a common origin. This situation seems to have been compounded by the creation of states

fuelled by the artificial mental and psychological division. This division is made worse by a section being referred to as 'south south', 'South East', and the mischievous introduction and practice of "Adelphobia"(fear and suspicion of a brother) and Ibophobia(fear and suspicion of the Ibo by non Ibos) by foreign colonial agents among those who make up the former "Ibo Country". Unfortunately the Ibo Peoples have failed to interpret this mischievous "adelphobia" as another dangerous ploy to divide them in order to silence and rule them. The target is to easily exploit their natural resources including their human talents and favours from G-d. The sooner the Ibos acknowledge this fact the easier it will be to integrate politically. Systematic and well planned education will be the key to creating this awareness among the Ibo peoples wherever they might be found including so called South South Nigeria, Delta State, Benue State, Ondo state, Kogi State, South East States, and over the seas in foreign lands including Mexico, Southern American, India, Japan, China to mention just these.

4.   The Ibos do not need to seek seccession as this is perhaps not the will of G-d for them; at least not at the present time. To everything there is a season. They should wait for G-d's "Kairos." At the present time they need to remain within the enclave called Nigeria but must seek to carve out a niche for themself as a People of G-d. Where ever the People of G-d are, they are known to be unique in enhancing development and growth. And with the cooperation of other Jews they should be able to excel even among their neighbours as they had been known to in the past. Correct political alignment means economic progress as this should remove or neutralize the stifling experiences of the past and present they have been experiencing within the enclave called Nigeria.

5.   Finally permit me to state that the Ibos can be in the lead for the propagation of the return of their Messiah as the Bible states the Messiah of the world would return. It is true that the Messiah Yeshua came to the world thousands of years after the Jewish ancestors that later founded the Ibo had left that territory. However they were able to embrace the teachings

of his followers who though treated them with dismay have made them to rediscover themselves as actually different from what their fathers expected of them as a people. The followers of Yeshua according to the New Testament were firstly Jewish people. In fact it is believed that Yeshua taught that he came for the liberation of the Jews. However Yeshua also said that he had other sheep that he must bring into the fold; they too would listen to his voice, and there shall be one flock and one shepherd. John 10.16. Neverthe less as the gentiles came into fold problems emerged and prompting the need for a council to be called to seek to resolve the issues. Some of the issues centred around the the place of the gentiles as converts. Should they be circumcised or not to attain full conversion into the new movement of Yeshua.

James indicated that gentile believers should learn the Law of Moses, so they would grow in their understanding of how to live a holy life Act 15: 21. James continues to state that the gentiles are to abstain from food sacrificed to idols, from blood, from the meat of strangled animals and from sexual immorality Acts 15: 29. He expanded upon the prophetic significance of the gentiles coming to faith in Yeshua, linking it to the end-time restoration of Israel and the appearance of gentiles who are called by his name. Acts 15: 16-18; Amos 9:11-14. Meanwhile meetings were held every Sabbath in the synagogue of every city for both Jews and gentiles believers.

Paul himself explains his own position in Romans 11. 11-31 stating that believers are grafted into one tree which he reharded to be Jewish into which all are nourished from the same root. Gentiles have been grafted into this tree as wild olive branches while the Jewish believers are grafted into the same tree, which is their own tree. He did not fail to point out to the Gentile the need to avoid being arrogant because their status is that of faith while that of the Jews is natural. Thus there should be no need to look down on the Jews as if they had been removed by Yeshua in order to make room for the gentiles. He warned both sides that just as God did not spare his own people what more would he not spare the gentiles if they fail Romans 11:19-21.

The unity of faith and service seem to have begun to wane by certain factors that introduced division among the brethren leading to a split.

It first began with argument over that the Passover should be replaced with the celebration as Easter. While some Gentile believers kept very close to the Jewish roots, celebrating Yeshua as the Passover Lamb on the first night of Passover, which is the 14th of the Hebrew month of Nissan. Most of them lived in the Asia Minor region. Others emphasized the resurrection, which occurred on the first day of the week. The believers in Rome moved the observance of the resurrection to Sunday and began the celebration of Easter.

A controversy arose when those called the Quartodecimans (Latin, referring to "fourteen") followed the Jewish practice of fasting on the eve of Passover.

History shows that the tradition was established by the Apostle John and practiced by his disciples, including Polycarp (c. 69-c. 155) who was the bishop of Smyrna, one of the seven churches of Asia, and by Melito (died c. 180) of Sardis, another church in Asia.

This fast was followed by the Passover celebration beginning at sundown on the 15 of Nissan in close adherence to the Jewish tradition.

Yeshua's followers met together to break bread after Sabbath, on Saturday evening. This is exemplified by Paul preaching late into the night and a boy falling to his death that Paul raised from the dead. However Gentile believers began to meet on Sundays morning and the Jewish believers who continued to attend the synsgogue began to experience pressure, especially after the destruction of the Temple. The emergence of the Jewish revolt of the 60s seems to have introduced disruption. The Jewish believers escaped to the mountains crossing over the Jordan and went to Pella, a Nabataean fortress. They escaped the onslaught of Titus and his army who destroyed the city of Jerusalem and the Temple. Consequently their fellow Jews began to accost them as deserters and some Rabbis began to excommunicate them. One factor that led to Gentiles separating from the Jewish believers was the introduction of the Jewish tax by the invaders. It was a tax imposed on the Jews for belonging to Judaism. This tax replaced the Temple tax and was used to keep the Temple of

Capitoline Jupiter in Rome. The Gentile believers therefor dissociated themselves from the Judaism. Another force that contributed to the division in the first century was the inclusion of the Birkat Ha Minim- the 19th blessing in the Amidah, a request of divine punishment (a curse) from God directed against the paroshim- those said to have separated themselves from the communit. The paroshim were associated with the minim or heretics, which were understood to be the Jewish believers in Yeshua and perhaps the Essenes.

Thus the Jewish believers were no longer able to lead prayer without actually avoking a curse on themselves. The benediction went a long way to make Jewish believers feel unwelcomed in the synagogue, causing them to worship separately(see Justin Martyr's 2nd c Dialogue with Trypho and Origin, who lived in the 3rdc AD) Epiphanius, who lived in the 5th c wrote, "Three times a day they say: 'May God curse the Nazarenes."

The Nazarenes Notzrim, referred originally to the first believers in Yeshua; however, it also refers to the 4th century sect of Nazarenes, believers who considers themselves Jewish and were thought to have originated with the believers who fled Jerusalem, and kept the Torah. The term could also apply to Gentile followers of Yeshua in general.

Over time Gentile believers began to incorporate pagan observances and rituals over Jewish oractice in thgeir worship. In AD 325, the first Council of Nicaea was convened by the Roman Emperror Constantine in order to set church doctrine.

None of the 318 bishops attending were of Jewish ancestry. One of the main acts of the council was to establish a separate celebration of the Passover from the Jewish Passover. This later became identified by the pagan name Easter from the Bsbylonian fertility goddess Ishtar. The council also established Sunday as the new Sabbath, as opposed to the biblical seventh day Sabbath.

The following Council of Antioch prohibited Christians from celebrating the Jewish Passover.

The Council of LAODICEA shortly after, prohibited celebration of the biblical Sabbath. Christians were even prohibited under penalty of death, to marry Jews, Jews became second-class citizens.

Anti-Semitism was so rampant at this time that a 4th c church in Constantinople held the following creed:

I renounce all customs, rites, legalisms, unleavened breads and sacrifices of lambs of the Hebrews, and all other feasts of the Hebrews, sacrifices, prayers, aspersions, purifications, sanctification and propitiations and fasts, and new moons, and Sabbatha, and superstitions, and hymns, and chanmts, and observances, and Synagogues, and the food and drink of Hebrew; in one word I renounce everything Jewish, every law, rite and custom and if afterwards I shall wish to deny and return to Jewish superstition, or shall be found eating with the Jews, or feasting with them, or secretly conversing and condemning the Christian religion instead of openly confuting them and condemning their vain faith, then let the trembling of Gehazi cleave to me, as well as the legal punishments to which I acknowledge myself liable. And may I be anathema in the world to come, and may my soul be set down with Satan and the devils (The Conflict of the Church and the Synagogue, by James Parks quoted in Messianic Synagogue Bible Haftara emailed to me July 2017)

The result of this conflict has been the propounding of "Replacement Theology" of the Roman Catholic Church that claims that the Roman Catholic church has replaced the Jewsih nation in God's Economy. This is contrary to prophetic utterances of Isaiah 49:6, Zech 8:22; Ezek 34: 23-24, 37:27, 28; Jer 23: 5-6.

The Bible teaches that it is the return of Yeshua the Messiah that will restore the unity between all peoples again. This wiil be preceded by the massive conversion of the Jews to accepting him as the expected Messiah.

The Ibos could be instrumental to achieving this massive conversion of the Jews to Yeshua as thier expected Messiah.

APPENDIX

SOME WORDS THAT MAY NEED BE GIVEN EXTRA ATTENTION AS RELEVANT IN THIS STUDY. MOST OF THE WORDS CONSIDERED IN THIS APPENDIX ARE NAME WORDS

GAD: Deuteronomy 33: 20, Gnenesis 46: 16: Father of Eri, the great Ancestor of some of the major Ibo groups according to a known Ibo legend.

Levi: 1 Chronicles 2:2: Father of all those responsible for the spirituality of the Ibo peoples. In the Hebrew Bible they are given the thummim and Urim. Deut 33: 8. Thus Levi is also the ancestral father of those communities in Iboland where these spiritualists are found. Their presence is almost universal among the Ibo groups. They are associated with powers to even command rainfall, and to heal and teach the laws and ways of God, ensuring the people kept the covenant, "omenala" (Berit) of Chukwu Abiama.

Joseph and his descendants among the Ibos: The Ephraim and Manasseh communities are named together among the Ibos as in the Hebrew Bible Joshua 16:2. We have the town or people of Achi in Enugu state and Asa, perhaps Asa in Abia state and else where

Perhaps Zebulun's descendants in Iboland could be identified as the Ubulu, Uvuru, Iburu, communities. We hear of the OzoUbulu, Nze Ubulu, Ubulu community in Ebonyi State, Ubulu Ukwu, Uvuru in Imo State

1 Chronicles 3: 10 features names of Judah towns that are similar to names of Ibo towns we have today. These include Asa in Abia state, Ahian 1Chronicles 7: 18ff (possible Ahia). Thus we have UmuAhia as children of Ahia. Also descendant of Judah include the Etam clan 1 Chron 4: 2. Perhaps this is same as Item in Abia State and/or Itam in Akwa Ibom State.

Other significant names of towns that may be noted as significant include

"Ishi" in 1 Chronicles 5: 24; thus we have Ishiagu, Amaishi, Ishi Nnewi, Ishiokpo

"Uzzi" in 1Chronicles 7: 2ff of the tribe of Isaachar. There are Uzzi communities in Iboland.

Also "Aziza" in Ezra 10: 7 is a common personal name among the Ibos

"Aniam": 1 Chron 7:18ff may be likened to Ibo "Anam"

"Machir" son of Manasseh in 1Chron 7: 15 and Micri 1 Chron 9:8 may be likened to "Amakiri", "Amachiri" –a common name among the Ibos.

The third son of Benjamin was named "Aharah" 1 Chron 8:1 also the name "Ahira" could be likened to "Ahiara" among the Ibos. However "Ahiara" does not mean "Aharah" neither is the meaning of "Ahiara" similar to "Aharah."

"Abiyah (Abijah)": has been written as Abia and has been likened to "Abia" a common word among the Ibos usually used to express a delight to a piece of music and a well spoken word. There should be some evidence or indication that Ibo "Abia" and Hebrew Abia, and "Abiyah" mean the same or are similar in meaning or point to the same sensibility. "Abiyah" is literally, "My father is Yah" and implies "Yah is my father", That means "Yahweh is my father." Zechariah is said to be a priest of the Order of Abia in Luke's gospel (Luke 1). Abia is the name of one of the Ibo states in Nigeria. I do not know the meaning of "ABIA" other than as an exclamation of delight. Some think it is derived of abbreviation of multiple names that make up the Abia state. The two words are pronounced the same way but are written differently. Also it is doubtful that the Holy name "Yahweh" could be used to merely express "delight" for something by a people who revere that name and were instructed that they must not "take the name of the Lord in vain." I also expected the word "ABIA" to end with the honorific letter "h" as practiced by the Ibos if its root was "Abiyah". The suffix "H" placed at the end of a vowel was used to expressed the worship and reverencing of the Holy G-D and LORD among the Ibos until enemies of the Israelite origin of the Ibos put a stop to it. A related name to "Abiyah" is "Eliyah" which some claim is the same as Ibo name "Alia." The name "Eliyah" means literally "Yahweh is my God" while "Alia" which is a common word among the Owerre Ibo used in a legend to teach the message of hard work and self denying attitude. "Alia," in the legend was the wife of "Mbe," the wisest creature on earth. The legend is used to teach that a wise young man should seek for a hard working self-giving lady for a wife. It has nothing to do with Yahweh as God. Similar problem is found in associated "Ahiyah" with "Ahia". Ahiyah is related to "Yah is my brother" literally. It has nothing to do with "ahia" used among the Ibos for market. Rather Umuahia and such like names that have ahia particle as part of their rendition could be related to the Hebrew name "Ahian." This will mean that Umuahia would probably mean children of "Ahian," (see also 1 Chroni 11: 26-47 where "Ahiam" is mentioned as one of the warriors under David).

Owere (anglicized to Owerri): is another word that has been rendered Owu-eri. However the correct rendition of the word by the people concerned is "owere"; so the origin of the word should be sought elsewhere, perhaps Portuguese "oruwari." The closes name is Er one of the sons of Judah in Genesis 46: 12. But he and his brother Onan are said to have died in Canaan. The other is perhaps to render Ir the son of Naphtali mentioned in 1 Chronincles 7: 12 as Er. This will render the expression owu-ere relevant to the study. However we must take note that Owuere is an expression and not a name word. Yet still if owu ere can be acceptable there is no reason why Owu eri could not also be acceptable. Above all the name Owere could be a shorter form of the statement "o were la" that means "he has made a choice", "he/she has chosen"- a common expression among the owere people. Is the Portuguese Oruwiari, meaning thickly forested place of Hebrew derivation? Perhaps, not.

Eker: is Hebrew word that reminds one of the Ibo communities of Ugwueke; and personal name Ekeh, Madueke, Manueke, Muoneke, as well as the Eke market day.

Ezer: is a Hebrew word that reminds one of Akaeze community

Ana: in Nehemiah 10: 26 is a Hebrew word that reminds one of the Anang communities of Akwa Ibom and the name "Anna Pepple" in Rivers State.

Hur is a Hebrew name that reminds of the Ibo communities called Ohuru, Ohahur, and perhaps also Ohuhu.

Bani: in Ezra 10: 34 reminds one of the common Ibo name 'Ubani'. It also brings brings to mind Boni communities in Rivers State.The question one might ask is, How did a word "Bani" change to "Boni"? How did the 'a' vowel change to 'o'? I would respond by pointing out that words do change in contextual meaning but still carrying the same root meaning originally given to it. This is a characteristic of Hebrew and Ibo words. "Ba" in Hebrew means "he came" just as the Ibo equivalent "Ba baa", means "come in". In Hebrew the word Bo' means "he entered" implying "he came and entered". Thus "Ba ani" means "I come". In Hebrew ('ani' is the Hebrew word for 'I' but in Ibo it means "we"). "Bo ani" in Hebrew means "I entered". Thus "Boni" would mean same as "Bani" in its root meaning. In Ibo that would mean "we have entered" or "we entered." Thus the root of "Boni" is more likely to be the name "Bani" than otherwise.Also Boni could be the Polel inflection of the verbal noun "Bani." Perhaps this similarity points to a needful conclusion that the ancestral community of the Boni people must have borne the name Bani originally. This word perhaps became changed to take the form "Boni" with time. Does this also imply that the Boni people are descendants of a Hebrew ancestor called "Bani" "Ubani"? Possibly,"Yes".

In Hebrew as in Ibo, words do change according to the verb order or the case retained by any particular clan or communities from the ancient root of that word. Verbs also can change by inflection that is retained in a particular dialect within a community. Thus in Hebrew grammar we come across Qal, Niph'al, Pi'el, Pu'al, hiph'il, hoph'al, hithpa'el and Polel. A particular community or part of a community's dialect might consciously or unconsciously retain any words in one of these particular renditions of conjugational verbal roots. Also influence of foreign interactions might alter the meaning and usage of a word from its original application. This might be necessitated by long distance connection and interactions with various dialects and foreign words and cultures. Thus studying relationship or genealogical connection between ancient languages such as Hebrew and Ibo, heebro, heebo, may prove to be a wild goose chase. However what is unique about the present study is that there was not as much difficulty as I had envisaged in observing connected words as this study has to some extent demonstrated. Perhaps this underscores the veracity of the claim that "Ibo" heebo, is anglicized "Hebrew"implying that we are talking of the same people rather than two different peoples. The spliting of the same people seemingly as two different peoples is treated as an accident of history caused by wars, evacuations, colonizations, the slave trades and cultural enculturation and acculturation of a people. However it is still needful to state again that similarity of words does not automatically mean the two peoples are genealogically related. There is therefore the need to prefer those words that are pronounced in the same or similar way and mean the samething or similar in meaning or connotation. Perhaps the least useful should be personal names. There is the possibility that some of the personal name words may not even have had Hebrew roots originally. In fact they may not even be Hebrew. This is especially the case with names that are not native to the tribe of Judah where most of the names that end in the reverencial 'h', 'iah', are known to be Hebrew obviously e. g Azariah, Isaiah, Ahaziah etc Ibo peoples are numerous and varied; so are the dialects. For example to understand some dialects as Ibo I have to listen very carefully to pick the words at first hearing them. An example are some Delta Ibo dialects, Anambra dialects, Ebonyi dialects, Nsukka dialects, Udi dialects, Ika Ibo dialects, Ikwere dialects, Etche dialects, Owerri dialects, Igala dialects, etc. Even Hebre spoken today is full of dialectal variations. For example I had to learn that 'v' is derived from pronouncing some Hebrew letter such as 'wau,' 'b' and some Yiddish and Modern Hebrew words as Hebrew.

Olaudah: Olaudah is a personal Ibo name that reminds one of the tribe of Judah. This is because it literally means 'Ola'- ornament, glory, sacrifice, a thing of beauty "'udah." 'Udah is regarded as a short form of "Yudah" anglicized as Judah. Thus Olaudah means "the Glory (ornament), sacrifice, of Judah" given to Judah,; Hebrew word for sacrifice is 'ola'

In 1Chron 3:10 the sons of Solomon are listed among whom is Asa son of Abiyah; which has been written as Abiah in the Ibo language. Asa is generally regarded as the father of AsaUmuteke in Abia State.

In Joshua 15: 42 we come across the name Ether, Eter, Ether as a town with their villages. Eter is a common name among the Ibos. Thus we have towns and villages named Akwete, Ogbete, Obite, and personal names Ete, Ekaete, EteEte and such like.

Perhaps to be included in this appendix is the Ibo word rapu and its different dialectal renditions, haphu, hafu. This word means "to leave." It could be applied to mean 'to set free." It brings to mind the Hebrew word "rapha." This Hebrew word is used to mean "to heal." The Ibos usually address an illhealth especially the sort of illhealth that defies all known curative measures, by saying: May this illness leave so and so. The word rapu, haphu, hafu, raphu, rafu is used depending on the dialect that is speaking.

NSIBIDI: IBO NATIVE PRECOLONIAL SCRIPT said to have been disallowed and banned because of its use by so called "secret societies"

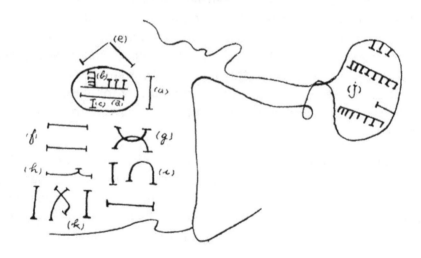

OTHER IBO INSRCIPTIONS COMMONLY FOUND IN THE PALACE

May not be ancient Hebrew letters or characters

Select Bibliography

Achebe C 1964: Arrow of God: Ibadan Nigeria: Heinemann Educational Books

Achebe C 1958: Things Fall Apart: Ibadan Nigeria: Heinemann Educational Books

Acholonu C 1989: The Igbo Roots of Olaudah Equiano Owerri, Nigeria: Afa Publications.

Adams J. 1822: Sketches taken during ten voyages to Africa London.

Adiele Afigbo 2005: Nigerian History, Politics and Affairs: The Collected Essays: African World Press.

Afigbo A 1981: Ropes of Sand: Ibadan Nigeria: University Press Limited

Africanus L 1896: History and Description of Africa translated by Pory 1600: Hakkluyt Society

Akaolisa H 2003: Igbo Race: Origin and Controversies: Awka Nigeria: Buckstar Publishers

Albright W 1951: British Association for the Study of Oriental Religions (BASOR) 144: 22

Alutu, J 1985: The Groundwork of Nnewi History Ndi Nri and Ora Eri in Particular. Ibadan: Claverianum Press

Anadi I 1972: The Kingdom they Knew Not: Enugu: Ocumba Press

Anadi I 1967: Our History and Cultural Heritage Onitsha: Etudo Limited

Anijielo A 1984: Theological Investigation into fear of Mystical Forces- with special reference to the Igbos Leverkusen- Opladen Bonn

Ancient Near Eastern Text 543:4

Arazu M 2005: Our Religion Past and Present: Awka Nigeria: Martin-King Press

Arinze F A 1970: Sacrifice in Ibo Religion: Ibadan, Nigeria: University Press.

A Welcome Address presented by the people of Ora Eri to their Israeli Brothers on their visit to Ora Eri on "Legends of the Lost Tribes of Israel on 6 October, 1997 by the Eze Nri at the Royal Palace.

Barth H 1965: Travels and Discoveries in North and Central Africa 3rd Vol: London: Frank Cass and Company

Barton: 1902: 98ff

Basden G 1921: Among the Ibos of Nigeria: London: University Publishing Company

Basden G Bristol Archives British Empire and Commonwealth collections 1920s 1930s films ref 2006/070

Basden G 1966: Niger Ibos: London: Frank Cass and Co. Ltd

Bernis J 2014: A Rabbi looks at the Afterlife: A New Look at Heaven and Hell with Stories of People who've been there Shippensburg, PA: Destiny Image Publishers.

Breasted J 1908: History of the Ancient Egyptians: New York

Breasted J 1927: Ancient Records of Egypt: Chicago

Botero J 1950: Revue Africue (RA) 44 112f

Brichto H 1973: 'Kin, cult, land and the afterlife: A Biblical Complex' in HUCA 44:22ff

Brichto H 1973: 'Kin, cult, land and the afterlife: A Biblical Complex' in HUCA 44:22ff

Brown F 1979: The New Brown-Driver-Briggs-Gesenius Hebrew and English Lexicon Peabody, Massachusetts: Hendrickson.

Bruce J 1804: Travels to Discover the Source of the Nile: Edinburgh

CA3/035/7 Niger Mission, Pastor Onitsha, 1872-1880. Report pf Rev. Soloman S. Perry, Native Pastor

Chomsky W 1957: Hebrew the Eternal Language Philadelphia: The Jewish Publication Society of America

Cole H 1982: Mbari Art and Life among North-East Igbo and Igala: Bloomington Federal University O P

Cassidy, F Gomes, Robert B Le Page 2002: A Dictionary of Jamaican English 2nd ed. University of the West Indies Press p. 168

Cassidy F G, Page R 2002: A Dictionary of Jamaican English 2nd ed. University of the West Indies Press p. 168

Cowper H 1897: The Hill of Graces: London

1985: Crisis and Leadership: Epistles of Maimonides; Texts translated and Notes by Abraham Halkin; discussions by David Hartman. Philadelphia: Jewish Publication Society of America

Davidson B 1966: Africa: History of a Continent: New York: The Macmillan Company

Davidson B 1966: African Kingdoms: New York: Time Incorporated

Davidson B 1959: The Lost Cities of Africa: Boston and Toronto: Little, Brown and Company

Dubois F 1896: Timbuctoo the Mysterious Translated by Diana White: New York

Deniker J 1900: The Races of Mankind: New York: Charles Scribner's Sons

Egekonye U 1999: Osus The Victims of Igbo Culture Jos, Nigeria: Trinity Graphics

Emeghara N: 2011 Baptism Power and the Miraculous in Contemporary Nigerian Christianity Milton Keynes UK: AuthorHouse

Equiano, Olaudah 1837: The Interesting Narratives of the Life of Olaudah Equiano 1, Knapp: 27(uses Eboe)

Eze Nri 1997: An Address of Welcome Presented by the People of Ora Eri to their Israeli Brothers on their visit to Ora Eri on "Legends of the Lost Tribes of Israel" on the 6 October 1997 at the Eze Nri Palace.

ERE vol 3: 1901:679ff;

Equiano, Olaudah 1837: The Interesting Narratives of the Life of Olaudah Equiano 1, Knapp: 27(uses Eboe)

Floyd, E Randall 2002: In the Realm of the Ghosts and Hauntings: Harbor House: p. 51 (uses Eboe)

Fischel W 1937: The Jews in the Political and Economic Life of Mediaval Islam: London

Forde D and Jones G 1962: The Ibo and Ibibio- Speaking Peoples of South-Eastern Nigeria: International African Institute: London

Floyd, E Randall 2002: In the Realm of the Ghosts and Hauntings: Harbor House: p. 51 (uses Eboe)

Gaster T. H 1969: Myth, Legend, and Custom in the Old Testament 41

Gitlitz David 2002: "Secrecy and Deceit: The Religion of Crypto Jews" Albuquerque, NM: University of New Mexixo Press

Green M 1947: Ibo Village Affairs: London

Gaer J 1956. How the Great Religions Began New York and Toronto The New American Library

Gibbon E 1931: The Decline and Fall of the Roman Empire Vol 11: New York: The Modern Library

Godbey A 1930: The Lost Tribes a Myth. Durham: N C Duke University Press

Grayzel S 1956: A History of the Jews 8th ed: Philadelphia: The Jewish Publication Society of America

Haran M 1965: "The Religion of the Patriarchs" ASTI 4: 42

Hawkins, J 1797: A History voyage to the Coast of Africa

Herbert Wendt 1964: It Began in Babel. New York: Dell Company: 403-405

Herdotus 1928: The History of Herodotus Translated by George Rawlinson: New York: Tudor Publishing Company

Hertz J 1937: The Pentateuch and Haftorahs 2nd ed: London: The Soncino Press

Horton J. A. B 1868: West African Countries and Peoples London.

Horton W 1956: "God and Man and Land in a Northern Ibo Village Group": Africa 17-28

'Ibo" in Encyclopedia Britannica 11th ed. 1911(uses Ibo)

Idigo M 1963: The History of Aguleri Ibadan: OUP

Ifesieh E 1989: Religion at the Grassroots: Enugu Nigeria: Fourth Dimension Pub Co. Limited

Ilogu E 1974: Christianity and Igbo Culture: New York: NOK.

Ilogu E 1983: "Iro mmuo and Ikpu ala" in Traditional Religion in West Africa E. A Adegbola ed Ibadan: Daystar Press: 138f.

Isichei E 1977: History of West Africa Since 1800: London: Macmillian Education Ltd

Israeli Embassy Lagos Nigeria 1997: Handouts: Hebrew lessons, Tapes and Manuscripts

Jeffreys M 1987: The Divine Umunri Kings of Iboland: Ekwulobia Nigeria: Ministry of Information

Jose' F 1992: In the Shadow of History: Jews and Conversos at the Dawn of Modernity. Albany, NY: State University of New York Press

Joseph F 1957: The Life and Works of Flavius Josephus Translated by William Whiston: Philadelphia and Toronto: The John C. Winston Company

Joseph M 1912: "Education" Encyclopedia of Religion and Ethics 5: 194-198

Kamen H 1997: The Spanish Inquisition: An Historical Revision. London: Weidenfeld and Nicolson

Kenneth R 1933: Ancient Hebrew Social Life and Custom As indicated in Law Narrative and Metaphor

Lindo H 1848: The History of The Jews of Spain and Portugal: London: Wertheimer and Company

Livingstone D 1859: Travels and Researches in South Africa: New York

Lodds 1948: 197ff

Lovejoy Paul 2000: Identity in the Shadow of Slavery: Continuum International Publishing Group: 58(uses Eboe)

Meek C 1989: An Ethnological Report of Peoples of Nsukka Division: Onitsha Nigeria: Etudo Press

Meek C 1939: Law and Authority in a Nigerian Tribe: London: Oxford University Press

Metuh 1985: African Religions in Western Conceptual Schemes. The Problem of Interpretation: Jos Nigeria: IMICO Press

Metuh I 1987: Comparative Studies of African Traditional Religions Onitsha, Nigeria: IMICO.

Munonye J 1966: The Only Son: Ibadan Nigeria: Heinemann Educational Books

Nwaiwu G 1987: "OSU Caste now against the Law" African Concord 12 no 108 June: 16.

Nwapa F 1966: Efuru: Ibadan Nigeria: Heinemann Educational Books

Nzeako T 1972: Omenala Ndi Igbo: Lagos Nigeria: Longman Nigeria PLC

Obi Regina 1998: Female Circumcision among the people of Ora Eri unpublished undergraduate essay submitted to the department of Religious Studies University of Jos Nigeria.

Obiechina E 1994: "Nchetaka: The Story: Memory and Continuity of Igbo Culture" Ahajoku Lectures Published by the Ministry of Information Imo State Nigeria.

Obichere, Boniface 1982: Studies in Southern Nigerian History: A Festschrift fur Joseph Christopher Okwudili Anene 1918-1968

Routledge 207 (uses 'Heebo')

Ogbalu F 1979: Omenala Igbo Lagos Nigeria: University Publishing Co Academy Press

Old Babylonian Text BM 78296

Onwuejeogwu M 1966: "Odinani" Nri: Onitsha Nigeria: Ideal Publishers Onwuejeogwu M 1981: An Igbo civilization: Nri Kingdom and Hegemony in Odinani Museum Journal: Onitsha Nigeria: Tabansi Press

Orji M 1999: The History and Culture of Igbo People: Nkpor, Nigeria: Jet Publishers Ltd.

Pedersen J 1940: Israel: Its Life and Culture. Oxford: OUP: 53

Peterson R 1995: Hell on Trial The Case for Eternal Punisment Phillipsburg, NJ: P&R Publishing

Poupard, Dennis, Scott: Literature Criticism from 1400 to 1800 1st ed. Gale

Prasch J www.moriel.org

Ratzel F 1898: The History of Mankind 3rd Volume translated by J Butler: London and New York: Macmillan and Company

Ridpath C 1897: Universal History 16 Vols: New York: The Jones Brothers Publishing Company

Roger J 1947: World's Great Men of Color: New York: Vol 1 Fturo Press Inc

Roth C 1932: A History of the Marranos: Philadelphia: The Jewish Publication Society of America

Sayyed T 2005: A Muslim in a Jewish Land: 13 Kislev 5766 December 14 Aish.com

Schaefer P 2007: Jesus in the Talmud Oxford and Princeton: Princeton University Press

Schweid E 1980: "The Authority Principle in Biblical Morality" Journal of Religion and Ethics 8, 2 Fall: 180-203

Se'adya ben Maimon Ibn Danan 16th century; Hhemdah Genuzah 15b
www.wikipedia.org/wiki/anusim

Slouschz N 1927: Travels in North Africa: Philadelphia: The Jewish Publication Society of America

1948: The Bible Dictionary: Philadelphia: The John C Winston Company

The Chronicles of Solomon bar Simon-The Chronicle of Rabbi Eliezer bar Nathan: The Narrative of the Old Persecutions (Mainz Anonymous)

The Columbian Encyclopedia 3rd ed: New York: Macmillan 1963. 1757

The Encyclopedia of Social Science: New York: Vol 1-11: 605.

1977: The Jews and the Crusades: The Hebrew Chronicles of the First and Second Crusades, translator and editor: Shlomo Eidelberg. Madison: University of Wisconson Press

1979: The New Brown, Driver and Briggs-Gesenius, Hebrew and English Lexicon: 1028

Torah" the Mishneh Torah, Sefer Shofetim

Thurstan S 1967: "The Mystery of the Buried Bronze at Igbo Ukwu" Account of the Archaelogical Discovery in Eastern Nigeria: Enugu Nigeria: Midland Press Limited. Also 1978 excavations with University of Nsukka team of excavators.

Uchendu V 1965: The Igbo of Southern Nigeria New York: Holt, Rinehard and Winston.

Udum Adah, Nkem 2016: A Brief Survey of the Patterns of Picking and Mixing (Syncretism) in Nigerian Christianity Xlibris Publishing Co.

van Gennep 1960: The Rites of Passage M Vizedom, translator: Chicago: University of Chicago Press

Vogt E 1956: Biblica 36: 1956: 56

von Rad, G 1966: "The Problem of the Hexateuch" in The Problem of the Hexateuch and other Essays E W Trueman Dickens –translator

Webster's Biographical Dictionary

Webster's Geographical Dictionary

Wedt H 1964: It Began in Babel: New York: Dell Publishing Company

Williams J 1928: The Hebrewism of West Africa: From the Nile to the Niger With the Jews: New York: Biblo and Tanen

Williams D et al 2008: Ebo Landing Painting Oil on Wood Coastal Centre for the Arts Ibo (e) Gale Research Company Literature Criticism from 1400 to 1800 1st ed. Gale Research co. pp 185-187 Retrieved 24 Nov. 2008.

Windsor R 2003: From Babylon to Timbuktoo A History of Ancient Black Races including the Black Hebrews: Atlanta, Georgia: Windsor Golden Series Research co. pp 185-187 Retrieved 24 Nov. 2008

INTERVIEWS

Papa Ulokanjo chief Priest of Amadioha 80 years of age of Umuoye village; was interviewed at various times in the months of June and July 1985

Nna Agu 102 years Umuoye village elder interviewed 1985 July 12

Adem Nwaogazi 101 years Umunakara village interviewed 20 June 1985

Papa Opera 85 Years Umuoye village interviewed 10 June 1985

Papa Augustine 90 village head of Umuoye village at various times

Rev Egeke 60 years interviewed at various times was forced to abandon his marriage to someone said to be OSU by his family

Clifford Maduike 70 years interviewed 2014

Chief Ekeocha 79 years interviewed 2015

Rev Okere Samuel of Salvation Army Church Umuoye Owerri 50 years was interviewed on the 10 July 1985

Anunobi Mgbafor, aged 89, of Mbuwa village, Akweze, interviewed 27/12/97

Dike Bridget aged, 40 years, Obinri village, interviewed 26/ 12/97

Emejuku Mgbeorie, 52, Umudike village 2/01/96

Ezeilo Gwamniru, 65 years, interviewed 1996

Ezekaka Hyacinth, Ibo inter-state herbalist, 40 years Obinri village 12/12/ 96

Ezeosika C, 48 years, Obinri village, interviewed, 16/1/98

Obiapusi Udoye Nweri, 79 years, Obinri village, interviewed 2/2/98

Oforkansi Alfred, traditional healer, 59 years, Obinri village, interviewed 8/8/98

Okafor Ezeugo Dibia, Chief Priest of Eke deity, 96 years, Obinri village, interviewed 29/12/97

Ofuo Oburukwa, Chief Priest of Ogwugwu deity, 71, Umuafia village interviewed 18/1/98

Udoye Ughanwa (Dibia) 69 years, Obinri village interviewed 11/11/97

MAP OF IGBOLAND IN NIGERIA

Communities such as, Ogoni, Opobo, Anang, Ibibio, Bonny, Ekoi, Igala Idoma, Umon also fall withn the Heebo, Ibo Country (Colonial Eastern Region). Interviews showed that some of these communities especially those within the Creeks emerged as settlements provided by natives to accommodate rescued slaves by the Ibo (Heebo) brothers. Igboland was historically known as the Ibo(e), Ebo(e) and Heebo country by early European explorers. Early settlement of Igboland is dated at 6000 B.C based upon pottery found in the Okigwe, Oka Igwe and known today as Awka, although another evidence claim 4500 B.C. It is also claimed that Ife was originally inhabited by Igbos prior to 1300 AD.(see black and white *films about the Ibo by George Basden 1920s and 1930s in British and Commonwealth Collection British Archives Bristol ref 2006/070, Ngodo excavations, Uturu by Anthropologist University of Benin; 1978 excavations led by Thurstan Shaw, University of Nigeria, Nsukka.*

Images of Some Ibo peoples before and during early colonial times show that they are black in complexion. DNA Haplogroup E1B1A Y-Chromosome has been identified among them. Haplotype E1B1A are said to belong to the Semitic stock. The Ibos are perhaps the original Hebrews of today. They are Jews only because their ancestors worshipped Ayah Ashar Ayah(also represented as YHWH), literally "The I am that I am", the true and only G-d identifying them as descendants of Jacob as the Old Testament text referred to children of Jacob as Jews. Ibos are not participants of Judaism whose main scripture is the Talmud. Ibo ancestors relied upon the Laws of "Ayah Ashar Ayah" called theTorah and other ancient scriptures which they carried about even while on their journey in exile, though enemies destroyed most of these texts (eg the Book of Joshua)

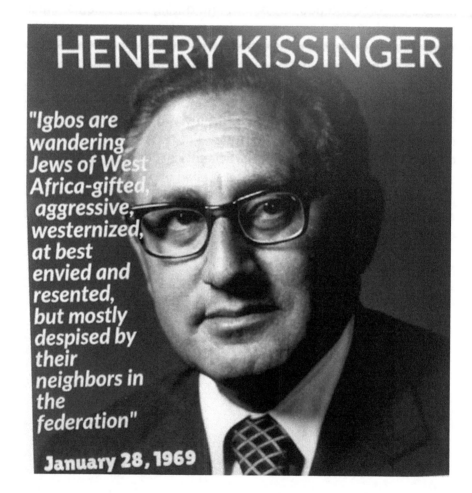

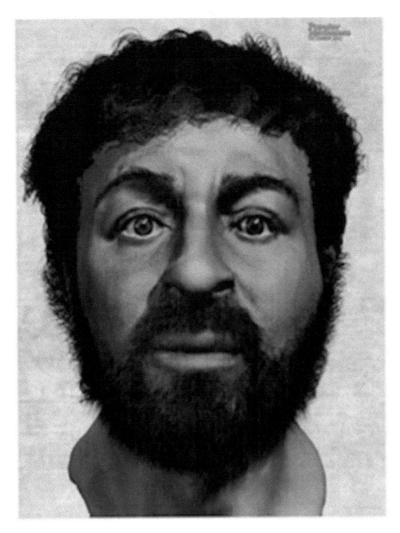

Portrait of Yeshua, (referred to as Iesous in Greek and Jesus in Latin and English languages). This portrait has today been generally accepted to be close representation of the true image of an adult Jew (Hebrew-Israelite male) of Yeshua's time and age by Professor Neave and his team of forensic Archaeological Scientists.

"THEY LEFT BLACK...."

The WAR for Israel

When he was asked about peace in the middle east... The late president of Egypt, Gamal Abdel Nasser, stated... "The Jews will never be able to live here in peace because they left here black but come back white."

Ibos are scattered all over the world because of slave trade as they were sought after ethnic group by the slave masters: They are found in:

Belize, where a city is named "Ebo(e) Town" after the Ebo inhabitants;

Cheasepeake Bay colonies

Dominique,

Barbados where the word 'bim' is colloquial term for Barbados commonly used among thr Brbadians(Bajans); this is Ibo "bem" that means "my place," "my people"

Jamaica: where the Jamaican Patois, the Ibo word "unu", that is plural for "you" is still being used Also there is the term "Red Ibo," "Red Ebo(e)" that refers to any light skin African because the Ibos were said to be generally light in complexion.

Trinidad and Tobago

Cuba

Gabon

Equatorial Guinea

USA including Maryland, Virginia, South Carolina, Georgia, Ebo landing

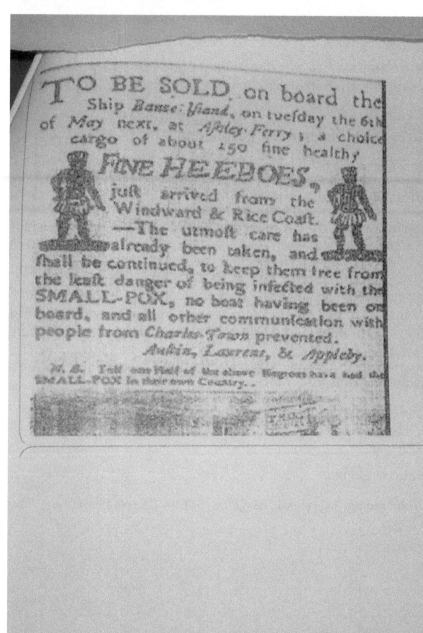

TO BE SOLD, on board the
Ship *Bance-Island*, on tuesday the 6th
of *May* next, at *Ashley-Ferry*; a choice
cargo of about 150 fine healthy

FINE HEEBOES,

just arrived from the
Windward & Rice Coast.
—The utmost care has
already been taken, and
shall be continued, to keep them free from
the least danger of being infected with the
SMALL-POX, no boat having been on
board, and all other communication with
people from *Charles-Town* prevented.

Austin, Laurens, & Appleby.

N. B. Full one Half of the above Negroes have had the
SMALL-POX in their own Country.

Yellow badge Star of David called "Judenstern": This star is part of the exhibition in the Jewish Museum Westphalia in Germany. "Jude" written in mock-Hebrew script, is the German word for Jew.

Lightning Source UK Ltd.
Milton Keynes UK
UKHW010705160223
417122UK00019B/1573